Recording Oral History

Recording Oral History

A Guide for the Humanities and Social Sciences

Second Edition

Valerie Raleigh Yow

ALTAMIRA
PRESS

A DIVISION OF
ROWMAN & LITTLEFIELD PUBLISHERS, INC.
Walnut Creek • Lanham • New York • Toronto • Oxford

AltaMira Press
A division of Rowman & Littlefield Publishers, Inc.
1630 North Main Street, #367
Walnut Creek, CA 94596
www.altamirapress.com

Rowman & Littlefield Publishers, Inc.
A wholly owned subsidiary of The Rowman & Littlefield Publishing Group, Inc.
4501 Forbes Boulevard, Suite 200
Lanham, MD 20706

PO Box 317
Oxford
OX2 9RU, UK

British Library Cataloguing in Publication Information Available

Library of Congress Cataloging-in-Publication Data

Yow, Valerie Raleigh.
  Recording oral history : a guide for the humanities and social sciences /
Valerie Raleigh Yow. — 2nd ed.
    p. cm.
  Includes bibliographical references and index.
  ISBN 0-7591-0654-1 (cloth : alk. paper) — ISBN 0-7591-0655-X (pbk. : alk. paper)
  1. Oral history—Methodology. I. Title.
  D16.14.Y68 2005
  907'.2—dc22   2004023848

Printed in the United States of America

♾™ The paper used in this publication meets the minimum requirements of
American National Standard for Information Sciences—Permanence of Paper for
Printed Library Materials, ANSI/NISO Z39.48-1992.

In memory of my father, Fletcher Raleigh Yow,
who showed me the power of words.

And in memory of my mother, Mae Moore Wyatt,
who revealed to me the power of imagination.

Contents

Preface

This book is intended for use by researchers who want information on carrying out the recorded in-depth interview. Ethical issues, questions about interpersonal relationships, and techniques for interviewing will be of interest to scholars and also to those who use the in-depth interview to enrich their knowledge of their own history. Because I am a historian, I often take a historian's point of view and discuss specific issues of concern to those researching contemporary history by means of oral history methodology. But I also address concerns of scholars in other disciplines when they differ from the historian's approach.

This is not a guide for conducting a diagnostic interview, although some aspects of that type of interview—such as building rapport—are similar to the work done in an oral history interview. And although it is not a book intended for researchers doing focused interviews, the chapters on interviewing skills, ethics, and interpersonal relationships may be helpful to them as well.

The in-depth interview is a research methodology with standards of excellence and guidelines for achieving these, and I present them here. Hard and fast rules, however, are not always appropriate in approaching the in-depth interview. Often problems arise that require considering the consequences of several strategies and then making a judgment. Nevertheless, a thorough knowledge of ethics, legalities, and techniques helps in this process of deciding what to do. And an awareness of what is happening in the interpersonal relationship during the interview situation can make the difference between a productive interview and a superficial, truncated interview.

Because little empirical research has been done on the efficacy of specific interviewing techniques, I must of necessity rely on the consensus (when there is one) of experienced interviewers on a solution for a particular problem. I give examples to illustrate what I mean with the attitude that we are all in this together and that we learn from one another. I hope my readers will forgive the prescriptive tone: it stems from an earnest desire to help the individual beginning to do this kind of research and also from the conviction that this is serious business—this dealing with living persons. On the other hand, I have tried not to be formal because I wanted the manual to be "user friendly." I do not disguise the speaker's "I": this is congruent with my belief that the writer of this kind of manual is a guide, not an unquestionable authority. And although it is impossible to pinpoint the absolute truth, I can strive to be honest with my reader, indicating how I arrived—in terms of my own values and experiences—at a conclusion.

Acknowledgments

Oral historians are a helpful group of people, perhaps the most helpful of my colleagues in history. I am grateful for help given me for the first edition by Sally Smith Hughes at the Regional Oral History Office, Bancroft Library, University of California, Berkeley; Paul Buhle, director of the Oral History of the American Left, Tamiment Library, New York University; Jane Adams, Department of Anthropology, Southern Illinois University at Carbondale; and Linda Shopes of the Pennsylvania Historical and Museum Commission, Harrisburg, Pennsylvania. Each of these generous scholars read several chapters and gave me perceptive criticisms. Ronald Grele, director of the Oral History Research Office at Columbia University, critiqued the first chapter. The late Carl Ryant, of the Oral History Program at the University of Louisville, read the chapter on public history; James Findlay, director of the State Oral History Project at the University of Rhode Island, read the chapter on ethics. They have all given me the benefit of their reflections. Especially enthusiastic thanks go to Charles Morrissey, director of the Oral History and Archives Office of the Baylor College of Medicine, for reading the entire manuscript. With his usual good humor and sharp critic's eye, he has made invaluable suggestions. I must, of course, accept responsibility for this book's shortcomings, but without these scholars' help, there would have been even more deficiencies. And I wish to take this opportunity also to thank my students at the University of Rhode Island and Northern Illinois University for their enthusiasm and interest and for good times in our class oral history projects.

In the middle of writing two new chapters for this second edition, I was struck by how much I needed the critical viewpoint of other scholars, experts in the fields I was sampling. I knocked on my friends' doors and am grateful, indeed, for their help. My colleagues in oral history, Ronald Grele and Alessandro Portelli, and sociologist Brian Roberts read the chapter on analysis and interpretation. Artist Marlene Malik generously gave me permission to print her oral history, read her testimony as printed, and commented briefly on my analysis of it in that chapter. Artist Alexandra Broches considered the chapter from the point of view of a founder of the Hera Gallery. James Peacock, anthropologist, Kim Rogers and Michael Gordon, historians, and Kenneth Sufka, biopsychologist, read critically the chapter on memory. Brian Roberts graciously scrutinized still another one—the greatly revised chapter on biography. And John Wolford examined the revised first chapter and kindly offered insights. John Neuenschwander helped me with the chapter on legal concerns in oral history. And Linda Shopes read critically the chapter on community studies and gave me the benefit of her experience and of the precision in her thinking. Dialogue with these individuals has greatly improved my understanding of subjects that have relevance to oral history. Editors at AltaMira Press, Susan Walters, Susan Scharf, and Erin McKindley were not only efficient and helpful, but supportive as well. Copyeditor Jen Sorenson showed such patience and tact that I ceased to fear the process. Of course, I alone am responsible for any errors or misinterpretations that remain in this text.

CHAPTER ONE

Introduction to the In-Depth Interview

Recently a development has been going on in the fields of education, anthropology, oral history, folklore, biographical literature, psychology, and humanistic sociology. This has been spurred in part by feminist psychologists, historians, and anthropologists and in part by men and women writing literary biography, humanistic sociology, and ethnography. This development is centered on a concern about the process of meaning making. Many of us who use the in-depth interview are interested in how the respondents interpret experience and how we, the questioners, interject ourselves into this process. We try to be conscious of the effects of the research process on both interviewer and narrator. Sociologist Judith Stacey described this as the realization that "ethnographic writing is not cultural reportage, but cultural construction, and always a construction of self as well as of the other."[1]

We are also concerned about the ways power relationships based on knowledge, gender, race, class, status, age, and ethnicity impinge on the interview situation. We strive to be aware of when and how these conditions affect the narrator and interviewer as they interact and how this influences the testimony recorded.

In ethnographic research in general and in oral history research specifically, there has been a shift in attitude about the relationship of interviewer to narrator. Formerly, the relationship of researcher (who plays the role of authoritative scholar) to narrator (who is the passive yielder of data) was one of subject to object. In the new view, power may be unequal, but both interviewer and narrator are seen as having knowledge of the situation as well as deficits in understanding. Although the interviewer brings to the interviewing situation a perspective based on research in a discipline, the narrator brings intimate knowledge of his or her own culture and often a different perspective. The interviewer thus sees the work as a collaboration.[2] This is an underlying assumption in this book; the term used to describe this dynamic is "shared authority."[3]

In striving to see the world as the narrator sees it, we realize that this stance compels some degree of compassion for the narrator. We cannot—and do not wish to—pretend to complete objectivity.

The guide is intended for all who use the recorded in-depth interview in their research and are open to reflecting on ethics and interpersonal relationships as well as to gaining information about interviewing techniques. Admittedly there is an emphasis on historical research because my own work has been centered on historical issues. For example, I emphasize the life history approach rather than the present-centered interview. However, my thinking has been enriched by research and debates in other disciplines, and I draw examples from the experience of scholars in anthropology, sociology, psychology, education, and folklore. I discuss specifically issues in in-depth interviewing that concern scholars in other disciplines when they diverge from those of historians.

This first chapter contains an explanation of terms used in referring to the recorded in-depth interview. There is a brief discussion about differences between qualitative and quantitative research methods; and the in-depth interview, or oral history, is presented in the context of the general field of qualitative research. I suggest appropriate uses of the in-depth interview and its limitations, as well as ways to deal with limitations.

Brief History of the Use of Oral History

Most writers begin books on oral history by reminding readers that the first oral historian was Thucydides, who sought out people to interview and used their information in writing the history of the Peloponnesian War. Use of personal testimony in the investigation of society has never ceased. But in the twentieth century, a new technology made the recording of testimony easier. Early in the century, recording onto wax cylinders by using heavy, cumbersome recording machines, folklorists recorded not only music but short interviews with the people making music. However, widespread use of the tape-recorded interview was possible only after World War II, when portable recording machines became available. So, although the use of data from individual memory is at least as old as the fifth century B.C., the mechanical recording of the in-depth interview is not so old—not much more than eighty years, in fact.

In 1948 Alan Nevins, at Columbia University, began to tape-record the spoken memories of white male elites: this was the first organized oral history project.[4] At that time, heavy, cumbersome reel-to-reel recording machines were being used. Soon lighter machines were invented and marketed, and by the 1960s the easy-to-carry tape recorder using cassettes had become the standard equipment. Also in the 1960s, an interest in recording the memories of people other than elites became paramount among academics.

Because of this interest and technical improvements in recorders, by 1965 there were eighty-nine oral history projects ongoing in this country, and the number of projects has grown in each year since then.[5] At the same time, the easy portability of cassette recorders enhanced the quantity and quality of interviews by folklorists, ethnographers, sociologists, and psychologists whose research was based on qualitative methodology. Although each discipline uses the in-depth interview in somewhat different ways, the practical and theoretical problems tend to cut across disciplinary boundaries. A simple search on the Internet via Google will show you the great number of oral history programs in the United States. Journals devoted to oral history and directories of oral history projects in English-speaking countries as well as Internet resources are listed at the end of the recommended reading section at the end of the chapter.

Definition of Oral History

The question, What is oral history anyway? has stymied nearly all of us at one point or another. Oral historians have probably devoted more energy to definitional issues and problems of application of this term than other disciplines. I'll venture a working definition: oral history is the recording of personal testimony delivered in oral form. Charles Morrissey, an oral historian, searched for the origin of the term *oral history* and traced it to a New York citizen of the nineteenth century.[6] Nevins called what he was doing "oral history."[7] But what is the oral history? Is it the taped memoir? Is it the typewritten transcript? Is it the research method that involves in-depth interviewing? The term refers to all three. Lamentations have been heard about the inadequacy, the imprecision, the misleading character of the term, but is it possible to find a better one? In this book, I use several terms interchangeably with *oral history*. James Bennett mentioned a string of them in his speech to the annual meeting of the Oral History Association in 1982, among them, *life history, self-report, personal narrative, life story, oral biography, memoir, testament.*[8] The terms used here—such as *in-depth interview, recorded memoir, life history, life narrative, taped memories, life review*—imply that there is someone else involved who frames the topics and inspires the narrator to begin the act of remembering, jogs memory, and records and presents the narrator's words.

Most of these terms have also been used in cognate disciplines. Although theorists have proposed a set of more technically specific meanings for each term, these meanings seem not to have caught on, and the terms remain interchangeable. *Oral history* seems to be the one most frequently used to refer to the recorded in-depth interview, although *life history* is also frequently used.

Oral History: Still a New Kid on the Block

Social scientists, in general, are trained to view manufacturing the evidence as the worst thing one can do. They will permit evidence to be "massaged" and "manipulated," but not made up. The recorded in-depth interview is a research method that is based on direct intervention by the observer and on the evocation of evidence. In the sense that the evidence was not tangible in these words exactly until the interviewer recorded it, and that the evidence is the result of the interviewer's questioning, this is the making of evidence.

But return to the first historians, the Greeks: they were not troubled about the issue of recording these answers and considering them evidence. They cheerfully (I guess) used the accounts related for them to write their histories. Nevertheless, many historians trained in research methods rooted in the Germanic "scientific school" of the nineteenth century cast a suspicious glance at oral history. They rely mainly on written records and on a critical examination of them. In the latter part of this chapter I will suggest ways of subjecting the orally transmitted document to the same critical examination with which written documents are evaluated.

Many sociologists and other social scientists today still hold the view that quantitative research is the only way to be certain about evidence. They have grave reservations about qualitative research because they view it as uncontrolled and lacking in the rigorous procedures followed by quantitative researchers. They are uncomfortable with the subjectivity inherent in qualitative research and strive to get rid of it as much as possible. But the subjectivity of the process did not bother the Greeks: they knew that their witnesses and they themselves were human beings involved in the process of living and observing what was going on around them and to them, even as they recorded memories and observations. They realized that they could not extract themselves from the story. I argue that awareness of our biases and preconceptions, the limitations of our experience and preferences, brings us closer to an understanding of how we influence our research and interpretation, whether it is qualitative or quantitative.

Qualitative methodology has its own body of strict standards for procedure and evaluation. Standards for the recorded in-depth interview as a research method and a critical evaluation of procedures are the subjects discussed in the chapters that follow.

Qualitative Research and Quantitative Research: Comparisons

Sharan Merriam, in the book *Case Study Research in Education: A Qualitative Approach*, explains that the quantitative researcher assesses a limited number of variables by examining researcher-controlled answers, trying to find out whether a preconceived hypothesis is operating, whether the prediction that certain variables cause certain effects will hold true.[9] By using a questionnaire requiring short answers, a researcher can query a large number of subjects. The subjects are selected in such a way that they are representative of the population studied. Therefore, researchers can make generalizations with a degree of confidence.

Qualitative research does not involve manipulation of a few variables. Rather, Merriam argues, this kind of research is inductive, and a multiplicity of variables and their relationships are considered not in isolation but as being interrelated in the life context.[10] The in-depth interview enables the researcher to give the subject leeway to answer as he or she chooses, to attribute meanings to the experiences under discussion, and to interject topics. In this way, new hypotheses may be generated.

The origins of the data used in these two ways of finding answers to questions about human society are at their foundations similar: observations of human behavior. British oral historian Paul Thompson reminds readers that the basic sources of information that statisticians use—census data, registrations of birth, marriage, and death—are suspect. Marriage registers, for example, contain false information about age because often couples did not want the official to know they were still of the age that required parental consent.[11] Birthdates are falsified to present a nine-month interval between marriage and birth of the first child. People give census takers false information, sometimes because they do not understand what the census taker means, sometimes because they do not trust the census taker. People answer questionnaires in a slapdash way because they are in a hurry or because they do not value the research topic. British historian Trevor Lummis sums up this idea: "So even 'hard' contemporary statistical data is only what somebody told somebody and if they have good reason and the opportunity to conceal the truth, then the 'facts' will be erroneous."[12] All of us who study humans— whether with quantitative or qualitative methods—know that we cannot hold our conclusions with absolute certainty.

One advantage in using qualitative methodology is that, because the researcher does not adhere to an unchangeable testing instrument, he or she is open to observing the informants' choice of topics. In this way, the researcher learns new things not in the original hypothesis—in fact, many qualitative researchers do not form hypotheses at the beginning of the research. An example of finding something outside the researcher's thinking comes from sociologist Arlene Daniels, who studies organization of work, especially unwritten codes of behavior. In a project on military psychiatrists, if she had used a questionnaire whose data she could then easily quantify, she would not have asked a question about sexuality. Earlier information would not have suggested that she do so unless the subject was sexual dysfunction, which the psychiatrist would treat clinically. Instead, in the in-depth interviews she conducted, she found that narrators wanted to talk about some secret sexual practices. Daniels realized that ways to handle these were indicative of informal controls. When wives of high-ranking officers began affairs with lower-ranking officers, the local military psychiatrist would send the offender to a hospital for evaluation and possible treatment. Thus, the psychiatrist provided a short-term but effective solution to a nonpsychiatric problem. By listening and allowing her narrators to teach her, Daniels discovered an aspect of behavior in the military that was not previously in her thinking.[13]

This possibility of discovering something not even thought of before is an advantage of the method. However, in-depth interviews are time-consuming, and so the qualitative researcher cannot examine the number of cases that the quantitative researcher can. Generalizations about a wider population have to be held tentatively.

One aim in quantitative research is to reduce as much as possible the influence of the researcher's bias. However, because it is the researcher who forms the research questions, the bias is present from the beginning. The researcher interprets the mathematical results: the probability of bias is there as well. Now, with the influence of postmodernism, many researchers are likely to acknowledge that "providing figures is as much of an act of social construction as any other kind of research."[14] I used to believe that subjectivity is more intrusive in qualitative research because the researcher is constantly interacting with the people being studied. Yet all research is biased in its subjectivity, simply because the research begins, progresses, and ends with the researcher, who, no matter how many controls she may put on it, will nonetheless be creating a document reflecting her own assumptions. Sociologist Jack Douglas describes the way the qualitative researcher acknowledges and uses his or her bias, but what he says could equally apply to the quantitative researcher: "Rather than trying to eliminate the subjective effects, the goal must be to try to understand how they are interdependent, how different forms of subjective interaction with the people we are studying affect our conclusions about them, and so on."[15] In later chapters of this book, ways to reflect on our own assumptions and biases are discussed.

The qualitative researcher learns about a way of life by studying the people who live it and asking them what they think about their experiences. The many examples they offer in their testimony are carefully studied. The term used to describe the close examination of examples that yields the hypothesis is *grounded theory*, an approach originated by sociologists Anselm Strauss and Barney Glaser.[16] *Thick description*, a term coined by ethnographer Clifford Geertz, is the goal—not a single view of the experience, but a large enough number of testimonies that great variety in detail is obtained.[17]

I do not intend to insinuate that quantitative research and qualitative research are necessarily antithetical approaches. Quantification has its appropriate use, as does qualitative research. The kind of question asked leads to the choice of research method. For example, oral historian Fern Ingersoll and anthropologist Jasper Ingersoll worked together on a project in southern Thailand, using field techniques from anthropology and oral history as well as population data gathered by sociologists. By observing behaviors and conducting in-depth interviews and focus group interviews, they sought an understanding of the way income was experienced in the daily life of the families.[18] If they had chosen to do so, they could have studied quantitative data and arrived at two dimensions of the society they studied—actual level of income as well as perceived level.

Qualitative methods and quantitative methods may also be profitably used together when data from several in-depth interviews are coded and expressed mathematically. In the example given above, the Ingersolls could have analyzed the total content of all the individual interviews in terms of answers to particular questions, assigning each answer to a category and giving each category a number. Statistical analysis could have then been feasible. Researchers may also use an in-depth interviewing project to suggest hypotheses that may be tested by using a questionnaire with a larger sample drawn from the population being studied.

The In-Depth Interview as a Qualitative Research Method

The recorded in-depth interview, or oral history, is a specific research method within the general designation of qualitative methodology and is close to the basic principle of grounded theory. However, grounded theory refers to other kinds of observations of behavior besides the interview. Another important difference between oral history and grounded theory lies in the emphasis oral historians place on the formation of questions that guide the research.

Proponents of grounded theory insist on approaching research without preconceptions—that is, hypotheses. Social scientists such as Leonard Schatzman and Anselm Strauss warn against having any preconceived notions before beginning the research.[19] For others, there is acceptance of the researcher's starting with articulated problems or questions that guide the interview process. This method may or may not result in the formulation of specific hypotheses during the research or at its completion. Ethnographer Renato Rosaldo describes this approach: "Ethnographers begin research with a set of questions, revise them throughout the course of inquiry, and in the end emerge with different questions than they started with. One's surprise at the answer to a question, in other words, requires one to revise the question until lessening surprises or diminishing returns indicate a stopping point."[20]

Some historians as well as other social scientists use hypotheses based on previous knowledge—these are tested and discarded as the evidence suggests other explanations. Other historians do not test hypotheses but have in mind some questions that they pursue with the aim of finding answers so they can construct a narrative that makes sense. British historian and philosopher R. G. Collingwood stresses that the historian does not collect data without questions to guide the search: "It is only when he has a problem in his mind that he can begin to search for data bearing on it."[21]

It is important to acknowledge that there are at least assumptions—if not hypotheses or questions—that direct the researcher's attention to some aspects of behavior or testimony and not to others. If assumptions are not acknowledged, how can they be examined? The qualitative researcher must be conscious of assumptions and interests that inform the work and be aware of how and why these change during the research process.

Differences in Ways That Disciplines
Approach the In-Depth Interview

Researchers from different disciplines use the in-depth interview differently, although interviewing techniques may be the same. According to your discipline, you will no doubt combine it with other methods. For historians, this will mean a thorough search for other primary sources. For many anthropologists, it will be close observation of behaviors over a long period of living in the field. For sociologists, it will probably be fieldwork as well as analysis of aggregate data such as census reports or survey research results. But these methods may be used by all three: the strict boundaries between disciplines are artificial. Often a more helpful question is simply, Given my research question, what do I need to do to find the answer?

The kind of general research question you ask, however, is often the result of the discourse you have studied in a particular discipline, and I do not wish to obscure differences. Ethnography—that is, participant-observation research whether practiced by anthropologists, folklorists, or sociologists—and history ask somewhat different questions of narrators. For example, historians cannot stop with asking questions about how things are but also must concern themselves with the general question, How did things get to be the way they are? This catapults them into an examination of sources of information about the past. Among disciplines, there is often a difference in the way the document (tape or transcript) is handled regarding the narrator's identity. There are differences in approaches to interpretation of the document. However, in practice the lines between disciplines are often blurred as scholars in one discipline use concepts or strategies from another.[22] In all of these disciplines, researchers who are using the recorded in-depth interview are seeking to understand the ways that the narrator attributes meanings to experience.

Uses of the Recorded In-Depth Interview

Whatever the particular approach or discipline, the recorded in-depth interview can offer answers to questions that no other methodology can provide. Consider here its appropriate uses.

The interview method permits questioning of the witness. In his book *Listening to History*, Trevor Lummis explains, "One precise advantage of oral evidence is that it is interactive and one is not left alone, as with documentary evidence, to divine its significance; the 'source' can reflect upon the content and offer interpretation as well as facts."[23]

This is especially important when we need to know underlying reasons for a decision. The official records state the decision blandly and in the most general terms. We might read that "the motion was made, seconded, and voted," but we have no way of knowing what the participants intended when they voted a certain way because the real motivation rarely appears in official written records. An ostensible reason may be given for public consumption. The in-depth interview is indispensable for probing behind the public-oriented statement. Once, when reading the minutes of a hospital board, I saw that a brilliant physician and creative administrator had handed in his resignation and that it had been accepted. As soon as I could interview the head of the hospital's board at the time, I asked him what happened those thirty years ago. He gave me a blow-by-blow description, explaining the underlying antithetical views of hospital administration held by the physician and the board members and the ways these views played out, as antagonism escalated. None of this was in the hospital board's minutes.[24]

The reasons why ordinary people made decisions that in the aggregate influenced history but are nowhere written down can also be ascertained. For example, why did parents in farm families continue to limit family size from the nineteenth into the twentieth centuries? Were there material reasons? Were there psychological reasons? Social reasons? Sociologists and other social scientists seek answers to these questions in the present; historians, for the past. Asking questions that involve this kind of personal, complex decision can best be done in the in-depth interview.

The life review reveals other kinds of information that do not get into the public record. People would rather not admit some things to the census taker—such as who is living with whom. Nearly everyone underestimates the value of renovations to property when filling out forms for the county tax office. And underlying the official accounts of "accidental death" are stories of despair on both the personal and societal level. If the interviewer presents no danger and is an empathic listener, these kinds of information may be articulated.

In the twentieth century and the present, much business is transacted orally. It is not a matter of supplementing the written record or explaining it because there are no written records for some decisions. For example, important decisions are arrived at over the telephone: there may not be written records. People rarely save electronic mail messages. (The technology of faxing documents may be changing this situation.) Business deals of importance for thousands of workers are discussed over lunch. A final decision on policy is settled while two people are riding up in the elevator. Out on the course, while carefully choosing the right golf club, an executive fires his subordinate who has come along anticipating a relaxing round. There is no record of the firing: indeed, the only written record is the positive portrayal in the recommendation the executive writes for him.

Certainly an obvious (but not intrinsic) use of oral history projects is that they often involve recording life histories among all socioeconomic levels of the population. In the past, only the well-to-do documented their lives. They not only had a sense of their own importance and were literate, but they also had the leisure and staff support to write. Because they were the ones who held power, their accounts of their lives were usually consonant with accounts in official documents. This was the situation British oral historian Bill Williams encountered when he began research among Jewish immigrants in Manchester, England. There were plenty of written records, but these had a particular slant: "Insofar as the immigrants survive in the written record they do so chiefly in accounts composed by an older-established Anglo-Jewish elite, with a vested interest in rapid assimilation, or of the majority society, where they appear most frequently either as the 'foreign refuse' of anti-alienism or as the pale reflection of middle-class liberalism. Written accounts by immigrants of their own experience are rare, and in the case of Manchester Jewry, all but non-existent."[25]

Paul Thompson comments on the paucity of written evidence for the history of working men and women: "The more personal, local, and unofficial a document, the less likely it was to survive." He lists the official documents that were deliberately saved to shape a view of the past wanted by those in power: legal documents, correspondence of landowners, account books from private firms. He concludes, "But of the innumerable postcards, letters, diaries, and ephemera of working-class men and women, or the papers of small businesses like corner shops or hill farmers, for example, very little has been preserved anywhere."[26] Oral history research thus becomes crucial to obtaining a picture of the total society because the viewpoints of the nonelite who do not leave memoirs or have biographers are presented.

On the other hand, sometimes in researching contemporary history, we are overwhelmed by the abundance of written documents. Much depends on the topic. Government requirements, such as documentation for the Equal Employment Opportunity Commission in the United States, result in a flood of paper. Oral history testimony can help us understand what was significant to the people who made the documents or lived through the times when the documents had power. Such testimony can reveal which documents are important enough to net from the waves of paper.

Oral history testimony is the kind of information that makes other public documents understandable. For example, we may know the average wage of unskilled male workers from looking at government data. What we cannot know unless we ask is how the man supplemented the wage with other work, how the woman found seasonal and part-time jobs and grew food in a kitchen garden and processed it and made over old clothes for the children, and how the children took baby-sitting jobs and ran errands for money and did unpaid work for their parents.[27]

Oral history reveals daily life at home and at work—the very stuff that rarely gets into any kind of public record. Thompson says that these are the areas where we can begin to see how social change is operating.[28] North Carolina mill workers, talking about courtship practices during and just after World War I, described not being allowed to be alone with a sweetheart. A chaperone was always in the parlor with them—one couple sat side by side and held hands under the sofa pillow. Then a few people were able to buy cars. At first, the chaperone went along, riding in the backseat. Then another couple went along—safety in numbers. Then two sweethearts started going out in the car alone.[29] Courting practices changed forever. Concrete details in these oral histories make understandable the textbook generalizations about the advent of the automobile changing social life.

The in-depth interview can reveal the informal, unwritten rules of relating to others that characterize any group. I reflect now on my interviewing project among artists in a women's cooperative gallery. The formal rule was that if an artist could not pay her dues after a stated length of time, she would be expelled from membership. In practice, the women were reluctant to expel anyone. They always found some strategy to keep the artist with them if she wanted to stay.[30] Another rule was that membership was open to both men and women, and indeed men regularly exhibited at the gallery. But when asked if they would vote for a man to become a regular member, the women hedged and finally indicated that that would be a hard decision to make.[31] (A few years after my research project was completed, they did vote men into membership.)

The ramifications of personal relationships that do not get told in official documents are revealed. Again I am reminded of the art gallery and of a heated discussion that went on for months over the difference between art and craft. Hard positions were taken: individuals seemed unmovable. As time went by, they softened their positions. Friendships mattered too much for anyone to maintain a rigid stance; in the end, personal relationships were more important even than the definitions of their work. And only in the in-depth interviews did the interweaving of personal relationships, work, and definitions of work become clear.[32]

It is through oral history that the dimensions of life within a community are illuminated. Studying the role of the two churches in the mill village of more than sixty years ago showed me how this can come about. The programs in which members offered songs and poetry emphasized family and mutual help: often my narrators sang their song for me or recited a few lines of poetry. Their testimony gave such accounts as that of taking into the house two maiden aunts when they were old and could not work. In the mill, people also helped one another. If a spinner was trying to tie a broken thread and another thread broke, a fellow worker would leave her machines and come over to help.[33] The philosophy of what it meant to be "a good person" was linked to a commitment to help one another and was experienced in several ways and dimensions in this mill village. There was nothing about this in the mill records or in superintendents' observations of workers. Lummis sums up this important use of recorded testimony: "There is no doubt that the strength of having the account of the various dimensions of life together in one lived experience gives all the data a particular strength lacking in virtually any other source of evidence; and certainly lacking in any other widespread documentary form."[34]

Individual testimony incorporates different aspects of experience at any moment, and these moments can be arranged chronologically to reveal development. Paul Thompson points out the use of oral history to help us understand change over time, to achieve not a static view of human experience but a dynamic view. Thompson writes, "Oral history is a connecting value which moves in all sorts of different directions. It connects the old and the young, the academic world and the world outside, but more specifically it allows us to make connections in the interpretation of history; for example, between different places, or different spheres, or different phases of life."[35]

Personal testimony enables the researcher to understand the meaning of artifacts in the lives of people. British historian Raphael Samuel, discussing artifacts such as a measuring book and a price list, explains: "Sources like this may only come to life when there are people to explain, to comment and to elaborate on them, when there are other kinds of information to set against them, and a context of custom and practice in which they can be set."[36] In the mill village just before World War I, a family saved enough money to buy an organ for the two daughters. If I had seen "organ" in a list of household goods, I would have regarded this artifact as a tangible symbol of "the arts" among working-class people. For the narrator it was the symbol of the intimate bond between her sister and her as they shared the organ in their adult lives after they married and lived in separate houses.[37] The organ had a significance for them in a way I did not at first imagine.

The in-depth interview also reveals the images and the symbols people use to express feelings about their experiences and give them meaning. In his book *Listening to Old Voices*, Patrick Mullen describes a man (born in 1900) who had come from a background of poverty to landownership and from a wayward life to that of a lay preacher. This narrator took Mullen to the top of the highest mountain on his land, the landscape symbolizing his rise from poverty to prosperity, from sin to spiritual elevation.[38]

The in-depth interview can reveal a psychological reality that is the basis for ideals the individual holds and for the things he or she does. There is no better way to glean information on how the subject sees and interprets her experience than to ask in the context of the life review. For past times, historians searched for a diary or personal journal, only to be disappointed by finding a daily account of weather and a brief synopsis of events. The ones that offered the writer's interpretations of the events on a psychological level were rare.

Such a situation arose during research John Bodnar conducted among Polish immigrants to the United States. He says that as a social scientist he might have seen immigration only in the context of economic and social forces. Using one of the oral histories to illustrate his point, Bodnar shows how the narrator expressed his experience in terms of the struggle to move from dependency on others to independence. In his personal psychology, independence was necessary to this narrator's sense of being a worthwhile person: the achievement of independence, rather than money, was the most important thing to him.[39]

Oral history research may also reveal the actions of individuals who have no one to witness for history their heroism or provide for future generations the evidence of their tragedy. Alessandro Portelli's book on a World War II tragedy, *The Order Has Been Carried Out: History, Memory, and Meaning of a Nazi Massacre in Rome*, presents the evidence of German troops' retaliation for the deaths of 33 Germans by killing 335 Italians they were holding as political prisoners. Portelli gives the names of the Nazis' victims, at least fifteen to twenty in each chapter, so that by the end every individual has been named. The narrators' description of the victims makes us see them as individuals who once had a life.[40] The words of the oral histories become a memorial perhaps more potent than stone.

The Use of Narrative as a Research Strategy

From childhood, I realized that I learned from others' stories and that I liked to tell my own. For a long time I thought this was just a characteristic of my working-class culture in the American South because, growing up, I heard stories everywhere, at all times. Grown up, I learned that people tell stories in every culture although form and purpose vary. I am reminded that the theorist Roland Barthes argued that narrative is always present in human groups.[41] More and more, scholars recognize that storytelling is a compelling endeavor that is universal: "The narrative gift is as distinctively human as our upright posture and our opposable thumb and forefinger," psychologist Jerome Bruner says.

Certainly narrative is an important component of oral history, along with description, explanation, and reflection. We ask our narrators questions, and they often answer in the form of stories. Of course, this has been going on for centuries, but respect for narratives as research data has waxed and waned. It waxed in the 1920s up through World War II. It waned in the years after the war up to the late 1960s.[42] Even in 1975 when psychologist William Runyan began to study life histories, he said, "A number of people reacted to these efforts at understanding life histories with responses ranging from indifference to contempt."[43] Only in the last thirty years has narrative as a research method become respected again by academicians. Psychologists Amia Lieblich, Rivka Tuval-Mashiach, and Tamar Zilber, in their book *Narrative Research: Reading, Analysis, and Interpretation*, describe what they see happening: "In the fields of psychology, gender studies, education, anthropology, sociology, linguistics, law, and history, narrative studies are flourishing as a means of understanding the personal identity, lifestyle, culture and historical world of the narrator."[44]

Why has this change of attitude come about? Qualitative researchers question positivistic approaches, that is, quantification of data with objectivity and certainty about results as the goal. They seek other means of learning about humans, including narratives.[45] Also, a current influence that affects acceptance of narrative research is the postmodernist view that observations of human actions are shifting, never conclusive, always the product of the culture in which they are embedded. Literary critic Robert Fulford explains why narrative is for postmodernists a deceptive practice: "The world is not a place of beginnings and endings and middles, a place of coherence—and when narrative arranges the world in that way in order to tell a story and reach out to an audience, narrative lies."[46] Actually, when we use stories to make sense of experience, and when we designate a beginning, middle, and end to an experience, that is true for us—there is no lie. In *Storied Lives*, the editors introduce their overall subject, narrative, by declaring that "coherence derives from the tacit assumptions of plausibility that shape the way each story maker weaves the fragmentary episodes of experience into history."[47] On the other hand, the postmodernist assumption that truth is not necessarily to be found in authoritative texts leads us to respect the individual account and to give serious consideration to how the individual sees her life story.

We can reflect on how we react to a life narrative and interpret it. This kind of endeavor is arresting. Linguistics scholar Harold Rosen recalls the power of telling stories about oneself and of listening to stories: "I know of someone who wrote about her childhood, setting out to recount the games and inventive pastimes which seemed to her both inexhaustible and full of meaning. At the end of it she said thoughtfully, 'It's about a lonely childhood.' Thus in the art of articulating autobiography we do not simply unmask ourselves for others, we too await to know the face under the mask."[48]

But even before the narrative form of research became acceptable, many oral historians and humanist psychologists and sociologists sought in the individual life story a specificity and a richness of experience that general accounts did not offer. Anthropologist Ruth Behar says that life histories give us the information that general studies, supposed to be typical accounts, obscure: "Rather than looking at social and cultural systems solely as they impinge on a life, shape it, and turn it into an object, a life history should allow one to see how an actor makes culturally meaningful history, how history is produced in action and in the actor's retrospective reflections on that action."[49]

Even if scholars in the past regarded work based on narrative as simple, many believe now that narratives are not simple and they are not innocent either because there is always an agenda. Bruner asks, "Why do we naturally portray ourselves through story, so naturally indeed that selfhood itself seems like a product of our own story making?"[50] He argues that narrative expresses our deepest reasonings about ourselves and our experience. Rosen suggests that we pay attention to personal accounts "because (1) the power of narrative in general corresponds to a way of thinking and imagining, (2) it speaks with the voice of 'commonsense,' (3) it invites us to consider not only the results of understanding but to live through the processes of reaching it, (4) it never tears asunder ideas and feelings; it *moves* us by permitting us to enter the living space of another: it is perceived as testimony, (5) it specifically provides for the complicit engagement of the listener."[51]

Narrative as a research tool is used by practitioners in many disciplines. Medical anthropologist Cheryl Mattingly, in her research concerning the use of narratives by occupational therapists, found that when they encouraged the patient to tell her or his life story, the patient could make sense of what was happening and fit the experience into a model, so that the story became part of a healing ritual.[52] Psychologist Carole Cain wanted to know how alcoholics change their self-identity so that they can begin to see themselves as nondrinkers, and so she studied storytelling among members of Alcoholics Anonymous.[53] Sociologist Ruth Finnegan studied life stories of people living in a British city to learn the multiplicity of experiences that could not be subsumed within the kind of general story such as academics tell. She wanted to gain an understanding of how "stories in practice interact in urban contexts" and express "our visions of urban life."[54] Historian Virginia

Yans-McLaughlin interviewed Italian and Jewish immigrants in New York City to find the stories that illustrate how culture (both ethnic and family) influences individuals' interpretations of experience.[55] Historian Lu Ann Jones interviewed farm women and men in the South in the twentieth century to understand "broad economic and social changes in personal terms," the "interplay between structural changes and family and community life."[56] Former English professor, now Catholic Worker, Rosalie Riegle sought stories from people who had known Dorothy Day, the founder of the Catholic Worker Movement, to understand Day's impact on the people she worked with and to assess her legacy.[57] Of course, I have scratched only the surface with these few examples—a lode of gold awaits us.

We, as oral historians, treat the narrative we record as a highly complex document. Sociologist Catherine Riessman advises that narratives are "essential meaning-making structures," and therefore researchers must not break them up but "respect respondents' ways of constructing meaning and analyze how it is accomplished."[58] You will find more information on analysis and interpretation of narratives later in this book.

Limitations of the Recorded Life Review

Narrative is a strength of oral history, but consider also the limitations of the life review and how to use these limitations. Trevor Lummis, in *Listening to History*, rightly says that oral history testimony can give us a detailed account of wages paid in a factory to a specific level of worker but may be "silent on the question of profits." We can learn in the interview what families spent their money on, but not how profits were invested internationally. Lummis expresses this limitation concisely: "Given that so many dimensions of economic life occur at the level of institutional, national and international finance and of technology it is not surprising that those aspects are not recorded in most oral accounts."[59]

The use of life reviews may result in a picture that is narrow, idiosyncratic, or ethnocentric. Studs Terkel's book *Hard Times: An Oral History of the Great Depression* presents more than 150 testimonies of what it was like to live during the Depression years of 1929 and the 1930s.[60] The informants talked about how they survived during the Depression, rather than about the failure of capitalism to provide the necessities of life for most of the people. As historian Michael Frisch points out, the narrators saw this as a personal experience.[61]

And yet there is the other side to this coin of limitations. In discussing the personal views presented in *Hard Times*, Frisch reminds the reader that taken together, the life histories reveal an important assumption in American culture: an individual can survive through hard work and ingenuity, no matter how bad the situation. He points out the advantage of learning individuals' reflections on their personal experience of history: "Anyone who has wondered why the depression crises did not produce more focused critiques of American capitalism and culture, more sustained efforts to see fundamental structural change, will find more evidence in the interior of these testimonies than in any other source I know."[62]

The in-depth interview is not necessarily idiosyncratic. In his article "What Is Social in Oral History?" Samuel Schrager points out that often there are references to the larger community and to national and international events, that the testimony is given in relationship to others. He gives this excerpt from an interview with immigrant Anna Marie Oslund: "I was born in eighteen ninety-one. And in eighteen ninety-two, the end of that summer—it was a late summer—my father went to America to find a better life for all of us. It was hard all over and he thought he'd try, he'd come."[63]

The narrator indicates she will offer two points of view, her own and her father's. She also refers to conditions being "hard all over" and articulates the reality of the wider society. She relates the story as she has been told it. And this is a family story, one that embodies a view of the past that sustains and guides the family in the present. It is assumed that it is in general terms like that of other families immigrating from the same place at roughly the same time. Schrager sums up the use to which this personal narrative can be put: "A migration story can be a very personal account and at the same time an incarnation of the peopling of an era, the exigencies of pioneering, and the aspirations of all who risk relocating to find a better life."[64] So the individual testimony may indeed contain references to the larger group and articulate a shared reality.

And it is possible by using the approach of grounded theory—the examination of a large sample of recorded life histories, the multiplicity of incidents that makes "thick description" possible—to make generalizations about a society. Paul Thompson and Thea Vigne did exactly this in their study of British society at the turn of the twentieth century: their project resulted in the recorded life histories of more than 900 narrators who represented contemporary occupational categories.[65] They used these interviews inductively to arrive at an understanding of several important aspects of Edwardian society.

A second limitation—one related to the ability to generalize from the testimonies—lies in the selectivity of narrators: it is the articulate who come forward to be participants. In interviewing clerical workers for a project in

Rhode Island, my fellow researchers and I found that our narrators were feisty, articulate, witty, sociable women. They had volunteered to talk.[66] Would we have gotten a different picture if those who were not enthusiastic had been represented in the collection of taped life reviews? We went on the assumption that the articulate spoke for the others, but I wish I had been more assiduous in seeking out the nonvolunteers and more persuasive when I found them. Probably, most interviewing projects are selective in that the shy or inarticulate individual—or the person valuing privacy—does not come forward.

Furthermore, as a historian interviewing the generation of mill workers who began work as children in a new North Carolina cotton mill at the beginning of the twentieth century, I only *heard* about those who had died. My sample was biased in the direction of the healthiest simply because they were the ones who survived. If this had been a study of safety conditions (they were nonexistent) in the mill, this selectivity of narrators would have seriously limited interviewing evidence and biased the conclusion.

A third limitation is the fact that the in-depth life review presents retrospective evidence. But before I discuss this problem, consider the questions always asked of a written document no matter how much time has elapsed: What motive does the witness have for writing this? For whom is this document intended? How close was this witness to the event itself? How informed is this witness about the event observed? What prior assumptions did the witness bring to the observation? What kinds of details have been omitted?

These are questions to be asked of any primary source, including an oral history. Traditionally trained historians see the oral history document as especially faulty because, in addition to the above questions, there is the question of how much the narrator slanted the story to make it interesting or at least acceptable to the interviewer. This is a valid question to ask. But slanting the story to make it acceptable to the receiver occurs even with the diary writer: even here the individual who writes only for him- or herself tries to protect the ego. People who write their accounts without an interviewer often make themselves heroes of the stories, justifying their actions to themselves, as they reflect on their experiences. Motivation for describing oneself in the best light is always there, no matter what the form of expression. The minute taker at a board meeting writes with a future reader in mind. The journalist's account for the morning paper is slanted to appeal to imagined readers. And letter writers always have in mind their correspondents' interests.

On the other hand, like other interviewers, I have found that people tend with the passage of time to be more, rather than less, candid. When a career is in progress, there is much to lose by an untoward admission. Near the end of a life, there is a need to look at things as honestly as possible to make sense of experiences over a lifetime: this need to understand what happened strongly competes with the need to make oneself look good.

As for deliberate omissions, this is as likely to happen with official documents such as government press releases or personal documents, letters, for example, as with oral histories. Perhaps the omissions are less likely with oral histories if the interviewer keeps probing.

And now to the issue of retrospective evidence. This is especially problematic for historians, who are the most concerned about the past and who evaluate the reliability of evidence according to the amount of time that elapses between the event and its written description. A journal entry on the day the event occurred is considered more reliable than the event remembered twenty years later and recounted in a memoir. Actually, research indicates that people forget more about a specific event in the first hour after it happens than during any other time and that much forgetting continues to go on nine hours afterward; in other words, more is forgotten the first day than in the succeeding weeks, months, and years.[67] Nevertheless, although much has been forgotten a couple of hours later when the diarist writes, some more has been forgotten after twenty years. All of us who have used the in-depth interview in research realize that ability to recall depends on the individual's health, on the topic under consideration, on the way the question is asked, on the degree of pain (or pleasure) required to dredge the topic up, and on the willingness of the narrator to participate in the interview in a helpful way. We notice that memories of childhood, adolescence, and early adulthood may be more easily recalled than those from middle and late years. Memory researchers have found that if the event or situation was significant to the individual, it will likely be remembered in some detail, especially if its associated feelings were intense. However, the narrator's interpretation may reflect current circumstances and needs. That old cliché about memory playing tricks has some truth to it. The next chapter is focused on an exploration of studies on memory relevant to oral history research.

Given the situation that human memory is selective and sometimes faulty in what is remembered, two aspects of the critical approach to the oral history are involved here: consistency in the testimony (or reliability) and accuracy in relating factual information (or validity). Consistency within the testimony can be easily checked, and questions about inconsistency pursued. Accuracy (the degree of conformity with other accounts) can be checked by consulting other sources and comparing accounts.[68]

After subjecting the oral history to such scrutiny, we may see that it does indeed offer information about an event that is consistent within the document and with other accounts. In other words, social scientists recognize that some "facts" have a shared reality with multiple means of verifying their facticity, no matter their interpretative frame.[69] And everyone views some facts as more reliable than others, and so a degree of acceptance is occurring, dependent on the means of verifying.

By accumulating sources of information and comparing them, we can arrive at an approximate understanding of what happened or is happening and hold this information with some certainty. But there is never absolute certainty about any event, about any fact, no matter what sources are used. No single source or combination of them can ever give a picture of the total complexity of the reality. We cannot reconstruct a past event, no matter how recent, in its entirety.

Another consideration is that the interpretation of the evidence depends on the interpreter. If we place kinds of evidence on a continuum, starting with the least mediation and ending with the most, such artifacts as vases, ditches in the land, tombs, and so on have had the least "mediation." A personal account has the most. A vase is what the researcher makes of it: a human being's past experience is what he or she makes of it before the researcher begins to interpret it.

We can, however, base a tentative conclusion on what the critical review of the evidence indicates. R. G. Collingwood describes this process: "For historical thinking means nothing else than interpreting all the available evidence with the maximum degree of critical skill."[70] This implies there is always the possibility that new evidence may appear, that new skills may be developed. Although Collingwood was referring to historical research, interpreting the available evidence with critical skill is applicable to any research that social scientists carry out.

And yet, is it not the meaning attributed to the facts that makes them significant or not? After all, history—or society—does not exist outside human consciousness. History is what the people who lived it make of it and what the others who observe the participants or listen to them or study their records make of it. And present society is what we make of it. Sociologist W. I. Thomas discusses "definition of the situation," arguing, "If men define situations as real, they are real in their consequences."[71]

Special Strengths of Oral History

So, what if the narrator is dead wrong about a number, a date, or an event? The factual information may be incorrect, but look more closely at the document to discover what significance the discrepancy may reveal. Oral historian

Alessandro Portelli reminds us that "untrue" statements are psychologically "true" and that errors in fact may be more revealing than factually accurate accounts. He insists that the "importance of oral testimony may often lie not in its adherence to facts but rather in its divergence from them, where imagination, symbolism, desire break in."[72]

To illustrate this, Portelli shows how narrators might get dates incorrect but hold steadfastly to an account of a historical event that fits their view of history. For example, over half of the workers interviewed in the industrial town of Terni, in telling the story of their postwar strikes, place the killing of a worker by the police in 1953 rather than, as it really happened, in 1949; they also shift it from one context to another (from a peace demonstration to the urban guerrilla struggle that followed mass layoffs at the local steelworks). This testimony is useful even though incorrect about the actual chronology and context. These factual matters, as well as dates, are easy to check. But discrepancy forces us to rearrange our interpretation of events in order to recognize the collective processes of symbolization and mythmaking in the Terni working class—which sees those years as one uninterrupted struggle expressed by a unifying symbol (the dead comrade), rather than as a succession of separate events.[73]

Portelli asked the question, Why is there discrepancy between dates recorded elsewhere and dates given in the oral histories? The researcher can use this discrepancy to learn something important by asking about the narrator's self-serving account: How does he construct this view? Where do his concepts come from? Why does he build this persona and not another? What are the consequences for this individual?

Closely related to this symbolization is the use of oral history to discover habitual thinking (often below the level of conscious thinking), which comes from the evolving culture in which individuals live. Although the term *culture* has differing shades of meaning according to its interpreter, most students of human society would accept the definition given by Charles Stephenson that culture is "a reality of shared values, common patterns of thought, behavior, and association."[74] Ethnographer Clifford Geertz says: "Believing, with Max Weber, that man is an animal suspended in webs of significance he himself has spun, I take culture to be those webs."[75]

French historian Jacques Le Goff explains the concept this way: "Automatic gestures, spontaneous words, which seem to lack any origins and to be the fruits of improvisation and reflex, in fact possess deep roots in the long reverberation of systems of thought."[76] The example he gives is from medieval history but is definitely applicable to the work of the scholar engaged in the search for an understanding of contemporary society. Pope Gregory the Great, in his *Dialogues* (written between 590 and 600), recounts the story of a monk who, on his deathbed, confessed to have kept for himself three gold coins. Keeping material possessions to oneself was against the rules of the order. Pope Gregory refused to let the man have the last rites, insisted on neglect of the dying man, and after the culprit's death, punished him still again by having his body thrown on the garbage heap. His stated reason was that he wanted to show other monks they must adhere to the order's rules, but this was definitely a negation of Christian ideology, which would have been to forgive. Le Goff concludes, "The barbarian custom of physical punishment (brought by the Goths or a throwback to some psychic depths?) proves stronger than the monastic rule."[77]

In the recounting of events, the deeper layers of our thinking may be revealed, indicating the centuries-long development of the culture in which we have our being. For this, oral history testimony is a research method par excellence. We cannot drag Pope Gregory from his tomb, prop him up, and ask, "What were you saying to yourself when you threw that monk in the garbage?" But we surely can ask a living witness.

Summary

Oral history is inevitably subjective: its subjectivity is at once inescapable and crucial to an understanding of the meanings we give our past and present. To reveal the meanings of lived experience is the great task of qualitative research and specifically oral history interviews. The in-depth interview offers the benefit of seeing in its full complexity the world of another. And in collating in-depth interviews and using the insights to be gained from them as well as different kinds of information from other kinds of records, we can come to some understanding of the process by which we got to be the way we are.

Recommended Reading

HEADS UP: Each chapter has a list of recommended readings, but be aware that these lists are incomplete. It would be impossible to list all of the good works on oral history, this rich field, without turning this book into a long bibliography. You will find in each recommended article or book leads to still other sources. The few lines accompanying each entry can give you a hint about the work but never do it justice.

Discussions on Research Methods

Denzin, Norman K. *Interpretive Ethnography: Ethnographic Practices for the 21st Century.* Thousand Oaks, CA: Sage, 1997. See especially chapter 9, "The Sixth Moment," pp. 250–89, in which Denzin discusses postmodernism's influence on views of the researcher–researched relationship.

——. *The Research Act: A Theoretical Introduction to Sociological Methods.* Englewood Cliffs, NJ: Prentice Hall, 1989. This book presents a discussion of qualitative methods that is focused on participant observation; there is information useful not only to the interviewer in the field of sociology but in other fields as well. You might also want to consult Norman K. Denzin and Yvonna S. Lincoln, *Landscape of Qualitative Research* (Thousand Oaks, CA: Sage, 2003) and Norman K. Denzin and Yvonna S. Lincoln, *Turning Points in Qualitative Research* (Walnut Creek, CA: AltaMira, 2003).

Douglas, Jack D. *Investigative Social Research.* Beverly Hills, CA: Sage, 1976. This is a general guide to fieldwork research; it presents a comparison of quantitative and qualitative methods in the introduction. Although it is not focused exclusively on the in-depth interview, it offers discussion on such concerns as self-deception and biases.

Glaser, Barney, and Anselm Strauss. *The Discovery of Grounded Theory: Strategies for Qualitative Research.* Chicago: Aldine Publishing, 1967. This is the original source for discussions about grounded theory. An early statement can be found in their article "The Discovery of Substantive Theory: A Basic Strategy Underlying Qualitative Research," *American Behavioral Scientist* 8, no. 6 (February 1965): 5–12.

Jensen, Richard. "Oral History, Quantification and the New Social History." *Oral History Review* 9 (1981): 13–25. The author states that the use of a questionnaire offers the advantage of providing systematic answers to identical questions, but it gives up the richness of narrative detail offered by the in-depth interview.

Merriam, Sharan B. *Case Study Research in Education.* San Francisco: Jossey-Bass, 1998. A lucid treatise, slanted toward scholars in education but containing information on using the in-depth interview applicable to other disciplines.

Price, Richard. *Ethnographic History, Caribbean Pasts.* Working Papers no. 9, Department of Spanish and Portuguese, University of Maryland, College Park, 1990. Insightful brief essay—and witty.

Sharpless, Rebecca. "The Numbers Game: Oral History Compared with Quantitative Methodology." *International Journal of Oral History* 7, no. 2 (June 1986): 93–108. The author suggests ways in which oral history and a testing instrument for quantification can be used together, and she compares intrusion of the interviewer in both methods.

General Works on Oral History

Allen, Barbara, and W. Lynwood Montell. *From Memory to History: Using Oral Sources in Local Historical Research.* Nashville, TN: American Association for State and Local History, 1981. See this book for discussions of the combined use of history and folklore and for the evaluation of an oral history.

Dunaway, David K., and Willa K. Baum, eds. *Oral History: An Interdisciplinary Anthology*. Walnut Creek, CA: AltaMira, 1996. This collection of articles from journals covers many aspects of oral history research; each article provides a quick overview of specific topics and an accompanying bibliography.

Friedlander, Peter. Introduction to *The Emergence of a UAW Local, 1936–1939: A Study in Class and Culture*. Pittsburgh: University of Pittsburgh Press, 1973. The author discusses the ways that narrators construct the narrative and, therefore, a view of history. The essay offers a convincing example of the benefits of repeated in-depth interviews with the same narrator.

Grele, Ronald, ed. *Envelopes of Sound: Six Practitioners Discuss the Method, Theory and Practice of Oral History and Oral Testimony*. 2nd ed. Chicago: Precedent Publishing, 1992. These articles contain numerous insights, such as why stories are revealing, how attitude affects memory, and how oral history affects the interviewer.

Henige, David. *Oral Historiography*. London: Longman, 1982. This is an especially helpful guide for researchers going into field research in non-Western cultures.

Lummis, Trevor. *Listening to History: The Authenticity of Oral Evidence*. London: Hutchinson, 1987. See especially the chapters on assessing interviews and on memory and theory.

Perks, Robert, and Alistair Thompson, eds. *The Oral History Reader*. London: Routledge, 1998. Collection of outstanding articles under these headings: "Critical Developments," "Interviewing," "Advocacy and Empowerment," "Interpreting Memories," and "Making Histories."

Portelli, Alessandro. *The Death of Luigi Trastulli and Other Stories: Form and Meaning in Oral History*. Albany: State University of New York Press, 1991. This is a collection of journal articles (several of which I have mentioned singly) that have helped to define the purposes of oral history.

Thompson, Paul. *The Voice of the Past: Oral History*. 2nd ed. New York: Oxford University Press, 2000. This is an insightful account of the uses of oral history by a veteran interviewer.

Oral History and Folklore

Davis, Susan G. "Review Essay: Storytelling Rights." *Oral History Review* 16, no. 2 (Fall 1988): 109–15. This article briefly discusses how oral history and folklore are different but can be used together.

Dorson, Richard. "The Oral Historian and the Folklorist." In *Selections of the Fifth and Sixth National Colloquia on Oral History*. New York: Oral History Association, 1972. This is a treatment of folklore's distinguishing characteristics and its differences from oral history. See also his book *American Folklore and the Historian* (Chicago: University of Chicago Press, 1971).

Ives, Edward D. *The Tape-Recorded Interview: A Manual for Fieldworkers in Folklore and Oral History*. 2nd ed. Knoxville: University of Tennessee Press, 1995. A classic study, now updated, with useful information delivered with a sense of humor. Ives talks about other subjects as well as oral history, such as recording music, using photographs, and carrying out interviews with groups.

Montell, William Lynwood. *The Saga of Coe Ridge: A Study in Oral History.* Knoxville: University of Tennessee Press, 1970. See the preface for a discussion of the ways that historians can use folklore. Montell argues that a folk tradition is itself a historical fact.

Schneider, William. *So They Understand: Cultural Issues in Oral History.* Logan: Utah State University Press, 2002. Schneider, an anthropologist and folklorist, divides his book into three main parts: "How Stories Work," "Types of Stories," and "Issues Raised by Stories." Chapter 4, "Sorting Out Oral Tradition and Oral History," pp. 53–66, gives a folklorist's point of view. He raises important questions about the way oral history is used in chapter 8, "Life Histories: The Constructed Genre," pp. 109–21.

Works on the Interviewer–Narrator Relationship and Subjectivity in Research

Anderson, Kathryn, Susan Armitage, Dana Jack, and Judith Wittner. "Beginning Where We Are: Feminist Methodology in Oral History." *Oral History Review* 15 (Spring 1987): 103–27. This is a discussion by a psychologist, sociologist, and two historians about the influence of "particular and limited interests, perspectives, and experience of white males" on research.

Cottle, Thomas. "The Life Study: On Mutual Recognition and the Subjective Inquiry." *Urban Life and Culture* 2, no. 3 (October 1973): 344–60. The author reflects on the "new selves" of researchers emerging because of the research.

Daniels, Arlene. "Self-Deception and Self-Discovery in Field Work." *Qualitative Sociology* 6, no. 3 (1983): 195–214. This is a candid, searching account of the author's behavior as an interviewer.

Gluck, Sherna Berger, and Daphne Patai. *Women's Words: The Feminist Practice of Oral History.* New York: Routledge, 1991. This collection of articles discusses listening, using words, relating to narrators, looking critically at one's work, and interviewing Third World women.

Kleinman, Sherryl. "Field-Workers' Feelings: What We Feel, Who We Are, How We Analyze." In *Experiencing Fieldwork: An Inside View of Qualitative Research,* ed. William B. Shaffir and Robert A. Stebbins. Newbury Park, CA: Sage, 1991. This is a sociologist's exploration of how the field researcher's feelings affect a study and how failure to recognize feelings affects a study.

Lebeaux, Richard. "Thoreau's Lives, Lebeaux's Lives." In *Introspection in Biography: The Biographer's Quest for Self-Awareness,* ed. Samuel H. Baron and Carl Pletsch. Hillsdale, NJ: Analytic Press, 1985. The entire collection is interesting in the questions it raises about the effects on the researcher of studying an individual life.

Patai, Daphne. *Brazilian Women Speak.* Rutgers, NJ: State University Press, 1988. In her discussion of methodology, the author explores her feelings about research among women in Brazil, pointing out how her intervention affected both researcher and the researched.

Yow, Valerie R. "Do I Like Them Too Much? Effects of the Oral History Interview on the Interviewer and Vice-Versa." *Oral History Review* 24, no. 1 (Summer 1997): 55–79. This article traces changes in the social sciences regarding the recognition and use of subjectivity in research.

Studies on the Philosophy of History and on Ethnography

Clifford, James. "Introduction: Partial Truths." In *Writing Culture: The Poetics and Politics of Ethnography*, ed. James Clifford and George Marcus, 1–26. Berkeley: University of California Press, 1986. This is a perceptive and influential essay on the "webs" of culture.

Collingwood, R. G. *Autobiography*. London: Oxford University Press, 1939. This uncommon autobiography presents the intellectual journey taken by an important theorist of historical research.

———. *Essays in the Philosophy of History*. Ed. William Debbins. Austin: University of Texas Press, 1965. See especially "The Limits of Historical Knowledge" and "The Philosophy of History."

Geertz, Clifford. "Thick Description: Toward an Interpretative Theory of Culture." In *The Interpretation of Culture*, 3–30. New York: Basic Books, 1973. This is an early, provocative discussion of the use of "thick description" in researching a culture.

Hay, Cynthia. "What Is Sociological History?" In *Interpreting the Past, Understanding the Present*, ed. Stephen Kendrick and Pat Straw, 20–37. New York: St. Martin's, 1990. Hay presents a brief essay on the relationship of history to the social sciences of sociology and anthropology.

Le Goff, Jacques, and Pierre Nora. *Constructing the Past: Essays in Historical Methodology*. Cambridge: Cambridge University Press, 1985. See especially the chapter "Mentalities: A History of Ambiguities" by Le Goff.

Rosaldo, Renato. *Culture and Truth: The Remaking of Social Analysis*. Boston: Beacon Press, 1989. In this provocative study of ethnographic research, the author discusses his own fieldwork to illustrate the importance of acknowledging and using one's own feelings and assumptions in the process of researching and analyzing.

Studies on the Use of Narrative in Research

Finnegan, Ruth. *Tales of the City: A Study of Narrative and Urban Life*. Cambridge: Cambridge University Press, 1998. See especially the first chapter for an illuminating definition of story. In subsequent chapters, the author presents oral histories and analyzes them. She shows the way narrative heightens "our understanding not only of urban theory but of our own lives and culture" (p. 3).

Fulford, Robert. *The Triumph of Narrative: Storytelling in the Age of Mass Culture*. New York: Broadway Books, 2000. Fulford, described as a "cultural journalist," sets out to critique master narratives like Toynbee's, works that feature the "unreliable

narrator," model literary narratives like those of Sir Walter Scott, and news programs and films as takeoffs of the narratives of Western culture.

Josselson, Ruthellen, and Amia Lieblich. "Fettering the Mind in the Name of Science." *American Psychologist* 51, no. 6 (1996): 651–52. Authors argue that psychology is between paradigms as logical, positivistic research gives way to narrative-
based psychology.

———, eds. *The Narrative Study of Lives.* Vol. 5. Thousand Oaks, CA: Sage, 1997. The
variety of articles attests to the range of uses of narrative in research.

Mattingly, Cheryl. *Healing Dramas and Clinical Plots: The Narrative Structure of Experience.* Cambridge: Cambridge University Press, 1998. This is a beautifully written
account of Mattingly's ethnographic research among occupational therapists in a
large Boston hospital, but the discussion of narrative gives it universal application.
Mattingly's theme is this: "The need to narrate the strange experience of illness is
part of the very human need to be understood by others, to be in communication
even if from the margins" (p. 1).

Montalbano-Phelps, Lori L. *Taking Narrative Risk: The Empowerment of Abuse Survivors.* Lanham, MD: University Press of America, 2004. With these narratives of
abuse survivors, the author assesses the relationship between narration and the
empowerment of the narrator.

Peacock, James, and Dorothy Holland. "The Narrative Self: Life Stories in Process."
Ethos 21 (1993): 367–83. This review article treats various approaches to using life
histories, stressing the importance of narratives as conveying the dynamic, rather
than static, view of a life. The authors critique ways to interpret the life history, arguing that each discipline's approach is limited and that a more creative, interdisciplinary approach is needed.

Watson, Lawrence, and Maria-Barbara Watson-Franke. *Interpreting Life Histories: An
Anthropological Inquiry.* New Brunswick, NJ: Rutgers University Press, 1985. An
informative, thought-provoking book, now a classic. Read chapter 1 for a historical survey of the use of life history research by anthropologists.

Journals Devoted to Oral History

Historia antropologia y fuentes orales. Universitat de Barcelona. Ed. Mercedes Vilanova
I. Ribas. Access information about this journal on the web at www.hayfo.com/
credits.html.

Oral History Association of Australia Journal. Published by the State Library of New
South Wales, Sydney. One issue per year.

Oral History Forum. (Previously the *Canadian Oral History Forum/Journal.*) Published
with assistance from Brescia University College of London, Ontario. One issue per
year.

Oral History: Journal of the Oral History Society. University of Essex. Two issues per year.

Oral History Review. Published by the Oral History Association. Dickinson College,
Carlisle, PA. Two issues per year.

And major journals that have sections devoted to oral history:

Journal of American History. Four issues annually; see September issue for oral history section.

Radical History Review. Published three times a year by the Taniment Library, New York University, and printed by the Duke University Press. Oral history section in each issue.

Bibliographies of Publications in Oral History and Oral History Collections

Cook, Pat, ed. *Oral History Guide: Bibliographic Listing of the Memoirs in the Micropublished Collections.* Sanford, NC: New York Times Oral History Program and Microfilm Corporation of America, 1983. See the review by Ronald J. Grele, "On Using Oral History Collections: An Introduction," *Journal of American History* 74 (September 1987): 570–78.

Havlice, Patricia Pate, ed. *Oral History: A Reference Guide and Annotated Bibliography.* Jefferson, NC: McFarland Publishing Company, 1985. This volume includes books, articles, and dissertations on oral history published from 1950 to late 1983. Annotations give brief summaries of content; entries are arranged alphabetically by author.

Meckler, Alan M., and Ruth McMullins, eds. *Oral History Collections.* New York: R. R. Bowker Company, 1975. Find by name and subject. Detailed information in each entry.

National Catalog of Manuscript Collections. United States government publication, last published in 1993. Citations give you the number that will enable you to locate each description. For example, looking at "oral history" in the index, you see 91-365, which sends you to volume 1991, entry number 365, "Eleanor Roosevelt oral history transcriptions."

Oral History Index: An International Directory of Oral History Interviews. Westport, CT: Meckler Publishing Company, 1990. The first section lists in alphabetical order the narrator's name and supplies a code for locating the tapes. The second section lists the codes and directs you to the oral history's location. This can only be a partial listing because many of the oral history archives queried did not reply. (This company has been sold, and a succeeding volume is unlikely to appear in this form.)

Perks, Robert. *Oral History: An Annotated Bibliography.* London: British Library National Sound Archives, 1990. Author does well with a task made difficult by the immense amount of sources. He focuses on Great Britain and includes both published works and references to archives containing interviews.

Smith, Allan, ed. *Directory of Oral History Collections.* Phoenix: Oryx Press, 1988. More a directory of institutions that hold oral history collections than a directory of individual collections, according to the review by William Moss in the *Oral History Review,* Fall 1988, pp. 173–74.

Please note: None of these can be inclusive because many collections are not reported to these editors. However, continue to search, seeking, for example, regional directories like *Oral History Collections in the Southwest Region: A Directory and Subject*

Guide, edited by Cathryn A. Gallacher (Los Angeles: Southwest Oral History Association, 1986).

Internet Resources

Indexes and Directories

Oral History Directory. Internet resource offered by Alexander Street Press at www.alexanderstreet2.com/oralhist/. Free resource that gives details of approximately 570 oral history collections in English.

Oral History Online. Internet resource offered by Alexander Street Press at www.alexanderstreet.com/products/orhi.htm. The press claims to index all important oral history collections in English available on the web or in archives. Fee required to access.

Oral History List Service. www.h-net.org/~oralhist. Free, nontechnical, user friendly. See especially for discussions of current issues and bibliography. See discussion log for past discussions.

Research Libraries Information Network (RLIN). See RLG Union Catalog, Recordings. This is an international, not-for-profit organization that serves libraries, archives, and museums. It shows location of collections of oral histories. There is a hefty fee for membership—it is not intended for individuals—so use this source in one of these institutions.

Notes

1. Judith Stacey, "Can There Be a Feminist Ethnography?" in *Women's Words: The Feminist Practice of Oral History*, ed. Sherna Berger Gluck and Daphne Patai, 111–19 (New York: Routledge, 1991); see p. 115.

2. I am indebted to Jane Adams for dialogue with me on this subject; Jane Adams, communication to author, June 22, 1993. And I draw from Renato Rosaldo, *Culture and Truth: The Remaking of Social Analysis* (Boston: Beacon Press, 1989), 19–21, 50.

3. Phrase which Michael Frisch uses and which sums up the underlying theme in Michael Frisch, *A Shared Authority: Essays on the Craft and Meaning of Oral and Public History* (Albany: State University of New York Press, 1990).

4. Louis Starr, "Oral History," in *Oral History: An Interdisciplinary Anthology*, ed. David Dunaway and Willa K. Baum, 3–26 (Nashville, TN: American Association for State and Local History, 1996); see pp. 10–12.

5. Starr, "Oral History."

6. Charles Morrissey, "Why Call It Oral History? Searching for Early Usage of a Generic Term," *Oral History Review* 8 (1980): 20–48; see p. 35.

7. Morrissey, "Why Call It Oral History?" 35.

8. James Bennett, "Human Values in Oral History," *Oral History Review* 11 (1983): 1–15; see p. 14.

9. Sharan Merriam, *Case Study Research in Education: A Qualitative Approach* (San Francisco: Jossey-Bass, 1988), 6–7.

10. Merriam, *Case Study Research in Education*, 16.

11. Paul Thompson, *The Edwardians: The Remaking of British Society* (Bloomington: Indiana University Press, 1975), 6.

12. Trevor Lummis, *Listening to History: The Authenticity of Oral Evidence* (London: Hutchinson, 1987), 75.

13. Arlene Daniels, "Self-Deception and Self-Discovery in Field Work," *Qualitative Sociology* 6, no. 3 (1983): 195–214; see p. 197.

14. Mary Maynard, "Methods, Practice and Epistemology: The Debate about Feminism and Research," in *Researching Women's Lives from a Feminist Perspective*, ed. Mary Maynard and June Purvis, 10–26 (London: Taylor and Francis, 1994); see p. 13.

15. Jack D. Douglas, *Investigative Social Research* (Beverly Hills, CA: Sage, 1976), 25.

16. Barney Glaser and Anselm Strauss, "The Discovery of Substantive Theory: A Basic Strategy Underlying Qualitative Research," *American Behavioral Scientist* 8, no. 6 (February 1965): 5–12.

17. Clifford Geertz, "Thick Description: Toward an Interpretative Theory of Culture," in *The Interpretation of Culture*, 3–30 (New York: Basic Books, 1973); see also a later discussion in this book, pp. 203–5.

18. Fern Ingersoll and Jasper Ingersoll, "Both a Borrower and a Lender Be: Ethnography, Oral History, and Grounded Theory," *Oral History Review* 15 (Spring 1987): 81–102; see p. 83.

19. Leonard Schatzman and Anselm L. Strauss, *Field Research: Strategies for a Natural Sociology* (Englewood Cliffs, NJ: Prentice-Hall, 1973), 19.

20. Rosaldo, *Culture and Truth*, 7.

21. R. G. Collingwood, "The Philosophy of History," in *Essays in the Philosophy of History*, ed. William Debbins, 121–39 (Austin: University of Texas Press, 1985); see p. 137.

22. See, for example, Dennis Smith, "Social History and Sociology—More Than Just Good Friends," *Sociological Review* 30, no. 2 (1982): 286–308.

23. Lummis, *Listening to History*, 43.

24. Valerie Raleigh Yow, *Patient Care: A History of Butler Hospital* (Providence, RI: Butler Hospital, 1994); see chapter 2, "A New Kind of Hospital."

25. Bill Williams, "The Jewish Immigrant in Manchester: The Contribution of Oral History," *Oral History* 7, no. 1 (Spring 1979): 43.

26. Paul Thompson, *The Voice of the Past: Oral History* (Oxford: Oxford University Press, 2000), 4.

27. Paraphrase of Lummis, *Listening to History*, 150.

28. Paul Thompson, introduction to *Our Common History: The Transformation of Europe*, ed. Paul Thompson and Natasha Burchardt (Atlantic Highlands, NJ: Humanities Press, 1982), 11.

29. Valerie Raleigh Yow (listed as Valerie Quinney), "Childhood in a Southern Mill Village," *International Journal of Oral History* 3, no. 3 (November 1982): 167–92; see p. 171.

30. Valerie Raleigh Yow, *The History of Hera: A Woman's Art Cooperative, 1974–1989* (Wakefield, RI: Hera Educational Foundation, 1989), 8–9.

31. Yow, *History of Hera*, 19.

32. Yow, *History of Hera*.

33. Yow, "Childhood in a Southern Mill Village," 184.

34. Lummis, *Listening to History*, 110.

35. Paul Thompson, "Believe It or Not: Rethinking the Historical Interpretation of Memory," in *Memory and History: Essays on Recalling and Interpreting Experience*, ed. Jaclyn Jeffrey and Glenace Edwall, 1–16 (New York: University Press of America, 1994); see p. 11.

36. Raphael Samuel, "Local History and Oral History," *History Workshop Journal* 1 (1976): 191–208; see p. 200.

37. Mrs. V. P., tape-recorded interview with author (listed as Valerie Quinney), Carrboro, North Carolina, May 29, 1974, side 1, tape counter number 300. Families of Carrboro, Chapel Hill Historical Society Records 4205, Southern Historical Collection, University of North Carolina Libraries, Chapel Hill, North Carolina.

38. Patrick B. Mullen, *Listening to Old Voices: Folklore, Life Stories, and the Elderly* (Chicago: University of Illinois Press, 1992), 189–90.

39. John Bodnar, "Reworking Reality: Oral Histories and the Meaning of the Polish Immigrant Experience," in *Workers' World: Kinship, Community and Protest in an Industrial Society, 1900–1940*, 59–68 (Baltimore, MD: Johns Hopkins University Press, 1982).

40. Alessandro Portelli, *The Order Has Been Carried Out: History, Memory, and Meaning of a Nazi Massacre in Rome* (New York: Palgrave Macmillan, 2003).

41. Roland Barthes, "Introduction to the Structural Analysis of Narrative," in *Barthes: Selected Writings*, ed. Susan Sontag, 251–95 (London: Fontana, 1982).

42. William McKinley Runyan, *Life Histories and Psychobiography: Explorations in Theory and Method* (New York: Oxford University Press, 1982), 9.

43. Runyan, *Life Histories*, viii.

44. Amia Lieblich, Rivka Tuval-Mashiach, and Tamar Zilber, *Narrative Research: Reading, Analysis, and Interpretation* (Thousand Oaks, CA: Sage, 1998), 3.

45. Lieblich, Tuval-Mashiach, and Zilber, *Narrative Research*, 1.

46. Robert Fulford, *The Triumph of Narrative: Storytelling in the Age of Mass Culture* (New York: Broadway Books, 2000), 103.

47. George C. Rosenwald and Richard L. Ochberg, introduction to *Storied Lives: The Cultural Politics of Self-Understanding*, ed. George C. Rosenwald and Richard L. Ochberg, 1–18 (New Haven, CT: Yale University Press, 1992); see p. 5.

48. Harold Rosen, "The Autobiographical Impulse," in *Linguistics in Context: Connecting Observation and Understanding*, ed. Deborah Tannen, 69–88 (Norwood, NJ: Ablex, 1988); see p. 77.

49. Ruth Behar, "Rage and Redemption: Reading the Life Story of a Mexican Marketing Woman," *Feminist Studies* 16, no. 2 (Summer 1990): 1–31; see p. 3.

50. Jerome Bruner, "Self-Making Narratives," in *Autobiographical Memory and the Construction of a Narrative Self: Developmental and Cultural Perspectives*, ed. Robyn Fivush and Catherine A. Haden, 209–25 (Mahwah, NJ: Lawrence Erlbaum, 2003); see pp. 213–14 and 222.

51. Rosen, "Autobiographical Impulse," 81.

52. Cheryl Mattingly, *Healing Dramas and Clinical Plots: The Narrative Structure of Experience* (Cambridge: Cambridge University Press, 1998), 14.

53. Carole Cain, "Personal Stories: Identity Acquisition and Self-Understanding in Alcoholics Anonymous," *Ethos* 19 (1991): 210–53.

54. Ruth Finnegan, *Tales of the City: A Study of Narrative and Urban Life* (Cambridge: Cambridge University Press, 1998), 56.

55. Virginia Yans-McLaughlin, "Metaphors of Self in History: Subjectivity, Oral Narrative, and Immigration Studies," in *Immigration Reconsidered: History, Sociology, and Politics*, ed. Virginia Yans-McLaughlin, 254–90 (Oxford: Oxford University Press, 1990).

56. Lu Ann Jones, *Mama Learned Us to Work: Farm Women in the New South* (Chapel Hill: University of North Carolina Press, 2002), 4.

57. Rosalie Riegle, *Dorothy Day: Portraits by Those Who Knew Her* (Maryknoll, NY: Orbis Books, 2003).

58. Catherine Kohler Riessman, *Narrative Analysis* (Newbury Park, CA: Sage, 1993), 4.

59. Lummis, *Listening to History*, 42.

60. Studs Terkel, *Hard Times: An Oral History of the Great Depression* (New York: Avon, 1970).

61. Michael Frisch, "Oral History and Hard Times: A Review Essay," in *A Shared Authority: Essays on the Craft and Meaning of Oral and Public History* (New York: State University of New York Press, 1990), 11.

62. Frisch, "Oral History and Hard Times," 12.

63. Samuel Schrager, "What Is Social in Oral History?" *International Journal of Oral History* 4, no. 2 (June 1983): 76–98; see p. 80.

64. Schrager, "What Is Social in Oral History?" 80.

65. Thompson, *Voice of the Past*, 146–47.

66. Valerie Raleigh Yow (listed as Valerie Quinney), "Office Workers and Machines: Oral Histories of Rhode Island Working Women," in *Life and Labor: Dimensions of American Working-Class History*, ed. Charles Stephenson and Robert Asher, 260–81 (Albany: State University of New York Press, 1986).

67. H. Ebbinghaus, *Memory: A Contribution to Experimental Psychology*, trans. H. A. Roger and C. E. Bussenius (New York: Columbia University Press, 1885). The findings of this early study have not been disproved by subsequent research.

68. Alice Hoffman, "Reliability and Validity in Oral History," in Dunaway and Baum, *Oral History: An Interdisciplinary Anthology*, 67–73.

69. Jane Adams, communication to author, June 22, 1993.

70. R. G. Collingwood, "Limits of Historical Knowledge," in *Essays in the Philosophy of History*, ed. William Debbins, 90–103 (Austin: University of Texas Press, 1965); see p. 99.

71. Quoted in "W. I. Thomas: On the Definition of the Situation," in *Sociology: The Classic Statements*, ed. Marcello Truzzi (New York: Random House, 1971), 274. Original discussion and quotation appeared in William Isaac Thomas, *The Child in America* (New York: Alfred A. Knopf, 1928), 572. See a treatment of this concept in Peter McHugh, "Defining the Situation: The Organization of Meaning," in *Social Interaction* (Indianapolis: Bobbs-Merrill, 1968), and Robert B. Stebbins, "Studying the Definition of the Situation: Theory and Field Research Strategies," *Canadian Review of Sociology and Anthropology* 6 (1969): 193–211.

72. Alessandro Portelli, "Peculiarities of Oral History," *History Workshop Journal* 96, no. 12 (Autumn 1981): 96–107; see p. 100.

73. Portelli, "Pecularities of Oral History," 100.

74. Charles Stephenson, "A Gathering of Strangers? Mobility, Social Structure and Political Participation in the Formation of Nineteenth Century American Working Class Culture," in *American Workingclass Culture*, ed. Milton Cantor, 31–60 (Westport, CT: Greenwood Press, 1979); see p. 36. Quoted in Lucy Taksa's discussion of Stephenson, "Spreading the Word: The Literature of Labour and Working-Class Culture," in *All Our Labors: Oral Histories of Working Lives in Twentieth Century Sydney*, ed. John Shields, 64–85 (Kensington: New South Wales University Press, 1992); see p. 65.

75. Geertz, "Thick Description," 5.

76. Jacques Le Goff, "Mentalities: A History of Ambiguities," in *Constructing the Past: Essays in Historical Methodology*, ed. Jacques Le Goff and Pierre Nora, 166–80 (Cambridge: Cambridge University Press, 1985); see p. 170.

77. Le Goff, "Mentalities," 170.

CHAPTER TWO

Oral History and Memory

For oral historians, memory is a vital concern. As in-depth interviewers, we provide an opportunity for the narrator to remember, to convey details, to provide explanation, and to reflect, because we listen. Of course, not all memories are positive; negative memories are also recalled and puzzled over, grieved over. Researcher Daniel Schacter remarks, "It has been observed that the act of remembering sad episodes can bring people to tears within moments, and remembering happy incidents can induce an almost immediate sense of elation. Why does memory have such power in our lives?"[1]

Remembering, an Important Act for the Narrator

It is clear now that we construct narratives from our memories. Even children as young as preschool age make stories of their experiences.[2] We use such stories not only to make sense of our experiences, but also to justify decisions, to profit from past experience in making current decisions about present and future, and to reassure ourselves that we have come through life's challenges and have learned something.

Psychologist David Rubin found that people begin reminiscing in their forties, but that from age fifty on this is an important and continuing endeavor. His research indicates that from middle age on, most people have more memories from childhood, adolescence, and young adulthood than from the most recent years of their lives. Why do these memories come back to us? He theorizes that they are especially important because they define us.[3]

During our early years we recognize that we are good at some subjects in school, but not as good at others; that we have interests unique to us; that we have certain personality characteristics. We choose a mate and we settle on what we think will be our life's work.

Psychologists Minda Tessler and Katherine Nelson conclude from their research that "the relation between autobiographical memory and a sense of self is a dynamic, interactive process in which self and memory organize, construct, and give meaning to each other in a way so intimate that we can truly say that we are what we remember and that our memories are ourselves."[4]

Memory—Fallible or Trustworthy?

When we oral historians judge evidence from interviews, we ask such questions as these: Is this memory accurate so that I can use it as evidence? How can accurate aspects of recollections be distinguished from inaccurate aspects? Can inaccurate aspects of a memory be regarded as evidence of a special kind? These are salient questions, but unfortunately there is no research that enables us to make a quick and definitive decision. There are criteria, however, that can help us evaluate oral history evidence. I will argue that human memory is both fallible and—when we approach the oral history document *critically*—trustworthy.

Since memory produces the oral testimony that is the basis of our work as oral historians, we need all the knowledge about memory we can get. This chapter is an interdisciplinary approach to memory, focusing specifically on the contributions of psychology, cultural anthropology, and history to the discussion of what affects remembering. I present some recent findings by researchers in psychology on individual or personal memory or, in psychologists' terms, autobiographical memory. For psychologists, autobiographical memory is "personal, long-lasting, and (usually) of significance to the self-system."[5] It is formed in interaction first with our parents, who consciously and unconsciously convey our culture to us. Developmental psychologist Katherine Nelson declares, "Autobiographical memory . . . is highly personal and idiosyncratic but never escapes its social and cultural boundaries."[6] I will suggest some ways research by historians and anthropologists, whose concern is social and cultural contexts, can contribute to the picture psychologists' research about individual memory has offered.

But we also remember as a group; that is, we listen to people who have shared the same experience with us, and we gain a feeling of identity with them when we remember as people in our group remember. This phenomenon is termed *collective memory*, or *social memory*, and will be considered in the second part of the chapter. David Thelen theorizes in his article "Memory and American History," "The study of memory exists in different forms along a spectrum of experience, from the personal, individual, and private to the collective, cultural, and public."[7] On this spectrum, psychology (which researches personal memory) can be thought of as operating on one end; history in the middle (since history is often based on documents of personal memory); and on the far end cultural anthropology and history again (since both are concerned with collective memory).

Psychologists' General Findings about How Memory Works

Let us focus first on individual or autobiographical memory. The new conclusions from memory research give a different picture from much that we had assumed in the past. Have you ever said when you could not remember something, "The computer in my head is overloaded"? The old model was that the human brain was a kind of computer, but since the 1980s this model has been replaced by a view that the brain is not like any machine or any other organ.[8] (Even though Woody Allen calls his brain his second most favorite organ.)

Nor do researchers any longer assume that one part of the brain handles one memory. Rather, the brain is seen as a complex web of interconnections of "multiple contributors."[9] For example, the amygdala, the small almond-shaped area deep within the brain, is involved in evaluating and regulating fear and engages in such fine-tuned activity as judging expression. It works with other areas of the brain that record image, smell, words, and touch—the hippocampus ties these together to send out a single memory.[10] So, remembering is not just a matter of receiving a cue and then responding with a stored intact text.

Memory researchers Ulrich Neisser and Daniel Schacter have a theory about the way we "convert the fragmentary remains of experience into the autobiographical narratives that endure over time and constitute the stories of our lives."[11] Neisser's analogy is that of a paleontologist who discovers bone fragments and reconstructs the dinosaur from them. The fragments and the reconstructed dinosaur are not the same thing. In the same way, Neisser and Schacter theorize, the engrams (various stored fragments of memory) and the memory (the organization of information) are not the same thing.[12] For oral historians, this means that a narrator may describe the memory differently with different cues or, in other words, reconstruct it differently when responding to different needs.

We can remember only what our brains have encoded, that is, recorded at the time of experiencing. Schacter sums up this process: "What we encode depends on who we are—our past experiences, knowledge, and needs all have a powerful influence on what we retain."[13] If you walk down the street with an architect, he will remember details of the buildings that you will not notice and therefore not remember. You will read words on a sign or overhear a conversation that he will not notice particularly or remember. The recording of a memory from the beginning preserves a *partial* record because we cannot take in every detail in a scene and therefore take in only what seems significant to us. Of course there are other kinds of memories that are not completely conscious, or buried deep within the unconscious, and they may be recorded during that walk, but oral historians deal with conscious remembering.

Aging and Memory

We used to think that forgetting went on all through our lives. Research indicates that much is forgotten in the first twenty-four hours. More is forgotten during the next three to five years. But after that, constituents of a memory may remain intact for fifty years and more.[14]

Recently, there have been some revisions in long-held notions about memory and aging, such as the idea that aging produces a decline in all memory functions. A ninety-three-year-old friend of mine who reads three newspapers every day and subscribes to several news magazines was asked by her physician in an initial visit in 2001, "Who is president of the United States now?" She replied, "I can't bear to say his name." He wrote down, "Does not know who the president is." It did not occur to him to question the generally held notion that elderly people cannot remember much.

In fact, performance on memory tasks for elderly persons varies widely across different situations.[15] Of course, since individuals of any age remember selectively, researchers have to conclude that remembering depends on individual interests and needs. In general, though, in nondepressed people, in good health, in their seventies, eighties, and even nineties, there is no difference between them and young adults in vividness of recall of details when the interviewer has given the narrator an open-ended question. The explanation is that people choose memories important to them: they repeat them over the years as they seek to reinforce meanings in their lives.[16]

Also important for oral historians, research indicates that older adults are better at telling stories of the past than are young adults.[17] Researchers found that when they recited events to subjects, young adults were better at verbatim recall, but older adults made better sense of the story. The older adults had richer vocabularies and could call on wide networks of facts and associations.[18] Experience, and also rehearsal of salient memories with their relevant information and associations, must count here.

However, subsequent memories may sometimes crowd out earlier ones. But memories of late adolescence and young adulthood are remarkably resistant to diminution—a phenomenon possibly best explained by Rubin's theory mentioned earlier that this is the stage in our lives when we are defining ourselves as adults.[19] Researchers have found that subsequent memories do not alter the original if that is an extremely salient memory for the individual.[20]

Finally, let us consider biological changes in our brains as we age. Semantic memory, which enables us to understand, draw inferences, and solve problems, continues to operate very well as we age. Frontal lobes, which are important in recalling, may sometimes show effects of aging: for example, the person may forget the source of the memory, such as who told him or her a particular story. Also, the frontal lobes are implicated in working memory, which contains the variety of things we need to remember so that we can carry out tasks. The possibility of some diminution there must be considered. Brain mass does shrink, beginning in the sixties, at roughly 3 percent over a decade. But loss of neurons now seems to researchers to have little effect on memory overall.[21] This may be because recent research demonstrates that new neurons continue to form, a process called "neurogenesis." Self-help books on aging urge people to memorize poems, even the grocery list, to keep memory active because this activity encourages neurogenesis.

The conclusion we can draw is that people, whether young or old, remember what is important to *them*. On items of less salience, it is possible that young adults can remember a little more accurately and in a little more detail. How is this relevant to us as oral historians? In oral history interviewing, it is feasible to begin with the most open open-ended questions whenever possible so that the aged narrator selects what he or she wants to talk about within the topic indicated.

Research Methods Concerning Individual Memory

Consider this brief overview of methods psychologists use now to test memory. The old way of testing memory was in a laboratory: the researcher handed the subject a list of unconnected terms, asked the subject to read it, and then tested him to see how much he could remember. Fortunately, about twenty years ago, researchers began to get a glimmer that these memory list experiments set up an artificial situation that had little to do with how memory normally works. For one thing, words on a memory list are not in themselves important to the subject. In a multidisciplinary, edited volume, *Memory Distortion: How Minds, Brains, and Societies Reconstruct the Past*, Lawrence Sullivan states another reason: "The ability to control conditions in experimental situations is of great value. At the same time, it must be said that the experimental setting, by definition, narrows, resets, and redefines memory in ways that remove it from the uncontrolled associations with which memory is entangled in life outside the experimental setting."[22]

Memory research no longer goes on solely in the laboratory, and now some research projects—the so-called naturalistic studies of memory—have relevance for what we do in in-depth interviewing.[23] One example of such naturalistic studies is the British experiment in which people viewed a historic event on television—such as Margaret Thatcher's resignation—and were tested for memory of details and feelings immediately afterward and then months later.[24] In other experiments, the researchers and their students kept diaries over a short time of three months in one study[25] and, in another, up to six years.[26] Questions to test individual researchers' and students' memories were drawn from these diaries. In still other experiments, researchers called subjects on their cell phones during a designated day and asked, "What are you doing?" Later the subjects were tested at different intervals of time to see how much of that day's events they could remember. Because of carefully controlled experiments like these, there is increasing respect among psychologists for the value of life-narrative remembering as research data.[27]

Since much of the current research in psychology is closer to the types of memory tasks that oral history practitioners are interested in, I will consider here the findings from this research and also from research by historians and anthropologists on (1) consistency of the factual content, (2) memory of habitual events versus single events, (3) consistency of feelings in memory, (4) consistency of meanings over time, (5) effect of mood and emotional needs on recall, (6) memories of traumatic events, (7) physical sensation and remembering, (8) vivid images, purpose, and false memory, (9) memory of chronological time, (10) gender differences in remembering, and (11) effects of the interview environment and relationships on remembering.

Consistency of Factual Content of Long-Held Memories

Is there consistency in memories about events, or, in other words, are memories about events reliable? Australian researcher R. Finlay-Jones found that there was consistency across reinterviews with adults in the general population with respect to separation from parents in childhood. The subjects were interviewed once, then again after eight months and by different interviewers. Ninety-one percent were consistent in their accounts; only 9 percent (23 out of 244) were inconsistent in their answers.[28] In the United States, sociologist Lee Robins interviewed people in their forties who had been patients in a child guidance clinic when they were eight to fourteen. Robins found, in comparing these interviews with the guidance records, that they remembered events remarkably well.[29]

In a project on long-term memory, historian Alice Hoffman, as interviewer, and psychologist Howard Hoffman, as narrator, recorded his memories of his military service during World War II. They decided that they would conduct three different series of interviews, separated in time, about his war experiences: the first series was completed in 1978, the second, in 1982, and the third, in 1986. For the first two sets, the questions were open-ended, and no cues were presented. Alice then sought documentary evidence and used this information as cues in the third set of interviews. She drew these cues from the company log and other official documents, as well as photographs taken by the United States Army Signal Corps and by Howard himself. In the third interview, Alice showed the photographs and other documents to Howard one at a time, asking questions after each exposure to a cue.

The Hoffmans compared this testimony with written documents and information from an on-site visit at the Edgewood Arsenal in Maryland, where Howard had volunteered as a subject in poison gas experiments. They found that "the majority of the events in his memory claim occurred and moreover occurred pretty much as he says they did."[30] They explain that these forty-year-old memories have resisted change and "appear to have been protected from decay by rehearsal and reinforced by salience so that they have become fixed in the mind."[31] His memories were not always correct when exact dates were required; nor did he always correctly remember his army's exact position or details such as the water temperature during the invasion of southern France. His memory did supply analysis of his experiences, an interpretation of their meanings, and an account of their emotional impact—all were consistent across time.[32]

Recall of Daily, Habitual Events versus the Single Episode

Dutch psychologists Willem Wagenaar and Jop Groeneweg compared two sets of testimony from concentration camp inmates. The opportunity to do this occurred in 1984 when a court case was initiated against a Dutchman accused of Nazi crimes: he was a Kapos, a fellow prisoner who became a guard in Camp Erika in the Netherlands, and an especially brutal guard at that. The first set of seventy-eight interviews had been conducted by Dutch police beginning in 1943 (when the Gestapo closed the camp) and continuing until 1948. In 1984 victims were urged on nationwide television to come forward and testify during this Kapos's trial, and so Wagenaar and Groeneweg were able to find fifteen surviving witnesses from the original seventy-eight. In comparing the survivors' accounts before and after a lapse of forty years, they found that the level of reliability and accuracy in recall of both conditions and details was high: "The accounts of the conditions in the camp, the horrible treatment, the daily routine, the forced labour, the housing, the food, the main characters of the guards, are remarkably consistent."[33] However, names were often forgotten, even the Kapos's face; and sometimes survivors attributed crimes to the wrong guard or became confused about other details, such as weapons used. To the researchers' surprise, they found that memories of especially brutal events were no more likely to be remembered than memories of day-to-day events. Episodic memory—that is, the recall of something that happened once, at a specific time and place[34]—has been thought to be more resistant to diminution than memory of habitual actions or events. But these victims sometimes forgot not only the murders and tortures they had seen but also the brutal treatment they themselves had endured. Wagenaar and Groeneweg concluded that "40 years of normal life in a modern Western society provided too many interfering experiences, and apparently there was not a sufficient amount of overt or covert rehearsal to counteract the interference."[35] I find this conclusion puzzling.

Psychologists believe that memory of repeated, everyday events will not be as vivid as memory of a single dramatic event, the rare action, the rare occasion.[36] And yet, this finding is contrary to Wagenaar and Groeneweg's concentration camp study, where daily routine was remembered very well. Perhaps this environment was so radically different from anything the victims had known or would know after the war that even though the daily events were repetitive, they constitute, nonetheless, vivid memories.

In my own experience of interviewing I have found—and you may have found—that certain kinds of daily events are remembered in detail. Women could recall the kinds of dishes they prepared for a Sunday dinner as well as the things the family ate during the week. Men could recall not only the year they bought a tractor but also how the tractor was used and how they fixed it when it broke down. They could remember daily work in a certain season. These were details of daily life—humdrum, yes, but important to survival. Perhaps salience (in this case, a behavior's survival value) may be an exception to psychologists' conclusion about forgetting daily events.

Along these lines is research on memory of the shocking, one-time event that occurs in the political and social world—"flashbulb memories"—and its consistency over years. Events of public significance may be easily recalled if they affected the individual and if there was an association with personal action. When someone asks, "Where were you when you heard John F. Kennedy was shot?" most people alive at the time can remember. They have a vivid picture in their minds of what they were doing and how they reacted to the news.[37]

But is such a memory consistent over time? Sven-Ake Christianson in Sweden asked young adults to tell him where they were and what they were doing when they heard of the 1986 assassination of Prime Minister Olof Palme. The first part of the research took place six weeks after the event; the second part, a year later. Christianson found that the accuracy of the description of their main reactions remained, but specific details of this flashbulb memory had declined over the year's interval.[38]

Daniel Schacter sums up the research findings on memories of events: "On balance our memory systems do a remarkably good job of preserving the general contours of our pasts and of recording correctly many of the important things that have happened to us. We could not have evolved as a species otherwise."[39] Oral historians may find that overall a narrator's account is accurate but some details may be missing or erroneous. Needless to say, some inaccuracies do not negate the value of the entire testimony.

Consistency in Memories of Feelings

In in-depth interviewing it is the very interpretation of the event and the remembered feelings about it that we seek. The findings suggest that feelings are usually consistent *within* an individual's testimony. Oral historian Paul Thompson found, for example, that a narrator in his study for *The Edwardians* might confuse details about where her father came from, but her memories about her feelings for her father were consistent over three different interviews.[40] My research for a biography of Betty Smith, who wrote *A Tree Grows in Brooklyn*, illustrates the consistency in recall of intense feelings. When Betty Smith was in her late thirties, she picked up a book, Thomas Woolf's *Of Time and the River*, and started writing in the flyleaf her anguish over her mother's sharp words to her. In her forties she wrote her autobiographical novel—*A Tree Grows in Brooklyn*—in which she showed the mother answering her daughter in a belittling way. Then Betty Smith in her sixties wrote an autobiography in which she described her mother's bitter words. By the time she was seventy, she suffered from aphasia, an inability to summon the needed word, a condition caused by leakage of blood in the brain's capillaries in a particular area. But she acted out for the two students who lived in her house the instances of her mother's speaking crossly to her and the terrible way this made her feel. I found this out through oral history interviews with the two men who were living in her house during her last few years. So, the memory of these intense feelings about her mother was consistent over a lifetime.

Looking at broader research studies, I see findings indicating that the intensity of the emotional content of the memory affects recall. Sven-Ake Christianson and Birgitta Hubinette at the University of Stockholm studied questionnaires filled in by people who had witnessed office robberies; the questionnaires were administered four and fifteen months after the robbery. These written documents were compared with police reports taken immediately after the robbery. The researchers found that witnesses' accounts, both four and fifteen months after the event, were consistent with the information given in police reports. Such details as date and time were not, however, as well remembered as the gist of the event. The researchers concluded that "highly emotional real-life events are well retained over time with respect to details directly associated with the emotion-arousing event, but less so with respect to details of the concomitant circumstances of the event."[41] Other long-term memory research studies corroborate these research results concerning the persistence of memory of unusually intense emotional events.

Consistency in Memories of Meanings

Oral history research is a prime source for understanding meaning making. But how consistent over time are the meanings we attribute to events? Alessandro Portelli shows us how the death of a young steelworker, Luigi Trastulli, in a demonstration in an Italian industrial town became a symbol for working-class people (discussed in chapter 1). Their inability to avenge his death caused them in memory to place the death in a different struggle and a different time so that they could give a meaning to it to suit their needs. The implication is that the meaning of his death changed over the years from the time of the death to the interviews years later.

Given the fact that we sometimes change perceptions of events as we move from one life stage to another, it is reasonable to assume that we may change meanings of remembered events. On the other hand, studies like the Hoffmans's suggest that meanings attributed to significant events can be consistent over decades of a life.

Moods, Emotional Needs, and Recall

Have you noticed that when you feel "down," it is easy to recall or imagine the outcome of events as negative experiences? You start thinking about bad things that have happened to you. On the subject of mood affecting memory, research data suggest that depressed people remember less detail and have memories that are less vivid than nondepressed people.[42] And even nondepressed people respond on the basis of mood. French anthropologists studied farm workers who had been displaced by machinery and who were feeling sad and worried. The researchers found that in their narrators' testimony about childhood, they frequently selected and dwelled on painful events.[43] On the other hand, when people are feeling happy, they tend to recall good-feeling memories.[44]

Also, when people remember past events, present emotional needs affect memory.[45] In the research for the Betty Smith biography, I interviewed one narrator who had been a drinker and party maker, and he described to me a good time he had had at the beach on a spree with a drinking buddy. He did not remember that this occurred at a crucial time in his marriage. During the interview, his wife walked into the room with their granddaughter and remarked that she was about to give birth to their first child when he disappeared for several days on that spree. He looked surprised. Apparently, he forgot that detail because at the present time he needed to think of himself as a model husband, father, and grandfather.

In Wagenaar and Groeneweg's concentration camp study, we saw that the victims forgot certain unusually brutal acts against other prisoners and against themselves. We could consider as one reason for this the victims' present emotional need—the preservation of their sense of dignity and the refusal to make of themselves strange beings now for having seen unthinkable deeds in the past.

Memories of Traumatic Experiences: Different from Ordinary Memories

Trauma is often defined as an event or series of events of such negative effect on the individual that there is a break with life before the trauma and an influence on the life as it goes on afterward.[46] Sometimes memory of a trauma is repressed and no amount of cueing inspires its recall: such a traumatic memory may not ever be recalled, or if it is, psychologists think it will come to mind when the individual is ready to bear the emotional pain of it. When

Freud wrote about repression of painful memories, the aim of analysts was to bring these memories to consciousness. Recently brain researchers have identified the biological changes that allow willful forgetting: "This work confirms the existence of an active process by which people can prevent awareness of an unwanted past experience." These researchers identified the neural systems that underlie this process of cutting off awareness. They believe that their research offers a "neurobiological model of a voluntary form of repression proposed by Freud."[47] Perhaps forgetting traumatic events is a survival mechanism. Possibly this is still another reason why Groeneweg and Wagenaar's narrators forgot certain incidents.

As oral historians, we encounter narrators who do recall traumatic events. How might the narrator deal with a traumatic memory?[48] Research suggests that to reduce present anxiety, people sometimes remember themselves as being safer than they actually were at the time of the traumatic event.[49] We may try to minimize the impact of negative events, if possible, by downplaying our distress over them.[50] For example, I once asked my mother about the time when both she and my father were out of work—I called it a desperate time. My mother said, "It wasn't so bad." But I know from other sources that it was.

For memories of extremely emotion-laden events such as traumas, there may be intrusive, persistent recalling. Psychiatrist Charles Wilkinson observed the reactions of 102 victims, observers, and rescuers in the weeks after the collapse of two skywalks at the Hyatt Regency Hotel in Kansas City on July 17, 1981. When tons of concrete fell on the lobby, 114 people were killed and 200 injured. Wilkinson found that 90 percent of the witnesses he interviewed said they could not stop remembering.[51] In *Holocaust Testimony: The Ruins of Memory*, Lawrence Langer reports that Holocaust survivors could not even take satisfaction in their children's accomplishments because terrifying memories from the past were so much a part of their present daily life.[52] Historian Kim Lacy Rogers, with two other researchers, carried out in-depth interviews with African Americans living in the Mississippi Delta who had participated in the civil rights movement. Her conclusion from this research, described in *Life and Death in the Delta: African American Narratives of Violence, Resilience, and Social Change*, was that despite current prosperity— their children were educated, their lives were secure—these narrators were living daily with grief resulting from persistent memories of the violence and losses of that earlier time.[53]

For experiences characterized by strong emotion, the oral historian can expect the "central core" or gist of the experience to be well remembered, but he or she should also be alert to the possibility that peripheral details may not be remembered accurately. Memory researcher Marigold Linton, who kept a daily personal log for six years and tested herself monthly and at the end of the six years, concluded the following from her findings and others' research: (1) "The event must be salient and be perceived as strongly emotional at the time it occurs (or it must be 'rewritten' shortly thereafter)." (2) "Your life's subsequent course must make the target event focal in recall; the event may be seen as a turning point, the beginning of a sequence, or as instrumental in other later activities." (3) "The event must remain relatively unique. Its image must not be blurred by subsequent occurrences of similar events."[54]

Physical Sensation, a Spur to Remembering

Do you recall a spanking you received as a child? Possibly, physical sensation coupled with the event's meaning reinforces memory. Among several sources for the condition of our family at the time when both my parents were out of work is a memory of my own. I must have been no more than five at the time. We had to stay with my father's brother and his family, and this uncle was a stickler for church attendance. His wife decided that I did not have a proper dress to wear to church and insisted that my mother put this aunt's daughter's dress on me. I was told several times that I would have to be careful not to "spoil it." I remember having a very uneasy feeling. Maybe wearing my cousin's dress distressed me because that meant in my child's mind that the aunt did not judge *me* acceptable. But undoubtedly, wearing that dress was connected to an awareness of my parents' situation of being dependent on others. I might also remember this event because it was reinforced by the physical discomfort I felt. Shortly after the dress was on me, I found a mud puddle and sat down in it and received the spanking I expected. (Curiously, I do not remember any feelings of injustice connected with the spanking.) Such a little, seemingly unimportant event, but I suspect that the feeling of extreme uneasiness was coupled with the physical sensations of a wet bottom and then a sting, and this "fixed" the memory in my mind for decades. Incidentally, I asked my mother if she remembered this event—she did, but not the spanking.

Taste and smell are other sensory experiences that spark remembering. Daniel Schacter considers the way Marcel Proust's tasting the madeleine and savoring these crumbs of cookie activated memories of incidents from his childhood. Schacter comments, "Memories that can be elicited only by specific tastes and smells are fragile: they can easily disappear because there are few opportunities for them to surface." Nevertheless, those that do survive are powerful stimuli, Schacter says: "Having remained dormant for long periods of time, the sudden appearance of seemingly lost experiences cued by tastes or smells is a startling event."[55]

Sometimes just a quick glimpse of something becomes a visual cue that causes the act of remembering. Memory researcher Thomas Butler recalls seeing at his mother's wake a very old man who approached him and asked, "Do you know who I am?" Butler was about to admit that he could not remember the man when he noticed "a malevolent bit of smile, a little curl in a corner of his mouth." Butler said, "Martin Pendergast, our coal man!" That one trait constituted what psychologists call a "memory trace" and caused the process of remembering to be touched off—a picture of the whole man as he used to be emerged for Butler.[56]

Vivid Images, Recall, and False Memory

If you can recall a scene vividly, can you be sure it happened? If the narrator remembers the details, even *sees* them so vividly that she describes them, should oral historians automatically trust the memory as an accurate recall? Sometimes it's a vivid memory of something that happened—but the time is wrong.[57] In the Betty Smith biography, I reprint a letter she wrote that indicates some kind of abuse, possibly sexual, that occurred in her adolescence. I suggest that her stepfather *might* have been the abuser and produce some literary evidence. (Incidentally, I checked on the first biographer's treatment of this incident of abuse and found we had independently arrived at the same conclusion, that it was possibly sexual abuse and the stepfather, the abuser.) Betty Smith's daughter liked the stepgrandfather and was upset. She said, "You lady researchers nowadays read sex into everything."

She then told me that she spent a year with her grandmother and stepgrandfather when she was in third grade and if anything like that had ever happened to her mother, she would never have allowed her own daughter to live in his house. She remembered certain experiences accurately from the year she spent with them—she could see in her memory her grandmother's kitchen table, for example. She told me what was on the shelves above it. I have a document showing that the daughter did indeed spend a year with her grandmother *after* this stepgrandfather died. The vivid details this narrator recalled indicated to me that this was an accurate memory, but I found out it was the wrong year—she had a purpose that influenced the way she remembered.

Have you ever written a letter in your head as you were driving along and then later thought that you had written it because you can remember the look of the words on the paper? This is the phenomenon known as "false memory." We are certain that the event happened because we remember the scene vividly. When we check other sources, it becomes clear that the event never occurred at all. The problem is that the brain not only registers what we actually see in the world around us but also what we *imagine* seeing. Since perception and image are usually laid down in close proximity in the same area of the brain, Schacter points out, we are sure it happened.[58] The conclusion for the oral historian is that no matter how vivid the memory, check on it if something does not seem quite right.

Also, when we can remember the *source* of a memory, we assume that this means that the event actually happened. Daniel Schacter gives an example: you remember not only what you wrote in a letter but even where you were sitting when you wrote it. Curiously, the respondent never received it. It's possible that you imagined yourself sitting down at the table after dinner and writing the letter, even thought out what you would say. The imagined event became so real in your thinking that you are sure it happened. Schacter advises that if you recall that the mailbox was stuffed when you put the letter in, you can have a little more confidence that you actually did mail it—it is unlikely that you would have imagined such a detail.[59] What should we conclude? Do not assume automatically that a memory is accurate because the narrator can describe its source or details about it.

Remembering the Time

As researchers, we would like to pinpoint the time so that we can know the sequence in the chain of events, but our narrators will not be concerned about precise time. Researcher William Brewer found that personal memory typically contains information about actions, location, and thoughts, but rarely precise information about time. And, as you would expect, Brewer found that *questions about time* are the least effective means of stimulating recall.[60]

Charles Thompson discovered in a three-month study that his subjects did not place events correctly in the exact time, but they grouped events in a "chronologically ordered, continuous past reality." In life review research, these groups of events often correspond to eras in an individual's life—grade school, high school, college, marriage, and so forth.[61] But Eudora Welty writes, "The events in our lives happen in a sequence in time, but in their significance to ourselves they find their own order, a timetable not necessarily—perhaps not possibly—chronological. The time as we know it subjectively is often the chronology that stories and novels follow: it is the continuous thread of revelation."[62] And a critic says of Alice Munro's short stories that "memory and passion reorder a life and cause events to fall meaningfully out of sequence in the mind."[63] Historians often encounter this phenomenon of subjective time. Tamara Hareven and Randolph Langenbach found that textile workers in the Amoskeag mills in Manchester, New Hampshire, said they ended work in 1922, but they actually worked until 1935. The year 1922 was the time when a brutal strike changed their work life forever, ending it as they had known it.[64] When we have information indicating that the offered time is false, we can ask ourselves what need our narrator had. As Alessandro Portelli suggests in his discussion of time in oral history testimony, the answer to this question is important information in itself.[65]

Differences in the Way Men and Women Remember

In reacting to narrators in an oral history interview, we should take into account that gender can affect what is remembered because what is salient for people of one gender is not necessarily salient for people of another gender. Women tend to remember details of personal experiences more often than men.[66] This may be a result of socialization because research indicates that mothers talk differently about remembering to girls than to boys.[67] Culture also has an effect because boys learn early that some things are important for men, but other things are not important.[68] Researchers observed that men's accounts of personal histories tend to be more purposeful and linear than women's accounts.[69] A recent large-scale research study showed a female advantage in memory for specific information about events, names, and faces. However, there was no gender difference concerning semantic memory, that is, memory of concepts and facts associated with general knowledge.[70]

In our culture women have been encouraged to express feelings, and so we would expect them to remember feelings better than men do. A team in Britain, sociologist/oral historian Paul Thompson and his colleagues, two family therapists and one child psychiatrist, interviewed adult men and women who had lost a parent in childhood and had had to adjust to a stepparent. They found "women's narratives to be fuller and richer accounts of changes in relationships and the feelings that were evoked by events in childhood." The researchers theorize that socialization affected remembering. Thompson and his colleagues remark on how hard they had to work to get full answers from their male narrators and how these narrators would end their stories by saying, "That's all really."[71] Their research findings are in accord with other studies that indicate that women's memories of feelings surrounding events are articulated in more detail than are men's.[72] As oral historians, we can appreciate male narrators' efforts to recall for us family relationships, feelings, and details—depending on the individual, this may not come "naturally."

Effects of the Interviewer–Narrator Relationship on Remembering

Finally, remembering in an in-depth interview is willful; and this kind of remembering takes place in a context, or, as psychologists express this, in a retrieval environment. A place comfortable for the narrator during the interview is essential. Especially important for oral historians then is the interpersonal relationship in the interview and the interviewer's questions. You may have noticed in your own interviewing that a positive relationship inspires the narrator to think hard, to try to remember. Communications scholar Deborah Tannen found in her research that when the narrator makes a point by sharing a personal, intimate memory—rather than offering some general statement—he indicates a high level of emotional involvement in the interview and a feeling of trust in the person spoken to.[73] (Interviewer's style and phrasing of questions are discussed in chapters 3 and 4.)

Summary of Findings on Personal Memory

We can arrive at some generalizations about this research: Memory researchers have found that memory for the gist of an event—that is, the most important, core information about the event—persists although peripheral details may be forgotten. Events in which narrators participate themselves will be better recalled than secondhand information. Events in which there were high levels of mental activity and emotional involvement will be remembered. In many cases (but not all), atypical events will be more readily recalled than typical events.[74]

I come from this review of the research with a renewed respect for autobiographical or individual memory as evidence that oral historians can use, as well as some caveats about what to look for in interviewing and in critiquing an oral history. Consider asking yourself: (1) What is the narrator's mood? (2) What emotional need might impinge on this process of remembering? (3) What seems to be the narrator's purpose in recalling this particular memory this way? (4) How is gender showing up in remembering? (5) Is the gist of the memory recalled accurately? (6) What details does the narrator seem uncertain about? (7) How did I, as interviewer, interact with this narrator? (8) How did the environment in which the interview took place affect remembering? (9) What checks exist for corroboration or refutation of a particular memory?

Individual Memory and Collective Memory

Having surveyed the research on individual memory, let us turn to an exploration of remembering as a group. When I was interviewing people who worked in a cotton mill in Carrboro, North Carolina, in the early twentieth century, I was amazed at the way their individual memories and collective memory were contradictory although both were seriously believed and simultaneously held. The mill was erected in 1898, and small, drafty mill houses were built nearby. A bell rang at 5:00 a.m.—everybody got up, dressed, stoked the fire, put the biscuits in the oven, and tended to animals (usually a cow and several chickens). The bell rang again at 5:30. People ate breakfast hurriedly and were running to the mill by the time the bell rang again at 5:55. They worked in the mill from 6:00 a.m. to 6:00 p.m. (or 7:00 p.m. during the summer because the light held out) and always from 6:00 a.m. until 1:00 p.m. on Saturday. Every night they came home and cooked, cleaned house, took care of animals, brought in water from a well, and chopped wood. Whole families worked in the mill, from grandparents to mother and father, to children. (The father's wages were so low they had to be supplemented by the work of all able-bodied family members.) Some of these children were only seven or eight years old: they went to school for a few hours and then came to the mill to be close to their mothers and worked beside them.

When I asked a woman what she ate in the little time she had at lunch, the answer was a biscuit and a pickle. Often a woman told me she made her dresses and her children's clothes from discarded feed sacks. Not many narrators mentioned seeing a doctor. All said they were often tired. In the mill, workers had only a communal bucket and dipper for water to drink during the day. At night, they pulled strings of cotton out of their eyes. Several remembered mill workers who had died of brown lung disease.[75]

But the narrators said the mill owner was a good person. He was a man who was kin to many workers, and several narrators called him uncle. He walked around in the mill in overalls just like everybody else. He was a hard worker, and they respected him. Respect was reinforced by the local Baptist and Methodist churches' ministers, who preached sermons about accepting one's station in life and accepting authority.

Narrators said that they liked working in the mill: their friends were there. They recalled that the mill sponsored a baseball team that played on Saturday afternoons. They had a Fourth of July picnic, and at Christmas, all the families received a turkey. So, the testimony of personal hardships associated with mill work, the individual or autobiographical memory, was at odds with the rosy picture of the mill that they remembered, the collective memory. It must be noted that my sample was skewed: these were the people who had lived to old age and who had continued to reside in that community. People who got fired and moved away or who died young were not among my narrators. But the narrators who endured saw no contradiction between memories of harsh personal experiences and positive memories of mill work. What happened?

Research by historians, sociologists, and cultural anthropologists suggests that collective memory affects personal memory. French sociologist Maurice Halbwachs, influenced by Emile Durkheim's emphasis on the power of the social group, defined collective memory in 1925. In his book *The Collective Memory* (published after his death in a Nazi concentration camp), he argues that we humans need an "affective community"; that is, we need to be with others with whom we have shared experiences and to think in common with them, to identify with them.[76] Therefore, others influence us to forget some experiences and remember others and to interpret these shared memories in a certain way. A memory is passed back and forth.[77] Often memories from personal life and social life intermingle. Halbwachs argues, "A man must often appeal to others' remembrances to evoke his own past."[78]

In general, American historians stress the mutual influencing of individual memory and collective memory. For example, historian John Bodnar found in his study of workers at the Studebaker plant in South Bend, Indiana, that individual memory was heavily influenced by interpretations stated in public. Individuals, he reminds us, discuss what happened at work with their fellow workers, read the union's version, and hear the owners' version.[79]

Some French historians and anthropologists do their work on the assumption that personal memories are at the same time unique *and* interdependent on other individuals' memories within their group.[80] On the other hand, other European scholars, especially those who follow certain Russian psychologists contemporary with Halbwachs, argue that *all* remembering and forgetting by an individual depends on social process. Oral historians, dealing with specific memories of events, follow a less abstract view, assuming the mutual influencing of individual and group memories but seeing them as different entities.[81] Historian Susan Crane emphasizes that ultimately all memories are created by individuals: "But when, in fact, has collective memory ever been uttered if not individually?"[82]

Under the Umbrella of Collective Memory: Official Memory and Popular Memory

Collective memory can be thought of as a term covering two different kinds of remembering: official memory and popular memory. Terms and definitions in research on collective memory are still fluid, but consider this working definition: An official memory is a version advanced by a group or person in a position of officially sanctioned power. A popular memory (sometimes referred to as vernacular memory) is a version held by a group of people who do not necessarily possess power—except cultural power as songwriters, storytellers, poets, speakers—but who have shared an experience. Memory that is different from official memory and challenges it is called countermemory. Often a popular memory is a countermemory.

Official Memory

Studies of the manipulation of collective memory for political purposes show the influence on personal memory. Memory and Totalitarianism, edited by Luisa Passerini, presents a study of official memory in the Soviet Union where researchers found that the Stalinist regime did not want the famine of 1932–1933 to be remembered on any level. The government created official collective memories, suppressed countermemories, and thus ensured that the famine would not be part of history. After 1988, when the accepted overview of Russian history was discarded, oral historians seized the chance to research effects of the famine in Kuban. They could find nothing on this in newspapers or other documents. During the interviewing process, the researchers realized that narrators still felt reluctant to talk about their experiences during the famine because for so long that was a dangerous thing to do. There was no popular memory. Their personal stories, which they had not told before, researchers thought were still "incomprehensible" and "uninterpreted by the narrators."[83]

Government can both withhold information and also offer information, as we are seeing in our own time, so that an official memory, disseminated by the mass media, results. In the recent war in Iraq, United States government soldiers carried out a raid on a hospital to obtain the release of an army private, Jessica Lynch, who had been taken prisoner by Iraqi troops. The raid was offered to the major television networks for the morning programs, and the American public saw a film of armed soldiers risking their lives in a daring nighttime rescue mission. The public was told by some reporters that Private Lynch had been shot.

The Canadian Broadcasting Corporation televised the interviews that journalists from the British Broadcasting Corporation carried out with two nurses, two doctors, and one hospital administrator in the Iraqi hospital that had received Jessica Lynch. They also interviewed separately several local residents. The doctors said they found no bullet wounds, but broken bones indicated a fall. Since they had run out of blood, they donated their own blood so that Jessica Lynch could have the surgery on her injured knee that she desperately needed. They informed United States officials that Jessica Lynch said she wanted to go home, and they arranged a transfer of their patient to United States forces. The doctors reported that there were no armed soldiers in the hospital, and local residents said they had told United States Special Forces troops that the Iraqi troops had already fled the area.

The United States forces' raid, accompanied by two cameramen and a photographer, occurred just before the date the two sides had fixed for the transfer. The American public believed an official memory—a memory based on the film their government delivered to the television networks. A different film was seen in Canada, and there the government was not involved. Canadian citizens have a collective memory of the same event far different from the American public's memory.[84]

Continuing his research on collective memory after the Studebaker study, John Bodnar examined the expressed purposes for the Vietnam Veterans Memorial and found that the veterans who initiated the project simply wanted to commemorate their comrades who had been killed in the war. They felt that the government had forgotten them. Politicians wanted to reinforce the value of sacrificing for the nation. They also wanted to heal the rift caused by dissent over the war. What government officials did not expect was that the parade and dedication ceremonies for the monument would evoke feelings unlike their own. Some veterans displayed placards that bore such messages as, "We Killed, We Bled, We Died For Worse Than Nothing." Or, "No More Wars—No More Lies." Afterward, people who came to view the monument left things like cowboy boots, teddy bears, baseball caps, pictures of teenage soldiers. Bodnar concluded that these objects were symbols of a countermemory to official memory, that this was an effort by individuals "to restate the human pain and sorrow of war rather than the valor and glory of warriors and nations."[85]

Power of the Media to Create Popular Memory

Historian George Lipsitz explored the ways collective memory, or, in this research, popular memory, inculcated by the media, affects personal memory.

He analyzed the urban, ethnic, working-class family comedies millions of Americans watched between 1949 and 1956—such shows as *The Goldbergs* (a Jewish family in the Bronx), *Amos 'n Andy* (a black neighborhood in Harlem), *The Honeymooners* and *Hey Jeannie* (Irish working-class families in Brooklyn), *Life with Luigi* (Italian working-class family life in Chicago), and *Mama* (Norwegian working-class family in San Francisco). He found that these narratives used working-class experiences and expressed some class resentments. But they also portrayed a new phenomenon: an isolated nuclear family whose satisfaction came from consuming material goods. Lipsitz argues that "those shows dealt with the aspirations of individuals as if ethnic rivalries and discrimination did not exist. Instead, ethnics attain a false unity through consumption of commodities."[86] Thus, they provided a homogenizing framework—inauthentic but realistic enough to be believed, and attractive—by which an individual could remember her own childhood in an ethnic working-class family, rather than remember the sharp pain of poverty and discrimination.

Paula Hamilton in her research on domestic service in Australia during the 1920s and 1930s found that domestic workers remembered their lives as being like episodes of the British television serial *Upstairs, Downstairs*. Domestic service in Britain was unlike the Australian experience, but her narrators discounted memories of their own experience and internalized the version seen on television. Hamilton explains that the program "struck a chord with many of these workers seeking to find sources of common experience with what had been for most of them a very isolating one."[87]

Consider ways that journalists for television and radio networks exercise cultural power and influence popular memory. Barbie Zelizer in *Covering the Body: The Kennedy Assassination, the Media, and the Shaping of the Collective Memory*, shows how journalists created a popular memory about John F. Kennedy when they repeatedly used the metaphor of Camelot to describe his presidential administration. Extramarital affairs, including a dangerous one with the girlfriend of an organized crime leader, as well as blunders such as the Bay of Pigs invasion, were not accommodated in this version of a romantic time in a land of mythical dimensions.[88] Even now anniversary commemorations stress the heroism of this president and leave many of us feeling queasy about criticizing him. If you compare journalists' treatment of Bill Clinton's extramarital affairs to this treatment of John F. Kennedy's behavior, you can see the power of mass media to create popular memory.

Returning to the problem of making sense of contradictions in the mill workers' testimony—their personal memories versus their collective memory—consider this explanation: we see our present in a framework of memories of the past. The period of these narrators' early work life was the first couple of decades of the twentieth century. They had recently come from a farming way of life where they expected to work twelve hours a day or more, and so twelve hours a day in the mill did not seem unusual. All members of the family at least by age seven did some kind of work when they were farming, so the situation in the mill was not different. Farming is dangerous work. If a person contracted brown lung disease from working in the mill, at least he did not get kicked in the head by a mule when he was preparing the soil for planting cotton. In brief, I was not thinking about their past, which provided their framework for judging mill work: the contradictions I saw were not what they saw.

Narrators remembered unique, positive, personal events, family tragedies, and specific hardships in their work in the mill. But collective memory about good times in the mill was just as strong because the mill owner made an effort to create a sense of "we're just one big family." Also important, he had power in this one-industry town because he owned not only the mill but also the mill houses. If he fired a worker, the whole family was out of a place to live. And pressure to "count your blessings" came from the churches—conformity must have been almost inescapable.

Because my narrators were child workers in the mill at the beginning of the twentieth century—I did not interview them until the late 1970s—they may not have experienced directly the worries that their parents had about making ends meet, but certainly they were aware of their parents' concerns. Undoubtedly they were influenced by their parents' collective memories held in common with other workers in that mill; and as the generation of my narrators grew older, they continued to be influenced by their lifelong neighbors and fellow church members with whom they had once worked in the mill. Certainly, their sense of identification was heightened by their shared attitude about mill work. Still, they did not relinquish their personal memories. How people view their past is always grounded in their experience, but how they frame their remembrances depends on the social context.[89]

Conclusion

The basic question we oral historians have asked is this: Does what is remembered constitute evidence that we can use? I use psychologists' research here to argue that oral history testimony based on memory can be informative about actual events. And just as important, it informs us about the significance of the events. When other oral testimonies and written documents do not corroborate the narrator's statements, we can surmise that the narrator's testimony is possibly not true historically, but we may have evidence for a different kind of truth, perhaps a psychological truth for the narrator. We can ask, What does the discrepancy between the speaker's truth and the truth of other evidence indicate?

Always, in critiquing an oral history document, the oral historian must look at the memory involved and ask questions—such as those concerning individual memory suggested earlier in this chapter. Especially we should be concerned about the historical context for recalling and sensitize ourselves to the influence of collective memory on an individual's testimony. Historians Natalie Zemon Davis and Randolph Starn offer a succinct rule: "Whenever memory is invoked we should be asking ourselves: by whom, where, in which context, against what?"[90]

Recommended Reading

Psychology
Brewer, William F. "Memory for Randomly Sampled Autobiographical Events." In *Remembering Reconsidered: Ecological and Traditional Approaches to the Study of Memory*, ed. Ulric Neisser and Eugene Winograd, 21–90. Cambridge: Cambridge University Press, 1988. Among many informative articles in this volume, Brewer's article specifically discusses two empirical studies of autobiographical memory and concludes that rare actions and rare locations are remembered more readily than everyday events.

Fivush, Robyn. "Constructing Narrative, Emotion, and Self in Parent-Child Conversations about the Past." In *The Remembering Self*, ed. Ulric Neisser and Robyn Fivush, 136–57. Cambridge: Cambridge University Press, 1994. This is an important article for understanding early childhood development of memory and storytelling.

Fivush, Robyn, and Catherine A. Haden, eds. *Autobiographical Memory and the Construction of a Narrative Self: Developmental and Cultural Perspectives*. Mahwah, NJ: Lawrence Erlbaum, 2003. These chapters are concerned with the way individuals "create a life narrative embedded in sociocultural frameworks that define what is appropriate to remember, how to remember it, and what it means to be a self with an autobiographical past" (introduction).

Neisser, Ulrich, ed. *Memory Observed: Remembering in Natural Contexts*. San Francisco: W. H. Freeman and Company, 1982. A collection of diverse articles, several of which are of interest to oral historians, such as Elizabeth Loftus and John Palmer, "Reconstruction of Automobile Destruction," about the effect of the phrasing of the question on memory, pp. 109–15.

———. "Self-Narratives: True and False." In *The Remembering Self: Construction and Accuracy in the Self-Narrative*, ed. Ulric Neisser and Robyn Fivush, 1–18. Cambridge: Cambridge University Press, 1994.

Pillemer, David. *Momentous Events, Vivid Memories: How Unforgettable Moments Help Us Understand the Meaning of Our Lives.* Cambridge: Harvard University Press, 1998. Excellent review of research on autobiographical memory, presented in an engaging writing style that makes the information accessible both to specialist and lay reader.

Reese, Elaine, Catherine A. Haden, and Robyn Fivush. "Mother-Child Conversations about the Past." *Cognitive Development* 8 (1993): 403–30. An important article about early socialization, language development, and memory.

Rubin, David C., ed. *Autobiographical Memory.* Cambridge: Cambridge University Press, 1986. See Rubin's introduction as well as William F. Brewer's review essay, "What Is Autobiographical Memory?" pp. 25–49, and Marigold Linton's chapter on "the questions relevant to a serious study of the mind," "Ways of Searching and the Contents of Memory," pp. 50–67.

———. Introduction to *Remembering Our Past,* ed. David Rubin, 1–15. Cambridge: Cambridge University Press, 1995. In this volume there are both reviews of the research literature as well as new research; readability varies.

Schacter, Daniel. *Searching for Memory.* New York: Basic Books, 1996. This book presents a review and synthesis of recent research on memory. It is written in a lively, clear writing style that the lay person can understand and even enjoy.

Thompson, Charles P. "The Bounty of Everyday Memory." In *Autobiographical Memory,* ed. Charles P. Thompson, 29–44. Mahwah, NJ: Lawrence Erlbaum, 1998. See also in this volume Gillian Cohen, "The Effects of Aging on Autobiographical Memory" (pp. 105–23), and Harry Bahrick, "Loss and Distortion of Autobiographical Memory" (pp. 69–78). These articles are not all reader friendly for the lay person, but the research results are important to oral historians.

History, Literature, and Anthropology

Bodnar, John. "Power and Memory in Oral History: Workers at Studebaker." *Journal of American History* 75, no. 1 (March 1989): 1201–20. Illuminating essay on the way that individual memory of work at the Studebaker plant was organized in three major plots, all "influenced by positions and interpretations stated in public."

———. *Remaking America: Public Memory, Commemoration and Patriotism in the Twentieth Century.* Princeton, NJ: Princeton University Press, 1992. Book based on Bodnar's research on different ways that collective memory in America has been shaped, especially focused on the use of public ceremonies by people in official position to shape patriotic fervor for their own ends.

Bozon, Michel, and Anne-Marie Thiesse. "The Collapse of Memory: The Case of Farm Workers (French Vexir, Pays de France)." *History and Anthropology* 2 (1986): 237–59. The authors show connections between individual memory and collective memory.

Caruth, Cathy. *Unclaimed Experience: Trauma, Narrative and History.* Baltimore, MD: Johns Hopkins University Press, 1996. Author examines literary work concerned with trauma and offers valuable insights: "Each one of these texts engages, in its own specific way, a central problem of listening, of knowing, and of representing that emerges from the actual experience of the crisis" (p. 5).

Crane, Susan A. "Writing the Individual Back into Collective Memory." *American Historical Review* 102, no. 5 (December 1997): 1372–85. Crane reviews the work of major theorists of collective memory and argues that collective memory begins as individual memory: "All narratives, all sites, all texts remain objects until they are 'read' or referred to by individuals thinking historically" (p. 1381).

Darian-Smith, Kate, and Paula Hamilton, eds. *Memory and History in Twentieth-Century Australia.* Oxford: Oxford University Press, 1994. A collection of research articles with discussions of theory—the volume has wider significance than the title suggests.

Davis, Natalie, and Randolph Starn. Introduction to "Memory and Counter-memory," special issue, *Representations,* no. 26 (Spring 1989): 1–6. Brief but cogent introduction to essays on memory. See especially in the same issue Pierre Nora, "Between Memory and History: Les Lieux de Memoire," pp. 7–24.

Debouzy, Marianne. "In Search of Working-Class Memory: Some Questions and a Tentative Assessment." *History and Anthropology* 2 (1986): 261–82. Author shows how differences in workers' memories vary according to trades, as well as cultural traditions and national experiences.

Fujitani, T., Geoffrey White, and Lisa Yoneyama, eds. *Perilous Memories: The Asia-Pacific War(s).* Durham, NC: Duke University Press, 2001. An excellent collection of essays centered on a specific geographical area but with wider implications as well. In this volume, see especially the introduction, pp. 1–29, by the editors; Marita Sturken, "Absent Images of Memory: Remembering and Reenacting the Japanese Internment," pp. 33–49; and Diana Wong, "Memory Suppression and Memory Production: The Japanese Occupation of Singapore," pp. 218–38.

Gillis, John, ed. *Commemorations: The Politics of National Identity.* Princeton, NJ: Princeton University Press, 1994. These research essays about commemorations in France, Germany, the United States, Israel, and Britain range from names of the dead to gold-star American mothers to public dedication of statues. They deal with both preservation of certain collective memories and the supplanting of others.

———. "Remembering Memory: A Challenge for Public Historians in a Post-national Era." *Public Historian* 14, no. 4 (1992): 91–101.

Glassberg, David. "Public History and the Study of Memory." *Public Historian* 18, no. 2 (Spring 1996): 7–23. Glassberg wrestles with unsettling issues in public history and memory. His statements are discussed by historians David Lowenthal, Michael Frisch, Michael Kammen, and Linda Shopes in *Public Historian* 19, no. 2 (Spring 1997): 31–56.

Irwin-Zarecka, Iwona. *Frames of Remembrance: The Dynamics of Collective Memory.* New Brunswick, NJ: Transaction Publishers, 1994. A brilliant in-depth study of collective memory, especially of the "community of memory" shared by "memory workers" of the Holocaust. Although her focus is on the obliteration of the memory of Poland's treatment of Polish Jews during World War II, the findings have wider implications. Any chapter could suggest topics for dissertations.

Jeffrey, Jaclyn, and Glenace Edwall, eds. *Memory and History: Essays on Recalling and Interpreting Experience*. Lanham, MD: University Press of America, 1994. A collection of articles from presentations at a conference of oral historians and cognitive psychologists in 1988. All of the articles are informative, but see especially Paul Thompson's "Believe It or Not: Rethinking the Historical Interpretation of Memory," in which he compares approaches to memory that historians have taken in different countries.

Kammen, Michael. *Mystic Chords of Memory: The Transformation of Tradition in American Culture*. New York: Knopf, 1991. Kammen traces how the United States acquired "a configuration of recognized pasts."

Leydesdorff, Selma, Luisa Passerini, and Paul Thompson, eds. *Gender and Memory*, vol. 4 of *International Yearbook of Oral History and Life Stories*. Oxford: Oxford University Press, 1996. See especially the introduction, where the authors argue that feminist approaches in historical research and oral history "grew up together" along paths that intertwine. There is diversity in the research sites in the articles in this collection, and they ask different questions about gender and memory, but the totality is entirely convincing in the premise that memories are gendered.

Lipsitz, George. "The Meaning of Memory: Family, Class and Ethnicity." *Cultural Anthropology* 1 (November 1986): 355–87. A trenchant analysis of the way popular entertainment, specifically television situation comedies, shapes our views of the history we lived.

———. *Time Passages: Collective Memory and American Popular Culture*. Minneapolis: University of Minnesota Press, 1990. Book-length treatment of the theme in the earlier article (cited above), expanding the research terrain to include other kinds of cultural offerings that influence popular memory, for example, novels.

Michman, Dan, ed. *Remembering the Holocaust in Germany, 1945–2000: German Strategies and Jewish Responses*. New York: Lang, 2002. These articles examine different strategies for forming—or obscuring—collective memory of the Holocaust, depending on the particular group.

Passerini, Luisa, ed. Introduction to *Memory and Totalitarianism*, vol. 1 of *International Yearbook of Oral History and Life Stories*, 1–19. Oxford: Oxford University Press, 1992. Thought-provoking introduction by the editor as well as articles that are research based and specific in their conclusions about collective memory; the contexts are wide-ranging. See especially Daria Khubova, Andrei Ivankiev, and Tonia Sharova, "After Glasnost: Oral History in the Soviet Union," pp. 89–101.

Portelli, Alessandro. "The Death of Luigi Trastulli: Memory and Event," and "'The Time of My Life': Functions of Time in Oral History." In *The Death of Luigi Trastulli and Other Stories*, 1–26 and 59–76. Buffalo: State University of New York, 1991. This volume offers essays based on the author's oral history research that illuminate subtle transformations in popular memory.

Roth, Michael, and Charles Salas, eds. *Disturbing Remains: Memory, History, and Crisis in the Twentieth Century.* Los Angeles: Getty Research Institute Publications Program, 2001. A collection of essays that reveal how shared trauma becomes collective memory, but a collective memory that is shaped by identifiable purposes. In their excellent introduction, the authors ask, "How can traumas that affect an entire community—events so dire that they exceed the categories it uses to take in the world—be adequately represented?"

Thelen, David. "Memory and American History." *Journal of American History* 75, no. 4 (March 1989): 1117–29. This is a thoughtful introduction to articles in this issue that concern collective memory—three of these articles discuss the use of oral history specifically.

Thomson, Alistair, Michael Frisch, and Paula Hamilton. "The Memory and History Debates: Some International Perspectives." *Oral History* 22, no. 2 (Winter 1995): 33–43. This very useful article presents an overview of scholarly debates about linkages between popular memory and official memory and historians' scholarship, with a focus on developments in Britain, the United States, and Australia. The authors conclude by saying that they have traced "some of the shifting debates about memory and history which are relevant to oral historians: the movements from initial celebration of 'history from below'; through arguments about the reliability of memory and the validity of oral testimony; toward concerns about the relationships between history, including oral history, and the contests for popular, collective or national memory" (p. 43).

Zelizer, Barbie. *Covering the Body: The Kennedy Assassination, the Media, and the Shaping of Collective Memory.* Chicago: University of Chicago Press, 1992. Written in a lively style, this well-researched book takes on some sacred—and manufactured—memories in American popular culture, showing how journalists created Camelot.

Notes

1. Daniel Schacter, *Searching for Memory: The Brain, the Mind, and the Past* (New York: Basic Books, 1996), 4.

2. Robyn Fivush, "Constructing Narrative, Emotion, and Self in Parent-Child Conversations about the Past," in *The Remembering Self,* ed. Ulric Neisser and Robyn Fivush, 136–57 (Cambridge: Cambridge University Press, 1994).

3. David C. Rubin, Scott E. Wetzler, and Robert D. Nebes, "Autobiographical Memory across the Lifespan," in *Autobiographical Memory,* ed. David C. Rubin, 202–21 (Cambridge: Cambridge University Press, 1986); see p. 212.

4. Minda Tessler and Katherine Nelson, "Making Memories: The Influence of Joint Encoding on Later Recall by Young Children," *Consciousness and Cognition* 3 (1994): 307–26; see p. 321.

5. Katherine Nelson, "The Psychological and Social Origins of Autobiographical Memory," *Psychological Science* 4, no. 1 (1993): 7–14; see p. 8.

6. Katherine Nelson, "Narrative and Self, Myth and Memory: Emergence of the Cultural Self," in *Autobiographical Memory and the Construction of a Narrative Self: Developmental and Cultural Perspectives*, ed. Robyn Fivush and Catherine A. Haden, 3–28 (Mahwah, NJ: Lawrence Erlbaum, 2003); see p. 23.

7. David Thelen, "Memory and American History," *Journal of American History* 75, no. 4 (1989): 1117.

8. Schacter, *Searching for Memory*, 4; William F. Brewer, "What Is Recollective Memory?" in *Remembering Our Past: Studies in Autobiographical Memory*, ed. David C. Rubin, 19–66 (Cambridge: Cambridge University Press, 1995); see p. 47.

9. Schacter, *Searching for Memory*, 217.

10. Schacter, *Searching for Memory*, 9.

11. Schacter, *Searching for Memory*, 71.

12. Schacter, *Searching for Memory*, 70.

13. Schacter, *Searching for Memory*, 52.

14. Harry P. Bahrick, "Semantic Memory Content in Permastore: 50 Years of Memory for Spanish Learned in School," *Journal of Experimental Psychology: General* 113 (1984).

15. Schacter, *Searching for Memory*, 283.

16. Gillian Cohen, "The Effects of Aging on Autobiographical Memory," in *Autobiographical Memory: Theoretical and Applied Perspectives*, ed. Charles P. Thompson et al., 105–23 (Mahwah, NJ: Lawrence Erlbaum, 1998); see p. 110.

17. Schacter, *Searching for Memory*, 299–300.

18. Schacter, *Searching for Memory*, 291.

19. Schacter, *Searching for Memory*, 298.

20. See, for example, Alice M. and Howard S. Hoffman, *Archives of Memory: A Soldier Recalls World War II* (Lexington: University Press of Kentucky, 1990), 150. A brief account of the Hoffmans's research and a discussion can be found in Alice M. Hoffman and Howard S. Hoffman, "Reliability and Validity in Oral History: The Case for Memory," in *Memory and History: Essays on Recalling and Interpreting Experience*, ed. Jaclyn Jeffrey and Glenace Edwall, 107–30 (Lanham, MD: University Press of America, 1994).

21. L. L. Light, "Memory and Aging: Four Hypotheses in Search of Data," *Annual Review of Psychology* 42 (1991): 333–76.

22. Lawrence E. Sullivan, "Memory Distortion and Anamnesis: A View from the Human Sciences," in *Memory Distortion: How Minds, Brains, and Societies Reconstruct the Past*, ed. Daniel L. Schacter, 386–400 (Cambridge: Harvard University Press, 1995); see p. 397.

23. David Pillemer discusses Ulrich Neisser's championship of naturalistic studies of memory as well as the criticisms of this kind of research. See David Pillemer, *Momentous Events, Vivid Memories: How Unforgettable Moments Help Us Understand the Meaning of Our Lives* (Cambridge, MA: Harvard University Press, 1998), 6–9.

24. Martin Conway, *Flashbulb Memories* (Hillsdale, NJ: Lawrence Erlbaum, 1995). Described in Schacter, *Searching for Memory*, 198.

25. For a book-length account of this diary research project, see Charles P. Thompson, John J. Skowronski, Steen F. Larsen, and Andrew L. Betz, *Autobiographical Memory: Remembering What and Remembering When* (Mahwah, NJ: Lawrence Erlbaum, 1996).

26. W. A. Wagenaar, "My Memory: A Study of Autobiographical Memory over Six Years," *Cognitive Psychology* 18 (1986): 225–52; see also Marigold Linton, "Transformations of Memory in Everyday Life," in *Memory Observed: Remembering in Natural Contexts*, ed. Ulrich Neisser, 77–91 (San Francisco: W. H. Freeman, 1982).

27. Pillemer, *Momentous Events, Vivid Memories*, 9–10.

28. R. Finlay-Jones, "The Reliability of Reports of Early Separation," *Journal of Psychiatry* (Australia) 15 (1981): 27–31. Cited in Lee N. Robins et al., "Early Home Environment and Retrospective Recall," *American Journal of Orthopsychiatry* 55 (January 1985): 28–29.

29. Lee N. Robins, *Deviant Children Grown Up* (Baltimore, MD: Williams and Wilkins, 1966).

30. A. Hoffman and H. Hoffman, *Archives of Memory*, 144. See also A. Hoffman and H. Hoffman, "Reliability and Validity in Oral History."

31. A. Hoffman and H. Hoffman, *Archives of Memory*, 145.

32. A. Hoffman and H. Hoffman, *Archives of Memory*, 144.

33. W. A. Wagenaar and J. Groeneweg, "The Memory of Concentration Camp Survivors," *Applied Cognitive Psychology* 4 (1990): 77–87; see pp. 84–87.

34. I use here the definition given by Katherine Nelson in "The Psychological and Social Origins of Autobiographical Memory," 7.

35. Wagenaar and Groeneweg, "Memory of Concentration Camp Survivors," 84–87.

36. Thompson et al., *Autobiographical Memory: Remembering What and Remembering When*, 64.

37. Norman R. Brown, Steven K. Shevell, and Lance R. Rips, "Public Memories and Their Personal Recall," in Thompson et al., *Autobiographical Memory: Theoretical and Applied Perspectives*, 137–58; see p. 157.

38. Sven-Ake Christianson, "Flashbulb Memories: Special, but Not So Special," *Memory and Cognition* 17, no. 4 (1989): 435–43. See also Conway, *Flashbulb Memories*.

39. Schacter, *Searching for Memory*, 308; William F. Brewer, "Memory for Randomly Sampled Autobiographical Events," in *Remembering Reconsidered*, ed. Ulric Neisser and Eugene Winograd, 21–90 (Cambridge: Cambridge University Press, 1988), 87.

40. Paul Thompson, *The Voice of the Past* (New York: Oxford University Press, 2000), 146–47.

41. Sven-Ake Christianson and Martin A. Safer, "Emotional Events and Emotions in Autobiographical Memory," in Rubin, *Remembering Our Past*, 222–23.

42. J. M. G. Williams, "Depression and the Specificity of Autobiographical Memory," in Rubin, *Remembering Our Past*, 244–67.

43. Michel Bozon and Anne-Marie Thiesse, "The Collapse of Memory: The Case of Farm Workers (French Vexir, Pays de France)," *History and Anthropology* 2 (1986): 237–59; see p. 242.

44. Christianson and Safer, "Emotional Events and Emotions in Autobiographical Memories," 229. Daniel Schacter summarizes research evidence for the effects of mood on memory in *Searching for Memory*, 211.

45. Schacter, *Searching for Memory*, 211.

46. See the introductory chapter in Cathy Caruth, *Unclaimed Experience: Trauma, Narrative, and History* (Baltimore, MD: Johns Hopkins University Press, 1996).

47. Michael C. Anderson, Kevin N. Ochsner, Brice Kuhl, Jeffrey Cooper, Elaine Robertson, Susan W. Gabrieli, Gary H. Glover, and John D. E. Gabrieli, "Neural Systems Underlying the Suppression of Unwanted Memories," *Science* 303 (January 9, 2004): 232–35; see p. 235.

48. In *Opening Up: The Healing Power of Confiding in Others* (New York: William Morrow and Company, 1990), James W. Pennebaker argues that confession is good for the soul, but not every soul.

49. Schacter, *Searching for Memory*, 205.

50. Charles P. Thompson, "The Bounty of Everyday Memory," in Thompson et al., *Autobiographical Memory: Theoretical and Applied Perspectives*, 29–44; see p. 42.

51. C. B. Wilkinson, "Aftermath of a Disaster: The Collapse of the Hyatt Regency Hotel Skywalks," *American Journal of Psychiatry* 140 (1983): 1134–39.

52. Lawrence Langer, *Holocaust Testimony: The Ruins of Memory* (New Haven, CT: Yale University Press, 1991), 34–35.

53. Kim Lacy Rogers, *Life and Death in the Delta: African American Narratives of Violence, Resilience, and Social Change* (New York: Palgrave, 2005).

54. Linton, "Transformations of Memory in Everyday Life," 89–90. See also Thompson et al., *Autobiographical Memory: Theoretical and Applied Perspectives*, 206.

55. Schacter, *Searching for Memory*, 27.

56. Thomas Butler, *Memory: History, Culture and the Mind* (London: Basil Blackwell, 1989), 17.

57. Brewer, "Memory for Randomly Sampled Autobiographical Events," 86.

58. Schacter, *Searching for Memory*, 23.

59. Schacter, *Searching for Memory*, 116.

60. Brewer, "Memory for Randomly Sampled Autobiographical Events," 86.

61. Thompson et al., *Autobiographical Memory: Remembering What and Remembering When*, 215.

62. Eudora Welty, *One Writer's Beginnings* (Cambridge, MA: Harvard University Press, 1984), 68–69.

63. Lorrie Moore, "Leave Them and Love Them: In Alice Munro's Fiction, Memory and Passion Reorder Life," *Atlantic Monthly*, December 2004, 126.

64. Tamara Hareven and Randolph Langenbach, *Amoskeag* (New York: Pantheon Books, 1978), 2.

65. Alessandro Portelli, "The Death of Luigi Trastulli: Memory and Event," and "'The Time of My Life': Functions of Time in Oral History," in *The Death of Luigi Trastulli and Other Stories*, 1–26 and 59–76 (Buffalo: State University of New York, 1991).

66. For a summary of this research, see Pillemer, *Momentous Events, Vivid Memories*, 21–22.

67. Elaine Reese, Catherine A. Haden, and Robyn Fivush, "Mother-Child Conversations about the Past," *Cognitive Development* 8 (1993): 403–30.

68. Pillemer, *Momentous Events, Vivid Memories*, 196.

69. M. M. Gergen and J. L. Gergen, "Narratives of the Gendered Body in Popular Autobiography," in *The Narrative Study of Lives*, ed. R. Josselson and A. Lieblich, 191–218 (Newbury Park, CA: Sage, 1993).

70. Agneta Herlitz, Lars-Goran Nilsson, and Lars Backman, "Gender Differences in Episodic Memory," *Memory and Cognition* 25 (1997): 801–11; see pp. 805 and 807.

71. Gwyn Daniel and Paul Thompson, "Stepchildren's Memories of Love and Loss," in *Gender and Memory*, vol. 4 of *International Yearbook of Oral History and Life Stories*, 165–85 (Oxford: Oxford University Press, 1996); see p. 167.

72. M. Ross and D. Holmberg, "Recounting the Past: Gender Differences in the Recall of Events in the History of a Close Relationship," in *Self-Inference Processes: The Ontario Symposium*, vol. 6, ed. J. M. Olson and M. P. Zanna, 135–50 (Hillsdale, NJ: Lawrence Erlbaum, 1990). See also C. Burck and G. Daniel, "Moving On: Gender Beliefs in Post-Divorce and Stepfamily Process," in *Gender, Power, and Relationships: New Developments*, ed. Charlotte Burck and Bebe Speed (London: Routledge, 1995); and David Pillemer, *Momentous Events, Vivid Memories*, 184.

73. Deborah Tannen, *You Just Don't Understand* (New York: Ballantine, 1990), 149.

74. Thompson et al., *Autobiographical Memory: Remembering What and Remembering When*, 64.

75. Valerie Yow (listed as Valerie Quinney), "Childhood in a Southern Mill Village," *International Journal of Oral History* 3, no. 3 (November 1982): 167–74. This collection of oral histories is in the Carrboro Public Library, Carrboro, North Carolina.

76. Maurice Halbwachs, *The Collective Memory*, trans. Francis Kitter and Vida Yazdi Ditter (New York: Harper and Row, 1950; original in French was published by Presses Universitaires de France, 1950), 25.

77. Halbwachs, *Collective Memory*, 31.

78. Halbwachs, *Collective Memory*, 51.

79. John Bodnar, "Power and Memory in Oral History: Workers at Studebaker," *Journal of American History* 75, no. 1 (March 1989): 1201–20; see p. 1202.

80. Marianne Debouzy, "In Search of Working-Class Memory: Some Questions and a Tentative Assessment," *History and Anthropology* 2 (1986): 270–71.

81. Communications scholar David Bakhurst summarizes their theory this way: (1) "memory is a psychological function which is essentially social in origin"; (2) "memories are socially constituted states"; (3) "certain forms of collective activity represent a form of social memory, irreducible to the happenings in any individual

mind, yet essential to the continuity of the mental life of each individual." David Bakhurst, "Social Memory in Soviet Thought," in *Collective Remembering*, ed. David Middleton and Derek Edwards, 203–26 (Newbury Park, CA: Sage, 1990); see p. 223.

82. Susan A. Crane, "Writing the Individual Back into Collective Memory," *American Historical Review* 102, no. 5 (December 1997): 1372–85; see p. 1382.

83. D. Khubova, A. Ivankiev, and T. Sharova, "After Glasnost," in *International Yearbook of Oral History and Life Stories*, vol. 1, 89–101 (Oxford: Oxford University Press, 1992); see p. 100.

84. Mitch Potter, Middle East Bureau, Nasiriya, Iraq, posted to the *Toronto Star* on May 5, 2003. British Broadcasting Corporation documentary, *War Spin: The Truth about Jessica*, aired May 25, 2003, on Canadian Broadcasting Corporation's television show *Newsworld's Passionate Eye*.

85. John Bodnar, *Remaking America: Public Memory, Commemoration and Patriotism in the Twentieth Century* (Princeton, NJ: Princeton University Press, 1992), 7–8.

86. George Lipsitz, "The Meaning of Memory: Family, Class and Ethnicity," *Cultural Anthropology* 1 (1986): 355–87; see pp. 378–79.

87. Paula Hamilton, "The Knife Edge: Debates about Memory and History," in Kate Darian-Smith and Patricia Hamilton, *Memory and History in Twentieth Century Australia* (Oxford: Oxford University Press, 1994), 9–32; see p. 26.

88. Barbie Zelizer, *Covering the Body: The Kennedy Assassination, the Media, and the Shaping of the Collective Memory* (Boulder: University of Colorado Press, 1992).

89. Iwona Irwin-Zarecka, *Frames of Remembrance: The Dynamics of Collective Memory* (New Brunswick, NJ: Transaction Publishers, 1994), 56.

90. Natalie Zemon Davis and Randolph Starn, introduction to "Memory and Counter-memory," special issue, *Representations*, no. 26 (Spring 1989): 7–24; see p. 2.

CHAPTER THREE

꒰ꕤ꒱

Preparation for the
Interviewing Project

Having defined this research methodology, oral history, and scrutinized memory, which it depends on, let us get down to work. Choose a subject for research that is of great interest to you. In the old view of research, the researcher was objective, noninvolved. However, even before the 1960s, when that model began to be questioned, the best research was done by people much involved because they were highly motivated to do a good job and were intensely committed to the project. They could thus endure the setbacks. They had an intrinsic interest in the topics under discussion, and the narrators sensed this. The narrators were in turn motivated to respond. (This does not mean that interest prevents us from stepping back and taking a critical look at the project when that is needed.)

Imagining what topics the project will focus on and how you will do this is, of course, the first step in the research. Becoming conscious of assumptions, formulating questions, even defining tentative hypotheses, and critically examining all of these are necessary activities even at the beginning. These are the things that influence us as we choose topics and specific questions.

This chapter contains the information that helps us move the research from this beginning to the interviewing phase. We cannot skip careful preparation and achieve anything but random conversations, so this is a crucial phase in the project. Doing careful background research, deciding what we want to find out, drawing up the interview guide, selecting narrators carefully, and getting tape-recording equipment ready are discussed in this chapter.

Conceptualization of the Research Project

Ask the question, What do I want to find out? Write out the list of questions, then express them as topics. Locate everything published on these topics and skim them until you decide which written sources will be helpful, and begin a close study of these specific works.

Some researchers using the approach of grounded theory object to the literature-review-first rule because this prevents the researcher from keeping an open mind and viewing evidence in new ways. I urge you to take advantage of the work that has been done before and critiques of it. Knowing the pitfalls and possibilities that other researchers have encountered can be helpful if you also maintain awareness of how preconceived notions may be influencing the course of your research.

Whether this is an event, movement, community, set of social problems, or individual biography you are researching, look for names of people involved. Start asking librarians, agency directors, ministers, teachers—whoever might know something about the history of the person or topic or whoever has been involved in some way with the topic—"Who was involved in this? Who would know something about this?" Write notes to the individuals named as having knowledge of the subject and ask if they would talk to you. Then follow up with a telephone call to say you would like to meet them briefly to talk about the event, movement, or individual. These are informal conversations: do not record, just take notes.

Because you are dealing with living persons, you have the opportunity to find out what is important to them in their history and in their present lives. As you carry out these informational interviews, ask, "If you were writing this study, what would you include?" and "Who would you recommend I interview?" In a community history, I carry out informational interviews with various individuals in that community, asking the questions above and, "If you were writing this history, what would you consider important?" I also ask, "Who was present at that event? Who was involved in making this happen? Who was affected by this?" In a family history ask, "What were the events in the family that you would expect to be in the history? What were the hopes and joys I should talk about? The sorrows?" In a biographical study, ask the person what he or she considers to be the most important events, which persons were significant in his or her life. Or if the individual is deceased, ask those who knew him or her well what they think were the pivotal events, the most significant relationships, the most important joys and sorrows, the aspirations, the defeats. Ask for names of people with whom you should talk. Find out if they have letters, photographs, or newspaper clippings.

How you go about conceptualizing the interviewing project depends on the kind of project you are doing. The chapters on community studies, family research, and individual biography later in this book present more detail on procedures relevant to the particular kind of project; this chapter offers a general strategy.

As you reflect on the information in these oral and written sources, your knowledge and understanding grow. You begin to have questions in addition to the ones you started with. Think about how the community, family, or individual is typical for the time and place and how it may be different. For example, a small group of people in an oral history methodology class I taught were interested in how DeKalb, the small Illinois town in which they lived, experienced World War II. They narrowed the project to an exploration of the ways that management and workers converted a Wurlitzer factory from the manufacture of organs to gliders and guided bombs. We invited men and women who had been workers there during the war to tour the now-defunct empty factory with us and then return to the classroom to talk. We listened to what they had to say about their experiences and found out what they considered important. We compared these local experiences with our readings in the social history of the United States during World War II. We began to think about the ways that the DeKalb workers' experiences might turn out to be similar to those of workers in other places and other kinds of war work and how they might be different.[1]

We composed a list of topics based on these issues as well as the events and situations that the workers noted as important to them. We also included questions of importance to us as historians, anthropologists, or psychologists, such as:

How did the men who had made beautiful organs adapt their skills to the manufacture of gliders?

How did they view the influx of unskilled women workers?

How were women workers treated in this plant?

How did the acquisition of manufacturing skills and increase in job responsibility affect the self-concept of these women, who had formerly done farmwork or retail sales?

To what extent and in what ways did coworkers help one another?

How were these workers affected by the national movement to unionize labor?

How did people react to wartime propaganda in the plant? To surveillance in the plant?

How did they respond to the news of the death of former coworkers overseas?

We had studied the information we needed to place the experiences of these workers in a historical context; and therefore we were able to write the interview guide so that both the unique aspects and the shared aspects were discussed. Planning the interview guide with care means that you will obtain testimony on a range of topics. After the project is over, you might wish you had asked questions about an overlooked topic, but you cannot go back to all of the narrators. If you have done the preliminary work with written and oral sources described above, you can compose an interview guide that is inclusive. This stage of conceptualizing the project is of utmost importance.

Composing the Interview Guide

An interview guide is not a questionnaire. A questionnaire is a series of questions that limit the range of answers the respondent can give, such as "agree, agree slightly, disagree slightly, or disagree." The questionnaire has a fixed set of questions, each with a stated limit on the kinds of answers acceptable. The interviewer may not depart from the questionnaire to follow different topics: if the answer does not fit one of the stated categories, he or she has to make it fit. An interview guide (sometimes referred to as the interview format) is a plan for an interview. The guide contains the topics the interviewer will pursue but does not limit the interview to those topics because the narrator will have the freedom to suggest others. The guide will have specific questions phrased in an open-ended way as much as possible—that is, there will often be no stated limit to the number of ways the narrator may answer. An order strictly following the guide will not be imposed on the narrator, who may wish to follow a different order that makes more sense to him or her. However, the guide provides topics and a strategy for following a line of questioning. You can change this plan, that is, what you think is significant enough to ask about. But with a plan, you do not flounder—you know what to ask next.

The interview guide is not just a plan the interviewer can throw away once the interview begins, however. The topics and their specific questions cover the information that the interviewer needs, but leeway is built into the situation to allow for the emergence of the unanticipated. This flexibility allows the narrator to teach the interviewer things he or she did not already know, while ensuring that the information the interviewer sought is also obtained.

A much higher level of skill is required in using the interview guide as compared to the questionnaire. The interviewer must understand the specific objectives of the interviewing project so well that even if the narrator suggests following other lines of investigation or chooses a different order of topics, the interviewer can still return to the unanswered questions he or she has come with if they still seem significant.

This is why it is imperative that the interviewer carefully think through and write out the interview guide. While some experienced interviewers may skip writing the specific questions, I believe that giving thought to the wording of the question is useful. I am more likely in the actual interview to phrase my questions in the clearest and strategically best way because I have thought about them ahead of time. (Spontaneous questions that arise in the interview situation—such as probes, follow-ups, challenges—are discussed in the next chapter on interviewing techniques.)

After I have become thoroughly familiar with the interview guide, I jot down headings of topics on index cards. I take the cards with me to the interview and glance down at them only at the end of a line of questioning and before I am ready to begin another. But having thought through the questions very carefully, I have them in my mind when I need them—before me, I have only the reminder in a simple phrase on an index card. This way, I can watch the narrator, respond to what he or she is saying, think about what is happening in the interpersonal relationship, and listen carefully so that I know when to probe, follow up, ask for clarification, or challenge. After you have used the interview guide several times in this condensed card form, you may not even need the cards because you will know the topics and questioning strategy so well. This confidence and ease will come as a result of careful preparation of the guide and your thorough knowledge of it.

In arranging topics for the interview guide, place the nonthreatening topics first. People generally like to talk about their birthplace, early childhood memories, and significant people and events in the years they grew up. Although this information may seem off the subject, a full life history is very useful. As I will stress several times in this book, the taped life history should not remain in your study closet: this is a social enterprise, and the collection of tapes from your project should be deposited in archives, where it will be available to other researchers. Whoever listens to the tape will want to know the background of the speaker, will want to place him or her in a specific time and place to understand how the narrator came to do what he or she did.

The necessity of a full life history was an early learning experience for me. In 1974 and 1975, during an interviewing project among three generations of mill village families in Carrboro, North Carolina, my coresearchers, Brent Glass and Hugh Brinton, and I recorded full life histories although we sought information chiefly on the transition from farming to mill work.

Later I published an article on childhood from the data, as well as other articles comparing the lives of three generations of women. My coresearchers also used the data in ways they had not envisioned, and our entire collection was used with many others' interviews in the book *Like a Family: The Making of a Cotton Mill World.*[2] Biographers feel very lucky when they find that someone interviewed the subject of the biography while he or she was still living and deposited the tape. Thus it is important that you record a life history rather than concentrate only on your specific objectives. You do not know how useful the information will be in the future to someone else, but you do know that you have the opportunity to record a range of information and that someone else may not get the chance to tape this narrator's experiences again.

A chronological order is one way to proceed: childhood, adolescence, work and relationships in youth, work and family in middle age, tasks of old age, reflections. This requires consciously integrating paid work with other activities and with human relationships at each stage. Another way is to organize the interview topically, such as early family memories, marriage, parenting experiences, preparation for a profession, active years in the profession, reflections on the profession, community involvement, hobbies, and so on. Appendix A offers a sample interview guide, but you must decide what the most logical progression should be, given the research project you are beginning.

Compose the core interview guide. Perhaps you plan to code parts of the narrators' responses and use the data for a quantitative analysis. In any case, the core will be the topics every informant will be expected to deal with. But you also tailor the guide to the individual narrator. The guide for the Wurlitzer plant study contained a core that we asked every narrator, but women and men were asked some questions specific to their experience. For example, several questions for the women dealt with the ways they were treated in the plant; men were asked different questions about the ways they perceived women being treated.

Remember that the guide is not an inflexible instrument. It is the nature of qualitative research that the researcher gains information not imagined at the beginning and uses the new information. As you learn new things from each narrator, insert new questions or even whole topics into the guide that you pursue in subsequent interviews.

It is possible to study interview guides used in other projects similar to yours because many colleges, universities, local historical societies, libraries, and museums offer information about their collections on websites. Mary A. Larson's article "Potential, Potential, Potential: The Marriage of Oral History and the World Wide Web" is an invaluable resource for finding information available on the web and the addresses of specific sites.[3] Larson names sites that contain finding aids, such as catalogs, indexes, and databases about holdings. On some sites there is an alphabetical index of interviewees and a cross-referenced subject index. For example, the Oral History Research Office at Columbia University has a list of interviewees as well as a list of projects at web.columbia.edu/cu/libraries/indiv/oral. This site has an "Ask Us Now" feature that gives you the chance to communicate with a librarian online. And often there is a possibility for dialogue online with a librarian, such as the library at the University of California at Los Angeles offers: visit www.library .ucla.edu/libraries or e-mail univ-archives@library.ucla.edu (or call 310-825-4068). Some institutions have published transcripts on the website; others may also show you the interview guide if you request it. The Bridgeport Public Library gives excerpts from transcriptions from its project "Bridgeport Working: Voices from the Twentieth Century," www.bridgeporthistory.org, including an audio portion of selected transcripts.

Strategies for Questioning

When you have the topical outline for the interview format, you are ready to plan the questioning strategy. Do you start with a broad question and proceed to the narrowly focused question? When do you use questions that elicit a simple yes or no? And when do you use questions that allow the narrator to handle the topic any way he or she wishes? Do you tip off the narrator to the answer you are looking for by using a "leading question," or do you just specify the subject you expect the narrator to deal with in the answer?

Consider first the use of the leading question—the kind of question that indicates what the interviewer wants as the answer. In the past, this has been a technique interviewers were taught never to use because the narrator will be likely to give the indicated answer. He or she wants to be cooperative or polite or just wants to finish the ordeal. The interviewer learns nothing new, only what he or she has asked for. I blush over a memory at the beginning of my interviewing career when I asked people who had worked as children in a cotton mill before World War I (project mentioned above), "You didn't like mill work?" Fortunately, they risked disappointing me by not giving the expected answer. One narrator explained, "Honey, if you had ever chopped cotton in the hot sun, you would see why I liked mill work."

Another way to tip off the narrator about what you want and expect in an answer is to set the stage. For example, the interviewer says, "Serbs are not for free trade. Are you?" If you know the narrator is from an ethnic background with a history of strife with Serbs, this is a sure way to bias the answer.[4]

Raymond Gorden argues that a leading question can be used to assure the narrator that he or she can go against the requirements of etiquette. You are fairly certain that the narrator knows the information and is so confident that he will not be influenced by your wording. The narrator already knows you well enough to realize his answer will not harm the relationship he has with you.[5] Look at this example from Gorden:

INTERVIEWER: What time did the meeting start, 8 or 8:30?
NARRATOR: We always start at 7 as we did last night.
INTERVIEWER: Did you just have an informal discussion?
NARRATOR: No, we also had a speaker from Columbus.
INTERVIEWER: Was his talk about the usual sort of things which education people have to say about child psychology?
NARRATOR: The topic was, "What can the taxpayer buy for his school tax dollar?"
INTERVIEWER: Oh, I see. Did you feel that the speaker had little of value to say as is so often true of people speaking on this topic?
NARRATOR: No, he had quite a bit to say; we selected him because of his objectivity.[6]

In this excerpt it is obvious that the narrator knows exactly what he wants to say and will not be swayed by the way the interviewer asks the question. However, the interviewer could have gotten the same answers in this case by asking the question without prejudging and thus making it a leading question. And even Gorden advises, "It is a good plan to avoid the use of leading questions rather than hope they are of the harmless variety unless the situation calls for their intentional use."[7]

A closed-ended question calls for a short answer such as yes or no, a date, or a number. It can be used profitably at the beginning of a line of questioning. If the interviewer needs to know what it was like to raise a family during the Depression, he or she must first find out whether the narrator was married at the time. "No" means you have to follow a different topic. Or if the interviewer needs specific, factual information before progressing along a line of questioning, he or she can ask a closed-ended question, expecting a short answer, for example, "How many people were living in the house at that time?" Or the interviewer may need to clarify something, such as a date: "Let's see, what year would that have been?" The problem comes when you elicit a string of one-word answers. When that happens, start thinking about questions that open up the possibilities for the narrator to choose the direction and to elaborate. (Otherwise, you could have given a paper-and-pencil test, which calls for limited choices and short answers.)

Whereas the closed-ended questions above gave the narrator only limited choice in the answer, the open-ended question allows the narrator to answer any way she wishes. If the narrator had answered "yes" to being married during the Depression, the interviewer would have asked one more closed-ended question, "Did you and your husband have children at that time?" If the answer was "yes," the interviewer would have followed with an open-ended question: "We want to know how mothers and fathers managed to raise families during the Depression. Could you tell me how you got by during the hard time when your husband was out of work?"

There are degrees of open-endedness. Consider these questions Stanley Payne offers from a wartime survey among farmers:

What would you say have been your main difficulties in farming during the past year?
How did those difficulties affect your farm production?
What are some of the shortages that have bothered you the most?
As you look forward to your farming this next year, what in the line of supplies or equipment is causing you the most concern?[8]

Each question becomes more restricted in the range of choice in the answer. In the first example, the narrator is restricted only to talking about the past year, but he can define difficulty in any way he wishes and talk about it in his terms. In the second, the narrator must focus on farm production. By the third, he must discuss not just production problems but specifically shortages connected with production. By the fourth, he must answer in terms of supplies and equipment. Each level of specificity in the expected answer has its use for the interviewer, but the questions remain open-ended because the narrator is still free to talk about his experience as he sees it and to elaborate as much as he chooses.

Think about the best strategy for you to choose, given your topic: Do you start with a broad question and gradually limit the scope of the answer? Or do you start with more focused questions and come to a broad question at the end of that progression?

Usually a broad question is the most open-ended you can ask, such as, "Please tell me about your life during the Depression." Much depends on the narrator's interest in and acquaintance with the topic and readiness to deal with broad questions. A workable strategy is to use a broad question at the beginning of a line of questioning and then pick up on what the narrator says and ask more specific questions. The advantage of the broad question coming at the beginning of a line of questioning is that the narrator follows his or her own thought processes or paths of association. You can learn much that you did not even guess about before the interview, including a new framework in which to view this topic. Rob Rosenthal, who interviewed people in Seattle to find out how their experiences in a general strike had changed their lives, explains the advantages of a broad question: "Letting people talk about their worlds with as little structure as possible is a good way to see things through their eyes, and ensure against interviewer bias."[9]

Figure out if the narrator is at ease with this approach (the broad question, then the specific questions): some are not and prefer that you ask specific questions; others relax and enjoy "picking up the ball and running with it." A broad question I have used successfully at the beginning of a line of questioning is, "I'm very much interested in knowing the details of daily life. What was a typical workday during the week like for you in those years?" Or "When you were a young girl living on the farm with your mother and father, what was a typical Sunday like?"

One kind of broad question to be concerned about is the comparative question. In interviewing academics in a liberal arts college in New England, I began with a broad question: "How do you compare your experience as a woman teaching at this college in the 1930s with your experience here in the 1970s?" The narrators enthusiastically launched into descriptions, anecdotes, and reflections that usually lasted at least half an hour. It was obvious that the narrators had talked about this among themselves; and not only were they used to this kind of comparative question but also they had considered this particular one already. I concluded that a comparative question at the beginning of a discussion is useful when you know that the narrator is invested in the success of the interview, tends to like this kind of question, will probably be interested in the particular question, and has much information in detail about the topic.

On the other hand, the comparative question at the beginning of the line of questioning may not be profitable if the narrator has not thought about this question before and is not used to this kind of analytical approach. At the beginning of the mill village project, I asked the women of the first generation, "How has your life been different from your daughter's?" They seemed dumbfounded. I thought about their reaction: if someone had asked me that question out of the clear blue sky, I also would have been stymied. I changed strategy and asked a series of focused questions about their lives, often asking how their daughters did the same things now. The very broad question I saved for the end; in that way, I was able to get full answers.

Providing a context for the question is very helpful. The narrator is trying to follow your train of thought just as you are trying to follow his. The narrator wants to know why you are interested in this topic. Oral historian Charles Morrissey calls this the two-sentence format and advises the interviewer to use similar wording in the question as was used in the introduction to the question. Morrissey gives the following example:

INTERVIEWER: In oral history interviews, after asking a person why a decision was made, we often ask why a different result didn't occur. During the merger discussions, did you at any time expect a different result to occur?[10]

Consider another example in which providing a context accomplishes two tasks. This kind of exchange took place in an interviewing project with farm families in northern Illinois in the mid-1980s:

INTERVIEWER: It's puzzling to social scientists that Americans in rural areas started limiting their families in the last century and then drastically in this century. No one knows who made that decision—father or mother—and why. We can't call them back and ask these questions but we can ask the generation who married in the 1920s and 1930s. So, I would like to ask you. I notice that your parents had 6 children, while you and your wife had 2. Did you make a conscious decision? (narrator nods yes) Who made the decision?

NARRATOR: Well, we pretty much decided together. Well, my wife would have liked more children, but I didn't. With her bad hip and all, we knew it wasn't a good idea to have another baby.[11]

Because of the explanation, the narrator understood why the question was important to the interviewer. Also, this is a situation that could come close to being too personal for this narrator's sense of propriety, but by putting it into the context of scholarly investigation, the interviewer was able to avoid offense.

In the same interviewing project among farm families in Illinois, my coresearcher Terry Shea and I decided our interview guide was too focused on material things. We began to add questions on perception of quality of life. One question we asked, in the context of religious life, was whether the narrator had had a spiritual experience. None had. Undoubtedly they thought I referred to a religious experience within the context of a church service—because we had just been asking about church-related topics—and the intense, emotional feeling of "being saved" was not part of their religion. Only later did I realize that I should have explained what I meant by a "spiritual experience" and left my definition open enough to allow them leeway in answering. Also, I should have placed my question in a different context because the sequence of questions implied a kind of experience I did not intend to refer to.

Kinds of Words and Phrasing to Avoid

Just as gaining skill as an interviewer depends on planning a strategy for asking questions, it also means becoming sharply aware of your own use of words. In *The Art of Asking Questions*, Stanley Payne has a witty discussion about this. Clarity is the rule of thumb here. All of us know not to ask the "can't win" variety such as, "Still beat your wife?" or to use a confusing question such as, "What is Mickey Mouse, a cat or a dog?" What is more difficult to discern are things such as "unintended specificity." When an interviewer asks, "How many books do you have on your bookshelf?" the narrator does not know whether he should run over and count them or not. And academicians use specialized words so often that they do not stop to think that these are not in everybody's vocabulary. "Do you eat the flesh of sensate mammals?" is an exaggeration of pompous speech, of course, but it is useful to scrutinize choice of words for appropriateness as you write out questions. Or the interviewer may blurt out a question before thinking about the possible double meaning: "Do you ever get down on the farm?" The narrator may think, "'Does he mean depressed?'"[12]

Worse still is when the interviewer uses words that indicate he or she thinks the narrator is not very intelligent: "How do you feel about your income tax—that is, the amount you have to pay the government on the money you take in during the year?" A better way to phrase a question when you are not sure the narrator will be familiar with a term you are using is to describe, then add the term: "How do you feel about the amount you have to pay the government on the money you take in during the year—I'm referring to the federal income tax here." Or the interviewer can go wrong by asking, "What year did you get the electric?" The narrator knows that the interviewer is not "just folks."[13] The interviewer strikes a false note by using slang words or colloquialisms and also insults the narrator.

Using a conversational style is fine. End the sentence with a preposition if you feel like that is informal and clear. And if in the interview, you fumble, that is all right, because people fumble in conversation and this implies that you are thinking things through, too, as you speak. You look a little more human, a little less in control of all the words flying about. It is confusion and talking down to the narrator that is the concern here.

Avoid the use of emotion-laden terms as you phrase the questions in the guide. If the narrator chooses to use such words, he or she reveals something important about attitude. But the interviewer should not suggest it. Research indicates that phrasing of the question influences the narrator's remembering. In one project psychologists Elizabeth Loftus and John Palmer reported two experiments conducted with people who viewed a film of a car accident. Later, in the memory task, the experimenters phrased one question, "About how fast were the cars going when they smashed into each other?" This question elicited higher estimates of speed than when the researchers asked the question using such terms as "collided, bumped, contacted, or hit" instead of "smashed." On a retest a week later, subjects who had been queried with the verb "smashed" were more likely to remember they had seen broken glass— although there was no broken glass shown in the film.[14]

In *Interviewing*, Gorden gives these sentences in which changing just two words makes a critical difference:

How do you feel about Negroes moving into this area?
How do you feel about Negroes invading your neighborhood?[15]

Scrutinize the questions you are planning to use for terms that have an effect that you do not intend.

Selecting Narrators

During the informational interviews in the first phase of the research, you have gleaned names of individuals to interview formally. You may need other ways to find narrators. For the mill village project, my coresearchers and I visited the ministers of the two churches and asked who the oldest members were. We wrote to these members. In addition, we put an advertisement in the local newspaper; we received a poor response, but other researchers have had better luck with this method. For the college history, I scanned the list of faculty for each year, then checked with the alumni office to find out which individuals were still living after the thirty- or forty-year interim. In researching the history of the Wurlitzer plant in DeKalb, Illinois, during World War II, we read the company newsletter, looking for names of employees. Then we checked the current city directory to see which of these names appeared. The best method in my experience, however, has been personal recommendation. Once we identified a few of the workers (the superintendents had died) at the plant, we asked them who among the employees still lived in the vicinity and were well enough to participate. We then asked the employees they named to whom they thought we should talk. This process of asking narrators to refer others who might be interested in the project is called snowball sampling by ethnographers.

The next step is to draw up a tentative list of narrators: I use the word *tentative* because you will probably add to the list as the interviewing project goes on and narrators think of others you should interview. In selecting narrators for recording, you will want to choose narrators who were involved in pivotal events. In a community history, you also choose narrators who have lived in the community the longest; for a family history, you might want to record the life story of every family member; for a biography, you will want to talk to the individual's associates, relatives, friends, and critics.

In the chapters on community studies, family research, and biography, there is information relevant to the appropriate kind of selection process. Here I will assume that the researcher is engaged in searching for information about an event or movement. Some individuals' recorded memories are essential: if one woman or man made a decision that changed the direction of the community, then that woman or man should be sought. When you seek to understand the effects of decisions on the community, a wider net is cast. But for recent periods, there may be so many narrators that you have to consider sampling techniques. Sampling design is simply the plan whereby the researcher selects cases for study; in oral history it is the choice of persons to be interviewed.

In quantitative research, such as a survey, 10 percent of the population might be designated by selecting every tenth name on an alphabetical list. These individuals would be called and interviewed. The researchers consider this a random sample. Such a random sample is often not helpful to a historian dealing with specific events: the 10 percent who are interviewed, for example, may tell you how the general public viewed the decision to drop the atomic bomb at the close of World War II, but they cannot say what was in the minds of the few people who made the decision.

In a qualitative research project, a different approach often will be necessary. If the project is concerned with decisions that changed the community, then the key decision makers must be interviewed. But these few at the top of the hierarchy do not make up the community. Certainly a study of a community or a movement requires interviewing in all strata because people at all levels not only felt the effects of decisions but also implemented them, sometimes changed them, and often made their own decisions, regardless of the ones handed down.

In the history of a psychiatric hospital—which I viewed as a work community—I insisted on interviewing narrators at every level in the workforce: grounds workers, housekeepers, maintenance people, psychiatrists, mental health workers, social workers, nurses, occupational therapists, cooks, carpenters, the administrative director, and members of the board of trustees. Patients were not included in this list because state law forbids access to patient records unless the researcher is directly involved in the individual's clinical care. The assumption was that the psychiatrist is the authority on diagnosis and prescription, but the mental health worker is the authority on the work that he or she does on the ward. By using this stratified sample, I was able to obtain information on a variety of experiences as well as many different perspectives on developments at the hospital. If I had interviewed only the directors and members of the board of trustees, I would have obtained a far different picture.[16]

I added to my stratified sampling technique purposive sampling: I also sought out people who no longer worked in the hospital, people who were for and against the union, people known to be favored by the administration, and those reported to be dissatisfied with the way things were going. In other words, I sought a variety of opinions on controversial topics and a variety of levels of allegiance to the formal organization as well as witnesses in each occupational category.

In the research project for *The Edwardians* (referred to in chapter 1), British oral historians Paul Thompson and Thea Vigne selected a group representative of the population in Britain early in this century. They designed a quota sample—one based on the 1911 census—that numbered 444 persons. Thompson describes the way the sample was drawn up: "The proportion of men and women was as in 1911; so were the proportions who had then been living in the countryside, the towns, and the conurbations; and so too the balance between the main regions of England, Wales, and Scotland. We tried to ensure a proper class distribution by dividing the sample into six major occupational groups, taken from the adjusted census categories of Guy Routh's *Occupation and Pay, 1906–65.*"[17]

In addition to stratified, quota, and purposive sampling, there are other ways to select narrators. In the history of workers in a mill village before World War I, I sought out every person mentioned to me as a worker in the mill early in the century. This method is referred to as a universal sample or nonprobability sample. At that point, the narrators were in their late seventies and eighties, and I contacted all living persons who had been part of that history and still resided in that town. The number was so small that it was feasible to contact all survivors. In fact, the narrators finally numbered thirty men and women who were able and willing to talk to us.[18] In a universal sample, the number of potential narrators is usually less than one hundred, and you contact each one, hoping a fair number will be in good health, have good memories, and be willing to participate.

Often the interviewer has to decide how many interviews are enough. When you find that narrators are repeating for the twentieth or thirtieth time, from about the same perspective, the same information, you know you have enough in that category. Glaser and Strauss refer to this as saturation.

A problem remains to be considered, however: some narrators may choose not to talk to the researcher at all. Laconic, isolated, or withdrawn individuals do not often appear in the sample of an oral history project.[19] Bear with the inarticulate: try to get them to talk when you know that they have been directly involved in the event you are studying. In your own sample, you will know the individuals you must seek out, no matter how laconic they may be. But if a narrator refuses to talk except in monosyllables and your good interviewing techniques are of no avail, do not be discouraged. Knowing that you have done your best to interview this key witness, turn to the next narrator and try to get the information from other witnesses and written records.

Finally, look at the list of narrators and prioritize. Individuals who were most involved in pivotal decisions, were most active in important events, or were most directly affected should be at the top. Also, those who are very elderly or those with health problems should be sought in the first phase of interviewing.

Contacting Narrators

Write a letter to prospective narrators. If anyone the narrator might know is supportive of your project, ask whether you may use his or her name in the letter. Describe your project and your training and interest in the project. Explain why it is important to learn from people who have firsthand knowledge of the subject. Tell them why you are contacting them, and ask for their help. Include your telephone number so they can call you if there are questions. End the letter with a statement that you will call.

If the narrator calls you to ask what this is all about, send a brief list of general topics to be covered in the interviewing session. Avoid sending the specific questions because you are likely to receive rehearsed answers.

This initial contact is almost always done best by letter rather than by telephone call. After the narrator has had time to receive the letter, then telephone; the narrator will know who you are. The exception to this procedure is a situation in which the individual has reason to distrust anything in print or to feel apprehension about such an invitation. Some elderly people have good reason to be skeptical about strangers, and the politically vulnerable will certainly want to know something about you. In either situation, having someone they trust explain the project to them will be the best method of contact.

Keep a file of index cards. On each narrator's card, record the name, address, telephone number, the name of the person who referred the narrator to you, and any pertinent information such as state of health. You need to know this information at the time you call. Keep a file folder on each narrator in which you can insert newspaper clippings or comments made by others about the narrator or any notes you take as you read through the written records. And, finally, make a huge chart, providing space for date of the preliminary interview (see the next chapter), date of the recorded interview, date when the release form was returned, when the thank you letter was written, whether there were photographs or any documents to be returned, and the date of their return. If a transcript is to be made, then allow space for the date transcribing began, who transcribed, when the transcript was finished, when this was sent to the narrator, and when returned. (A model for this form is given in appendix E.)

Scheduling the Interview

When you call, schedule the interview at the narrator's convenience as much as possible. With elderly narrators or narrators who have had health problems, ask what time during the day they like having a visitor. Scheduling is not easy with very busy people: the time they suggest may sound strange to you—6:45 a.m., for example, while the person crunches breakfast cereal. (Chat while he finishes the cereal, explaining that you do not want unintended sounds recorded. Use these few minutes to build rapport.) Because the narrator's goodwill is necessary for the interview to take place at all, be accommodating as much as you can.

Preparing the Equipment

As you prepare for the interview, you will be getting your recording equipment ready. Although I was at first cavalier about technical aspects of oral history, I soon found to my dismay that the sound quality of a recording was so poor that my work was of little use to anyone. And even as an experienced interviewer, I have had mishaps with equipment. I agree with oral historian

Dale Treleven's statement about this: "Sloppily done interviews are a menace to the historical record, a pain to archivists, a disservice to researchers, and, above all, an insult to respondents who so willingly share their memories for posterity."[20] If you are concerned about what is happening technically or if you have had problems with sound, then here are suggestions about equipment. However, I will not recommend a specific recording device because technology is changing so fast that by the time this book is published, there will be something new on the market.

The instructions I offer below apply to the use of a cassette recorder—called an analog recorder. Now some oral historians use digital technology. Review the pros and cons stated by archivist Robyn Russell: If you are looking for length of time the recording will last, reel-to-reel tape, which lasts forty years, is the best. But such a recording machine is too heavy to carry around. Sound on audio cassettes lasts about twenty years, and the recorders are easy to get, inexpensive, and easy to carry around and use, and repairs are relatively inexpensive. But for archival storage, the cassette recorder's tape should be transferred to reel-to-reel. Another disadvantage is that the hiss caused by the revolution of the tape gets recorded. The Digital Audio Tape recorder (often referred to as DAT) is easy to carry around; and the sound quality is better than that of a cassette recorder. It is easy to transfer the sound from a DAT recorder to computer, but you need special software to do this. Of course, everything has to be backed up immediately because of the possibility of computer failure. A worse problem is that the sound doesn't seem to last very long, and eventually you need to transfer the interview to a CD-ROM.[21] Folklorist Edward Ives has a very lucid explanation of kinds of recorders in his book *The Tape-Recorded Interview*.[22] For discussion of current technology for preservation of sound, see the last chapter. To stay up-to-date, subscribe to the Oral History List Service. (If you are an experienced interviewer who is comfortable with your equipment and sure of sound quality, then skip to the next chapter.)

Use two remote microphones (attached to the lapels of narrator and interviewer) or one remote placed between interviewer and narrator. The voices are clearer and there is not as much extraneous noise (such as the whir of turning tape) as with recorders having only built-in microphones. When you are using only one remote microphone, place it between yourself and the narrator near enough so that the voices of both will be loud and clear. Microphones are sensitive and pick up vibrations, so nestle it on a scarf or some soft padding.

Place the recorder so that you can see how much tape you have left as the interview goes on. (A recorder that gives you a signal that the tape side is about full is a great help.) Glance down to make sure the record button is pressed in. And then check again. After the interview has gone on a few minutes, stop and play back. Explain to the narrator what you are doing: "I need to check the machine to make sure the sound is OK and that we are recording." Get in the habit of checking to make sure the record button is pressed in. Use 60- or 90-minute tapes because 120-minute tapes have a greater chance of breaking when rewound and played back during transcribing. Always carry extra tapes: you never know if the interview you thought would last an hour goes into three hours.

The use of batteries eliminates the problem of interference from other things in the house on the same circuit. Once when I was using a plug-in, someone started a vacuum cleaner in the next room and blitzed the sound on the tape recorder. I had just checked the sound and did not check again for fifteen minutes—none of that part of the interview was audible. I discovered the problem, the maid changed rooms and vacuumed upstairs in the room above us, and another portion of the sound was obliterated. Other interviewers I've talked to prefer using the house's electric current, however. If you are using the house's current, check every twenty or thirty minutes or when there is a pause in the conversation to make sure there is no interference. The advantage here is that you are not relying on a battery, which may run down.

It is best to buy a recorder that has a battery-strength indicator. If not, one strategy with a tape recorder without such an indicator is to jot down the hours used in recording and change the battery before you use up the time. Then you do not have to use the house current, and you can feel confident that when you check the sound, the battery will be strong. You can expect that it will not weaken before the ninety-minute interview is up. (But always take along extra batteries, just in case the sound starts to get weak, and take an extension cord.)

When you use up one side of the tape, mark it quickly before you turn it over. This is a bother, of course, but you do not want to make a mistake and record over a side that is full. And it is very easy to make such a mistake: you record on both sides of a tape, put it aside, record on both sides of the second tape. By this time, you are tired, but the interview has not yet ended—the narrator is still going strong. Without noticing, you pick up the first tape and put it in the recorder, thinking you have a blank tape. The first side recorded is erased—but this is an unlikely thing to happen if you have labeled the side. As soon as the interview session is finished, remove the recording tab on the tape so no one can record over it.

Label each side with project title in brief, narrator's name, interviewer's name, date, and place. Immediately make a notation in your records so that you can, just at a glance at your chart, see which interviews are completed, which are yet to be done. Of course, if you are carrying out only four or five interviews, this is not necessary, but if the project requires more than that, good record keeping saves much time. You do not have to rummage through tapes and correspondence, racking your brain trying to remember. You avoid making unnecessary telephone calls or writing duplicate letters. (See appendix E for models of record-keeping sheets.)

Summary

The abundance of instructions of different kinds I have thrown at you necessitates a summing up at this point: Carry out informational interviews to find out what the people who lived the history judge important. In drawing up the interview guide, you have the opportunity to ask the questions that will enable you to situate your findings in a historical context. You can get information unique to individuals and also place them and the events of their lives in a wider framework: you can draw on your background reading to suggest questions that will reveal how the people you talk to were like the rest of the state or the nation, how they were different. Be aware, though, of how background reading may influence you to stay with original hypotheses rather than frame new ones as you hear the testimony.

In the wording of your questions, strive for clarity. Avoid talking down to the narrator. Avoid emotion-laden terms. Start with nonthreatening topics first. Closed-ended questions are often necessary at the beginning of a line of questioning to establish suitability of the narrator to deal with the topic or to clarify. Open-ended questions give the narrator scope to define the direction the answer will go in and to elaborate as much as he or she wishes.

Choose a strategy that will work best, given the topic and the particular kind of narrator: Ask focused questions first in a line of questioning and end with the broad questions when the narrator needs time to think the matter through in some detail before considering the broader picture. Choose a broad question when you know the narrator can easily handle it and when you need the narrator to be completely free in the response. Then you can follow up with questions on details the narrator has offered.

Careful attention to the mechanics of recording pays off in clear, strong sound. Use a remote microphone, placed between narrator and interviewer, or two microphones, one attached to the lapel of the interviewer, one to the narrator. Use batteries and test frequently to make sure they are strong enough, or if you prefer using electric current, check periodically to make sure there is no interference. Equipment in good working order and conscientious record keeping enable you to stay in control of the project.

Recommended Reading

The Interview Guide

Atkinson, Robert. *The Gift of Stories: Practical and Spiritual Applications of Autobiography, Life Stories, and Personal Mythmaking.* Westport, CT: Bergin and Garvey, 1995. This text is heavily influenced by Carl Jung and Joseph Campbell: there are chapters on the power of stories and myths as well as a long chapter on why and how to begin writing autobiography. See the last chapter, "Giving Others Their Story: Doing a Life Story Interview," pp. 115–34, which contains suggestions for organizing and an interview guide for a full life history interview.

Gorden, Raymond. *Interviewing: Strategy, Techniques and Tactics.* 4th ed. Chicago: Dorsey Press, 1987. This book has useful information on the phrasing of questions and on strategy.

Lummis, Trevor. *Listening to History: The Authenticity of Oral Evidence.* London: Hutchinson, 1987. The author discusses differences between the questionnaire and the interview schedule (or interview guide) and the usefulness of the guide.

Morrissey, Charles. "The Two-Sentence Format as an Interviewing Technique in Oral History Fieldwork." *Oral History Review* 15 (Spring 1987): 43–53. The author offers an important discussion on placing the question in context.

Payne, Stanley. *The Art of Asking Questions.* Princeton, NJ: Princeton University Press, 1951. This remains the best single source on how to ask productive questions.

Using Photographs to Suggest Questions

Modell, Judith, and Charlee Brodsky. "Envisioning Homestead: Using Photographs in Interviewing." In *Interactive Oral History Interviewing,* ed. Eva M. McMahan and Kim Lacy Rogers, 141–61. Hillsdale, NJ: Lawrence Erlbaum, 1994. Article suggests ways to use photographs to generate questions that stimulate memory during an interview.

Samuel, Raphael. *Theatres of Memory.* London: Verso, 1994. See especially "In the Eye of History," pp. 315–36, and "Scopophilia," pp. 364–77. These chapters by the late Raphael Samuel are about analyzing historic photographs but will give you insights into contemporary photographs—even afterward, we cannot "take photographs on trust or treat them as transparent reflections of fact" (p. 329). He remarks of family photographs, "They are posing not for the viewer but for themselves, projecting an image, however idealized, or fantasized, of what they believed themselves to be" (p. 366).

Classroom Oral History Projects

Dean, Pamela, Toby Daspit, and Petra Munro. *Talking Gumbo: A Teacher's Guide to Using Oral History in the Classroom.* Baton Rouge: T. Harry Williams Center for

Oral History, 1998. This teacher's guide offers specific information on how oral history can be integrated into the school curriculum and gives lesson plans as well as a bibliography of oral history materials suitable for secondary school teaching. There is an accompanying video, "You've Got to Hear This Story," which students will relate to because it features student actors.

Hickey, M. Gail. *Bringing History Home: Local and Family History Projects for Grades K–6*. Boston: Allyn and Bacon, 1999. Emphasis is on using local history and family history to reveal to students that they make history and also to foster an acceptance of others through understanding the diverse backgrounds of fellow students. Suggestions for activities and resources. Specific help in detail, such as a chart to show which activities described in the book are right for what grade level.

Sitton, Thad, George L. Mehaffy, and O. L. Davis Jr. *Oral History: A Guide for Teachers (and Others)*. Austin: University of Texas Press, 1983. Authors state, "Classroom oral history . . . brings history home by linking the world of textbook and classroom with the face-to-face social world of the student's home community" (p. 12). Specific discussions, such as "Project Options" and "A Model for Fieldwork in Oral History," offer practical advice and models.

"Voices of Experience: Oral History in the Classroom." Roundtable discussion with Marjorie McLellan, Cliff Kuhn, Rich Nixon, Susan Moon, and Toby Daspit. *Magazine of History* 2, no. 3 (Spring 1997): 23–31. Teachers talk about what prompted them to begin an oral history project for their classrooms as well as obstacles to the success of such projects.

Whitman, Glenn. *Dialogue with the Past: Engaging Students and Meeting Standards through Oral History*. Walnut Creek, CA: AltaMira, 2004. A guide for using oral history in middle school and high school classrooms. Discussions are clearly written, and lesson plans are specific and in detail.

Wigginton, Elliot. *Sometimes a Shining Moment: The Foxfire Experience*. Garden City, NY: Doubleday, 1985. Compelling autobiography about a pioneering project to bring oral history to the classroom—the student work that resulted in the Foxfire books. Worth a course in teaching methods.

Wood, Linda P. *Oral History Projects in Your Classroom*. Pamphlet in the series published by the Oral History Association, 1992. (To order, contact the Oral History Association, Dickinson College, P.O. Box 1773, Carlisle, PA 17013-2896, or e-mail: oha@dickinson.edu.) Useful suggestions for introducing and developing an oral history project in a secondary school classroom. Ideas for project topics, as well as useful forms, such as a project evaluation form, are offered. The project from the South Kingstown High School (Rhode Island), "What Did You Do in the War, Grandma?" and a subsequent project, "1968: The Whole World Was Watching," can be accessed online at www.stg.brown.edu/projects/1968.

Using the Internet in a Classroom Oral History Project

Benmayor, Rina. "Cyber-Teaching in the Oral History Classroom." *Oral History* 28, no. 1 (Spring 2000): 83–91. Creative approach, specific instructions. Students learned to design, carry out, present, and archive their project and to present their findings in print, in a public program, and on a website.

Online Workshop in Oral History

Several oral history programs offer online workshops in oral history. By necessity these are brief. For example, Baylor University offers a concise, three-part oral history workshop with information on organization of a project. Go to "Introduction to Oral History" at www3.baylor.edu/Oral_History.

Notes

1. Char Henn, Estella Metcalf, and Valerie Yow, eds., "Life at the DeKalb Wurlitzer Plant during World War II" (Northern Illinois Regional History Center, Northern Illinois University, DeKalb, Illinois).

2. Christopher B. Daly, James Deloudis, Jacquelyn Dowd Hall, Lu Ann Jones, Robert Korstad, and Mary Murphy, *Like a Family: The Making of a Cotton Mill World* (Chapel Hill: University of North Carolina Press, 1987).

3. Mary A. Larson, "Potential, Potential, Potential: The Marriage of Oral History and the World Wide Web," *Journal of American History* 88, no. 2 (September 2001): 596–603.

4. Raymond L. Gorden, *Interviewing: Strategy, Techniques and Tactics*, 4th ed. (Chicago: Dorsey Press, 1987), 332.

5. Gorden, *Interviewing*, 219.

6. Gorden, *Interviewing*, 217.

7. Gorden, *Interviewing*, 217.

8. Stanley Payne, *The Art of Asking Questions* (Princeton, NJ: Princeton University Press, 1957), 35.

9. Rob Rosenthal, "The Interview and Beyond: Some Methodological Questions for Oral Historians," *Public Historian* 1, no. 3 (Spring 1979): 58–67; see p. 66.

10. Charles Morrissey, "The Two-Sentence Format as an Interviewing Technique in Oral History Fieldwork," *Oral History Review* 15 (Spring 1987): 43–53; see p. 46.

11. Terry Shea and Valerie Yow, "Farm Families of DeKalb County" (Northern Illinois Regional History Center, Northern Illinois University, DeKalb, Illinois, unpublished collection).

12. Payne, *Art of Asking Questions*, 120–23.

13. Payne, *Art of Asking Questions*, 116.

14. Elizabeth Loftus and John C. Palmer, "Reconstruction of Automobile Destruction: An Example of the Interaction between Language and Memory," *Journal of Verbal Learning and Verbal Behavior* 13 (1974): 585–89; see p. 589.

15. Gorden, *Interviewing*, 332.

16. Valerie Yow, "Effects of Change in Treatment Philosophy on Clinical Practice in a Psychiatric Hospital" (paper delivered at the annual meeting of the Association for the History of Medicine, Cleveland, Ohio, May 1991).

17. Paul Thompson, *Voice of the Past: Oral History* (New York: Oxford University Press, 2000), 147.

18. Valerie Yow (listed as Valerie Quinney), "Childhood in a Southern Mill Village," *International Journal of Oral History* 3, no. 3 (November 1982): 167–92; see pp. 167–68.

19. Thompson, *Voice of the Past*, 149.

20. Dale Treleven, "Oral History and the Archival Community: Common Concerns about Documenting Twentieth Century Life," *International Journal of Oral History* 10 (February 1989): 50–58; see p. 53.

21. Robyn Russell, "Is It Archival? Considerations for Librarians and Oral Historians" (paper delivered at the annual meeting of the Oral History Association, Washington, DC, October 2003).

22. Edward D. Ives, "How a Tape Recorder Works," in *The Tape-Recorded Interview: A Manual for Fieldworkers in Folklore and Oral History*, 1–24 (Knoxville: University of Tennessee Press, 1995).

CHAPTER FOUR

Interviewing Techniques

Interviewer Ann Oakley said, "Interviewing is rather like marriage: everybody knows what it is, an awful lot of people do it, and yet behind each closed front door there is a world of secrets."[1] In this chapter, I will tell you some secrets. I will also present interviewers' wisdom based on hours of interviewing experience. I have gleaned what can be useful to the interviewer from various disciplines, from the work of oral historians, sociologists, journalists, anthropologists, folklorists, psychologists, and communication specialists.

I suggest steps to begin the interview and ways to build rapport. The chapter also presents a discussion on productive kinds of spontaneous questions to use as well as ways to handle delicate matters and to ask hard questions. I draw your attention not only to word use but also to nonverbal signals, especially the signs of impending difficulties. You will find some advice on what to do when there is trouble. Finally, there is a checklist you can use to critique your own interviewing style.

The Preliminary Meeting

Everything you do before the interview will contribute to the establishment of the character of the relationship between interviewer and narrator. It helps to make a brief visit to the narrator before the day of the interview (unless you already know the narrator well). Even though you have written and called, you are still a stranger. A meeting in person, however brief, means that you are not a stranger when you appear with your recorder.

Drop by at a time convenient for the narrator. Explain the project briefly and show enthusiasm about interviewing this person. Say something positive about the place and the person. Use some humor. This sets up the expectation that you are not a threatening person, that this could be a pleasant experience. In his book *Creative Interviewing*, Jack Douglas asserts that "small talk and chitchat are vital first steps on the way to intimate communion."[2]

I have arrived for a preliminary interview at a time when the narrator was washing the dishes. I dried them while we talked. Another asked if I had any canning jars, and I said I had a few empty ones I could bring, which I did. However, in scheduling an interview with a bank president, I was warned I would have only thirty minutes. Any preliminary meeting with him was not possible. In another project, I realized that a physician who was on the board of the college I was researching was too busy at the hospital for me to talk with her there. I asked her to stop by the archives and meet me when she came to the college for a board meeting. She did, and this gave me a chance to show her how the project was organized, how many tapes we had recorded to that point, and so on. She started saying more positive things about the project. This preliminary meeting is not always possible, but make it happen if you can.

At the preliminary meeting, you can talk about what work will be done during the recording session. Explain that the recorder will pick up sounds in the house. Insist on a noise-free environment. If the narrator wants to sit in her rocker on the back porch and the sound of car horns and heavy trucks is in the neighborhood, explain that the noise will be on the tape and will obscure words from time to time. Ask her to find a different place. If the narrator wants you to come to his office but the telephone keeps ringing and the secretary keeps popping in, then point out that constant interruptions will be on tape and that also they obstruct the flow of the conversation. You might explain, "We'll spend a lot of time after each interruption, trying to reconstruct the conversation to that point so we can go on." Ask, "How can we keep the telephone from ringing and stop the interruptions?" If you are sitting in a living room and the television in the next room can be heard, then request in a firm, serious tone that the television be turned down when you come back to record. And ask the narrator to move a barking dog to another place. I have even suggested muffling a grandfather clock that chimed loudly every fifteen minutes.

The place where you meet the narrator to record makes a difference. An individual who meets you in his office will present himself differently in the conversation and will emphasize different things from the way he would if you recorded in his living room at home. Once a student of mine, recording

in ethnic communities in Providence, Rhode Island, interviewed the propri-
etor of an Irish bar inside the bar he owned. The narrator declared several
times that it is a myth that Irish men drink a lot, but in the background were
the tinkle of glasses and the gurgle of liquids. His testimony would have been
more convincing if the recording had been done in a different setting. And
if he had recorded at home, he might not have chosen that topic to discuss
at all: his life at home and in his neighborhood would have been more prominent in his thinking.

About eight times out of ten, it is best to record just the two of you, without a third voice. The presence in the room of another person changes the
interview. On rare occasions, however, a third person can be helpful. I have
interviewed a mother in her nineties whose daughter insisted on being there.
The daughter was very quiet unless there was some information for which the
mother wanted confirmation, such as, "I think that was 1934—do you remember your Dad talking about this?" The presence of the daughter seemed
reassuring to the mother, and she might not have talked to me otherwise.
And sometimes an interpreter is required or the culture prevents an outsider
from interviewing a woman alone so that a female relative must sit by the
narrator's side.

On the other hand, I have had the experience of a husband insisting on
staying in the room. He dominated the interview. My advice is: never permit
a husband and wife to be interviewed together unless the project specifically
calls for joint interviews. As much as married couples like the illusion that
they are of one mind, they are not. The presence of one often inhibits the
performance of another or at least slants it.

However, in some kinds of interviewing, especially projects in the sociology of the family, the research strategy requires conjoint interviews. Anthropologist Linda Bennett and social worker Katharine McAvity discuss their
research methods for a psychosocial research project on alcoholism and family heritage. They argue that there are advantages to interviewing couples together when "marital negotiation of family identity" is the general aim of research. This is the easiest way to detect lack of consensus on an issue. The
spouses provoke each other to expand on information and to clarify differences.[3] Other researchers, however, have found that information comes out
that creates or exacerbates problems. (This subject is discussed further in the
chapter on ethics.)

A different situation occurred when two women who had worked together
in a munitions plant during World War II wanted to be interviewed together.
They had been best friends for forty years. As long as the conversation was
focused on their war work, they sparked each other's memory. Answers to

questions about their personal lives were truncated, however. Possibly, they thought of the interviewer as a member of the out-group and used this to solidify their feeling of being in their own in-group.

So, although I have insisted on the necessity of being alone with the narrator, there are exceptions to this:

When the presence of a companion is needed, as in the case of an elderly parent needing a daughter or son by her side
When the research strategy requires couple interaction
When the presence of an interpreter is necessary
When the culture prevents an outsider from having exclusive conversation with the narrator

Beginning the Interview

On the day of the interview, before you take out the recorder, your comments can reduce tension. Douglas explains, "When you talk about the weather, the view from her mountain top chalet, or the lack of view from her cellar den, a certain offhandedness indicates that nothing earth shattering (like headlines) is going to happen here."[4] Explain the purpose of the project again, and tell the narrator how it is coming along. Assure the narrator that he or she is not obliged to answer all of the questions. Because people do not wish to be impolite, let them know that you will not be offended if they decline to answer a question.

After the recording begins, give the narrator the chance to talk: except for introducing and asking the questions and answering the narrator's questions, don't keep chatting about your own experiences. Otherwise, your story gets recorded thirty times (or as many tapes as you make in a project). Some interviewers see the interview as a "dialectic with speech and counterspeech."[5] I argue that the recorded in-depth interview is not a conversation in the usual sense: both people are aware that this testimony is going on a record. It is the narrator's story that is important to record; however, when the narrator *wants* to hear your story, tell it. This is possibly a request for reciprocity, for sharing, which the narrator needs to build trust.[6]

If the narrator does not like the idea of your using a tape recorder, then explain that you cannot take notes fast enough and that you lose ends of sentences or beginnings of the next. If you are doing historical research, remind the narrator that the taped memoir is a historical document that others will listen to and benefit from. (Or, in case studies requiring confidentiality, remind the narrators that you will not use their names on tape or reveal their identities to anyone.) You might say something reassuring such as, "In these interviews, we just ignore the recorder. Usually we forget it's on." If there is some hesitation because the narrator does not know how the conversation will sound, play the tape back after a few moments to let her or him hear the voices. Of course, if the narrator absolutely insists that you put away the recorder, then you will have to take notes. Type them up as quickly as possible before you forget specific sentences. If you are a historian, deposit them in the archives with your tapes: at least others will have some means of checking your evidence, but notes are not an adequate substitute for the taped interview.

Begin the taped interview by stating the name of the interviewer, the name of the narrator, the location of the interview, and the date. To any listener in years to come, explain the purpose of the interview very briefly. If you have a special relationship to the narrator, inform the listener, because this will make a difference: "The narrator and interviewer have been friends for twenty years." Then ask for the narrator's oral consent (a nod will not suffice) to the taping of your conversation that day. If this is a research project where confidentiality is required, of course you do not give the real name. But if you are using a pseudonym, explain that; you still need acknowledgment on tape that the narrator knows the conversation is being recorded.

Begin with routine questions such as, "Where were you born?" Follow with uncomplicated questions about the place or family. These nonthreatening questions help both of you ease into the interview.

Building Rapport

In *The Ethnographic Interview*, James Spradley observes four stages in the interview situation: (1) apprehension, (2) exploration, (3) cooperation, and (4) participation.[7] Every first interview begins with uncertainty on the part of the interviewer and the narrator. The interviewer does not know how the interview will go. The narrator does not know what is expected of him or her. Often the narrator says something like, "I don't think I know enough to be of any help to you."[8] The interview begins, and soon the interviewer and narrator are exploring the situation; this is a period of listening and observing. Spradley suggests that running through the minds of these two are questions such as, "What does he want me to say? Can she be trusted? Is she going to be able to answer my questions? What does she really want from these interviews? Am I answering questions as I should? Does he really want to know what I think?"[9]

The narrator will soon decide whether or not to trust the interviewer. It is thus crucial for the interviewer to be honest and straightforward about the project and to answer the narrator's questions honestly and respectfully. This may require repeated explanations of what the project is about and why he or she is there interviewing this particular individual. Douglas recalls a moment in an interviewing session that had been preceded by several sessions. He thought everything was understood. Suddenly, the narrator asked, "What is the point now? Why are we doing this?" Douglas realized that he would have to explain in far more detail than he had earlier exactly what he was doing and why.[10]

Taking the time to make sure the narrator understands also builds trust. It is not productive to echo repeatedly the narrator's statements, but sometimes if you are not sure of the meaning, ask, "Do I understand you right? You had mixed feelings about the decision to take the plane that morning?" The narrator appreciates your effort to understand and to represent the meaning correctly.

Give the narrator reassurance that he is responding in a helpful way. Spradley suggests communicating to the narrator, "I understand what you're saying; I am learning; it is valuable to me."[11] The interviewer should express appreciation that the narrator is offering his or her time to answer questions. And especially the interviewer should make it clear that the narrator's expertise or special effort is appreciated: "I know I am asking you some questions that are not easy to answer, and I really appreciate your helping me with these." "You know the details of that situation better than anybody else. Talking to you really helps me understand." "You've explained this so clearly that I feel like I understand it." Positive appraisal of the narrator's work in the interview contributes to the narrator's motivation to continue and to cooperate in the endeavor.

Although this may seem too obvious to mention, listen carefully. Listening with only part of your mind will be detected, and who wants to talk to someone who is only halfway listening? This means not following an interview guide slavishly but instead following the narrator's thought processes. In the old style of questioning by social scientists, the interviewer's attitude might have been like this description given by Douglas: "How much more proud and worthy—serenely confident and powerful—we feel when we can impose the structure of discourse and of reality itself upon our little 'subjects': 'Sit there, subject. Now here is a questionnaire with five hundred questions on it. They are written in stone and encompass the entire realm of possible questions concerning these realities. There are only five possible responses to each one.'"[12]

In in-depth interviewing, because you seek the unexpected, the information you do not already know, you give the narrator scope to develop his or her train of thought. The narrator may tentatively offer another line of investigation, and careful listening enables you to pick up on this. Consider this interchange after the interviewer asks the narrator if his father was involved in the Irish Republican Army.

> NARRATOR: My mother was active. She received several medals for bravery from the Irish government.
> INTERVIEWER: Very good! And how about your father?[13]

The interviewer missed a very promising line of questioning. However, this does not mean that you can allow the narrator to digress to the extent that he or she uses the interview for a catharsis for some current problem not connected to the subject of the interview. (Of course, if you are writing a biography, every concern of the narrator will be of interest.) Gorden points out that afterward, in listening to the tape, the narrator may feel embarrassed or resentful that the interviewer let him talk on and on about irrelevant or trivial matters.[14] I realize that I have stressed equal sharing in the direction of the interview and it seems like a contradiction for me now to advise you to return to the intended topic. You must depend on your judgment here: if you judge that this is totally irrelevant, listen, but when there is a pause, tactfully draw the narrator back to the subject under discussion.

When you change topics in the interview, explain what connection there is to the previous topic or how the new topic fits into the overall plan of the interview. The narrator appreciates your letting him know what you are doing. After all, he or she is trying to follow your train of thought.

Indicate that you are interested in the unique point of view the narrator can give you by personalizing the request. You can say outright, "I want to be sure I understand your point of view on this issue."[15] Or "I'd like to know what *you* did that day."

Needless to say, you do not interrupt or finish a sentence for the narrator. The matter of silence is not so easy to state categorically, however. You have to sense the narrator's pacing and keep your own compatible. If the narrator is a reflective person, pausing to think something through, wait for her to take the time she needs. On the other hand, if the narrator answers with a clipped efficiency and seems to expect a rather brisk pace, you can proceed a little faster than you would ordinarily. Gorden suggests that before you ask the next question, you should give the narrator at least a ten-second pause to see if he or she wants to add anything.[16]

Sherry Thomas, who had just completed an interviewing project with farm women, talked to her audience at a National Women's Studies Association conference about learning to keep silent, to give the narrator time to think. She said, "Sometimes the answer to a question from fifteen minutes before comes the next hour if you'll let the silence drag on."[17] Too long a pause, however, is a way of putting pressure on the narrator to add, and I suspect that this produces resentment after a while.

Your nonverbal responses are important. Avoid responding with "Uh huh," because it is recorded and transcribed. Nod, smile, shake your head to show that you are following. It is important to maintain eye contact. Looking down to take notes and not looking into the person's eyes makes you seem to be more concerned about taking perfect notes than understanding at the moment. And it prevents you from observing the narrator's nonverbal behavior. Often it is necessary to keep a small pad of paper and a pencil handy to jot down names or terms for which you need to ask correct spelling after the interview or to jot down a word to remind yourself of a line of questioning to pick up on later; but make this note taking quick.

Both people, however, look away from time to time because that is what we do in any conversation. Communication researchers Byron Lewis and Frank Pucelik found that people often look up and to the right when they are constructing images, up and to the left when they are remembering images, level and to the right in constructing speech, level and to the left remembering sounds, down and to the right in concentrating on feelings, down and to the left in holding an internal dialogue.[18] (The researchers warn that this represents a generalization about human behavior, one that may be reversed for some left-handed people.) You might keep these possibilities in mind as you observe the narrator's behavior.

Sometimes the interviewer can anticipate how difficult it will be for a narrator to answer a question and that the narrator may be strongly tempted to lie. Gorden advises letting the narrator know immediately that you have some information on this topic already and that you are making no judgment about it.[19] Another way is to depersonalize the question. For example, "I know that some women in the neighborhood donated their gold wedding rings to Mussolini's cause; of course, they did not know what was to come later in Italy. Did you know people who were asked to donate their rings?"

The usual advice is to communicate positive regard. It is difficult to do this when you are interviewing people whose values you abhor. Consider, for example, the interviewing project with former Nazis that William Sheridan Allen undertook for his book *The Nazi Seizure of Power*.[20] Allen interviewed a range of adherents and opponents to the Nazi regime, and these first-person accounts do indeed enlighten the reader about the reasons why the movement gained supporters. Allen had to show that he wanted to understand and that he appreciated the fact that their dilemmas were not the same that he had faced in his life. This does not mean that he had to show approval or agreement—just a willingness to listen without immediate judgment.

Take the time to review background material thoroughly on the subject of the interview. You should not show off your knowledge, but the narrator will sense that you are informed and that you take the interview seriously. Do not try to convey the impression that you are in the in-group by using jargon. This is false, and the narrator knows it. But learn as much as you can about terms specific to the topics to be discussed before the interview begins. During the interview, ask if you do not know. Sometimes, even if you know a dictionary meaning, you may want to ask for the narrator's ideas about the term's meaning. (See the discussion on asking for meanings later in the chapter.)

These techniques will help you win the narrator's cooperation, but the most important basis for a good interview is sensitivity to the narrator's feelings. Show the narrator that you have empathy; say, "I can imagine how you felt." The narrator is grateful for this understanding. Gorden shows how the interviewer can respond with empathy to a narrator:

NARRATOR: At that time I had three babies still in diapers, and that made it a bit difficult to adjust to the divorce.
INTERVIEWER: Three babies all in diapers! How did you manage?[21]

Diminishing Rapport

Up to this point, the discussion has been focused on ways to build rapport. Consider also the ways that rapport can be damaged. Contrast the interviewer's reply in the next example with the previous one:

NARRATOR: At that time I had three babies still in diapers, and that made it a bit difficult to adjust to the divorce.
INTERVIEWER: What were some of the problems?[22]

The second example creates the message, "I am detached from this. I just need some information." Here is a similar interchange:

NARRATOR: Jim and I were going down highway 67; we didn't see the tornado, but just as we came to one of those banked turns we couldn't make it because the car was off the ground. We were jerked up in the air and I remember seeing a flash as our car hit the high-tension lines. Then we landed bottom side up in a swamp about four feet deep. One more gust of wind came and just flipped the car right side up again.

INTERVIEWER: Were you going north or south on highway 67?[23]

Would you wish to continue to talk to someone you had just met who responded to you in the way the interviewer did in the last example? You can see that this interviewer showed no sensitivity to the feelings of the respondent, no appreciation of what this experience was like for the person going through it.

The subtle communication of a negative attitude also can damage rapport. The narrator can sense disapproval. Gorden cites an interview with an individual in a metropolitan slum. The interviewer was taken aback by the casual attitude displayed toward middle-class ideals of parenthood and of legalities such as adoption procedures. His disapproving attitude was somehow communicated. Gorden observes, "From this point on, the respondent ceased to express herself so candidly, and any constructive working relationship was made more difficult."[24]

Communicating attitude by your nonverbal response is a real possibility. In interviewing farm women, Sherry Thomas found issues that the ideal picture of our society does not permit us to acknowledge. She said that she had expected her narrators to talk about pregnancy, child rearing, and even sexuality, but she received surprises: "What I didn't expect was, I got a lot of wife battering, incest, lesbianism, from women aged fifty to 100 in midstream America." She advised, "You have to be real comfortable about dealing with [such issues] and real able to keep that conversation going, and not by your face or your body manner or anything else put a stop to it, because it's some of the most powerful material that's going to surface, and to me, it's the material that blows the statistics wide open."[25]

I have talked about being animated—nodding, smiling, for example—during the interview; now I am advising that you control your face and body language. It is one thing to show interest, another to show judgment.

In his discussion of inhibitors of conversation, Gorden explains that negative attitudes toward the narrator also show up as errors of omission—such as forgetting what the narrator has said and just passing over topics important to the narrator. The use of a condescending tone of voice or "cautious rigidity" (a reluctance to depart from the interview guide) also has a negative effect.[26]

When the interviewer shows interest and respect, a desire to understand, and a sensitivity to the feelings of the narrator, a real partnership in the interview may develop. Spradley defines participation as a situation in which the narrator accepts the role of teaching the interviewer.[27] I see this as occurring when the narrator takes on some of the responsibility for making the interview productive. As you may have observed in your conversations with friends, an earnest and intense involvement in the process on the part of one conversational partner sparks the other's engagement.

Using Skill in Questioning

Gorden lists as interviewing skills (1) wording the question so that it is clear and appropriate for the topic, (2) listening to the narrator, (3) observing the narrator's nonverbal behavior, (4) remembering what the narrator has said, and (5) judging the relevance, validity, and completeness of the answer so that you know when to follow up, probe, and so on.[28]

Probe

Probing is used when you sense that something has been left out, that the narrator could give a more complete answer. In an example in the preceding chapter, the interviewer rightly gave a context for asking the question about family limitation. The narrator answered with the explanation that he and his wife limited their family because the wife had a bad hip. The interviewer thought there might be additional reasons:

INTERVIEWER: Were there any other considerations that dissuaded you from having a larger family?

NARRATOR: Hell, it was expensive. I knew I wanted both of mine to go to college. And farming's an "iffy" thing. If it's not too wet, if it's not too dry, if the price of machinery doesn't go up. (laughs) You can't count on being able to take care of the ones you've got.[29]

Because of the interviewer's probe, another level of motivation was articulated: higher expectations for the next generation that would require so much of the resources of this family that having more than two children would diminish the chance of realizing those expectations.

By probing, you invite the narrator to go into greater detail. Linda DiLuzio and Harry Hiller, in their study of Canadians who had to move from one place to another, found that probing can force the narrator to think more deeply about what he is trying to say, "perhaps even to admit things he had never verbalized before to another person."[30] This is what a narrator said to them after a probing question was asked: "This is the first time that I have ever really lev-eled with anyone about this move. It was always easier to just say what peo-ple expect to hear, and that way I didn't have to deal with it myself. But you asked me about all the details, who said what, and what happened when. Peo-ple don't really care enough to want to hear all that, but you seemed to want to hear it and that kind of forced me to say it like it really was."[31]

Another kind of probe is asking for the meaning of a word when the in-terviewer suspects it has a special meaning in a subculture or for that narra-tor. In defining meaning, the narrator will tell you a lot about her values. Look at the following partly hypothetical exchange (it's based on a question I once asked in a project on women artists in Chicago, and the answer is a composite of answers I received):

INTERVIEWER: Everybody thinks about the meaning of this word differ-ently. I suspect it means something different to everybody. What does *sisterhood* mean to you?

NARRATOR: Well, I guess it means we all go out of our way to help an-other woman, that we look on her like we do a sister, help her when we can.

Often, asking the meaning of a technical word you do not understand will give you an insight that the narrator takes it for granted that you have. At the beginning of the last century, Beatrice Webb, social investigator par ex-cellence, learned that she had to become familiar with the technical terms appropriate to a line of investigation. She says, "Technical terms and techni-cal details . . . are so many levers to lift into consciousness and expression the more abstruse and out-of-the-way facts or series of facts; and it is exactly these more hidden events that are needed to complete descriptive analysis and to verify hypotheses."[32]

Sociologist Arlene Daniels describes such an event in her research on psy-chiatrists in the military:

Once, for example, a key informant said, with lowered, confidential voice, "Since Colonel X has been to Vietnam, he's caught a bad case of Oudai fever." I had no idea what that meant; but I said nothing. In the course of another conversation, I said, "I understand he has a bad case of Oudai fever," hoping that I would find out what that meant. But this offended officer frowned and changed the conversation. Later, I learned that Oudai fever refers to the re-lentless pursuit of Vietnamese women: the Oudai is the name of the silken gar-ment the women wear. And this I learned only when I discovered that the of-ficer whom I offended was giving me a bad reputation for spreading malicious gossip. So much for the use of a standard technique for trying to learn insiders' ways without asking directly for information.[33]

Sherry Thomas described her puzzlement over the meaning of the definition farm women gave about themselves. They never called themselves farmers; rather, they said something like, "Well, really I only helped out on the farm." Thomas thought this over: "And by about the third interview I realized that I needed to find out what that phrase meant, because either I was wrong in what I was seeking to find out or something else was going on." She sensed that there was cognitive dissonance. She began asking questions such as, "Tell me what you did in 1926 on a typical day." These questions evoked responses that brought her nearer to the truth:

> And "helping" turns out to mean that those women got up at five in the morning, milked as many as twenty-four cows by hand, did all of the cream separating and milk preservation, ran a poultry herd, sold eggs for money, which was a significant part of the cash income, produced all of the vegetables and fruit for the family, and did at least a third, and frequently a half, of all the field crop work for the family, as well as doing all the housework, all the cooking, all the food preservation, and all the child care.[34]

Thomas's advice is not to stop with the socially accepted response but to keep probing until the narrator reveals the reality of the situation.[35] She was able to probe by asking a different kind of question, trying a different tactic. This is a delicate matter because you neither want to "lead the witness" by eliciting the answer you desire nor make the witness feel that he or she has failed to live up to your expectations. Often, however, a general probe following a line of questioning can elicit information without prejudicing the answer. As interviewer, you sense that the narrator is still thinking about the topic or seems to be expecting further questions or might talk more if encouraged. Then ask, "You have done an excellent job in giving me insight into this problem. Is there anything else you would like to add?"[36]

An interviewer can also use a probing question when a narrator has given a factual account but no indication of feelings. The interviewer senses that something important is being left out.

NARRATOR: So, we sold the farm and moved to town. I got a job at the dairy.

INTERVIEWER: I am imagining how I would have felt in that situation. Would you tell me how you felt about this change in your life?

Probing for a response about feelings can be problematic, however. First of all, a level of trust is required, but also the narrator's culture and gender roles may affect the response. Men in our culture will sometimes have a hard time articulating feelings, and women also will be most hesitant to admit certain ones. Interviewer Dana Jack explained: "Oral interviews allow us to hear, if we will, the particular meanings of a language that both men and women use but which each translates differently. For women, the ability to value their own thought and experience is hindered by self-doubt and hesitation when private experience seems at odds with cultural myths and values concerning how a woman is 'supposed' to think and feel."[37]

Follow-Up
Consider now a different kind of question, the follow-up question, which is closely related to the probing question. The interviewer picks up a clue in the narrator's statement and pursues it. The narrator may just slide past the topic, indicating in an offhand manner that he could tell you more, as he does in the following example:

NARRATOR: Well, the Thirties were lean around here. People weren't actually starving, but they weren't eating very much. By the way, I know how that DeKalb winged ear of corn sign got started. But as I said, people tried to live off hope and you get mighty thin on that.

INTERVIEWER: I'd be interested in hearing how the winged ear of corn began. Please tell me.[38]

Sometimes, a follow-up question phrased as a gentle suggestion can evoke information. This is helpful especially when you have come to the end of the line of questioning and you believe the answers have been honest but that the narrator could be encouraged to reflect and go beyond a factual account. It's tricky, though, because you run the risk of "leading" the witness. Here is a typical answer my coresearchers Brent Glass and Hugh Brinton and I received and a typical follow-up in our project on mill workers in Carrboro, North Carolina:

NARRATOR: They had a ball field for the workers. Christmas, gave out a turkey for each family. Picnic in the summer.

INTERVIEWER: Did you feel at the time that was enough or did you wish the mill had done more for the workers?

By our follow-up question, we subtly suggested that the mill owner could have done more.

Reason-Why

Another kind of question is the "reason-why." The reason-why question is useful when you need to know motivation. For example, the narrator has told you that a decision was made but has not told you the reason for it:

> NARRATOR: We decided to go along with the administration, whole committee did.
> INTERVIEWER: Why did the committee make that decision?

In some cases, the simple reason-why question can open up a new line of inquiry. By asking, "Why did you prefer that uncle to the other one?" the interviewer obtained a detailed account of family interaction.

Clarification

Still another kind of question is aimed at clarification. The simplest kind is to make sure you and the narrator are talking about the same thing:

> INTERVIEWER: Was that the situation in World War I or World War II?

The interviewer also may be confused because something has been left out: "I'm a bit confused here. Would you explain the relationship between these two people that existed prior to this particular meeting?" Another kind of clarification question is the request for the source of the information. You need to know whether the event described is a firsthand account or a handed-down story. The credibility of the account must be established. Ask something like, "Did you see it happen?" Establish the location of the narrator relative to the action described: "How close were you to the man who was making that speech?" "Was he using a microphone?" If the narrator was there but was yards away and no microphone was in use, then he may not have heard correctly.

The narrator may be used to taking shortcuts in conversation, such as saying, "You know what I mean." Usually the person listens politely and just nods or says, "Uh huh." During a recording session, you will have to be less polite and say, "I'm not sure of your meaning here. Could you tell me more about it?"[39]

If the narrator gestures to show you how large the fish was or says the stream was only as wide as the living room and dining room together, the next person listening to the tape will have no understanding of this. As interviewer, you must indicate on tape what the nonverbal communication means: "Would you say the fish was three feet long?" Or, "I think these two rooms together measure about twenty-four feet, so the stream was about twenty-four feet wide?"

What If? Question

The hypothetical question is interesting for finding out the narrator's wishes or aspirations or the things she thinks would have made her happy. "If you could have gone to work wherever you wished, where would you have worked?" Or, "You chose to go into medicine. What would your life have been like if you had followed your love, art?" You can get surprising and re-vealing answers about the actual situation with a what-if question.

Comparison

The comparison-type question gives the narrator a chance to explore a topic further. Some narrators are not analytical, and this type of question may not appeal to them, which you will be able to judge after a brief period of interview time. The question, "How do you compare working in the telephone office and working in the munitions plant?" brought out some interesting observations on social life in a small office composed of women as compared to social life in a large plant where both men and women were working. (See the discussion of broad questions, including comparisons, in chapter 2.)

Challenge

The challenge question is risky. Use your judgment as to whether the narrator can tolerate a challenge and be very careful in wording it. Make sure that your tone of voice and nonverbal gestures soften the challenge. For example, imagine that you are interviewing the mill superintendent about a strike in 1936 at his mill. He has just told you that the strikers were armed and that a striker accidentally shot the strike leader. The newspapers reported that the eyewitnesses said the strikers were not armed. You know that the mill owner had hired armed men, and you would like to find out how, in retrospect, the mill superintendent feels about what happened, even though he has given you the official line. Indeed, to ask him is to challenge the official line, and you are putting him on the defensive:

INTERVIEWER: We do know that the mill had hired armed guards. Just about everybody questioned saw their guns. I'm wondering how you felt about having these men with guns there?

NARRATOR: Needed to protect the building. Didn't want any burning, wrecking.

INTERVIEWER: Was the decision to bring in armed guards your decision?
NARRATOR: No.
INTERVIEWER: Were you against it or for it?
NARRATOR: (brief silence) I never had any trouble talking, I'd rather we kept talking. Don't like to see anybody get killed. I was afraid that would happen. (narrator shifts feet, looks at watch, looks directly at interviewer, not smiling now)

Here the interviewer took a chance and kept pushing to get information beyond the official version. But reading the nonverbal signals told her to stop there, at least for the time being. He has indicated, however, that he did not go along with the mill owner's decision to bring in armed men.

Below is a narrator who also could be challenged, even though this is going to puncture her long-held myth. She is describing a neighborhood in Providence, Rhode Island, in the early part of the century and her Italian American heritage:

NARRATOR: The Irish people and Italian people lived in the building with my mother and they lived next door, all along the lane. They got along so wonderfully you would think that they were all one family.
INTERVIEWER: Your family moved when you were two years old, did you say?
NARRATOR: Yes, only about five or six houses down. And they were all Irish people down there, too. Then as the Italian people started to move in, the Irish started to move out.[40]

The discrepancy in the narrator's two statements tip the interviewer off that a challenge is needed here: "Why did the Irish move out?" As in the preceding example, the interviewer must observe the nonverbal communication and listen to the tone of voice. If the narrator is annoyed, stop this line of questioning and return to it later, phrasing it differently.

Coping with Troublesome Situations

In any interview situation, the narrator keeps having to decide what to disclose, how much to tell, and what to keep silent about. There is always a kind of tug going on within the narrator and between narrator and interviewer. You must sense from the nonverbal response as well as from the spoken words how uncomfortable you are making your narrator and stop challenging before you get ordered out.

One strategy in asking troubling questions is to stop that line of questioning at the moment you can tell from tone of voice or look that the narrator is getting upset. Wait, then return to it later in the interview, phrasing it differently, more gently, maybe more obliquely. Once, in interviewing an Italian American woman on Federal Hill in Providence, Rhode Island, I asked where she had obtained the money to start her flower business. This was a project where I was recording the life histories of ethnic women, and I was especially interested in ethnic women who had "made it in America" as businesswomen. She ignored my question but continued talking. From her tone I knew she was offended. I did not pursue that but instead asked the next line of questioning, about how she built up her business. At the end of the hour, my student who had accompanied me said innocently, "You sure made the business a success but you never did tell us how you got your start." I felt my heart drop to my knees. The narrator, who had meanwhile warmed up to us, said, "Oh, I stole it from my husband's funeral parlor business—I kept the books for both."

Jack Douglas describes a similar situation when he was trying to ask a personal, troubling question during an interviewing project with beautiful women. He refers to the narrator here as "the Goddess":

> I try to put these [delicate questions] off until optimum trust and intimacy are established by going around them, if necessary. But always the point is to return to them by an indirect route. The hope is always that the Goddess will herself find her own way to talk about it, at her own time, and in her own words and tones. Allow her the lead once she has learned what you want to know. Then, if she does not find her own way back to what you need to know, gently nudge her with the reins toward the potentially sore spot. Do not lunge for it. Weave a circle of relevance around it, homing in on it in a downward spiral. If the disease becomes great, pull back and circle further away, or take up another point, keeping it in mind to come back and try another day when intimacy and trust are greater.[41]

Look at still another way to ask a troubling question. Asking a string of questions at once or even two questions at the same time can confuse the narrator. You usually get an answer to only one—the last one asked. The exception to this rule against asking two questions at the same time occurs when you are approaching an emotion-laden topic. You let the respondent "off the hook." In interviewing in the Italian American neighborhood in Providence mentioned above, I learned to say, "Were some people in the community for Mussolini and some against him?"[42]

Sometimes the narrator wants to be helpful, but the questions come so long after the event that his or her memory is not clear. Artifacts are very useful in this situation. Sven Lindquist, in his article about in-depth interviewing aptly titled "Dig Where You Stand," describes this technique: "If you come with a document, like the household book, or a report from the Factory Inspectorate, or a plan of the workplace from the archives of the insurance company, or a collection of photographs, or something else that captures the interest of the old person, this will awaken their memories and make the interview more worthwhile for both of you."[43]

If you have none of the above, ask the narrator whether she or he has photographs or souvenirs that you could look at together. You might ask, "Did this have a special meaning for you?" "What was that event like?" At one point during an interviewing project on farm families, I asked a farmer to draw a diagram of the family's house. Questions around this drawing (suggested to me by anthropologist Jane Adams), such as, "When the new bride came, did you build on?" revealed a lot about family change.[44] During the same project, a narrator mentioned that his mother kept a diary and asked me if I would like to see it. Reading some lines out loud stimulated his memories of her as he explained to me what she was referring to. In a class project on the history of a local, defunct Wurlitzer organ plant, the students visited the plant with former employees. The employees explained the part of the manufacturing process that was done in each room. These narrators became interested in the project, indeed, highly motivated to help, and their recall was very good when they were interviewed. Probably seeing the setting again stimulated memory.

Sometimes the narrator is just wrong about some detail. You do not wish to point that out in such a way that you hurt his feelings. Unless the error is seriously confusing the narrator and preventing the conversation from going forward, keep silent. You can put a note correcting the error in the transcript or the interviewer's comments to the tape. If it is causing serious trouble, say, "Just a second. Let's check this date—I'm a stickler for dates. Let's see, if the war ended in 1945, do you think this might have been . . . "

Chronology is indeed one of those areas where narrators are apt to depart from the expected answer because people often remember things according to significant life events rather than dates, as we noted in the chapter on memory. Alessandro Portelli explains this process in his article "'The Time of My Life'": "Historians may be interested in reconstructing the past; narrators are interested in projecting an image. Thus, historians often strive for a linear, chronological sequence; speakers may be more interested in pursuing and gathering together bundles of meaning, relationships and themes, across the linear span of their lifetimes."[45] Portelli quotes from an oral history transcript to show how this may be done:

AMERIGO MATTEUCCI: One more thing I remember, about Bianchini's farm. It was a farm with thirty-four hands. On Sunday mornings, the overseer would come in and say, "Say, you guys, no going to town today. We have work to do." Can you believe that? It was slavery. That's what it was, slavery. Sunday mornings—so many they seem without limit.

Portelli comments, "He wishes us to perceive the slowness of change in the lives of farm workers."[46] Interviewers must ask when this occurred so they can establish a general time frame; but the narrator has another objective— to indicate what was significant from his or her point of view.

Very often, it is neither time nor chronology but the association of events that is important, as Barbara Allen points out. In reflecting on her experience interviewing in middle Tennessee and south central Kentucky, she writes:

> The stories the narrators related that afternoon were not told in chronological order, nor were they linked together topically, for they dealt with more than just the episodes of violence that were the ostensible subject of the interview. Rather, they seemed to be grouped according to the association the narrators made among the events they were recounting, the individuals involved in those events, and the relations that bound those individuals to each other and to others in the community.[47]

Follow the thought process of the narrator, and allow him or her to develop the story as needed. The narrator may well answer all the questions you have; if not, you can return to them later in the interview. If a date is not correct, but the narrator insists on it, ponder this question: What significance might this switch have for the narrator?

Another troubling situation occurs when the interviewer assumes a meaning the narrator has not given to something. Beware of expressing the narrator's feelings or drawing a conclusion that he or she has not stated. Instead of saying, "I conclude that . . . ," just ask, "What do you conclude from that experience?"

Listening and Understanding

Earlier in this chapter, I stressed the importance of listening. I bring this up again, now with a different meaning. We may listen but not understand. Sometimes our own anxieties or assumptions prevent us from grasping the significance of what the narrator is saying. You may feel vaguely troubled at some point in the interview but not realize what happened until the interview is over. An excellent interviewer told me about a project she had undertaken with a Russian Jewish immigrant. She asked him if he had experienced anti-Semitism in pre–World War I Russia. He talked about quotas for attending high school and added, "I was never pressed," intimating that the worst had not happened. Because the worst had not happened, she went on with the interview but felt uneasy. In the second interview, she returned to the subject, this time probing. He talked about restrictions on movement, pogroms, derogatory names for Jews. She asked what being "pressed" meant. He explained that he had never been forced to consider discontinuing his practice of Orthodox Judaism. Her vague discomfort with his answer during the first interview tipped her off: she sensed that somehow she had not understood his meaning, the significance of this for him. She explained that the subject of anti-Semitism is an emotionally charged one for her and that she might not have wanted to hear.

In the above example, the interviewer was attuned to an internal voice. For all of us who do in-depth interviewing, being aware of our own fears, aversions, and assumptions and checking to see where we might have failed to hear and understand fully is a beneficial strategy.

Detecting Trouble

To figure out what is going on inside the narrator, pay attention to nonverbal signs. Squirming, glancing at a wristwatch, and making a comment about what he still has to do that day signifies that the narrator is losing interest. Switch to something he really wants to talk about. Drooping eyes, yawning, and stretching might prompt you to ask if the person is tired and would like to continue at another time. The narrator who crosses her arms over her chest and stares at the interviewer is working up some hostility. Soften your challenges, give the narrator an expression of appreciation for what she has offered, and forgo for the time being asking questions that you know will cause discomfort.

The narrator who resents your questions at some level, conscious or unconscious, will attempt to gain control of the direction of the interview. Turning your questions into his questions is one way to do this. Being vague in her answers, mumbling "I don't know," is another way. Sometimes the narrator will keep the interviewer on the defensive by continually asking him or her to clarify the question. Sometimes the narrator will talk in such a low tone of voice that the interviewer can barely hear.[48] Or he will encourage constant interruptions that will sabotage the interview. Usually, the anxious narrator just talks about a remotely related subject and does not answer directly. Or else he takes the conversation on a completely irrelevant tangent. Or she gives short answers and refuses to elaborate.

These are tough situations. If you continue to get "I don't know," try some open-ended questions about a nonthreatening topic. You might say something like, "Tell me more about your childhood. I'd like to hear more about those trips to the Farmers' Market with your grandmother." (Of course, you should not jump around in the conversation: your question has got to be on the topic discussed or you must give a reason for changing suddenly.) If you are getting answers in a scarcely audible voice, try saying cheerfully, "Let's just listen and see if we are getting a good sound quality." Listening to the tape may reveal to the narrator how strange this mumbling person sounds, and she may decide to speak a little louder. Ask only nonthreatening, routine questions until you sense that she is relaxing. If the narrator keeps obstructing the interview by going off on a tangent, explain again, in different terms this time, why these questions are important to you and how she will have the right to restrict use of the tape. Or, you might confront her by saying something like, "I notice that you change the subject when I mention your father. Would you prefer not to discuss this right now?"

On one occasion, I persisted in the interview even though the narrator's questions to me and her answers indicated she trusted no one, including me. At the end, she demanded the tape and threw it into her fireplace, which had a blazing fire going. On another occasion, I wound down the interview because the narrator kept asking me questions and was consistently evasive. I realized the interview was useless. Sometimes, when you have done everything you know to do and the narrator is still distrustful, resentful, and hostile, give up. Thank the narrator politely and leave. Further struggle with so little promise of constructive work is a waste of your time.

Consider one last situation: the narrator breaks down and weeps. You could not have known that you would touch on a topic that would evoke such sad memories for the narrator. At one point in our mill village project, I blithely asked the standard question about courtship practices in the early part of the century. The narrator started to cry as she remembered a sweetheart she had loved fifty years ago. When this happens, be silent for a few minutes. Every person is entitled to express his or her private grief. British oral historian David Jones, in his article "Distressing Histories and Unhappy Interviewing," points out that one of the reasons why people cry is that this is a way to communicate the importance of the remembered experience[49]—yes, but it still hurts. Acknowledge the narrator's distress and apologize for stumbling onto a topic that was painful. Ask the narrator if he or she would like to go on with the interview. If the narrator gives assent, change the topic and go on.

But there are even more serious topics that may come up in an interview. Jones says, "Perhaps there are times when it might be better, for the interviewee, not to encourage them to discuss some things that would be useful to know. A common dilemma therefore is whether to probe, or encourage someone to expand on an issue that appears to be upsetting, or potentially upsetting."[50] He describes an interview in which the narrator talked about sexual abuse by her father. She said that when her young daughter suffered such abuse by a friend of the family, she talked to her daughter about her own experience to show that she truly understood. Jones concludes, "Something about the way she told me here, made me feel that it was safe territory. Very simply she is telling me that she has *talked* about it."[51] In another project interviewing families with a mentally ill member, he asked himself whether anybody should be doing this kind of interviewing. He realized that his own distress in hearing such painful things influenced him. But also, he realized some good might come of this work: "I came to think that I owed those people. I owed them that I should help others understand their point of view, and some of the very mixed and difficult feelings they have to manage."[52] He concluded that the interviewer has to consider whether getting this painful information is justified by the use he will make of it. More important, try to figure out if *the narrator's purpose* in recording outweighs the pain of dredging up severely painful feelings. If the narrator does not think it is worth it, stop.

Ending the Interview

As the interview winds down, thank the narrator on tape. As you reach for your belongings and chat with the narrator, leave the tape running. Inevitably, the narrator thinks of something else to add. Don't turn off the recorder until the last minute. And if he or she starts talking again, unpack the recorder and turn it on again. Always ask, in addition, for names of other people to interview and written documents that will lead you further in your research. If there is any indication at all that the narrator has more to tell you, ask for a second interview. On the second and third interviews, rapport improves. Your questions have stimulated memory, and the narrator will continue to think about them during the intervening time. You also will think of questions you would like to ask. Interviewer and narrator now have a history together on which they can build.[53]

Hand the release form to the narrator and explain it. Give him or her time to read it and ask questions. Obviously, the advantage of having the signing take place then is that you can take the release form with you. If the narrator insists that you leave it so a son or daughter or husband or wife can look it over, try to get a date specified when you can return to pick it up. Otherwise, give the narrator an addressed, stamped envelope and request that you receive it in the mail by a specified date.

As soon as you get home, write a thank-you letter and the notes about the interview. Write the notes immediately while the information is fresh in your mind. If you are a historian, you will need these for the interviewer's comments that are deposited in the archives with the tape. Putting off writing the field notes and procrastinating about the thank-you letter will result in a backlog of work. And the longer you wait, the harder it gets because you will forget observations. As you reflect on the interview, consult the checklist for critiquing interviewing skills (see box 4.1). You can assess your interviewing techniques—for me, every interview is a learning opportunity.

In this chapter, I have stressed attention to details and discussed techniques that are essential to expert interviewing. It is worthwhile to learn them. Beyond techniques, however, you bring to the interview your own unique approach to others and to life. Beatrice Webb said it best: "Hence a spirit of adventure, a delight in watching human beings as human beings

---

A. POSITIVES (Add 10 points for each item checked.)
  1. Indicated empathy when appropriate.
  2. Showed appreciation for the narrator's help.
  3. Listened carefully.
  4. Followed the narrator's pacing.
  5. Explained reason for change in topic.
  6. Used a two-sentence format when introducing a line of questions that might be problematic for the narrator.
  7. Probed when appropriate.
  8. Used a follow-up question when more information was needed.
  9. Asked a challenge question in a sensitive manner.
  10. Requested clarification when needed.
B. NEGATIVES (Subtract 10 points from the score above for each item checked.)
  1. Interrupted the narrator.
  2. Kept repeating what the narrator had just said.
  3. Inferred something the narrator had not said.
  4. Failed to pick up on a topic the narrator indicated was important.
  5. Made irrelevant, distracting comments.
  6. Ignored narrator's feelings and failed to give an empathic response.
  7. Failed to check the sound on the recorder.
  8. Let the narrator sidetrack the conversation with a long irrelevant aside.
  9. Asked a leading question.
  10. Asked several questions at the same time.

Box 4.1. Checklist for Critiquing Interviewing Skills

quite apart from what you can get out of their minds, an enjoyment of the play of your own personality with that of another, are gifts of rare value in the art of interviewing."[54]

Summary

A meeting before the day of the interview means that you do not appear at the interview as a stranger. It permits you to survey the interviewing environment and establish some expectations about a good environment for recording. You have the chance to explain the purpose of the project and give some indication of what will be discussed.

Begin the recording session by giving pertinent information on tape and get the narrator's verbal consent to the taping. Start with nonthreatening topics and questions that are easy to answer. The first interview with a narrator usually begins with apprehension on both sides. After a period of exploration, if the interviewer can build rapport, the narrator may feel like fully cooperating and may end up taking responsibility for the success of the interview. Rapport is built by being sensitive to the narrator's feelings, showing appreciation, listening carefully, following the narrator's pacing, communicating interest and respect, and taking time to explain why you change topics and why you ask a line of questions.

Know when to probe, when to use a follow-up question, to ask for clarification, to try a suggestion, to ask a reason-why question, and to pose a hypothetical question. Challenging questions are appropriate but must be pursued with caution. Be aware of your own assumptions that might prevent you from probing when that is needed. Try to get dates correct but understand that narrators have their own organization of experiences and may be less concerned with chronology than you are.

In troublesome situations, watch the nonverbal communication and listen to the tone of voice. If the narrator is getting angry or uncomfortable, stop that line of questioning. Return to the topic later, using a different approach if possible. Resentful narrators try to sabotage an interview by giving only short answers, getting the conversation off track, encouraging interruptions, and mumbling. Steer the conversation to a nonthreatening topic. If the obstructing persists, ask outright in as friendly a manner as possible what is bothersome in the interview.

At the end of the interview, get a signature on the release form if you can. Ask for names of other possible narrators. If you think the narrator has more to tell and is willing, schedule a second interview. As soon as possible, write the interview notes and thank-you letter.

Recommended Reading

Banaka, William. *Training in Depth Interviewing.* New York: Harper & Row, 1971. This manual is slanted toward the interviewer in an employment counselor situation or a psychological intake interview; nevertheless, Banaka has things to say that are appropriate to interviews in general.

Chirban, John T. *Interviewing in Depth: The Interactive-Relational Approach.* Thousand Oaks, CA: Sage, 1996. Chirban does not have in mind an oral history interview, and yet his interviews have been not only clinical, psychological interviews but also life history interviews. He emphasizes the importance of the interviewer's awareness of his own involvement in the process and stresses developing authenticity and sensitivity.

Douglas, Jack D. *Creative Interviewing.* Beverly Hills, CA: Sage, 1985. Douglas has in mind the sociological or anthropological investigation, but interviewers in other disciplines also will find helpful information.

Gorden, Raymond L. *Interviewing: Strategy, Techniques and Tactics.* Chicago: Dorsey Press, 1987. First published in 1969, this book is slanted toward the needs of sociologists doing survey research, but there is excellent advice on interviewing strategies, techniques, and ethics that is applicable to the in-depth interview no matter what your discipline.

Lindquist, Sven. "Dig Where You Stand." *Oral History* 7 (Autumn 1979): 26–30. (Also in *Our Common History: The Transformation of Europe,* ed. Paul Thompson and Natasha Burchardt [Atlantic Highlands, NJ: Humanities Press, 1982].) The author provides admonitions and examples on probing.

Morrissey, Charles T. "The Two-Sentence Format as an Interviewing Technique in Oral History Fieldwork." *Oral History Review* 15 (Spring 1987): 43–53. This is a helpful article on phrasing a question so that you provide a context.

Payne, Stanley. *The Art of Asking Questions.* Princeton, NJ: Princeton University Press, 1951. This is a readable guide for phrasing questions for both survey research and the in-depth interview.

Portelli, Alessandro. *Death of Luigi Trastulli and Other Stories: Form and Meaning in Oral History.* Albany: State University of New York Press, 1991. This collection of essays forms a thoughtful and provocative treatise on in-depth interviewing in general.

Sitton, Thad, George L. Mehaffy, and O. L. Davis Jr. *Oral History: A Guide for Teachers and Others.* Austin: University of Texas Press, 1983. This useful guide for using oral history in the secondary school classroom presents ideas for projects, ways to proceed using oral history in classroom teaching, and methods of archiving and disseminating the information.

Spradley, James P. *The Ethnographic Interview.* New York: Holt, Rinehart & Winston, 1979. This book presents useful information in general, but concerning the in-depth interview it is very good for discussion of cooperation and participation and for techniques of building rapport.

Thomas, Sherry. "Digging beneath the Surface: Oral History Techniques." *Frontiers* 7 (1983): 50–55. Thomas speaks candidly about her experiences interviewing farm women across the United States; she stresses the need for probing and for keeping silent to allow the narrator time to think.

Weiss, Robert S. *Learning from Strangers: The Art and Method of Qualitative Interview Studies.* New York: Free Press, 1994. Written for sociologists, this book will also be of use to interviewers in other disciplines. See especially chapter 4, which gives excerpts from interviews with a running critique of the interviewer's questions, and chapter 5, the section "Interviewing Difficulties."

Notes

1. Ann Oakley, "Interviewing Women: A Contradiction in Terms," in *Doing Feminist Research*, ed. Helen Roberts (London: Routledge, 1981), 31.

2. Jack Douglas, *Creative Interviewing* (Beverly Hills, CA: Sage, 1985), 79.

3. Linda A. Bennett and Katharine McAvity, "Family Research: A Case for Interviewing Couples," in *The Psychosocial Interior of the Family*, 3rd ed., ed. Gerald Handel, 75–94 (New York: Aldine, 1985); see pp. 76–84. See also Ralph LaRossa, "Conjoint Marital Interviewing as a Research Strategy," *Case Analysis* 1, no. 2 (1978): 141–49. For a discussion of the opposite point of view, see Marie Corbin, "Problems and Procedures of Interviewing," appendix 3 in *Managers and Their Wives: A Study in Career and Family Relationships in the Middle Class*, ed. J. M. and R. E. Pahl, 286–306 (London: Penguin, 1971); see pp. 294–95.

4. Douglas, *Creative Interviewing*, 82.

5. Martha Ross, "Interviewer or Intervener," *Maryland Historian* 13 (Fall–Winter 1982): 3–5.

6. Kristin M. Langellier and Deanna L. Hall, "Interviewing Women: A Phenomenological Approach to Feminist Communication Research," in *Doing Research on Women's Communication: Perspectives on Theory and Method*, ed. Carol Spitzach, 193–220 (Norwood, NJ: Ablex Publishing, 1989); see p. 207.

7. James Spradley, *The Ethnographic Interview* (New York: Holt, Rinehart & Winston, 1979), 79.

8. Spradley, *Ethnographic Interview*, 79.

9. Spradley, *Ethnographic Interview*, 80.

10. Douglas, *Creative Interviewing*, 100.

11. Spradley, *Ethnographic Interview*, 81.

12. Douglas, *Creative Interviewing*, 55.

13. Valerie Yow (listed as Valerie Quinney) and Linda Wood, *How to Find Out by Asking: A Guide to Oral History in Rhode Island* (Providence: National Endowment for the Humanities Youth Planning Grant and the Rhode Island Board of Education, 1979), 20.

14. Raymond L. Gorden, *Interviewing: Strategy, Techniques and Tactics*, 4th ed. (Chicago: Dorsey Press, 1987), 251.

15. Gorden, *Interviewing*, 232.

16. Gorden, *Interviewing*, 188.

17. Sherry Thomas, "Digging beneath the Surface," *Frontiers* 7, no. 1 (1983): 54.

18. Byron Lewis and Frank Pucelik, *Magic Demystified: A Pragmatic Guide to Communication and Change*, 2nd ed. (Lake Oswego, OR: Metamorphous Press, 1984), 121.

19. Gorden, *Interviewing*, 303.

20. William Sheridan Allen, *The Nazi Seizure of Power: The Experience of a Single German Town, 1922–1945* (New York: F. Watts, 1984).

21. Gorden, *Interviewing*, 226.

22. Gorden, *Interviewing*, 226.

23. Gorden, *Interviewing*, 227.

24. Gorden, *Interviewing*, 225.

25. Thomas, "Digging beneath the Surface," 51.

26. Gorden, *Interviewing*, 249.

27. Spradley, *Ethnographic Interview*, 81.

28. Gorden, *Interviewing*, 43.

29. Terry Shea and Valerie Yow, "Farm Families of DeKalb County" (Northern Illinois Regional History Center, Northern Illinois University, DeKalb, Illinois, unpublished collection).

30. Linda DiLuzio and Harry H. Hiller, "The Interviewee and the Research Interview: Analysing a Neglected Dimension in Research," *Canadian Review of Sociology and Anthropology* 41, no. 1 (February 2004): 1–26; see p. 17.

31. DiLuzio and Hiller, "The Interviewee and the Research Interview," 17.

32. Beatrice Webb, *My Apprenticeship* (New York: Longman, Green, 1926), 409.

33. Arlene Daniels, "Self-Deception and Self-Discovery in Field Work," *Qualitative Sociology* 6, no. 3 (1983): 195–214; see p. 198.

34. Thomas, "Digging beneath the Surface," 51.

35. Thomas, "Digging beneath the Surface," 51. In a similar way, James Spradley advises interviewers to ask for the use of the word rather than for meaning, but this strategy may depend on the situation. Spradley, *Ethnographic Interview*, 156–57.

36. Gorden, *Interviewing*, 234.

37. Kathryn Anderson, Susan Armitage, Dana Jack, and Judith Wittner, "Beginning Where We Are: Feminist Methodology in Oral History," *Oral History Review* 15 (Spring 1987): 103–27; see p. 114.

38. Shea and Yow, "Farm Families of DeKalb County."

39. Gorden, *Interviewing*, 234.

40. Yow and Wood, *How to Find Out by Asking*, 20.

41. Douglas, *Creative Interviewing*, 138.

42. Yow and Wood, *How to Find Out by Asking*, 9.

43. Sven Lindqvist, "Dig Where You Stand," in *Our Common History: The Transformation of Europe*, ed. Paul Thompson with Natasha Burchardt (Atlantic Highlands, NJ: Humanities Press, 1982), 326.

44. Jane Adams, "Resistance to 'Modernity': Southern Illinois Farm Women and the Cult of Domesticity," *American Ethnologist* 20, no. 1 (February 1993): 89–113.

45. Alessandro Portelli, "'The Time of My Life': Functions of Time in Oral History," in *Death of Luigi Trastulli and Other Stories: Form and Meaning in Oral History* (Albany: State University of New York Press, 1991), 63.

46. Portelli, "'Time of My Life,'" 67.

47. Barbara Allen, "Recreating the Past: The Narrator's Perspective in Oral History," *Oral History Review* 12 (1984): 1–12; see p. 11.

48. William Banaka, *Training in Depth Interviewing* (New York: Harper & Row, 1971), 17.

49. David W. Jones, "Distressing Histories and Unhappy Interviewing," *Oral History* 26, no. 2 (1998): 49–56; see p. 54.

50. Jones, "Distressing Histories and Unhappy Interviewing," 51.

51. Jones, "Distressing Histories and Unhappy Interviewing," 52.

52. Jones, "Distressing Histories and Unhappy Interviewing," 54.

53. Eva M. McMahan, *Elite Oral History Discourse: A Study of Cooperation and Coherence* (Tuscaloosa: University of Alabama Press, 1989), 6.

54. Webb, *My Apprenticeship*, 411.

CHAPTER FIVE

Legalities and Ethics

Like a cat about to go into a yard full of dogs, step with full attention into this matter of legalities and ethics. The amateur just turns on the tape recorder and lets the tape roll. The professional reads as much as possible about the law, uses a release form, and saves hours of worry. Writing this, I feel like the Ghost of Christmas Yet to Come, pointing a bony finger at you: "It was shrouded in a deep black garment, which concealed its head, its face, its form, and left nothing of it visible save one outstretched hand. But for this it would have been difficult to detach its figure from the night, and separate it from the darkness by which it was surrounded. . . . 'You are about to show me shadows of the things that have not happened, but will happen in the time before us,' Scrooge pursued. 'Is that so, Spirit?'"[1]

Yes! this spirit you are dealing with now answers. I want to save you a lawsuit. The main areas of legal concern to researchers recording people's words are copyright, libel, and privacy. This chapter will consider these legal areas. But often a legal issue is an ethical issue, as well. Such ethical issues as responsibilities of interviewer to narrator, considerations of harm to others, and truthful presentation of research will be discussed.

Legal Issues

Copyright
Who has legal ownership of the tape? First consider ownership of copyright as defined by the most recent United States copyright law, the Copyright Act

of 1976 (which went into effect January 1978) and the Digital Millennium Copyright Act of 1998. At the moment you turn off the machine, the tape belongs to the narrator. John Neuenschwander, a history professor, lawyer, judge, and oral historian, in his book *Oral History and the Law* states the current interpretation of the law: "At this point in the process, the interviewee is usually deemed to be the sole author of the tape and the singular copyright holder."[2] So, we, the interviewers, ask the narrator to sign a legal release form. This is a written statement to the effect that the narrator transfers his or her ownership of the interview to the interviewer or to the institution that has commissioned the interview or to the archives that will receive it. We used to think that the interviewer automatically had rights to the interview also, but this question of whether the person who conducts the interview has any copyright interest in the interview has unfortunately not been resolved by the courts. Neuenschwander does note that when the United States Copyright Office receives an application to register an interview, its standard policy is to determine whether both the narrator and interviewer are joint authors. Given the possibility that at some point interviewers may be deemed by the courts to have a joint interest in an interview with the narrator, the safest way to proceed is for you, as interviewer, to sign a release agreement when you get ready to turn over the tapes to a third party.[3]

You need release forms for two purposes: If you want to use the information in published writings or in public presentations, you must secure from the narrator the right to use the information. If the taped life history is to be deposited in archives, the archivist will need permission to let the public listen to it. A release form is not a guarantee against all lawsuits, but it will surely help in court. Sample release forms are included in appendix F, and you may be able to use these models to tailor a form for your project. The best protection is to have a lawyer scrutinize the form you draw up. Neuenschwander reminds oral historians that it is cheaper to hire a lawyer at the beginning of a project than to hire a lawyer later to defend you in a lawsuit.

Before you begin recording, inform the narrator that you will have a release form that you will ask him or her to sign at the end of the recording session. Do not ask the narrator to sign before the recording, which would be tantamount to asking someone to give up control of his or her words before the questions and the answers were known. It is like telling someone to sign and hand over a blank check. When the recording has been completed, give the form to the narrator. Explain how the release form is to be used: "This will allow me to use the information in my book." "This will allow people interested in this community who come into the library to listen to your tape." If you plan to place the collection of interviews on a website, this information, as well as information about other kinds of public presentations that you have in mind, should be included on the release form. Add a general phrase like, "such educational presentations as the interviewer shall deem appropriate." Explain options concerning use of the interview: unrestricted access to the tape, sealing the entire tape for a specified number of years, or sealing portions of the tape for a specified number of years. Be sure to write the narrator's decision under the designation "Restrictions." A final possibility is anonymity, which must be stated on the form if this is the narrator's choice. If there are no restrictions, ask the narrator to write "None" and initial it.

If, at a later date, you use the information in a special way not mentioned on the release form, you have to make a judgment about whether to go back to the narrator for permission. For example, if the release form covered scholarly publications, I would not ask for permission to publish a brief article in a magazine, but I would make a new request for permission if I presented the information in a play or put it on a plaque in a public building.

If you intend to deposit the tapes in archives, note this in the release form, which relinquishes copyright to the interviewer, by adding a statement such as, "I also grant the interviewer, Dr. Jekyll, the right to deposit this taped interview and any transcript made from it in the Archives of the Institute for Change." When the tapes are deposited, you must give the archivist a release form from each narrator. A general release covering the whole collection will not be sufficient. It is helpful if, at the beginning of the project, you decide which archives will receive your collection of tapes and request their deed of gift form. Then you can save everybody time by asking the narrator not only to sign a release stating that he or she relinquishes copyright but also the deed of gift form. Otherwise, at a later time, either the archivist or you must track down the narrators and request they sign the deed of gift form.

If you are employed by an institution or group to carry out an interviewing project, your interviews are defined as "work made for hire." Your employer owns copyright when the narrator signs a release form relinquishing his or her rights. An interviewer may wish to acknowledge the employer's copyright formally by signing a form, "Work Made for Hire Agreement," for the institution before interviewing starts.[4] (See appendix F for a model form.)

If anonymity is promised, you must lock up this release form, make a duplicate of the tape, and on this copy, erase the name and substitute a pseudonym. This duplicated copy will be made available to the public with the explanation that a pseudonym is being used.

If the narrator chooses not to sign the release form, you must not pressure him or her to do so. This would be a denial of the narrator's right to choose to do whatever he or she wishes with his or her property. Without a release form, you are allowed by the 1976 copyright law to use the tape in your own classroom for educational purposes.[5] You may not lend the tape to anyone else. You may, however, deposit a copy of the tape in the archives if you seal it for a period of seventy years after the narrator's death. (Sound deteriorates, and so it is better to deposit a transcript with the tape.)

Whenever you deposit a tape, remember that some archives have loose security systems. Make sure that if you promise the narrator that a tape will be sealed for ten years, it will indeed be locked up and the public denied access to it for ten years. If portions are to be sealed, make a duplicate copy, erase the sealed words, and place the original under lock. In the silence created by the erasure, indicate to the listener what has happened: "Here, Miss Lizzie Borden requests that information of a confidential nature regarding her relationship with her parents be sealed for one hundred years."

Also be aware that courts can subpoena tapes, and government agencies can demand tapes made during government-sponsored research. The best protection you can give the narrator is to stop recording for a second if the conversation veers toward a topic that could be self-incriminating or result in a libel suit. Warn the narrator. If he or she continues unrestrained, after the recording advise sealing portions of the tape that are libelous. And still another possibility is to delete the identity of the person discussed if this is the narrator's wish, but indicate on tape that at this point the narrator requests deletion of a name.

When the first edition of this book was published, I did not give thought to the ways oral histories would be appropriated and used publicly—for example, in exhibits in museums or other public buildings, in filmed documentaries, and on websites. I once walked into a public building and saw on the wall a plaque with an excerpt from an interview I had recorded years earlier. After reading it, I realized that no harm had been done to the narrator (who had signed a release form indicating that her interview could be used publicly for educational purposes), and the copyright had been handed over to the archives that had received the tapes. Also, I decided public use of the words was fine with me because my purpose in the project was to make these individuals' contributions to the community known.

Now such use is so widespread that the possibility of your seeing excerpts from your interviews in a public place or on television or the Internet must be addressed. You have some protection, as Neuenschwander asserts: "An oral history tape is protected expression as soon as an interview is completed."[6] But it will be up to you to decide whether the topics or the persons interviewed might provide juicy material for a media presentation. If you have not relinquished this copyright, and if you want to have some control over what is presented, you may wish to secure a formal copyright. It is possible to copyright an entire collection if it has a single title and the interviews follow one theme or deal with one general topic.[7] One method is to place on the title page of the collection or the individual oral history a copyright notice, which looks like a *c* in a circle. Another method is to register an oral history interview or collection with the United States Copyright Office (or appropriate government office in your country). The requirement is an application, a fee of thirty dollars, and two copies for deposit (or one copy if the work is unpublished). Request Form TX, which covers literary work other than drama. Write to the Library of Congress, Copyright Office, 101 Independence Avenue, SE, Washington, DC 20559-6000, or on the Internet go to www.copyright.gov, which offers forms and instructions that you can download. Or, you may decide that you want the transcript to be in the public domain, open to everyone without requiring any permission. In that case, stipulate in the release that you renounce all copyright ownership.[8]

A situation that we will all probably face is that a collection of interviews—many of them you may have done yourself—is placed on the World Wide Web. These interviews were usually carried out before anyone foresaw the publication of the interviews on the Internet. The release form did not state "Internet publication," but if the language was inclusive—like, "whatever use the director of the archives may determine"—the publication on the web is legal. Still, as a matter of courtesy, the archivist would do well to tell the narrator whose words are being so published what is happening. The lesson here for all of us is to make the language in the release form general enough to cover future uses that we may not in the present anticipate.

Libel

I have implied the possibility of going to court to sue against infringement of copyright. Be aware of the possibility of *being sued* on a charge of libel. Libel is a *published* statement that is false and that is intended to harm a person's reputation. If the defamation is spoken, it is slander. You cannot libel a deceased person, but since as oral historians we often deal with the recent past and living persons, legalities concerned with libel are important to consider.

You may think that what the narrator chooses to say about someone else is the narrator's problem. But it is also your problem because the court's assumption is that "anyone who repeats, republishes, or redistributes a defamatory statement made by another can be held liable as well."[9] What would a court of law find defamatory? Neuenschwander sums up five categories of possible libel, that is, published statements that involve

1. imputing criminal action;
2. describing disgraceful or despicable conduct or irresponsible association with immoral people;
3. charging immoral or unethical actions;
4. attempting to demonstrate financial irresponsibility; or
5. implying a lack of competence or misconduct while in office or employment.[10]

And if, by misfortune, you find yourself in court, what must the prosecution prove? The words must be lies. The lies must have been communicated at least to a third party. The person offended must be identifiable. The person's reputation must have suffered harm. And finally, the person bringing suit must establish that the defendant has been to some degree at fault.[11]

"Degree of fault" sounds problematic, and it is. Neuenschwander explains that the issue here is whether the person maligned is a public figure or not.[12] If a person has become a public figure, apparently the court considers that so many accusations have been made that one case will not ruin a reputation about which there is already so much known and openly discussed.

Several other conditions are important criteria for establishing "degree of fault." Intent is a crucial test. If the defendant can prove that he or she was simply mistaken and that no malice was intended, then the court will not convict. (However, absence of malice is difficult to prove.) Or if the accusation was just an opinion and there was no attempt to recite false information to prove the opinion, the defendant may be off the hook.

A case that began in 1983, was judged in 1993, and still remained unsettled for another year illustrates the difficulties of carrying on a libel suit, even if you win in the end. In the early part of the 1980s, journalist Janet Malcolm interviewed psychotherapist Jeffrey Masson for approximately forty hours. She published a two-part article in the *New Yorker* titled "Annals of Scholarship: Trouble in the Archives" on Masson's work at the archives for Freudian research.[13] Masson brought suit against Malcolm and the magazine, charging libel. He pointed out five quotations attributed to him falsely and argued that these had damaged his reputation and professional life. The jury read the transcripts of the forty hours of taped interviews as well as Malcolm's notes. The decision was that all five quotations were fabricated and that two fit the definition of libel.[14] The case dragged on until November 1994, when the jury decided that although Malcolm had included two fabricated quotations that fit the definition of libel, she had not acted willfully or recklessly.[15] Janet Malcolm won, but we can imagine the legal fees she had to pay.

Privacy

Consider the matter of privacy. Herbert C. Kelman, a social scientist who studied legal and ethical issues in social science research, defines invasion of privacy as "exposure of damaging information, diminishing a person's control and liberty, and intrusion into a person's private space."[16]

Secret listening by means of electronic bugging is an invasion of privacy. Any recording without the speaker's knowledge and consent is an invasion of privacy. In oral history interviews, begin the recording by asking on tape if you have permission to record. Make sure you have the spoken consent on tape. The release form should state that the information was recorded, and the narrator's signature on the release at the end of the interview will prove his or her awareness of this.

Another kind of invasion of privacy is the public revelation of information about an individual's intimate, private life. This is information that may be true but is intensely personal. Often it is not important that the public know about it because this very personal, private situation did not affect the individual's conduct in office or job performance.[17] Or perhaps in such research as studies of family life, intimate details from life histories are not necessary to the publication of the research findings.

I confronted this issue when I was writing the history of a psychiatric hospital and had to make a decision about a personal rivalry between two staff people. One psychiatrist drove spikes in the ground around his parking place so that his rival, who had the spot next to his, would blow out his tires if he went so much as an inch over the line. I left that out of the published book because it was not part of the institution's history—their rivalry had not affected the course of the hospital. By pointing out these eccentricities in private life, I would have damaged the psychiatrist's reputation. This could have been interpreted as invasion of privacy because the incident reveals a personal, ruinous obsession that few knew about.

Ted Schwarz, who published several biographies and *The Complete Guide to Writing Biographies*, cautions that narrators can openly reveal their own intimate secrets and agree to publication; but be careful when they tell you someone else's. Discussing someone else's secrets in public is an invasion of privacy and would be cause for a libel suit.[18] In the same hospital study, I heard a lot of stories about the personal lives of the upper echelon in that work community. These personal stories would have enlivened the book, but I judged they would not have contributed much to understanding the institution's history. I did quote a lot of information concerning professional behavior and treatment philosophy and practice, and I pointed out the negative consequences of some of this behavior. I may have opened up the possibility of a libel suit but certainly not on grounds of invasion of privacy because the actions I discussed were public.

Institutional Review Boards

One last note about protection of narrators: oral history projects are often carried out under the auspices of a university or another kind of institution, and this means appearing before an institutional review board (IRB) whose mission is to protect human subjects who are going to be studied. This mission is a worthy one, but in practice, research such as medical professionals carry out—which originally necessitated such review boards—differs greatly from the kind of research social scientists do. All research should not be lumped together and scrutinized in the same way: important differences should not be ignored. Even within the social sciences, the in-depth interviews that oral historians conduct are different from quantitative social scientists' testing of large groups by means of questionnaires.

You may find yourself arguing this before a powerful group that has ultimate control over whether your research project can go ahead or not. Not only the United States but other national governments, as well, have offices for scrutiny of research testing human subjects; and so the matter concerns us in many countries and in all disciplines that use the in-depth interview as a research method. I will use as my example the situation in the United States because I am familiar with this one. I recommend to you *Walking the Tightrope: Ethical Issues for Qualitative Researchers*, an interdisciplinary anthology of articles by researchers in Canada, Great Britain, and the United States.[19] The reflections on governmental review of social research in this volume are invaluable for an understanding of these very complicated issues.

The United States' Office for Human Research Protection requires IRBs to scrutinize research that fits this definition: "A systematic investigation, including research development, testing and evaluation, designed to develop or contribute to generalizable knowledge." But this is a confusing statement—what is generalizable knowledge? The Oral History Association's "Guidelines for the Review of Oral History Research Projects" argues: "Open-ended, individualistic interviewing about events that have occurred in the past represents a different form of research than federal regulations were intended to encompass."[20]

Furthermore, the IRB's requirement that anonymity be maintained does not take into account the characteristics of qualitative research. In survey research, it is possible to promise anonymity and adhere to that. But often in qualitative research, the number of subjects has to be limited: we do not carry out in-depth interviews with five hundred to one thousand narrators. We interview face to face—we know very well who the individual narrators are. When sociologists or anthropologists provide an account of a group, based on participant observation and interviews, they cannot always totally disguise an informant's identity. His or her position in the group must be noted for the discussion of level of power to make sense, and often this is a unique position. An important aim of the oral historian's research is to make known an individual's actions in history and also to hold the individual accountable for his testimony. In the United States in August 2003, the Office for Human Research Protection accepted a policy statement provided jointly by representatives of the American Historical Association and the Oral History Association that oral historians' research methods do not fit the type of research covered by the federal regulations.[21] (See appendix D; and for a bibliography of articles on institutional review boards, go to www.historians.org/press/2003-11-10-IRB-Bib.htm.)

However, institutions within the United States vary in the ways that they consider and adhere to historians' statements about appropriateness of institutional review of research in contemporary history. And sociologists and anthropologists today find themselves trying to get approval for research from boards that ten years ago would have simply exempted a particular research study because it was clear that intention to harm was not there and that safeguards were in place. In Canada and Great Britain, the agencies exercising control are somewhat different from those in the United States, but the situation of an overreaching body exercising control is operating—often with results that squelch research. The problems are not solved yet.

Ethical Issues

General Principles in Professional Guidelines

Ethical and legal issues are often intertwined, and it is appropriate to consider them in the same chapter. Ethical issues, however, are even more difficult to solve than legal issues. John A. Barnes defines ethical problems as those we try to solve not in terms of expediency or gain but in terms of morality, of standards of right or wrong.[22] Immanuel Kant's guide to ethical behavior remains the basic principle of research ethics: people must be treated as ends in themselves, not as means to an end. The reality is that as interviewers we do use people for our ends. Kant's meaning is that we cannot let our ends override considerations of our narrators' well-being.[23] In "Ethical Issues in Different Social

Science Methods," Herbert Kelman explains this rule: "We . . . have a moral obligation to avoid actions and policies that reduce others' well-being (broadly defined) or that inhibit their freedom to express and develop themselves."[24]

The resolution of ethical problems in in-depth interviewing requires a solid understanding of professional guidelines and an ability to reflect on and critique one's own behavior. Readers should consult the guidelines and codes of ethics relevant to their discipline: the Oral History Association, American Historical Association, American Sociological Association, American Anthropological Association, and American Psychological Association all have statements on ethical conduct in research. (See, for example, "Principles and Standards of the Oral History Association" in appendix C. See also "Statement of Ethics: Principles of Professional Responsibility for the American Anthropological Association" on the Internet, www.aaanet.org/. For the ethical standards of the American Sociological Association, go to www.asanet .org/members/ecostand2.html. The "Statement on Standards of Professional Conduct" for the American Historical Association is at the site www .historians.org/pubs/Free/ProfessionalStandards.htm.) All of these normative restraints, across disciplines, express concern about protection of the well-being of the persons studied and truth in publication.

The historical profession insists that the practitioner of oral history has an obligation to tell the narrator honestly what the goals of the project are, the stages of the research as the researcher expects them to unfold, and the uses to which the taped information will be put. The researcher must inform the narrator of her or his rights: especially, the narrator must be assured that she or he may refuse to answer any question or discuss any topic. The researcher must say where the tape will eventually be placed and who will be able to listen to it.

In a similar way, guidelines for sociologists, anthropologists, and psychologists seek to protect the narrator by insisting that the researcher must clearly explain the purpose of the research and what will be expected of participants. This permits the narrator to judge whether or not participation may be harmful. The narrator must be told that he or she can withdraw from the project at any time. If the narrator decides to participate, this constitutes informed consent. Furthermore, the researcher must provide for anonymity and confidentiality of information if that is promised. If there is any possibility that the privacy of the narrator cannot be maintained, then the narrator must be so informed. Risks of harm to the participants must be small in comparison to the good resulting from the research.

Feminist researchers have pointed out that, while general principles are necessary, real life tends to be far more complex than these principles imply.

Ethicist Elizabeth Porter, in *Feminist Perspectives on Ethics*, asserts that there has to be a "dynamic interplay between justice and care, rights and responsibilities." She explains, "Feminist ethics places personal experience, context, care and good relationships as central features of morality."[25] Thus, Porter's emphasis is on putting the individual's well-being at the center of decisions, not as a second consideration where searching for truth is first. Such a process requires the researcher to reflect on her or his own code of ethics and humanitarian concerns so that the researcher understands how these impinge on the project and especially to value and not to negate these. In *Ethics in Qualitative Research*, the editors present a way of reconciling this ethics of care with an ethics of justice: "Principles guide our perceptions of how to conduct ethical research and yet ultimately, specific circumstances and contexts inform our decisions."[26]

As a historian, I feel the necessity of presenting all information gained from my research that is relevant to the topic. There is an audience, albeit in the abstract, with whom I have that tacit contract—by identifying the writing as history, I set up the expectation that I will not suppress evidence. What kind of history is it if salient information is omitted? And yet, as a feminist, during the decision-making process in the research and writing, I have uppermost in my mind the good of the persons involved. Most often, this has been the most satisfying way for me to proceed, but sometimes I may bend too far to avoid harming a person. Consider the application of an ethics of justice and an ethics of care in specific situations described in the following sections of this chapter.

Often the consequences of the research process for the narrators are phrased in terms of the long-range good outweighing immediate harm. This attitude is summed up in the term *cost–benefit analysis*. Joan Cassell asserts, "Risk and benefit in fieldwork occur at 2 different times, during interaction and when data becomes public."[27] The cost–benefit approach is highly problematic because you cannot always anticipate costs. Some ethicists think this precept should be thrown out (not a bad idea), but look at its application in specific situations in this chapter.

Informed Consent
Informed and free consent on the face of it looks like a protection. The problem is that informed consent has to be voluntary, but sometimes it may only seem voluntary. As Norman Denzin says, "The powerful university-based scientist ventures out into some local community to do research, carrying the mantle of authority that comes with university sponsorship."[28] The narrator may be too much impressed by this authority to utter any reluctance to cooperate.

In other situations, the freedom of the narrator may be restrained. One situation occurs when students in a college class feel like they have to agree to be interviewed lest their reluctance be seen as a refusal to help the researcher and they incur a lower grade. Barrie Thorne points out an extreme example: prison administrators give consent for the prisoners to be interviewed, but the prisoners themselves have not consented.[29] The researcher must find out whether a refusal to be interviewed would have negative consequences for the individual. If you detect coercion, correct that situation or end the project.

Some researchers have argued that the narrator cannot be told in any detail what the project is about lest the information prejudice the research results. For example, you want to discover if there is a persistent bias against women in a company. When the interviewees know this, they try to hide their own bias as they recount their observations. In effect, you shape the data by telling them the research aim. In this case, if masking specific aims does not harm the narrator, give a general explanation rather than a specific one. Barnes suggests that the researcher can explain to the narrator that as a scientist, he or she does not want to influence answers by explaining the purpose of specific research questions but will give a general explanation as soon as possible and a specific answer at the conclusion of the project if the narrator is interested.[30] The salient question here is, "If I don't tell the narrator the truth about this project, do I leave the narrator vulnerable to harm?"

Consent in a qualitative research project is problematic also because we do not know exactly where the project is going. Conversations may take an unanticipated turn; information from several interviews may result in new hypotheses so that the whole research project takes a different turn. What can be done? Some qualitative researchers consider the consent form as an acknowledgment of willingness to participate and permission to begin. They advise checking in with narrators during the interviewing process to find out if they still want to proceed. William E. Smythe and Maureen J. Murray explain in "Owning the Story: Ethical Considerations in Narrative Research" that the narrator should be free not only to stop talking but also to take the tape back.[31] I think that if the interviewer keeps checking, the narrator will begin to think something really wrong is happening or going to happen. If you see that the narrator is extremely troubled, that is the time to ask about his feelings about continuing.

After an interview, the oral historian can advise the narrator to seal the portion of the tape that could cause harm. And the researcher can voluntarily decline to publish the information. But in conjoint interviewing, such as researchers studying the family carry out, information may be articulated during the interview itself by one partner that shocks the other and changes the marriage relationship.[32] The benefit is that you have gotten what you want and *maybe* the publication resulting will help somebody—and after all, they gave their consent to be interviewed. But the cost for the individuals is high. The best time to ward off problems is during the recording: if you can see that the conversation is edging toward a topic that could cause trouble, change topics and schedule individual interviews to deal with that one troublemaking topic.

On rare occasions, although you have a release form and are legally correct in publishing something a narrator said or depositing the tape in public archives, you suspect that he or she might not have understood the consequences of signing the release form. (Sometimes the narrator will want to please you—you are such a nice person—and will be agreeable without thinking things through.) It would be ethical to go back to the individual and describe the segment you think might cause problems.[33] Once again, ask if it is acceptable to make this knowledge public. If not, seal that portion.

Anonymity and Confidentiality
Guaranteeing anonymity for the narrator and maintenance of confidentiality of information is also problematic. M. G. Trend describes what can happen when research is done under government contract. He had been involved in ethnographic research on low-income households, gathering data with a promise of confidentiality. The General Accounting Office (GAO), which audits expenditures of public funds for the United States Congress, requested the data. Trend found that the Privacy Act of 1974 (Public Law 93-577) provided that information collected by government agencies or their contractors should be released in certain cases. Among these was the enforcement of civil or criminal law and requests under the Freedom of Information Act from congressional investigating committees and from the GAO's comptroller.[34] Now, under the Homeland Security Act in the United States, there is even less protection of individual freedom. If you do research under government contract, keep this in mind and do not promise confidentiality.

But for any research project, the courts can subpoena your tapes or pressure you to give information. Consider the case of Rik Scarce, who had been doing research on radical environmental movements for a graduate degree in sociology at Washington State University. The court wanted him to testify concerning the activities of an animal rights activist who was accused of forcibly entering and marring a federally funded laboratory on campus. Scarce said, "What I told them was that any information that I may have

about this break-in was obtained by me only through promises of confidentiality with research participants." Scarce went to jail for five months, but he
did not give up his information.[35]

Anonymity is also problematic in specific research situations. David Jordan asserts that the anthropologist making the only record of a population
needs to ask whether it is ethical to disguise the name of a village or a whole
ethnic group—or withhold the study from the people when they need it. He
points out that subsequent researchers should have access to names so that
they can restudy the data and challenge data, methods, and conclusions.[36]

Also, there are degrees of anonymity: although you do not publish individuals' names, you may have to inform a small group of researchers about
them, trusting their adherence to professional ethics in not making the
names public.[37] For example, in longitudinal studies, David Jordan notes, the
interviewer has to identify the narrators so that the researchers who continue
the project can locate them.[38]

Anonymity is especially problematic for the historian. Oral historian
Linda Shopes remarked that the issue of anonymity was the most difficult the
committee developing the Oral History Association's ethical guidelines had
to deal with.[39] One of the necessities in reviewing a historian's conclusions is
that others have access to the same documents. If the source is anonymous
and identified only by a pseudonym, how can the veracity of a statement be
judged? The narrator is unknown and therefore does not take responsibility
for his or her statements. The narrator's relationship to the events under discussion remains vague. In biographies and narratives of events and movements, you slide away from credibility when narrators do not identify themselves and take responsibility for their words.

If you do promise anonymity, use a pseudonym on tape and omit identifying details, as described earlier. If the real name is left in, however, and the
narrator requests only that the name not be used in print, you have to rely
on the archives to enforce the narrator's wishes. Once I came on staff when
an oral history project was already finished; the project had concentrated on
mill work and included questions about how families survived the Depression
that began in 1929. A newspaper reporter was admitted to the archives and
listened to the tapes. He published an account of how families survived, giving actual names. The members of one family had not wanted anybody to
know how hard it was for them personally or to know the desperate strategies to which they had resorted. They had stated on the release form that
they did not want to be identified publicly. The director apologized, but feelings were already hurt; the damage was done. Remember that protection of
the individual's privacy depends on the security system in the archives.

Training of staff in an oral history project is crucial because staff members may be dealing with information whose spread will have regrettable consequences. It is important to caution all members of the project—other interviewers, transcribers, and office staff—to keep silent about information of a confidential nature and to resist using the real names of narrators who requested anonymity. Just as important is the feeling of respect for the narrator that you inculcate in those working with you on the project.

On the other hand, anthropologists, sociologists, and historians agree that it is important to name individuals when they want to be identified. Historian Brent Glass was preparing informational plaques for the Carrboro, North Carolina, cotton mill (which was being preserved as a shopping mall) and wanted to use testimony from an oral history project with people who had worked there. In this project, he and I had carried out the in-depth interviews with another coresearcher, sociologist Hugh Brinton, recording information not only about work, but also about family interaction: we promised anonymity. Glass went back to the narrators to ask if he could use their names and testimony, and they were pleased to have this chance to inform the public about their work and life in general in the village early in the century. He rerecorded conversations about work and mill village life for public information and identified the narrators. Now all of our narrators are deceased, but this public witness to their skill and labor remains.

Relationships and Reputations

Relationships among narrators are in your hands. Sometimes the interviewer can forestall harm by warning a narrator of consequences he or she may not know about. While I was taping the oral history of a physician in an oral history project on a college, she began a critique of the undergraduate education she had received there. Some of it contained negative comments about individual professors. I stopped recording for a few seconds and suggested that she not name or identify individuals. I explained that those individuals came into the oral history office to listen to tapes of famous alumni, especially if they had taught them. The narrator did not realize this, and because it was not her intention to hurt anyone's feelings—she just wanted to influence change in the curriculum—she altered the approach. She made her points without hurting feelings in that rather small community of scholars and former students.

Take care not to exacerbate existing enmities by saying things like, "When I talked to Mr. Smith, he said that you wrecked his career." Figure out how you can get information on the topic without mentioning Mr. Smith's charges. Try something indirect, such as, "I'm wondering if you had any reservations about the action Mr. Smith took in this matter." And then, "Did you express your concern to anyone at the time?"

Ethics in Relationships of Unequal Power

Permeating the process of in-depth interviewing are subtle ethical issues in the interpersonal relationship. These may not be easy to define, and sometimes the researcher has trouble reaching conclusions even about what is happening, much less what to do.

Power in the relationship is not equal but tipped to favor the interviewer. Consider that the researcher takes and moves on, using the information to get a degree or a publication and a better job situation. The process of recording and using other people's words is described by a group of British oral historians in "Popular Memory: Theory, Politics, and Method": "On the one hand there is 'the historian,' who specializes in the production of explanations and interpretations and who constitutes himself as the most active, thinking part of the process. On the other hand, there is his 'source' who happens in this case to be a living human being who is positioned in the process in order to yield up information."[40] I do not deny that the narrator has some power, though. Anthropologist John Gwaltney, in his book *Dry-longo: A Self-Portrait of Black America*, quotes a narrator who told him, "I know you must have sense enough to know that you can't make me tell you anything I mean to keep to myself."[41]

Daphne Patai, interviewing women in Brazil in the early 1980s, was led to reflect on the ethics of this kind of research. Patai's original question was, Do both narrator and interviewer profit equally according to time spent? Certainly, the researcher accomplishes his or her purpose, and so the reward is easier to see. But you can give something tangible back to the narrator: Give a copy of the narrator's taped history to him or her. Write a letter summarizing the research findings so the narrator can learn too. Publicly acknowledge the narrator's help unless he or she wishes to remain anonymous or there has been a promise of confidentiality of certain specific information. Beyond this, oral historian Alessandro Portelli found that his working-class narrators were gratified to find their oral histories read and even quoted in additional historical work on the Resistance. Portelli suggests, "The real service I think we provide to communities, movements, or individuals, is to amplify their voices by taking them *outside*, to break their sense of isolation and powerlessness by allowing their discourse to reach other people and communities."[42]

Most important in research ethics is consideration of the possibility in a dominant-subordinate relationship of taking advantage of the subordinate person. Patai describes this situation inherent in interviewing:

We ask of the people we interview the kind of revelation of their inner life that normally occurs in situations of great intimacy and within the private realm. Yet these revelations are to be made within the context of the public sphere—which is where, in an obvious sense, we situate ourselves when we appear with our tape recorders and note pads eager to work on our "projects." The asymmetries are marked, further, by the different disclosure that our interviewees make and that we are willing or expected to make—this goes back to the fundamental rules of the interviewing game. While shyly curious, interviewees never, to my knowledge, make a reciprocal exchange a condition of the interview. And researchers almost always are much less frank than they hope their subjects will be.[43]

The narrators have to trust us because they do not know how we will use the information. Will we describe the narrator in print as an ugly woman in late middle age, subsisting on irregular work as a cleaning woman? Will we use the details of narrators' intimate lives to sell books? Will we publish studies about their particular group or community that change the ways they think about themselves in a negative direction? As interviewers and authors, we know what we intend to do; we have the advantage of this knowledge.

We also determine to some extent the quality of the interpersonal relationship, and we use rapport to get information. In her essay "Can There Be a Feminist Ethnography?" Judith Stacey cautions against seducing the narrator into "telling all" by being such a good confidante and defining the relationship as one between equals so that all defenses are removed.[44] A similar issue arises especially in in-depth interviews with couples for those researching topics in the sociology of the family or family history. A couple in crisis or experiencing stress may divulge more than they might in ordinary circumstances. The researcher seems to know a lot about families; he or she has promised confidentiality, and this is taking place in the home, suggesting that a friendship is developing. The couple may begin to think that if they tell "all," advice or help of some kind may be forthcoming.[45] It is unethical to so disarm the narrator that he or she puts on tape information that will hurt. It is unethical to insinuate that you can help if you cannot. (For further discussion of friendships in research, see the chapter on interpersonal relations in research in this book.)

And one more caveat in dominant-subordinate relationships in research: while most interviewers would not consider indulging in such behavior as sexual action, it would be naive not to acknowledge the potential for this in such a confidential, one-on-one situation as in-depth interviewing requires. Esther Newton, an anthropologist, says, "In graduate school in the early

1960s, I learned—because it was never mentioned—that erotic interest between fieldworker and informant either didn't exist, would be inappropriate, or couldn't be mentioned; I had no idea which."[46] Recently, however, there has been a lot of discussion in the literature concerning sexual relations during ethnographic research, with varying opinions voiced. Sociologist Amanda Coffey, in an article titled "Sex in the Field: Intimacy and Intimidation," discusses researchers' sexual engagement with people studied in fieldwork and contends that the problems are inherent in research because age, gender, and sexual orientation are in the picture, as well as the process of establishing relationships and boundaries. The researcher engaged solely in oral history interviewing will go back to the narrator for subsequent interviews but will not be living in the field; nevertheless, there is even then an interpersonal relationship, which may awaken sexual interest. Coffey mentions different kinds of sexual relationships discussed in anthropological literature—from a relationship with a single informant that resulted in a committed partnership, to several casual sexual relationships because the researcher wanted to pursue her "ongoing identity work," to many promiscuous relationships because the researcher wanted to transcend "the separateness" that distanced him from his subjects.[47]

These behaviors, as Coffey states, have to do with personal gratification, no matter what the rationalization. The purpose of the research becomes not the primary focus but secondary. The boundaries that made the process clear to interviewer and narrator are blown away and confusion results: the informant, at the least, must be puzzled, thinking, "This is not what I was told this project was about." The possibilities for drawing the narrator into a situation in which he or she will be used in a way that was not part of the original bargain are inherent in this kind of researcher behavior. Appearing in one guise and then using this guise to satisfy sexual needs is an ethical issue. Acceding to a narrator's desires for sex in order to get information is an ethical issue.

If you feel attracted to the person you are interviewing, admit this to yourself—both feelings and intellect inform and enrich your work. But accepting feelings is different from acting on them. Remind yourself of your purpose for being there. Make the boundaries clear and respect them: this is a professional relationship. Be aware, though, that because anthropologists live in the field and share many aspects of daily life with informants, some have a different slant on this subject.[48] Anthropologist Kate Altork, in her article "Walking the Fire Line: The Erotic Dimension of the Fieldwork Experience," suggests a way to integrate emotions and intellect in fieldwork while maintaining boundaries.[49]

Publication of Information Harmful to the Narrator

The problem of publishing material from taped life histories for which you have a release form but that nonetheless could cause harm to a living person comes up often. In a court of law, you could argue that you have ownership of copyright because you have a release form from the narrator. Before other scholars, you argue that your account presented all available evidence and the statements are true, according to corroborating evidence. You prove that you correctly attributed the statements to the speaker by producing your transcripts or tapes. So! you have fulfilled your obligation to your profession by presenting an honest account—no evidence was suppressed and the in-terpretation was fair to the best of your ability. But although ethically and legally correct, you have to live with the knowledge that you have caused much distress to the person involved. You have satisfied your profession's re-quirements but violated your need to be a compassionate person.

Consider a few specific situations in which this dilemma occurred. When I was researching the history of an institution, I found out that a di-rector had a serious substance abuse problem at the time he was in office. What turn his life and career had since taken I did not know. I studied the historical situation carefully and decided that the institution was well man-aged then by the department heads and that the director's incapacity did not have an adverse effect. (A brilliant man, he had himself set up the ad-ministrative structure that had worked so well.) At the end of the chapter, in discussing his resignation—which did affect the course of the institu-tion's history—I wrote about his troubles briefly. I used the description "emotional and physical problems becoming more and more serious over the last year which finally prevented him from continuing his work." I did describe the last board meeting, when he passed out, because this was dra-matic proof to the trustees that he could not continue in the job. Without a description of the events at this meeting, their decision would have been incomprehensible.

In a similar situation in writing an institutional history, I soon became aware as I was taping that there was a bitter enmity at one time in the past between the medical director and the administrative director. Their private conversations were unknown to me, but the echoes of their confrontations rumbled through the hospital and in their own oral histories as well as in the taped recollections of their associates. I saw the conflict as situational: there were many areas of decision making in the administrative structure of a dual headship that had been left undefined. It was inevitable that they would have confrontations. I decided not to blame this on personality but to show how the administrators and staff coped and how another structure evolved.

An exposé of personal faults would not have helped anybody and certainly would have harmed the individuals involved. Information about flaws in administrative structure might have helped—this history was educational in that it had relevance beyond the particular institution.

On the other hand, sometimes failure is unmistakably due to personal actions, and this is difficult to deal with. Following the strategy of using oral history testimony for information about the individual's role in the work community and concentrating on the individual's objectives—considering always the state of knowledge at the time—I tried to give a fair account without damaging anybody's reputation. But in one case, lacking warm, affectionate, or positive descriptions of a man from the oral histories, I used appraisals of his clinical work. I studied his published research, read reviews of it, and listened again to his own taped recollections of his objectives. I felt uneasy about this approach (which had worked so well before) because I had practiced such selectivity in the history that I had skewed the account in his favor and glossed over real problems related both to personality and administrative style.

Saul Benison, an oral historian in the field of the history of medicine, says that when he was writing a history of a famous physician, he included a wild escapade the young intern had in 1910. The doctor had approved of Benison's telling the story, but after his death his widow did not approve. Benison reasoned as follows: "Should I retell the story when the book was printed? I felt that I didn't want to hurt this seventy-six-year-old lady. There was enough in the interviews to indicate that he was a hard drinker and I took out the story to save the sensibilities of this lady."[50]

Here are two dilemmas, both involving omission of personally damaging information. Raymond Gorden describes his process of figuring out what to do: "[Ethics] does not merely involve some fixed hierarchy of abstract ideas isolated from knowledge of cause and effect in the empirical world; ethics involves decision making guided by both values and knowledge."[51] Looking at the two examples, I think Benison was right to omit the story of the intern's account. I was wrong not to indicate the individual's personality and administrative style because these characteristics had negative effects on the hospital work community. I practiced self-censorship to a harmful extent because I omitted information crucial to understanding the history of that institution. Patricia Adler and Peter Adler in "Ethical Issues in Self-Censorship" ask, "How can we know the nature of behaviors, the extent of behaviors, and the connections between social factors when they are not reported?"

May we ever make public knowledge that invades privacy? The Adlers caution, "Potential social problems may go unreported by researchers who protect their subjects, leading to harm against others."[52] They give as examples failing to report violence against children or sexual abuse of children or violence against other family members, whose effects we witness when we enter a home to conduct an interview. This may be a betrayal of trust from the narrator's viewpoint, but such an action to protect the vulnerable is taken because the researcher's ethical values require protection of those who cannot help themselves. (Often localities have laws that order you to report child abuse.) Dilemmas like this must be solved in their context: I would have to ask myself whether there was anyone in the home who would be willing to report the abuse if I offered to help her or him do so. In the case of an abused child, I would report the danger, regardless of whether the information was in the recorded interview or not or whether there was denial in the whole household.

And we assume that good comes from the publication of results of the interviewing project, but sometimes publication of a study causes distress instead. For example, individuals who had been promised anonymity are identified by themselves and by others according to the roles they played. Researchers may not anticipate this result. Howard S. Becker says that the interviewer must refuse to publish when individuals are bound to be harmed seriously. Only if the harm is judged minimal can the information be published. For situations that fall in between, the researcher and the individuals he studied must come to some decision together.[53]

Anthropologist Jean Briggs carried out research in a native Alaskan community with the intention of preserving anonymity. Later, in publishing an account of her six years of research, she decided to identify the group and the geographical location: "I reasoned that the work would lose ethnographic value if the statements could not be put in historical and geographical perspective." She disguised the identity of individuals by using pseudonyms, but she realized that at least four people could be identified by their roles in the community. She omitted any information that could be used against individuals and any information told to her confidentially. She asked a missionary couple there whom she had known well to distribute an explanation of her reasons for writing the book as she did. She also asked the people, through the missionaries, if she could put their pictures in the book. The missionary wrote back that the people did not object to the book and agreed to have their pictures in it. After the book was published, she returned to the community and was welcomed. But even clearing some things with those studied may not have been sufficient: she had nagging feelings that some had been offended.[54]

In some cases, anonymity is maintained, but very personal information is published. The researcher must be aware of the shock a narrator feels on seeing in print intimate details about his or her life. Elizabeth Bott and her coresearchers studied intensely the social relations of two married couples. In the resulting publication, they disguised identities and used pseudonyms. They took the draft back to the narrators. The four people involved agreed to publication (even though they did not agree with the interpretations of the findings). The researchers could, in that way, go ahead with publication of very personal information; they had disguised identities, informed the individuals involved, explained why the information was necessary, and gained consent. By taking these steps, they hoped that publication would cause no surprise and therefore less harm.[55]

The possibility of exploitation, historian Daphne Patai concludes, is built into every research project that uses human beings as sources of information.[56] Earlier in this chapter, legal ownership of the oral history was discussed, but ownership of an oral history is also an ethical issue. What we as scholars do with an individual's story will affect that individual in some way. We interpret the underlying, implicit meanings[57] and we have the authority of our education and training to back us up. We hope that our narrators will reject the interpretation if they believe it does not fit. And yet, it is still out there, published for anyone to see. "How do we explain the lives of others without violating their reality?" feminists say.[58]

When the village schoolmaster was asked what was gained by a study of his village, Ballybran (Ireland), published in *Saints, Scholars and Schizophrenics*, he said, "It's not your science I'm questioning, but this: don't we have the right to lead unexamined lives, the right *not* to be analyzed? Don't we have the right to hold on to an image of ourselves as different to be sure, but as innocent and unblemished all the same?"[59]

After this sobering consideration, any advice seems superficial, indeed, but this is the best I can come up with: ethicists Smythe and Murray advise educating the narrator at the beginning of the project that there will be multiple interpretations of the oral histories, that no one has the last word. They urge sharing the report with the narrators before it is published, even publishing their views if substantially different from the researcher's.[60]

Correct Representation of the Narrator's Meaning

It is possible, ethicist Gesa Kirsch argues, that interpretive conflict is inevitable in qualitative research. In an interviewing project on homemakers' returning to the workforce, the researchers found that their perspectives differed from those of the women they studied: the women thought of themselves as independent, but the researchers saw them as having lives characterized by both a structural and personal dependence. Whose interpretation should prevail in a published report? Kirsch advises, "Negotiation with participants seems to be key in addressing interpretive conflicts of all kinds."[61] Ideally, both interpretations would be reported.

But there are times when an ethics of justice should not be cast aside, even when you are aware of a need for compassion toward individuals. Kathleen Blee, having interviewed women members of the Klan, analyzed the accounts for a book about them.[62] She found the narrators' downplaying the racism of that movement, normalizing their activities in the Klan, exonerating themselves for being members. Blee would have violated her sense of justice if she had just accepted their interpretations of the Klan. I do not think there would have been any possibility of reconciling her narrators' interpretations with her own.

Regardless of differences in interpretation, correct representation of the narrator's meaning is necessary, and this requires attention to words. In quantitative research, computations are made to check the statistics: it is assumed that anyone could duplicate the experiment and get the same statistical results. In qualitative research, errors are not so easily checked. Rereading the documents to see whether the transcription was accurate and whether interpretation was on the mark is one way to prevent misrepresentation.

For the oral historian, additional checking with the oral source is a necessity. And all who have used living witnesses as primary sources take the transcript back to them, if at all possible, so they can correct for transcription errors. When no transcripts have been made, send the chapter in which the oral testimony appears back to the principal narrators and ask, "Have I misinterpreted your words? Have I made factual errors in this chapter?" In the case of marginally literate narrators, you may want to call or visit and read the quotation or paragraph pertaining to their testimony. (Further discussion of this process can be found in the last chapter.)

And again, on important points, compare written and oral sources with one another. Sometimes a narrator is just wrong. If you quote in this case, present the facts that right this incorrect statement or contextualize it so that it is clear the statement represents one person's memory rather than a verifiable account of the situation. Respect for the witness is necessary, but this does not mean unquestioning acceptance of the veracity of the testimony.

Truth in Presentation of Findings: Commissioned Research

Researching and writing commissioned studies—where someone else pays the bill and demands the goods for the money paid—presents problems the academic scholar independently investigating does not encounter. Historian Ronald Tobey asserts that the academic historian is expected to research and analyze the data as objectively as possible, recognizing and correcting for his or her bias.[63] The historian whose work is commissioned and destined for a nonacademic audience and any social science researcher doing commissioned research must also work in the same rigorous way.

Tobey compares the academic historian and the commissioned researcher: the academic historian is not supposed to plead a cause; however, a hired professional is expected to plead a cause—but one cause only. The implication is that the public historian or any commissioned researcher does this. For example, a lawyer must defend the interests of one client only; objectivity and disinterestedness would be considered unethical.[64] I contend that the scholar and lawyer have different tasks to perform. The historian, sociologist, or anthropologist has the obligation to be truthful. A metaphor often used is that the scholar pleads before the "bar of history." That bar endures: when the present uproar over research some group does not like passes, the documentation will be as useful as the day it was published, to the extent that it was carefully gathered. Neither academic nor commissioned researchers can remain completely disinterested, but neither should they suppress evidence crucial to an understanding of the event studied. In that sense, neither is an advocate.

Nevertheless, there is greater pressure on the public historian or sponsored social scientist to bend the evidence: this is where the real difference exists, and it is one of degree. The problem is that no company or institution or governmental body wants to publish a study that shows the leaders in a bad light or increases respect for a competitor.[65] The commissioner may withhold written records or object to interviews with certain narrators or insist on omitting evidence from the published work. If the researcher presents evidence the commissioner does not like, there is the risk that the manuscript will not be published. And many of us who write public history have had the experience of completing a manuscript only to have bureaucrats in the institution say that things in it would damage their public image. Many worthwhile scholarly histories have probably been quietly deposited in company files never to be seen again, and many research reports have been "lost" among some agency's papers.

Consider some specific situations in which pressure has been applied. Raymond Gorden discusses an incident from his own research in which pressure was put on the researchers to suppress information. He was engaged in a study of social problem rates in a certain city, a research project funded by a college, a private welfare council, and a city planning commission. Gorden reported that data indicated the Boy Scouts were not serving lower-class areas. Local scout officials, who needed support from the United Fund, wanted to suppress that information. The researchers refused to do that. And when data indicated that the boys who were Protestant were most likely to be delinquent, the Protestant Council of Churches wanted to suppress that information. The researchers again refused. In the end, support came from the college, which insisted on publication of the entire report.[66]

One situation that involves ethics in researching commissioned histories is access to information. A company or college or institution may want to seal its private archives against public use. The very documents you need you may not be able to see, but this is a problem every scholar working in the period of the last fifty years may face. You can do some negotiating, however. In writing one institution's history, I wanted to see the union contract in effect then. That request was refused. I could have gone to union headquarters to read it, but I felt like that would have been going behind my employers' back—this seemed to me to be a betrayal of trust. I again requested access to the union contract, stipulating the clauses I needed to see. Their compromise was that these particular clauses would be read to me. Because I needed to know what was in them in order to compare oral history testimony with the wording in the clauses, I accepted this solution. This was not an easy compromise to agree to: my ethical obligation to my profession was to seek all extant documents on the topic; my ethical obligation to the institution was to honor its rules. Because I did have access to the clauses that were significant, I judged this compromise acceptable. But if they had not offered this compromise, I might have gone to union headquarters and asked people there to read me the clauses, having informed my employers that I would do this and braved their displeasure.

Access to narrators is fully as important as access to written sources. You may find that the company would prefer that you not talk to union leaders or to individuals who are central figures in incidents of dissatisfaction with the company. Sometimes, company executives are afraid that workers "on the line" do not understand the overall objectives of the company and will give you a jaundiced view. You have some educating to do: explain what the purpose of the study is from your point of view and describe the research procedures you see as necessary. Insist on your need to record testimony of witnesses at every level of the community.

On the other hand, the researcher may see trouble coming and use professional judgment to decline a commission. When I was interested in writing a history of the rural health centers in North Carolina, I encountered a pivotal individual in the health care research bureaucracy who was concerned about his reputation in the state. He demanded that he have a right to veto the publication if I did not write the book he wanted. I declined the project on the grounds that free inquiry and freedom from censorship in publication are necessities in a scholar's research. The project was important to me because of the developments in rural health care that affected people I cared about. However, I realized certain things: Without his cooperation, I would have had difficulty gaining access to several important narrators and to necessary documents. With his cooperation, I would have become a hired lackey, turning out the usual laudatory account of "great white men."

Finally, the company may cheerfully change your manuscript and go ahead and publish a version that the officers want the public to have. The public relations people may want a more positive public image, or the institution's lawyers may scrutinize a manuscript for cause of a possible lawsuit. Truth in the published narrative is not their goal: they have been hired to protect the institution, and this is their only concern. I faced such a conflict when I was researching and writing the history of a college. The new campus had been built in the 1970s and consisted of a giant unistructure. In the middle of the building on the ground floor was a large swimming pool, and anyone walking the perimeter of the unistructure could look down and see the pool. At one time, the president was a single man in middle age who felt greatly attracted to young women. One fine summer day he took off his clothes and went swimming in the college pool with a woman companion. He was observed, of course.

This episode caused a shock wave that rushed through campus and public groups. Newspapers were full of descriptions of the incident. The president stayed on, but the incident damaged his credibility. In protest against his refusal to leave the college, all three vice presidents resigned. This private deed could not be omitted from the written history because it affected the course of subsequent developments at the college. I did considerable oral history research and research in the written records, trying to write an honest account of the total administration, describing both positive and negative aspects. At the lawyers' request, I changed one phrase from "nude swimming" to "alleged nude swimming." On reading the galleys, I saw that the account of nude swimming in the college pool had been deleted entirely. Only one phrase remained: "alleged incident."[67] These two words had been substituted by the college lawyers for my phrase, and several paragraphs had been omitted. I was powerless: as agent for this institution in the researching and writing of the history, I did not hold copyright to the tapes or the book. I insisted that the title page of the book bear the disclaimer "Edited by So and So." Obviously, this was not a satisfactory solution.

It is also necessary to take a closer look before you begin a project to discover the source of funds and the use to which information from the research will be put. The infamous Project Camelot is an extreme example of research being used for a political purpose not beneficial to the people studied. This research was aimed at providing information for determining the nature and causes of revolution in underdeveloped areas with the objective of preventing revolution. The funding agency was the U.S. Department of Defense.[68] The project was terminated for reasons of political expediency but not before prominent social scientists had agreed to do the research. Consequences to the people studied—manipulation for another nation's political interests—should have been considered.

Unconscious Advocacy

Still another pitfall in any research is unconscious advocacy. For one thing, in commissioned research we are being paid and may feel reluctant to "bite the hand that feeds us." For another, we want to do a good job in the commissioner's eyes. And sometimes the thought that we have to continue to live or work in the community we write about may make us cautious enough to consider omitting some evidence.

In reflecting on your own biases in the study, think about how your feelings about the community and the individuals who helped you might have affected the research. When you like and admire the people you are interviewing, you are also subtly influenced in the direction of seeing things positively instead of realistically. When I was doing the research for the psychiatric hospital history mentioned earlier, I had an office that happened to be across a courtyard from the emergency entrance. I would see people with serious illness enter the hospital, and several weeks later I would meet them walking around, looking calm and in control. The chief cook would come over in the middle of the night to prepare a meal for a patient just admitted if the nurses thought the patient should have something to eat. Or the director of nurses would come over on Sundays, her day off, to see if anybody needed help. Of course, I admired the work the hospital staff did. I cannot put a finger on any place in the history where I consciously ignored evidence or falsified an account, but respect for individuals working in that hospital influenced what I wrote. And hospital personnel—my narrators—having worked there for years, must have toned down some negative aspects when they were recording because they identified with the place.[69] The ways these biases impinge on the work should be pointed out to the readers.[70]

The late historian Carl Ryant called this reluctance to damage the reputation of a place or people we like "goodwill advocacy." He did not have trouble gaining access to documents or narrators in researching the histories of three companies. He explained that in each case the company had reorganized or expected to do so, diversified, or even moved out of state. The companies' executives did not have any fear that information that could damage current reputations would emerge.[71] They were not looking for an advocate at that point.

However, Ryant saw a drawback when the institution is amenable to the writing of a truthful history: the pressure to present a favorable picture may come, not from the funding institution, but from inside the researcher. He explained, "Sympathy for a corporation (particularly when it is helping to fund a project) may cause an interviewer to leave certain questions unasked, in the belief—perhaps honest—that protecting the subject's image will do no real damage to the integrity of the research."[72] My bony finger emerges from the black shroud to point at you: leave no question unasked.

Protection of Interviewer in Contracts

In the situation described above of the college deleting sections of the man-uscript, I should have had a contract that would have prevented publication without the author's consent. When you begin to negotiate a contract with an institution or agency, make it clear that as a professional, you must write as truthful an account as you can. Explain that research results may not be altered. Get a commitment in writing that defines access to documents and narrators so that the employer will know what a professional requires and you will know, from the outset, if there are any limitations.

Find out where the money is ultimately coming from and anticipate where control on the research might be applied. Try to figure out what motives the commissioner has and how the information from your project will be used. If you can foresee that the information might be used in such a way that the narrators are harmed, refuse the commission. If the commissioner offers a contract, look at the fine print to discover who has ultimate control over publication. Try to get a guarantee that if the commissioners choose not to publish, you may still use the information in a form that you deem feasible.[73]

Conclusion

Ken Plummer, in coming to the end of his chapter on ethics and power in life history research, says, "We have rummaged through a minefield of ethical traps."[74] I feel like this is what we have done in this chapter. Although I have tried to state unequivocally a solution to an ethical dilemma when I could, often I have hemmed and hawed because solutions depend on principles, context, and personal values and require much reflection. There is no "one size fits all."

We cannot, however, ignore the fact that power in the interviewing situation is often on the side of the interviewer, even though the ideal is equal sharing. But whatever the power structure in a particular interviewing situation, the narrator's immediate and long-range good should never be sacrificed for the researcher's gain. Oral historian Alessandro Portelli best sums up the meaning of research ethics for each of us personally:

> Ultimately, in fact ethical and legal guidelines only make sense if they are the outward manifestation of a broader and deeper sense of personal and political commitment to honesty and to truth. In the context of oral history, by commitment to honesty I mean personal respect for the people we work with and intellectual respect for the material we receive. By commitment to truth, I mean a utopian striving and urge to know "how things really are" balanced by openness to the many variants of "how things may be."[75]

Recommended Reading

Appell, G. N. *Ethical Dilemmas in Anthropological Inquiry: A Case Book.* Waltham, MA: Crossroads Press, 1978. The author presents individual accounts of ethical problems in field research, some of which involve oral history interviewing.

Barnes, John Arundel. *Who Should Know What? Social Science, Privacy and Ethics.* Cambridge: Cambridge University Press, 1979. This is an informative, thorough treatment of ethics in field research.

Beauchamp, Tom L., Ruth R. Faden, R. Jay Wallace Jr., and LeRoy Walters. *Ethical Issues in Social Science Research.* Baltimore, MD: Johns Hopkins University Press, 1982. See especially the articles by Terry Pinkard and Herbert Kelman concerning ethics in interviewing and Joan Cassell on risk–benefit analysis.

Blee, Kathleen M. "Evidence, Empathy, and Ethics: Lessons from Oral Histories of the Klan." *Journal of American History*, September 1993, 596–606. Thought-provoking account of the dilemma of having empathy with narrators whose values you abhor.

Delamont, Sara. "Whose Side Are We On? Revisiting Becker's Classic Ethical Question at the Fin de Siecle." In *Ethical Dilemmas in Qualitative Research*, ed. Trevor Welland and Lesley Pugsley, Cardiff Papers, 149–60. Burlington, VT: Ashgate Publishing Company, 2002. Author raises again Becker's strategies for valid research. She traces eras of research and evaluates their conclusions in terms of current research vis-à-vis postmodernist attitudes.

Denzin, Norman K. *Interpretive Ethnography: Ethnographic Practices for the 21st Century.* Thousand Oaks, CA: Sage, 1997. See the pages on ethics of positivism versus ethics in a postmodern age, 252–87.

Edwards, Rosalind, and Melanie Mauthner. "Ethics and Feminist Research Theory and Practice." In *Ethics in Qualitative Research*, ed. Melanie Mauthner, Maxine Birch, Julie Jessop, and Tina Miller, 14–31. London: Sage, 2002. This excellent introduction to the subject presents an overview of feminist models of research.

Authors provide a useful table contrasting an ethics based on care (which is context based) and an ethics based on the abstract concept of justice. They suggest thoughtful questions on ethics in interpersonal relationships (pp. 28–29), which are then dealt with in specific chapters.

Ellen, R. F., ed. *Ethnographic Research: A Guide to General Conduct*. London: Academic Press, 1984. See especially the section "Ethics in Relation to Informants, the Profession and Governments" by Anne V. Akeroyd, pp. 133–54.

Erikson, Kai T. "A Comment on Disguised Observation in Sociology." *Social Problems* 14, no. 4 (Spring 1967): 366–73. Insightful, brief essay.

Feldman, Kerry D. "Anthropology under Contract: Two Examples from Alaska." In *Anthropologists at Home in North America: Methods and Issues in the Study of One's Own Society*, ed. Donald A. Messerschmidt, 233–37. Cambridge: Cambridge University Press, 1981. Interesting for the general reader, a "must" for anthropologists.

Fluehr-Lobban, Carolyn, ed. *Ethics and the Profession of Anthropology: Dialogue for a New Era*. Philadelphia: University of Pennsylvania Press, 1991. See especially the article by Jay Szklut and Robert Roy Reed, "Community Anonymity in Anthropological Research: A Reassessment," pp. 97–114; and Barbara Frankel and M. G. Trend, "Principles, Pressures, and Paychecks: The Anthropologist as Employee," pp. 175–97.

Gorden, Raymond. *Interviewing: Strategy, Techniques and Tactics*. 4th ed. Chicago: Dorsey Press, 1987. The chapter on ethics is slanted toward the sociologist rather than the historian. There is discussion showing how the researcher weighs benefits and costs in making a judgment.

Hopkins, Mary Carol. "Is Anonymity Possible? Writing about Refugees in the United States." In *When They Read What We Write: The Politics of Ethnography*, ed. Caroline B. Brettell, 121–29. Westport, CT: Bergin and Garvey, 1993. Hopkins points out how difficult it is to maintain the anonymity of informants when the researcher wants to include members of the community studied in critiquing the prepublication drafts of the research findings.

Horowitz, Irving L. *The Rise and Fall of Project Camelot: Studies in the Relationship between Social Science and Politics*. Cambridge: Massachusetts Institute of Technology Press, 1974. This book offers a history and analysis of this example of government funding, control, and abuse of social science research.

Jordan, David K. "Ethnographic Enterprise and the Bureaucratization of Ethics: The Problem of Human Subjects Legislation." *Journal of Anthropological Research* 37, no. 4 (1981): 415–19. This article deals with serious problems under debate now.

Karamanski, Theodore, ed. *Ethics and Public History: An Anthology*. Malabar, FL: Krieger Publishing, 1990. In this collection of informative articles on ethical issues, see especially Carl Ryant's "The Public Historian and Business History: A Question of Ethics."

Kelman, Herbert C. "Privacy and Research with Human Beings." *Journal of Social Issues* 33 (1977): 169–95. This article defines invasion of privacy as "exposure of damaging information, diminishing a person's control and liberty, and intrusion into a person's private space." The insights are not out of date but continue to be relevant.

Kirsch, Gesa E. *Ethical Dilemmas in Feminist Research: The Politics of Location, Interpretation, and Publication*. Albany: State University of New York Press, 1999. A thoughtful, clearly written, jargon-free, in-depth study of ethical problems in specific research situations. See especially "What Do You Know about My Life, Anyway? Ethical Dilemmas in Researcher-Participant Relations," pp. 25–44, for a discussion of feminist research ethics.

Klockars, Carl B. "Field Ethics in Life History." In *Street Ethnography: Selected Studies of Crime and Drug Use in Natural Settings*, ed. Robert S. Weppner, 201–26. Beverly Hills, CA: Sage, 1977. Klockars draws on his experiences in researching the life history of a dealer in stolen properties to examine the risk–benefit principle.

Kulick, Don, and Margaret Wilson, eds. *Taboo: Sex, Identity and Erotic Subjectivity in Anthropological Fieldwork*. London: Routledge, 1995. The editors' introduction gives a brief history of how erotic attraction in fieldwork has been treated by anthropologists, and the articles explore ways erotic subjectivity affects fieldwork. See especially Kate Altork, "Walking the Fire Line: The Erotic Dimension of the Fieldwork Experience," pp. 13–39, which suggests ways to integrate emotions and intellect in fieldwork while maintaining boundaries.

Langness, L. L., and Gelya Frank. *Lives: An Anthropological Approach to Biography*. Novato, CA: Chandler & Sharp, 1981. See the section "Ethical and Moral Concerns" for a discussion of the principles of professional responsibility adopted by the American Anthropological Association.

Markowitz, Fran, and Michael Ashkenazi, eds. *Sex, Sexuality, and the Anthropologist*. Urbana: University of Illinois Press, 1999. Markowitz and Ashkenazi's introduction briefly traces the history of the subject and suggests reasons why erotic attraction has not been openly discussed in anthropological literature until recently. Their aim in producing this collection of articles is to "demystify the field and show it as a process of intersubjective communications that sometimes work and sometimes do not" (p. 10).

Messerschmidt, Donald A., ed. *Anthropologists at Home in North America: Methods and Issues in the Study of One's Own Society*. Cambridge: Cambridge University Press, 1981. See especially "Constraints in Government Research: The Anthropologist in a Rural School District," pp. 185–201.

Neuenschwander, John. *Oral History and the Law*. 3rd ed. Carlisle, PA: Oral History Association, Dickinson College, 2002. READ THIS BOOK. (To order, contact the Oral History Association, Dickinson College, P.O. Box 1773, Carlisle, PA 17013-2896 or e-mail: oha@dickinson.edu.) Very helpful discussions because Neuenschwander, both oral historian and judge, presents specific cases and explains how each case was viewed from a legal point of view.

Patai, Daphne. "Ethical Problems of Personal Narratives, or, Who Should Eat the Last Piece of Cake?" *International Journal of Oral History* 8 (February 1987): 5–27.

This is a focused and clear discussion of ethics, the in-depth interview, and field research methods, especially the interviewer's exploitation of the narrator.

Plummer, Kenneth. "The Moral and Human Face of Life Stories: Reflexivity, Power and Ethics." Chap. 10 in *Documents of Life 2: An Invitation to a Critical Humanism*. London: Sage, 2001. In this brilliant chapter, Plummer examines important personal and ethical issues: self-reflexivity in research, emotions and biases that impinge on the project, roles in research, ethics and morality in research, informed consent, harm.

Portelli, Alessandro. "Tryin' to Gather a Little Knowledge: Some Thoughts on the Ethics of Oral History." Chap. 4 in *The Battle of Valle Giulia: Oral History and the Art of Dialogue*. Madison: University of Wisconsin Press, 1997. Discusses the importance of a personal and political commitment to honesty and to respect both for the information we gather through oral history as well as for the narrator.

Punch, Maurice. *The Politics and Ethics of Field Work*, vol. 3 of *Qualitative Research Methods*. London: Sage, 1986. This is an account of the problems Punch encountered as he attempted to write a history of a private school in Britain.

Renzetti, Claire M., and Raymond M. Lee. *Doing Research on Sensitive Topics*. London: Sage, 1993. See especially Patricia Adler and Peter Adler, "Ethical Issues in Self-Censorship," pp. 249–66; and Rosalind Edwards, "An Education in Interviewing: Placing the Researcher and the Research," pp. 181–96.

Thorne, Barrie. "'You Still Takin' Notes?' Fieldwork and Problems of Informed Consent." *Social Problems* 27, no. 3 (February 1980): 284–96.

Trend, M. G. "Applied Social Research and the Government: Notes on the Limits of Confidentiality." *Social Problems* 27, no. 3 (February 1980): 342–49. Very useful information.

Notes

1. Charles Dickens, *A Christmas Carol* (New York: Franklin Watts, 1969), 111–12.

2. John Neuenschwander, *Oral History and the Law*, 3rd ed. (Carlisle, PA: Oral History Association, Dickinson College, 2002), 30.

3. John Neuenschwander, e-mail communication to author, July 28, 2004.

4. Neuenschwander, *Oral History and the Law*, 33.

5. I based this on commonly accepted practice in the profession of oral history and on the doctrine of "fair use." See discussion in Andrea Hirsch, "Copyrighting Conversations: Applying the 1976 Copyright to Interviews," *American University Law Review* 31 (1982): 1071–93; see pp. 1085–92.

6. Neuenschwander, *Oral History and the Law*, 36.

7. Neuenschwander, *Oral History and the Law*, 40.

8. Neuenschwander, *Oral History and the Law*, 41.

9. Neuenschwander, *Oral History and the Law*, 18.

10. Neuenschwander, *Oral History and the Law*, 26.

11. Neuenschwander, *Oral History and the Law*, 19.

12. Neuenschwander, *Oral History and the Law*, 21.

13. Janet Malcolm, "Annals of Scholarship: Trouble in the Archives," *New Yorker*, part I, December 5, 1983, 59–152; part II, December 12, 1983, 60–119.

14. Jane Gross, "Jurors Decide for Psychoanalyst but Split Award," National Desk, *New York Times*, June 5, 1993, sec. 1, pp. 1, 6.

15. David Margolick, "Writer Wins a Bittersweet Verdict," *New York Times*, November 6, 1994, sec. 4, p. 2, col. 1.

16. Herbert C. Kelman, "Privacy and Research with Human Beings," *Journal of Social Issues* 33 (1977): 169–95.

17. Neuenschwander, *Oral History and the Law*, 4.

18. Ted Schwarz, *The Complete Guide to Writing Biographies* (Cincinnati, OH: Writer's Digest Books, 1990), 111.

19. Will C. Van den Hoonaard, ed., *Walking the Tightrope: Ethical Issues for Qualitative Researchers* (Toronto: University of Toronto Press, 2002).

20. Linda Shopes, "Oral History Association Guidelines for the Review of Oral History Research Projects" (draft submitted by the Oral History Association to the Office of Human Research Protections, October 2002).

21. Linda Shopes and Donald A. Ritchie, "An Update: Excluding Oral History from IRB Review," *OHA Newsletter* (Oral History Association) 38, no. 1 (Spring 2004): 1.

22. John Arundel Barnes, *Who Should Know What? Social Science, Privacy and Ethics* (Cambridge: Cambridge University Press, 1979), 16.

23. For a slightly different explanation of Kant's meaning, see Barbara Johnson, "Using People: Kant with Winnicott," in *The Turn to Ethics*, ed. Marjorie Garber, Beatrice Hanssen, and Rebecca L. Walkowitz, 47–63 (London: Routledge, 2000); see pp. 48–49.

24. Herbert C. Kelman, "Ethical Issues in Different Social Science Methods," in *Ethical Issues in Social Science Research*, ed. Tom L. Beauchamp et al. (Baltimore, MD: Johns Hopkins University Press, 1982), 41.

25. Elizabeth Porter, *Feminist Perspectives on Ethics* (Harlow: Pearson Education, 1999), 25.

26. Melanie Mauthner, Maxine Birth, Julie Jessop, and Tina Miller, eds., *Ethics in Qualitative Research* (London: Sage, 2002), 6 (introductory chapter by the four editors).

27. Joan Cassell, "Risk and Benefit to Subjects of Fieldwork," *American Sociologist* 13 (August 1978): 134–43; see p. 137.

28. Norman Denzin, *Interpretive Ethnography: Ethnographic Practices for the 21st Century* (Thousand Oaks, CA: Sage, 1997), 272.

29. Barrie Thorne, "'You Still Takin' Notes?' Fieldwork and Informed Consent," *Social Problems* 27, no. 3 (February 1980): 284–96; see p. 292.

30. Barnes, *Who Should Know What?* 110–11.

31. William E. Smythe and Maureen J. Murray, "Owning the Story: Ethical Considerations in Narrative Research," *Ethics and Behavior* 10, no. 4 (2000): 311–36; see pp. 319–20.

32. Ralph LaRossa, Linda A. Bennett, and Richard J. Gelles, "Ethical Dilemmas in Qualitative Family Research," in *The Psychosocial Interior of the Family*, 3rd ed., ed. Gerald Handel, 95–111 (New York: Aldine, 1985); see p. 100.

33. Sally Smith Hughes, letter to author, December 4, 1992.

34. M. G. Trend, "Applied Social Research and the Government: Notes on the Limits of Confidentiality," *Social Problems* 27, no. 3 (February 1980): 342–49; see p. 342.

35. *Chronicle of Higher Education*, "Keeping His Promises," May 16, 2003, A11–12.

36. David K. Jordan, "The Ethnographic Enterprise and the Bureaucratization of Ethics: The Problem of Human Subjects Legislation," *Journal of Anthropological Research* 37, no. 4 (1981): 415–19; see p. 417.

37. Jane Adams, conversations with author, Chapel Hill, North Carolina, June 18, 1993.

38. Jordan, "Ethnographic Enterprise and the Bureaucratization of Ethics," 416.

39. Linda Shopes, letter to author, July 20, 1992.

40. Popular Memory Group, "Popular Memory: Theory, Politics, and Method," in *Making Histories: Studies in History Writing and Politics*, ed. Richard Johnson et al. (Birmingham, UK: University of Birmingham Center of Contemporary Cultural Studies and University of Minnesota Press, 1982), 219.

41. John Gwaltney, *Drylongo: A Self-Portrait of Black America* (New York: Random House, 1980), xxiii.

42. Alessandro Portelli, "Tryin' to Gather a Little Knowledge: Some Thoughts on the Ethics of Oral History," in *The Battle of Valle Giulia: Oral History and the Art of Dialogue*, 55–71 (Madison: University of Wisconsin, 1997), 69.

43. Daphne Patai, "Ethical Problems of Personal Narratives, or, Who Should Eat the Last Piece of Cake?" *International Journal of Oral History* 8 (February 1987): 5–27; see p. 21.

44. Judith Stacey, "Can There Be a Feminist Ethnography?" in *Women's Words: The Feminist Practice of Oral History*, ed. Sherna Gluck and Daphne Patai, 111–19 (New York and London: Routledge, 1991); see p. 113.

45. LaRossa, Bennett, and Gelles, "Ethical Dilemmas in Qualitative Family Research," 101.

46. Esther Newton, "My Best Informant's Dress: The Erotic Equation in Fieldwork," *Cultural Anthropology* 8, no. 1 (1993): 3–23; see p. 4.

47. Amanda Coffey, "Sex in the Field: Intimacy and Intimidation," in *Ethical Dilemmas in Qualitative Research*, ed. Trevor Welland and Lesley Pugsley, 57–74 (Burlington, VT: Ashgate, 2002); see p. 66.

48. Fran Markowitz and Michael Ashkenazi, eds., *Sex, Sexuality, and the Anthropologist* (Urbana: University of Illinois Press, 1999); Don Kulick and Margaret Wilson, eds., *Taboo: Sex, Identity, and Erotic Subjectivity in Anthropological Fieldwork* (London: Routledge, 1995).

49. Kate Altork, "Walking the Fire Line: The Erotic Dimension of the Fieldwork Experience," in Kulick and Wilson, *Taboo: Sex, Identity, and Erotic Subjectivity in Anthropological Fieldwork*, 13–39.

50. Ronald Grele, Studs Terkel, Jan Vansina, Alice Kessler Harris, Dennis Ted-lock, and Saul Benison, "It's Not the Song, It's the Singing," in *Envelopes of Sound: The Art of Oral History*, 2nd ed. rev., ed. Ronald Grele (Chicago: Precedent Publishers, 1985), 71.

51. Raymond L. Gorden, *Interviewing: Strategy, Techniques and Tactics*, 4th ed. (Chicago: Dorsey Press, 1987), 16.

52. Patricia A. Adler and Peter Adler, "Ethical Issues in Self-Censorship: Ethnographic Research on Sensitive Topics," in *Researching Sensitive Topics*, ed. Claire M. Renzetti and Raymond M. Lee, 249–66 (Newbury Park, CA: Sage, 1993); see p. 262.

53. Howard S. Becker, "Problems in the Publication of Field Studies," in *Reflections on Community Studies*, ed. Arthur J. Vidich, Joseph Bensman, and Maurice Stein, 267–84 (New York: John Wiley & Sons, 1964); see p. 272.

54. Jean L. Briggs, "A Problem of Publishing on Identifiable Communities and Personalities," in *Ethical Dilemmas in Anthropological Inquiry: A Case Book*, ed. G. N. Appell, 202–4 (Waltham, MA: Crossroads Press, 1978); see pp. 203–4.

55. Elizabeth Bott, *Family and Social Network*, 2nd ed. (London: Tavistock, 1971), 47; cited in Barnes, *Who Should Know What?* 142.

56. Patai, "Ethical Problems of Personal Narratives," 16.

57. Smythe and Murray, "Owning the Story," 324.

58. Joan Acker, Kate Barry, and Johanna Esseveld, quoted in Gesa Kirsch, *Ethical Dilemmas in Feminist Research: The Politics of Location, Interpretation, and Publication* (Albany: State University of New York Press, 1999), 45.

59. Nancy Scheper-Hughes, *Saints, Scholars and Schizophrenics: Mental Illness in Rural Ireland* (Berkeley: University of California Press, 1982), introduction to paperback, vii; quoted in Caroline B. Brettell, *When They Read What We Write: The Politics of Ethnography* (Westport, CT: Bergin and Garvey, 1993), 13.

60. Smythe and Murray, "Owning the Story," 329 and 332.

61. Kirsch, *Ethical Dilemmas in Feminist Research*, 54.

62. Kathleen Blee, "Evidence, Empathy, and Ethics: Lessons from Oral Histories of the Klan," *Journal of American History*, September 1993, 596–606.

63. Ronald C. Tobey, "The Public Historian as Advocate: Is Special Attention to Professional Ethics Necessary?" in *Public History Readings*, ed. Phyllis K. Leffler and Joseph Brent, 127–34 (Malabar, FL: Krieger Publishing, 1992); see p. 128.

64. Tobey, "Public Historian as Advocate," 128.

65. Donald Page, "Ethics and the Publication of Commissioned History," in *Ethics and Public History: An Anthology*, ed. Theodore Karamanski, 65–71 (Malabar, FL: Krieger Publishing, 1990); see p. 66.

66. Gorden, *Interviewing*, 86.

67. Valerie Yow (listed as Valerie Quinney), *Bryant College: The First 125 Years*, ed. Peter Mandel and Elizabeth O'Neil (Smithfield, RI: Bryant College, 1988), 98.

68. Norman Denzin, *The Research Act*, 2nd ed. (Chicago: Aldine, 1978), 329–31.

69. Valerie Yow, *Patient Care: A History of Butler Hospital* (Providence, RI: Butler Hospital, 1994); see author's preface.

70. Carl Ryant, "The Public Historian and Business History: A Question of Ethics," in Karamanski, *Ethics and Public History*, 62.

71. Ryant, "Public Historian and Business History," 60–61.

72. Ryant, "Public Historian and Business History," 61.

73. Susan W. Almy, "Anthropologists and Development Agencies," *American Anthropologist* 79 (1977): 280–92.

74. Ken Plummer, *Documents of Life 2: An Invitation to Critical Humanism* (London: Sage, 2001), 226.

75. Portelli, "Tryin' to Gather a Little Knowledge," 55.

CHAPTER SIX

Interpersonal Relations
in the Interview

In this chapter, interpersonal relationships and the effects of the interviewing process on both interviewer and narrator are discussed. As an investigator, you may want to get "just the facts, Ma'am," but conversations are much more than a recital of facts, and you, as an in-depth interviewer, can open a treasure chest that will enrich your own life—or maybe a Pandora's box of troubles.

Many of us, trained in traditional research methods using written sources, have little preparation in relating to the living witness. Because of the very nature of the main sources of information—living people—the interviewer has to delve into a study of interpersonal relationships in the research process. In this chapter, I will discuss ways the relationship between interviewer and narrator directly affects the quality of the recorded life history.

First, the recording of an oral history is a collaborative venture. This does not necessarily make the two people, interviewer and narrator, feel equal, however. In any interviewing situation, a vague awareness of the power relationship impinges. As pointed out in the preceding chapter, the interviewer has formal knowledge, an agenda, and the ability to represent the narrator to a wider audience. Other than that, the power relationship is affected by age, race, class, status, ethnicity, gender, and knowledge. These conditions in the interpersonal relationship are discussed in this chapter. Most often, I use the term *narrator*, rather than *interviewee*, because *narrator* places primary importance on the person telling the story. *Interviewee* uses the suffix *ee*, which is a derivative form, secondary to the primary noun, *interviewer*.

Second, present after the interview are the lingering reflections on what has happened. The interviewer has asked the narrator to tell things he or she would not normally tell a stranger. During this process, both interviewer and narrator are changed in some way. These changes are considered.

Effects of the Interview on the Narrator

The interviewer walks into a home. She or he asks questions the person living there has not thought to ask about her life. Suddenly, the process of analyzing, of answering someone else's questions about a life, of standing outside it and looking at its experiences in a different way, makes the narrator feel strange. British oral historian Wendy Rickard says, "Oral history offers the possibility of both affirming and destabilizing a personal narrative."[1] And you, as interviewer, also feel strange because you have asked questions that have taken you into another's world, and you are not sure of your place there.

Can the effect on the narrator be positive? Certainly the oral history interview gives the narrator an opportunity to make sense of scattered events. The narrator has a serious, eager listener. This is an opportunity to tell one's life story to another person who accepts that this version is true for the teller and that it is important. There is validation for the narrator that he or she is worth listening to.

This validation is especially important to people our society often devalues—women, the elderly, political dissidents, working-class people, and minorities. Interviewing working-class women for a study of mill work in Carrboro, North Carolina, I often heard the narrators say, "I don't know what I can tell you. There are people smarter than I am who will know more." During the course of the interview, they discovered that they knew a lot about the topics under discussion.

Certainly, in the process of telling the life story, the narrator describes things that happened and the reaction to them and learns something about himself by articulating things not consciously thought about before. In his book on autobiography, James Olney explains that "the act of autobiography is at once a discovery, a creation, and an imitation of the self."[2]

In describing events and struggles, the narrator creates a story and gives her or his life a meaning. Judith Modell concludes that anthropologists assume that the individual is an "active creator of his surroundings each time he puts thoughts into words." Probably, she says, the narrator has already begun in his mind to compose the story: "As informant, the individual self-consciously unravels a plot and presents a character he has been constructing and coloring all along. Storytelling goes on with a relentlessness which illustrates, I would suggest, a special human strategy of survival."[3]

The process of reflecting during an oral history interview can be a way to understand anew some things that happened and a means of coming to accept the things that have hurt. Each person is creative in the way that she or he weaves from various life experiences—both the pleasant and the devastating—a whole cloth. Recording the life story gives the narrator not only formal encouragement, but also a structure for doing this. Robert Butler, a psychiatrist and former director of the National Institute on Aging (United States National Institutes of Health), told members of the Gerontological Society at an annual meeting, "By reviewing the past events of their lives, old people put their lives in perspective, prove to themselves that their lives have been worthwhile and prepare themselves for death with a minimum of fear or anxiety."[4] He concluded, "Oral history can be a boon to both the patient and the practitioner—helping both to 'see and see again.'"[5]

And the narrator learns something from the interviewer. He or she gets a perspective that was not there before. The narrator will look at the experience in a different way and reflect on this long after the interview has been completed. (I assume here that the interviewer respects the narrator and that what the narrator learns is a different way to see things and not necessarily a negative way.) William Foote Whyte, in interviewing for *Street Corner Society*, found that his informants were becoming sophisticated in their observations about their own lives as they responded to his questions and thought about their experiences in new ways.[6] Years after publication of the book, one of the narrators, born in the Boston slum neighborhood Whyte was studying, said that Whyte showed him that the community was well organized with a certain structure and social patterns. (But others spoke of less beneficial effects.)[7]

The presence of a listener who records the narrator's words for a story of the past gives the process a sense of drama and importance a casual conversation cannot impart. Through the use of the tape recorder, the narrator can speak to the present community and to generations to come. Politicians make speeches that they assume will be recorded for posterity in history books, but most of us never make that assumption. It is tantalizing to think that we might have the chance to say to future generations, "This is the way it happened. This is the way we were." Speaking of his book *All God's Dangers*, Theodore Rosengarten says of the narrator Nate Shaw (Ned Cobb), the principal witness to the history of the southern tenant farmers' struggles for justice,

> He was racing against time to give his last confession. From me he wanted the affirmation he felt he had never gotten from his children—that he had always

tried to do the right thing. Moreover, he was speaking to a higher judge. By offering his good works as proof of his intentions, he pinned his salvation on God's justice, not mercy. If he erred on the side of righteousness, he gambled that his last deed would win him forgiveness. The lies he exposed were monumental compared to the lies he concealed. He wanted his testimony to oppose the stories told about people like him in newspapers, court records, congressional reports, merchants' ledgers, and school books.[8]

What have narrators themselves said? Lynn Echevarria-Howe reports her narrator's reactions to a series of in-depth interviews:

INTERVIEWER: You trusted me enough to share with me. How did you feel about me taking away this material? It's all about you and someone is taking it, and working with it.

PHOENIX: Well trust wasn't a factor, that wasn't something I even thought about. I wanted so much to have left you with something potent. Other than that, if this piece of work can touch people in some way then I feel good about that. I am not ashamed about what I have said.[9]

Ann Oakley interviewed women in depth in a research project on transition to motherhood. At the end, she questioned them about the effects of the project on them. She found that nearly three-fourths of the women said that being interviewed had affected them, and the three most common forms this influence took were in leading them to reflect on their experiences more than they would have done; in reducing the level of their anxiety and/or reassuring them of their normality; and in giving a valuable outlet for the verbalization of feelings. None judged that the interviewing had had a negative effect.[10]

In all of the situations discussed above, there is the assumption that the interviewer can communicate the following to the narrator:

1. You have something to say that I think is important.
2. I listen and accept that your version of the story is true for you.
3. I seek to understand rather than to judge.

This kind of encouraging, noncritical listening based on mutual respect between narrator and interviewer is crucial to a productive interview and important to the narrator's self-esteem. The interviewer who goes into an interview assuming that the narrator is nothing more than a bigot may get very little information. (He may indeed be a bigot, but each of Shakespeare's villains has the complexity of character that makes him human and interesting.) The interviewer who communicates to the narrator that she is just a lower-class, inarticulate woman who happened to witness a historical event will do much more harm to the narrator than he or she can imagine. And the interviewer's communication of disdain will discourage the narrator from being helpful. This disdain can kill the chance for a frank, full discussion in an oral history interview.

Sometimes in the midst of answering questions, the narrator turns the tables and asks the interviewer a question. This may be a request for information about the interviewer or advice. The interviewer suddenly finds herself in a different role—friend or adviser. The old model in the social sciences was to keep silent. The reasoning was that the researcher should not say anything because it might bias the narrator's answer. However, oral historians Kristin Langellier and Deanna Hall believe that the interviewee's questions are "requests for reciprocity from the interviewer." They explain, "They [the interviewees] ask the interviewer to invest some of herself in the research relationship within and outside of the interview frame."[11]

Furthermore, the old model possibly biased information anyway because the narrator sensed that the interviewer was being less than candid. Ann Oakley, in her study of transition to motherhood (mentioned above), interviewed fifty-five women four times each—twice during pregnancy and twice after childbirth. She had found in previous research that refusing to answer questions damaged rapport. In this project, she answered questions, and these were usually about pregnancy and childbirth, matters she had studied. She believed that the narrators, without the satisfaction of having their pressing questions answered, would not have been motivated to continue after the first interview.[12]

In his book about interviewing workers in Argentina, *Doña María's Story*, Daniel James recounts a time when he wanted a narrator to go back over his union story. The narrator did tell the story again, but when James interrupted to request clarification on a point, the narrator said in exasperation, "You just want to get things from me, but you don't tell me anything about yourself, about what you think, about your ideas. What do you value? What do you think of Perón?" The interviewer realized his narrator was expressing something important: "He was, in fact, challenging the entire premise of my activity, the power relationship I had taken for granted and which underlay my sense of myself as the author, the constructor, the editor of the historical knowledge that would come out of our encounter. He wanted some form of genuine dialogue and interchange, but also, more than that, he wanted this to be the basis of my listening to what he most wanted to say."[13]

This remarkably astute narrator understood what was happening and asked the interviewer to share his thoughts with him, thereby putting the two on a more equal footing but also creating a climate of reciprocity and trust. Sensitivity to the narrator's feelings and intentions is the key here. If you have information, give it. (Of course, I do not refer to information told to you in confidence.) If your own understanding of the topic is vague and you do not feel well informed, tell the narrator. Be frank about the limitations of your own knowledge. If you can refer the narrator to other sources of information on the topic, such as books, agencies, and so on, do so. If narrators want to know you better before they answer all your questions, answer theirs.

The narrator may want to know if you agree with him. During an interview in the project on work in a North Carolina cotton mill in the early twentieth century, I was suddenly stymied. The narrator had just asked, "Do you feel like I do about black people?" I replied as gently as I could, "No, I don't, but I grew up in a different time." I tried to express disagreement without disapproval—a kind of "this is the way things are" attitude. I went on to the next topic. Traditionally, social scientists were told to avoid any expression of opinion: "I'm here to get your opinion—mine doesn't matter in this research project." However, I believe that when you expect your narrators to be open and honest with you, then you must be open and honest with them, even about your opinions when they really want to know.

On the other hand, consider that your intervention in their lives may have unintended consequences. The researcher asks questions that compel people to think in new ways about their relationships to others. The researcher then leaves, but the narrators must come to terms with new perspectives about people significant in their lives and must continue to live with them. At the extreme, the researcher who asks questions that lead to new awareness of serious problems and then leaves has been compared to someone who indulges in "slash and burn agriculture."[14]

When I was beginning to interview, I suggested to a woman that she had worked hard for her political party and deserved some reward, that perhaps she herself should run for office. I must have started the ball rolling; undoubtedly she consulted others, and she decided to run for mayor. She won, but it proved to be a difficult and most unrewarding experience. I learned that there is a difference between giving information and giving advice.

Effects of the Interview on the Interviewer

Up to this point, we have considered effects on the narrator of the process of being interviewed. Consider now the effects of interviewing on the interviewer. The interviewer may begin to feel a kind of strangeness, too, because he or she is welcomed into a home and treated like a friend. Information is confided that is often told only to a friend. And yet the interviewer is there to get information for her or his own use; and in the traditional training of a social scientist, the interviewer should be an impartial observer. No matter what we have been told, the interviewer is affected by this intense communication with another person. Mary Stuart, coming to the end of an interview, asked the narrator how she had found the experience of being interviewed. The narrator replied, "And how was it for you, Mary?" Stuart was thrown off guard for a second, but she marveled over her narrator's insight: "No intimate research moment can be one-sided."[15]

Often the interviewer may feel a friendship developing. When the interviewing project is over and the interviewer leaves the area, there is guilt over terminating a friendship. So, what is the interviewer—friend or researcher? Is it possible to be both?

Arlene Daniels notes that she gravitated to particular narrators who caught her imagination, and she made close friends of them. Daniels describes the way she became fascinated with an officer during her interviewing project with military psychiatrists. Later, during a research study on women in volunteer work, she accompanied a particular woman to various engagements, listening to her every word. Later Daniels reflected on the process of cementing friendships with these two narrators: "It was difficult to see how the glitter of interesting personality that surrounded these figures was a product of how much I needed them. I did not realize how I had psyched myself up to admire extravagantly in order to enjoy the advantages they offered me."[16]

She realized that she had not confronted honestly the "self-serving nature" of these friendships, but she felt discomfort, an underlying sense of unease, and perhaps guilt about the unconscious manipulation involved. She tried to carry out "ritual expressions of friendship" to prove she was a good friend as well as a researcher.[17]

Feminist researchers have continued to discuss this delicate problem of friendship developing in the interview situation, especially the tendency to use intuition and empathy to build such a close relationship that the narrator reveals more than she would normally. Julie Jessop and Jean Duncombe discuss such a situation in their article "'Doing Rapport' and the Ethics of 'Faking Friendship'": when Jessop asked a narrator what she had gained from the interviews, she replied, "Well, apart from anything else, I've made a friend." Jessop was troubled that the woman did not realize how much "faking of friendship" had been part of her work as researcher. Later, when Jessop met this narrator on the street, she could not recall her narrator's name.[18] Researcher Jane Ribbens notes, "While we may seek to establish clearly the nature of the research relationship at the outset, the subtle distinctions between listening with empathy and actually responding with care and concern, may be hard for the interviewee to appreciate, against her more general experience that listening implies caring."[19]

Possibly, the role of researcher obstructs the development of a friendship: the researcher is there to get information, and after the interview, the researcher has the tremendous power of interpreting the narrator's experience for others.[20] It is possible that a true friendship may develop after the research comes to a close, but in the midst of a research project, the researcher has a purpose in talking with the narrator that is not friendship. Pamela Cotteril, in "Interviewing Women: Issues of Friendship, Vulnerability, and Power," reminds us, "For one thing, close friends do not usually arrive with a tape-recorder, listen carefully and sympathetically to what you have to say and then disappear."[21] It is not honest or wise to indicate that there will be an ongoing friendship after the research ends unless you are sure that you want to continue the relationship and can do so.

In some situations, however, you know that there will be an ongoing relationship. A biographer has a unique situation: the biographer does not become a member of the family but rather an interpreter of a family's life, a strange relationship because it is both close and distant. In research for two biographies of women writers, I realized that once the biography was published, my relationship with family members would not end. I knew I would be in touch with them for years to come, and that has been the case. Another exception occurs when you live in a small community where your narrators live and can expect that the friendship you had before the interviewing project will continue after the project is finished. And finally, when the interviewer goes back to the narrator many times, a relationship gradually develops that is not exactly a friendship but not strictly an interviewer–interviewee relationship either. Wendy Rickard says about such a relationship, "There always remains an issue for me about where we set those boundaries with each individual interviewed, why we often choose to set them very differently depending on the person, and how we maintain or change those boundaries over time, either consciously or unconsciously."[22]

Generally in an interviewing project, though, the relationship is limited in time. As Ribbens points out, the narrator, no matter how well educated, may not understand the rules for a professional relationship. What you can do is indicate that this is a collaboration in a project that will have an end. Communicate your respect and liking and thank the narrator for this gift of memories. To the narrators I felt close to, I stated outright that they would always be significant to me not only in this research project but also in my life. I assured them that the time we had spent together was enjoyable and rewarding for me, that they had taught me a lot, that I would not forget them. In this way, I tried to bring about closure in the immediate situation but assure them of their ongoing importance in my thinking. And at the same time, I was aware that there is a tension inherent in this kind of research and that the tension must be lived with.

In addition to this tension, there is guilt attached to learning about someone's misery and doing nothing to help. And merely revealing a group's plight by publishing the research study does not necessarily improve the situation. The traditionally trained social scientist avoids this by assuming that his or her role is appropriately that of objective researcher. Those of us trained in qualitative research methods acknowledge that we are human beings as well as social scientists and that to be untouched by the sufferings of our fellow human beings is to be less than human ourselves. But the dilemma is there: one must be cognizant of the sufferings and feel empathy but also be aware that there are limitations on what an individual can do.

When I was interviewing farm women in DeKalb County, in northern Illinois, I was struck by how many elderly widows lived alone on isolated farms. They were glad to see me because they needed another person to talk to. If they were lucky, a daughter or daughter-in-law lived nearby and would drive them to the grocery store once a week, or a church member would drive them to church on Sundays. But they longed for companionship. There was no way I could be a companion to the twenty or more women in the research design. I felt a failure in that respect. My only rationalization (a limp one) was that for that week, I was somebody to talk to. I found myself winding down the project and realized later that I had felt overwhelmed by their needs. As an isolated individual, there was not much that I could do.

Often the researcher does not live in the community, but if that is your own place and you can see possibilities for ameliorating a bad situation and this is a priority for you, organize. Collectively you can accomplish something and that is probably the most constructive way. But obviously you cannot organize for every cause: realize and accept limitations. Set priorities based on what you can actually do. At the least, you can become informed about the social services available in the area and tell the narrator about these.

Learning something about yourself in interviewing is always a strong possibility. As Thomas Cottle notes, in the interviewing process we watch ourselves as much as we watch the narrators.[23] Observing your thoughts about the interviewing you are doing can be facilitated by keeping a personal journal. Write whatever comes to mind about yourself, the narrator, the interviewing process. Write the details that you remember. Later, read these entries again and reflect on them. That is how I came to realize in the project with widowed farm women described above that I was winding down because I felt overwhelmed.

During an interviewing project Arlene Daniels observed her behavior. She began to scrutinize her clothing: she had thought of herself as a "mud hen" (a rather drab bird) and dressed like one. But she wanted the military psychiatrists she was interviewing to think that she was a sophisticated person, so she began to dress in a chic way and to see herself as a peacock.[24] Sherry Thomas, who interviewed farm women, began to reflect on her attitudes. She found that she was much more skittish about discussing sexual experience than she had thought. She admitted, "I publish my sex life in feminist journals, and I'm a prude when I sit in front of an eighty-year-old woman and she starts to tell me about hers."[25]

The interviewer enters the narrator's world and learns another way of life and some things about her or his own assumptions. A professional woman herself, sociologist Arlene Daniels assumed when she studied society women who were volunteers in philanthropic causes that this was just a way to pass the time because their days were useless. She came to understand that these philanthropic endeavors were "hidden worlds of serious careers invisible to the sex-stratified and cash nexus economy." She began to see her narrators as women who performed needed services for the community and at the same time developed their own competencies. And in coming to this realization, she confronted her own "sexist views of nonworking (not gainfully employed) women."[26]

I learned some things about myself during an interviewing project for a college history. I taped faculty women, many retired, some still teaching, all significant in the college's history. One day when I began an interview with a young woman, she said, "I've had a stroke and I may not remember everything—sometimes I lose a word, too." This was a statement, not an apology nor a plea for sympathy. Her frankness toward me and acceptance of herself was so reassuring that I immediately relaxed and said, "OK." We both smiled. It turned out to be a productive interview. I started to work on admitting and accepting my own shortcomings and bad luck without feeling sorry for myself.

Interviewing can enlarge the sympathies of the interviewers as they hear the struggles of people in a world they have not known firsthand. Taping life histories of women clerical workers for the Rhode Island chapter of 9to5 (a national organization of clerical workers), I talked to a lot of single mothers. As I listened to the details of how they juggle work and child care and budget to the penny, I gained an appreciation of their practical knowledge, financial acumen, and courage.

Blanca Erazo recorded the life stories of Puerto Rican women working in the garment industry in New York. She soon detected a pattern: the omission of testimony about victimization. Instead, the women gave her images of strength and combat. They sent to the younger generation of women a message to persevere. Erazo describes the effect on her: "In our oral history work, we have acquired a renewed respect for the struggles of garment workers, for their steadfastness, ingenuity, and resolve in the midst of an alienating, oppressive, and often hostile environment. If these stories prepare a younger generation of listeners for anything, it is to understand how we have survived as a people: through persistence, perseverance, struggle, ingenuity, and hard work."[27]

A researcher can feel drawn to narrators and even inspired, as in the examples just given, or he or she may be repelled. Sometimes there arises real resentment about the way a narrator behaves toward the interviewer. Daniels recalls the sexist manner in which the military psychiatrists treated her: "But, even without knowledge of the women's movement yet to come, I knew the responses I was getting had something to do with competition, resistance to taking instruction from a woman, resistance to a civilian and non-M.D., all combined in a general desire to minimize and neutralize my presence."[28] Their flirtatious overtures made her uncomfortable and put her on the defensive. Their tactics made her less effective as an interviewer. Daniels reasoned that she needed to soften her style in order to seem less like a competitor to the military psychiatrists she was interviewing. Indeed, she was not their competitor, and she realized she needed to convey that fact. She was conducting the interview to get information, not to get the better of the narrator in a game.

Ann Phoenix, a black woman, interviewed young people in two research studies, "Mothers under Twenty" and "Social Identities." One narrator, a white woman, began talking about how she disliked black people, especially black men. Phoenix was understandably upset: "I had established a warm feminist interviewing relationship with this woman and gone beyond the interviewee/interviewer relationship in attempting to help her begin to sort out a potential predicament."[29] Phoenix reminded herself that "accounts that respondents give are not unitary and there are generally parts of their accounts with which researchers feel in sympathy."[30] She focused on the aspects of the narrator's personality that she liked.

If you feel toward the narrator a rising dismay or increasing dislike, stay with your purpose to record a history. And be conscious that your proper role is that of listener, but that you also have feelings. It is all right to dislike the person—admit it to yourself and go on with your work. And as a compassionate human being, you do not have to give back what he or she dishes out. Remind yourself that the narrator has to live with the mistakes that he or she has made, while you do not—you live with your own. Look with compassion on this fellow traveler in the journey of life and pass on in search of your own destination.

There are also subtle feelings about narrators that play at the back of the mind. We have preconceived ideas about what a person or a situation should be, and that affects the way we feel about them. And we have a self-concept that influences the way we react to others. We may not always be conscious of these influences as Daniels and Phoenix were in the examples above. Sometimes a narrator says something that evokes a memory in you that had lain dormant. Mary Stuart, interviewing women left as children in a convent because they were thought to be learning disabled, suddenly came to a realization about herself. She says, "On one occasion, as a woman spoke of her past experiences of being left at a convent, I was thrown back to my own experiences of being left at a convent. The sudden rush of desperation and childhood fear quite surprised me."[31] That memory had not surfaced in years because there had not been up to that time words that stimulated remembering.

Sometimes, transference, a concept from analytical psychology, can be useful in figuring out what is going on. One way transference occurs is in the narrator's placing of the interviewer in a relationship familiar to her or him. Micaela di Leonardo says that her middle-aged narrators often related to her as a daughter.[32] Or, a perfectly ordinary, nice narrator comes to the door, extends his hand in greeting, and the interviewer draws back for a split second. It is possible that some little characteristic of the narrator that the interviewer is not even conscious of evokes a fleeting memory or feeling of someone in the past. Researcher Michael Roper defines transference as "the enactment of emotional fragments of past relationships in the present."[33] Roper argues that transference occurs in all relationships; the oral history interview is, by definition, a relationship. Roper points out that interviewers can figure out what is happening and thereby tolerate their anxiety.[34] When you write these feelings in your journal, you can reflect on them later so that a deeper understanding of the interview relationship emerges. (I have shied away from using the term countertransference because it refers to the role of the analyst—a role inappropriate for the interviewing situation.)

While transference often goes on in human interaction, there is a situation unique to oral history: the very act of recording compels both narrator and interviewer to be mindful of the presence of other listeners. Both have a need to speak for the communities they identify with, and both have an ideology. When interviewer and narrator share the same ideology, the interview may go smoothly; when the ideologies are not held in common, the interpersonal relationship is affected. Oral historian Ron Grele argues that the interviewer will show by questions which side he is on and the narrator will certainly explain in answers which side she is on.[35] I do not imply that you should actively start a political debate in an interview and take over. You have invited the narrator to record his or her experience and reflections, and you must allow that and listen, but you are bound to ask challenging questions. Make yourself aware of how this conflict influences the interaction.

Here are some specific questions we can ask ourselves that might help us understand what was happening when we reflect on the interview:

What am I feeling about this narrator?

What similarities and differences impinge on this interpersonal situation?

How does my own ideology affect this process? What group outside of the process am I identifying with?

Why am I doing this project in the first place?

In selecting topics and questions, what alternatives might I have taken? Why didn't I choose these?

What other possible interpretations are there? Why did I reject them?

What are the effects on me as I go about this research? How are my reactions impinging on the research?[36]

The best effect on the interviewer has been saved for the last statement in this section: the process of interviewing can be an exhilarating experience, an epiphany. Paul Buhle, a social and cultural historian, describes his interviews with Yiddish screenwriters for his project "An Oral History of the American Left." He says they gave him views of the making of popular culture from the inside, insights he could have gotten from no one else: "Seeing these people made me feel new again with oral history—I was both humbled and honored."[37]

Effects of Race, Gender, Age, Class, Ethnicity, and Subculture

Race

Be aware of power relationships based on race and gender. When people from the Works Progress Administration (WPA) interviewed people who had been in slavery before the Civil War, they found that research results depended on the race and gender of the interviewers. Black interviewers were not participants in the WPA project in the southern states except in Virginia, Louisiana, and Florida. John Blassingame, in reviewing these life histories, concludes, "Generally, the stories are most revealing when the informant and the interviewer were of the same sex; black interviewers obtained more reliable information than white ones; and white women received more honest responses than white men."[38] When black scholars from Hampton Institute, Fisk University, and Southern University conducted nearly nine hundred interviews with ex-slaves between 1929 and 1938, the narrators talked much more freely than in the WPA project: they spoke candidly about miscegenation, hatred of whites, courtship, marriage and family customs, cruel punishments, separation of families, child labor, black resistance to whites, and admiration of Nat Turner.[39]

Racial differences impinged on the interviewing situation, but power and race were inseparable. Black narrators saw white males as having the power to hurt them if they said something those interviewers interpreted as criticizing the social order. White women were less threatening because they did not share in the formal power structure in the South in the 1930s, and thus it was somewhat easier for a group that was powerless to identify with them. But white women, although they had no formal role in the power structure, were nevertheless intimately connected to those in power. This reality could not have escaped the former slaves. On the other hand, women are often easier to talk with because they tend to have a less authoritative manner, and so gender difference in styles of communication, as well as race and power, had an influence on the interviewing situation.

In Ann Phoenix's study, she found that some white narrators were "visibly shocked" when she appeared at their door. She noticed that they recovered quickly and she was able to establish rapport: she adds, "However, I cannot rule out the possibility that for some white interviewees having a black woman in their home, perhaps for the first time, has an impact on how forthcoming they are."[40] She was interviewing women, but she found that sometimes color made a difference that overshadowed their common gender. On the other hand, some young black women who were her narrators wanted to ask her questions like, "What do you feel as a black person? About living in Britain?"[41]

Cultural Norms

Cultural norms also impinge. When I interviewed mill women in Carrboro, North Carolina, I received a very different description of sexual practices than did my male colleagues, who interviewed the men. I heard from the women that there was no premarital or extramarital sexual behavior. The male interviewers were told about prostitution in the community. In this case, gender—and not power—affected the answers, but so did cultural norms. Men of that generation, who came of age about the time of World War I, did not talk to women about sexual matters. They could talk to other men about even risqué sex, however. And women did not talk about such things to other women unless they were their closest friends. At the beginning, my coresearchers and I decided it would be useless for me to ask male narrators about sexual practices or for them to ask women. But even the women I talked to were unwilling to discuss the topic.

On the other hand, interviewing farm families of a later generation (those who came of age during World War II) in a wealthy county in northern Illinois, I found that the men more readily talked to me about birth control than did the women. The men carefully chose the words to use, however, and never went into details. This was a later generation than the Carrboro narrators, and there also was a difference in level of education: cultural norms were different than in the earlier situation. Now men could talk in general terms about birth control to a woman.

Gender

Recent research on gender and communication indicates a difference in style in informal conversation that men and women use. In fact, some scholars argue that men and women come from different sociolinguistic subcultures.[42] Communication experts' research findings are based on observation of casual conversation, and researchers stress that they are specific to the situation. The findings cannot all be applicable to the in-depth interview because of its formal nature, but some may be. And although researchers use categories of male and female to show patterns of behavior, they are not assuming sex-linked traits; their theories on speech behaviors are based on the assumption that gender differences are learned in a sociolinguistic context. (Of course, individuals do not stay neatly in categories, and interviewing each individual is always a unique experience in some aspects.)

Consider some situations in which characteristics of casual conversation may not apply to the formal interview. In informal conversation men interrupt women more often than women interrupt men.[43] In the formal situation of the recorded interview, the interviewer—no matter what the gender—is conscious of the rule that the interviewer does not interrupt (although the narrator might interrupt as soon as the question is understood). Sometimes, however, men use silence as a way of exerting power;[44] but in the interview situation, the narrator quickly learns that the expectation is that he will answer or refuse to answer and use silences only to think. In informal conversation, women ask more questions than men, and women do more listening than men. In the interview situation, the expectation is that the interviewer—no matter what the gender—asks most of the questions and listens the most.

Speech communication researchers stress the asymmetry that is established between two speakers in informal conversation; for example, the one asking for information is requesting help, and that puts him or her lower on the power ladder than the person with information to give.[45] In the formal interview, the one asking for information is following the expectation for that activity and may not necessarily be viewed as "one down" from the narrator. In casual conversation, men control the choice of topic more often than women;[46] but in the interview situation there is often an assumption or clearly stated procedure that both interviewer and narrator will choose topics. Still, because the interviewer has a research plan, it is expected that he or she will introduce more topics than the narrator.

Nevertheless, some characteristics of gendered communication in casual conversation may carry over to the formal interview. Men often feel in interacting with another man or with a woman in their profession or at their rank that the situation is competitive, that they must establish themselves in a higher position.[47] Oral historian Sally Hughes found that the male physicians and scientists she interviewed did not see her as a competitor even at the outset because she has a doctorate in the history of medicine, rather than in a physical science, and so they placed her in a different profession from theirs.[48]

On the other hand, these male elites were inclined to "talk down" to her because she is a woman. Research findings indicate that this is often the situation in male–female conversation because our society does not value women's work, expertise, or statements as highly as men's.[49] However, Hughes made sure she was thoroughly prepared for the interviews, which included familiarity with the history of the narrators' branch of science or medicine and a working knowledge of their key publications and professional contributions. Thus, gender could have operated to her disadvantage, but her preparation made it obvious that she understood what was going on in their field.[50] Against their expectations, they became convinced that she was intelligent and informed—but not a competitor—and they stopped being condescending.

Also, as a woman, Hughes uses an interviewing style that is a "directed conversation, rather than a hard-boiled interrogation," which may help put male elite narrators in a nondefensive posture.[51] Because some men feel challenged when they are questioned and unconsciously "spar" with the interviewer, such a softening of style could mitigate the challenge whether the interviewer is male or female.

However, women in general may have an advantage in this kind of situation because women often learn as children to establish an ambiance of thinking things through together. Daniel Maltz and Ruth Borker summarize research on characteristics of women's cross-sex conversational behavior: Women are more likely than men to say things that encourage responses. Women are more likely to use positive minimal responses, such as "mm hmm," that indicate "I'm following you." And women are more likely to use the pronouns *you* and *we* to indicate awareness of and solidarity with the other.[52] (Like the style I have unconsciously used in this textbook.)

On the other hand, men may interpret a woman's "mm hmm" as agreement and may be surprised when that is not the case.[53] Women may use "overlap" in speech—that is, before a sentence is finished, the listener says something that indicates she understands. Men may see this as an interruption. Or, a woman may express empathy. This is often interpreted by a man as condescension.[54] However, in general women have learned to interpret correctly nonverbal signals, and there is some safeguard in this.[55]

Whereas women hesitate to disagree, feeling that disagreeing or challenging might break the rapport they have built up, men see disagreeing in a different light. For men, this is an opportunity to exchange information, to have the satisfaction of a debate, to solidify a relationship rather than to disrupt it.[56]

Women seek to be supportive, and we feel empowered when we can be helpful. We try to discern if we have rightly understood the narrator's question and if we are making our meaning clear: conversation is a way to establish connection. Men like to give information—this process establishes authority. Psychologist H. M. Leet-Pellegrini discovered in her research a "subtle interplay" between gender and expertise: "Women with expertise in the present study generally avoided responding in dominant ways. Particularly in the presence of non-expert men, they responded with even more supportive, collaborative work than usual. Whereas the name of man's game appears to be 'Have I won?' the name of woman's game is 'Have I been sufficiently helpful?'"[57]

In my own experience, however, most male narrators have genuinely wanted to be helpful—whether I was interviewing northeastern bankers or midwestern farmers. Perhaps the definition of the situation of the in-depth interview operates here: the stated and implicitly agreed-on goal requires a helping role on the part of the narrator.

Men in our culture learn as children to control expression of feelings. However, "keeping cool" takes on other dimensions. Jack Sattel argues that the problem "lies not in men's inexpressiveness per se, but in the power and investment men hold as a group in the existing institutional and social framework."[58] Men who are expressive may incur the disrespect of others because they are not maintaining the stance needed to reinforce power. Sattel offers the example of presidential candidate Ed Muskie, who cried in public and afterward was perceived by others as being unfit.[59] Therefore, the interviewer who asks a male narrator about feelings is asking for more than this particular bit of information: she or he is asking the narrator to make himself vulnerable.

But again, my experience has been different; in interviewing men in the later decades of their lives, I found that they wanted to express feelings. I remember asking an eighty-year-old Illinois farmer the standard question in our interview guide, "What do you consider the best time in your life?" He replied with tears in his eyes, "When I was courting Edith, of course." Edith, his wife of fifty years, was in the kitchen; we were recording in the living room, so this was not said for her hearing but for his pleasure in recalling and expressing this. He was not ashamed of his tears. Possibly, because my interviews with men have mostly been with narrators in their seventies and eighties, a developmental need impinges. The published research does not take into account developmental stages. Or another possible explanation is that by agreeing to be interviewed, these narrators are, by definition, willing to talk about their lives, even their feelings.

In conversation, women often establish a quality of sharing. They exchange personal information and expressions of feeling as a way of creating a friendship bond.[60] There is not as much exchange of personal information in the formal interview situation because the narrator does most of the talking, but often an affinity between a woman interviewer and a woman narrator develops. This affinity may also develop between an empathic man interviewing and a narrator of either gender.

Women are pleased when the other person expresses interest in the routines of daily life. Men prefer to talk about politics or sports or intellectual subjects and may find "homey" topics inappropriate or boring. They feel most comfortable talking about personal topics in the abstract.[61]

What can the interviewer learn from this research on gender and communication? Although some of it may not be applicable to the formal interview situation, interviewers have experienced aspects of these research findings while interviewing. Certainly, research findings can suggest to us things to watch out for. Men interviewing can note and learn from the ways that women establish an ambiance of thinking things through together. They can soften the challenging stance of questioning. Both men and women as interviewers need to introduce the project as an opportunity for a collaboration in a mutually interesting endeavor. Both men and women may sense some jockeying for status in their interviews with men; the conversation may become a competitive situation. The interviewer should be careful to stop and in a friendly way define again the interview as "teamwork" and express appreciation for the narrator's contribution.

A male narrator may tend to talk down to a female interviewer; and a male interviewer may unconsciously talk down to a female narrator. A male interviewer, by acquainting himself with the research literature on gender and communication, becomes aware of this and changes his attitude. A woman interviewing can establish her own credentials and knowledge of the topic and thus prove her competence. But in the end, we women may have to work on seeing male condescension more as the result of societal influence than individual arrogance.

Since men may be uncomfortable about expressing or hearing talk about feelings, interviewers questioning men about feelings must take this into account. A sensitive interviewer listening to a male narrator talk about personal topics or domestic topics can be patient if the narrator is having trouble dealing with these. And women and men should maintain eye contact and nod to show interest. But women must be wary of overlap. And the interviewer should be watchful in expressing empathy—if the male narrator shows annoyance, he may be perceiving this as condescension. Generally, women like to be helpful, and this may carry over to the formal interview situation; men like to give information, and this may contribute to moving the interview along.

Sexual Attraction

Still another influence that may intrude is sexual attraction. I am reminded of the occasion when a ninety-two-year-old man patted my knee and asked, "You're not married, are you?" Two anthropology professors recount the story of their graduate student who said that at the end of an interview, the narrator took her hand for a handshake but passionately embraced her instead. She asked, "What did I do wrong?" They said, "Nothing!"[62] The reality is that if you are a good interviewer, you are a good listener and an empathic one. The narrator may indeed feel closer to you emotionally than he or she does to most people because generally good listening skills are rare.

Women have heard the nuances in a conversation that indicate the male narrator is pleased to have a younger woman show interest in him. And probably many men have found that a woman narrator is flattered to have attention. Does this affect the course of the interview? Probably. But the ways that this sexual "chemistry" is manifested vary with the individuals. With tact and sensitivity to the narrator's feelings, take time to define once again your expectations in the interviewing situation: "I appreciate your answering these questions. This will probably take an hour. I will send you a brief paper on the results of the research." In the situation described above of the embrace, thank the narrator for the interview and don't linger. (For a discussion of sexual relationships with informants during a research project, see the chapter on ethics.)

Social Class

In interviewing elites, the interviewer may feel that it is the narrator who is most in command and is just doing the interviewer a favor by granting a half hour of precious time. In interviewing working-class people, the interviewer may sense that the balance of power often is on the interviewer's side because the interviewer seems to know all the questions to ask and, by implication, the answers.

Sometimes the effects of social class can impinge on the interpersonal relationship without the interviewer's being conscious of it. While interviewing mill workers in the village of Carrboro, North Carolina, I asked during a conversation about leisure activities among adolescent women workers, "What did you serve at the card parties?" The narrator replied, "Oh, we picked up hickory nuts and made fudge—we weren't such bad paupers." I knew immediately that somehow the issue of the level of their poverty had crept in. Did I cause that? Was it just inherent in the situation where a middle-class woman was asking a working-class woman about her life? (I had mentioned my own working-class upbringing, but my speech and dress and level of education marked me as middle class.)

When interviewer and narrator come from a different subculture, that fact also encroaches on the interpersonal situation. Rosemary Joyce found that early in her recording of Sarah Penfield's life story, she became aware of the "subtleties of connotative differences in culture—and correspondingly in speech." She told Sarah Penfield she was interested in learning about the "lives of women in our society." Sarah Penfield laughed and replied that she and her sister "weren't social people and never went to parties."[63]

The feeling that "we're alike and we're in this together" was shared by the narrators and me, I thought, when I was interviewing other professional women about my age, coming from the same subculture. But even then, equality was not always the situation, and I would be reminded of this when the narrator would inform me that her husband was "chief of staff" in a local hospital and thus indicate her higher social status. The reality is that the gender of narrator and interviewer may be the same, but an important difference—social status, or color, or age, or level of education—may affect the relationship.

Effects of Ethnicity

Interviewing in your own ethnic group may be easier than interviewing in a different one; but even so, habitual ways of relating that you take for granted, or are not conscious of, need to be examined critically. If you are interviewing in a different ethnic group, learn as much as you can about speech communication characteristics of this group. Researcher Deborah Tannen advises that conversational style is such an important aspect of ethnicity that only by understanding characteristics of the group can you be "on the same wave length."[64] For example, if your narrator is argumentative, you may wonder what is happening and ask yourself, "Have I done something wrong?" But in that ethnic group, argument may be a way of developing sociability. Deborah Schiffrin found in studying conversations in a working-class, eastern European Jewish group in Philadelphia that the speakers frequently debated one another, a process that served to strengthen the bonds among them.[65] Other researchers, such as Mark Hansell and Cherryl Ajirotutu, have demonstrated that someone outside the group can detect different styles in speaking but miss their significance, that sometimes just figuring out whether a conversation is serious or humorous can be a problem.[66] However, Arthur Hansen, based on his interviews with third-generation Americans of Japanese descent, cautions that the interviewer must be aware that characteristics expected of a particular culture may not be present with all individuals and in every situation.[67]

Conclusions about Differences Impinging on the Interview

I conclude that differences may be overcome to some extent, but you as researcher must give attention to the particular age group, gender, social class, race, ethnic group, and subculture. You can look at the interviews critically, asking these questions:

Is there a possibility that the narrator is not comfortable?

How is the difference in age, race, gender, or class operating here to influence responses?

Have I, coming from another subculture, missed the special meaning of a word or failed to understand the significance of an experience so different from my own?

Effects of the Interview on People Close to the Narrator

And last, be aware of how the interviewing process—and resulting publication of the information—affects people close to the narrator. Theodore Rosengarten found out that Ned Cobb's sons had a meeting to decide whether they would allow him to ask their father questions. Rosengarten understood their concerns: "When fathers talk about their lives, they must talk about their children; and what is social history to the outside reader is really Papa talking about family affairs."[68] After the book was published, Rosengarten was surprised by the reaction of Ned Cobb's family. He remarks, "When I went back to see them, they told me straight out: they were deeply offended." He realized that, from their point of view, "Ned had told too much and I lacked the sensitivity to leave it out."[69] Ned Cobb's son Wilbur especially objected because Rosengarten told family business, like his own quarrel with his father, that he believed should not have gone outside the family. Still, a daughter accepted the book because, although the ugliness was there, the "good is so overwhelming."[70]

Folklorist and ethnographer Jan Vansina recalled a student who wanted to study the history of two Russian Jewish immigrant families. The grandmother of one family had been murdered. The other branch knew who the murderer was, and the murderer belonged to their branch. The student delved into the tragedy and laid bare all the facts. She caused irreparable harm to the family members living now.[71] Thus, intervention by means of the tape recorder can change relationships within a family and within a community.

Summary

Let us sum up the disparate ideas discussed in this chapter: The oral history interview can be rewarding for the narrator because there is an opportunity to make sense of events. And in the narrator's understanding anew things that have happened, there is the possibility of a resolution or at least acceptance. In telling the story, the narrator gives her or his life meaning. The narrator may also learn a different perspective from the interviewer that might be helpful. These positive effects are possible if the interviewer conveys a noncritical listening attitude and respect.

The interviewer has an opportunity to expand her or his knowledge and understanding of a different world of experience. The interviewer learns about himself or herself as the interviews go on because, as Cottle says, we watch ourselves as much as we watch others.

In the interpersonal relationship of the oral history interview, there is the danger of role confusion. The interviewer must keep in mind that a professional relationship is not a friendship and make that clear, if need be, to the narrator. When the interviewer has a negative reaction to what the narrator is saying or is distracted by some interpersonal chemistry, he or she must consciously keep in mind the purpose of the interview.

Interpersonal relationships are affected by age, race, gender, social class, status, ethnicity, and subculture. Generally, there is more open communication when age, gender, class, and race are the same, but in any interviewing situation the interviewer must be conscious of the ways in which these basic social attributes impinge. Sensitivity in interpersonal relations and respect create the climate most conducive to a productive interview.

In our culture, behaviors for men and women in conversation are learned in the early socialization process and are maintained in a society where men expect to assert power. The interviewer must be watchful of the possible effects of gender on the communication process in the formal interview. Ethnicity also impinges: awareness of conversational style in the particular ethnic group you are interviewing can make puzzling situations understandable.

Recommended Reading

Effects of Interviewing on Interviewer and Narrator

Cotteril, Pamela. "Interviewing Women: Issues of Friendship, Vulnerability, and Power." *Women's Studies International Forum* 15, nos. 5–6 (1992): 593–606. In this thoughtful, candid discussion on feminist values applied to specific interviewing situations, Cotteril, a sociologist, argues that "interviews are fluid encounters where balances shift" and that interviewers and narrators are all vulnerable. Although she refers to women interviewing women, there is much to learn from this article about interpersonal relationships, in general, in the interview.

Cottle, Thomas J. "The Life Study: On Mutual Recognition and the Subjective Inquiry." *Urban Life and Culture* 2 (1973): 344–60. This is a beautifully written, insightful essay on interpersonal relationships in the interviewing situation.

Daniels, Arlene. "Self-Deception and Self-Discovery in Field Work." *Qualitative Sociology* 6, no. 3 (1983): 195–214. Daniels presents a candid account of her own experiences as an interviewer—amusing, fascinating, and informative.

DiLuzio, Linda, and Harry Hiller. "The Interviewee and the Research Interview: Analysing a Neglected Dimension in Research." *Canadian Review of Sociology and Anthropology* 41, no. 1 (February 2004): 1–26. Authors use their research on internal migrants in Canada to study reactions of narrators to the interviewing process. Extensive bibliography in social science literature included, most of it on moving, but also some items of interest to oral historians.

Echevarria-Howe, Lynn. "Reflections from the Participants: The Process and Product of Life History Work." *Oral History* 23, no. 2 (Autumn 1995): 40–46. Account of in-depth interviewing by a white woman with two black women in Canada. Striking excerpts and insightful analysis.

Grele, Ronald, Studs Terkel, Jan Vansina, Alice Kessler Harris, Denis Tedlock, and Saul Benison. "It's Not the Song, It's the Singing." In *Envelopes of Sound: The Art of Oral History*, 2nd rev. ed., ed. Ronald Grele, 50–105. Chicago: Precedent Publishers, 1985. In this article, veteran interviewers discuss the effects of interviewing on themselves. This roundtable discussion was recorded for radio station WFMT in Chicago, April 13, 1973.

James, Daniel. *Doña María's Story: Life History, Memory, and Political Identity.* Durham, NC: Duke University Press, 2000. Excellent discussion on listening with empathy. Illuminating on interviewer–narrator interaction. See especially the chapter "Listening in the Cold."

Langness, L. L., and Gelya, Frank. *Lives: An Anthropological Approach to Biography.* Novato, CA: Chandler & Sharp, 1981. Especially helpful in this book is the discussion of transference and countertransference in the interview situation and the effects of researcher intervention.

Olney, James. "Autobiography and the Cultural Moment: A Thematic, Historical, and Bibliographical Introduction." In *Autobiography: Essays Theoretical and Critical*, ed. James Olney, 3–27. Princeton, NJ: Princeton University Press, 1980. This is an excellent introduction to autobiographical discourse.

Pang, Alex Soojung-Kim. "Oral History and the History of Science: A Review Essay with Speculations." *International Journal of Oral History* 10 (November 1989): 270–85. This article discusses, among other topics, responses of scientific elites to the interview situation.

Phoenix, Ann. "Practising Feminist Research: The Intersection of Gender and 'Race' in the Research Process." In *Researching Women's Lives from a Feminist Perspective*, ed. Mary Maynard and June Purvis, 49–71. London: Taylor and Francis, 1994. Phoenix uses her own experiences as a black woman interviewing white and black women in Britain to illustrate how negotiation between interviewer and narrator is affected by gender, race, and social class. Insightful and impressive article.

Plummer, Ken. *Documents of Life.* Contemporary Social Research Series, ed. M. Bulmer, 7. London: Allen & Unwin, 1983. This is a sensitive approach to interpersonal relationships in the interview but especially to the struggle within the narrator as he or she composes the self-story.

Popular Memory Group. "Popular Memory: Theory, Politics, and Method." In *Making Histories: Studies in History Writing and Politics*, ed. Richard Johnson et al. Birmingham, UK: University of Birmingham Center of Contemporary Cultural Studies, 1982. This is a serious search into the possibilities of exploitation of narrators by interviewers.

Reay, Diane. "Insider Perspectives or Stealing the Words out of Women's Mouths: Interpretations in the Research Process." *Feminist Review*, no. 53 (Summer 1996):

57–73. Reay, a British sociologist, takes a searching look at how the interviewer's social class impinges on the interviewing and on interpretation. A revealing, candid essay.

Rickard, Wendy. "Oral History—'More Dangerous Than Therapy'? Interviewees' Reflections on Recording Traumatic or Taboo Issues." *Oral History* 26, no. 2 (1998): 34–48. Presentation of a discussion of four narrators about their reflections on the interviews in Rickard's project. Well-reasoned conclusions by author.

Yow, Valerie. "'Do I Like Them Too Much?' Effects of the Oral History Interview on the Interviewer and Vice-Versa." *Oral History Review* 24, no. 1 (Summer 1997): 55–79. Article describes historical developments in the social sciences that defined a new paradigm whereby the former emphasis on objectivity was discarded for an emphasis on acknowledgment of subjectivity in the interviewing process. Ways that both interviewer and narrator may be affected are discussed.

Gender and Ethnicity Impinging on the Interview Situation

Ardener, Shirley. "Gender Orientations in Fieldwork." In *Ethnographic Research: A Guide to General Conduct*, ed. R. F. Ellen, 118–29. London: Academic Press, 1984. This article discusses the influence of gender on the way researchers are perceived and on the ways they gather and analyze data.

Bennett, Adrian. "Interruptions and the Interpretation of Conversation." *Discourse Processes* 4, no. 2 (1981): 171–88. The author analyzes different kinds of interruptions.

Hansen, Arthur A. "A Riot of Voices: Racial and Ethnic Variables in Interactive Oral History Interviewing." In *Interactive Oral History Interviewing*, ed. Eva M. McMahan and Kim Lacy Rogers, 107–39. Hillsdale, NJ: Lawrence Erlbaum, 1994. Hansen uses his interviews with Nikkei (Americans of Japanese ancestry) to illustrate the necessity of being sensitive to the influence of stereotypes on the interviewer–narrator relationship, but also taking notice of the individual and the situation. He concludes that "those of us studying such (ethnic) communities would have to attend to age, generational, class, gender, and ideological divisions within them if we wanted to gain a more complex sense of past reality and avoid the charge of racism" (p. 136).

Henley, Nancy, and Cheris Kramarae. "Gender, Power, and Miscommunication." In *"Miscommunication" and Problematic Talk*, ed. Nikolas Coupland, Howard Giles, and John M. Wiemann, 18–43. Newbury Park, CA: Sage, 1991. This is a thorough review of theories of male–female miscommunication.

Lakoff, Robin. *Language and Woman's Place*. New York: Harper & Row, 1975. This early, widely read book on gender and communication brought together many research studies and contributed insights that inspired much subsequent research.

Leet-Pellegrini, H. M. "Conversational Dominance as a Function of Gender and Expertise." In *Language: Social Psychological Perspectives*, ed. Howard Giles, W. Peter Robinson, and Philip M. Smith, 97–104. Oxford: Pergamon, 1980. The author contrasts the way men use expertise to gain power with the way women use expertise.

Maltz, Daniel N., and Ruth A. Borker. "A Cultural Approach to Male-Female Miscommunication." In *Language and Social Identity*, ed. John J. Gumperz, 196–216. Cambridge: Cambridge University Press, 1982. This article summarizes research on this topic and integrates it to draw conclusions.

Sattel, Jack W. "Men, Inexpressiveness, and Power." In *Language, Gender, and Society*, ed. Barrie Thorne, Cheris Kramarae, and Nancy Henley, 119–24. Rowley, MA: Newbury House, 1983. Author argues that men's conversational style, although learned in early childhood, is maintained as a way of asserting power.

Schiffrin, Deborah. "Jewish Argument as Sociability." *Language in Society* 13, no. 3 (1984): 311–35. Speakers in this subculture may frequently disagree with each other, but this is a form of talk and social interaction that actually increases solidarity.

Tannen, Deborah. "Ethnic Style in Male-Female Conversation." In *Language and Social Identity*, ed. John J. Gumperz, 217–31. Cambridge: Cambridge University Press, 1982. The author's interesting observations stress that the "sharing of conversational strategies" creates satisfaction, a "sense of being understood."

———. *You Just Don't Understand: Women and Men in Conversation* (New York: William Morrow, 1990). The author draws on her own research as well as that of others in the fields of communication and gender studies. Popular and readable, but based solidly on research, this is important reading for any interviewer.

Zimmerman, Don H., and Candace West. "Sex Roles, Interruptions and Silences in Conversation." In *Language and Sex: Difference and Dominance*, ed. Barrie Thorne and Nancy Henley, 105–29. Rowley, MA: Newbury House, 1975. Discussion of "striking asymmetries between men and women with respect to patterns of interruption, silence, and support for partner in the development of topics."

Feminist Theory on Interpersonal Relationships in Interviewing

Feminist scholars have raised questions about the nature of interpersonal relationships in fieldwork: an understanding of this dialogue is essential to an understanding of current theory and practice. See below some of the articles that I have found helpful in understanding this dialogue.

Anderson, Kathryn, Susan Armitage, Dana Jack, and Judith Wittner. "Beginning Where We Are: Feminist Methodology in Oral History." *Oral History Review* 15 (Spring 1987): 102–27.

Forrest, Lesley, and Judy Giles, "Feminist Ethics and Issues in the Production and Use of Life History Research." In *Women's Lives into Print: The Theory, Practice and Writing of Feminist Auto/Biography*, ed. Pauline Pokey, 44–58. New York: St. Martin's, 1999.

Lugones, Maria G., and Elizabeth V. Spelman. "Have We Got a Theory for You!" *Women's Studies International Forum* 6, no. 6 (1983): 577–81.

Patai, Daphne. *Brazilian Women Speak*. Rutgers, NJ: Rutgers University Press, 1988.

———. "U.S. Academics and Third World Women: Is Ethical Research Possible?" In *Women's Words: The Feminist Practice of Oral History*, ed. Sherna Gluck and Daphne Patai, 137–53. New York: Routledge, 1991.

Ribbens, Jane. "Interviewing: An 'Unnatural Situation'?" *Women's Studies International Forum* 12, no. 6 (1989): 579–92.

Stacey, Judith. "Can There Be a Feminist Ethnography?" In *Women's Words: The Feminist Practice of Oral History*, ed. Sherna Gluck and Daphne Patai, 111–19. New York: Routledge, 1991.

Stanley, Liz, and Sue Wise. *Breaking Out: Feminist Consciousness and Feminist Research*. London: Routledge, 1983.

Notes

1. Wendy Rickard, "Oral History—'More Dangerous Than Therapy'? Interviewees' Reflections on Recording Traumatic or Taboo Issues," *Oral History* 26, no. 2 (1998): 34–48; see p. 35.

2. James Olney, *Autobiography: Essays Theoretical and Critical* (Princeton, NJ: Princeton University Press, 1980), 190.

3. Judith Modell, "Stories and Strategies: The Use of Personal Statements," *International Journal of Oral History* 4, no. 1 (February 1983): 5–6.

4. Robert Butler, "The Life Review: An Unrecognized Bonanza," *International Journal of Aging and Human Development* 12, no. 1 (1980–1981): 35–39; see p. 36.

5. Butler, "Life Review," 38.

6. Raymond L. Gorden, *Interviewing: Strategy, Techniques and Tactics*, 4th ed. (Chicago: Dorsey Press, 1987), 27.

7. William Foote Whyte, *Street Corner Society*, 3rd ed. (Chicago: University of Chicago Press, 1981), 365. For a debate on the methodology used for *Street Corner Society*, see "*Street Corner Society* Revisited," special issue, *Journal of Contemporary Ethnography* 21, no. 1 (April 1992). For criticisms from some of Whyte's informants, see W. A. Marianne Boelen, "*Street Corner Society*: Cornerville Revisited," pp. 11–15 in the same special issue.

8. Theodore Rosengarten, "Stepping over Cockleburs: Conversations with Ned Cobb," in *Telling Lives: The Biographer's Art*, ed. Marc Pachter (Washington, DC: New Republic Books, 1979), 115.

9. Lynn Echevarria-Howe, "Reflections from the Participants: The Process and Product of Life History Work," *Oral History* 23, no. 2 (Autumn 1995): 40–46; see p. 42.

10. Ann Oakley, "Interviewing Women: A Contradiction in Terms," in *Doing Feminist Research*, ed. Helen Roberts, 30–61 (London: Routledge, 1981); see p. 50.

11. Kristin M. Langellier and Deanna L. Hall, "Interviewing Women: A Phenomenological Approach to Feminist Communication Research," in *Doing Research on Women's Communication: Perspectives on Theory and Method*, ed. Carol Spitzach, 193–220 (Norwood, NJ: Ablex Publishing, 1989); see p. 207.

12. Oakley, "Interviewing Women," 49.

13. Daniel James, *Doña María's Story: Life History, Memory, and Political Identity* (Durham, NC: Duke University Press, 2000), 130.

14. D. Clark and D. Haldane, *Wedlock* (Cambridge, UK: Polity, 1990), as quoted in Rosalind Edwards, "An Education in Interviewing: Placing the Researcher and the Researched," in *Researching Sensitive Topics*, ed. Claire M. Renzetti and Raymond M. Lee (London: Sage, 1994), 194–95.

15. Mary Stuart, "'And How Was It for You, Mary?': Self, Identity and Meaning for Oral Historians," *Oral History* 21, no. 2 (Autumn 1993): 80–83; see p. 82.

16. Arlene Daniels, "Self-Deception and Self-Discovery in Field Work," *Qualitative Sociology* 6, no. 3 (1983): 195–214; see p. 209.

17. Daniels, "Self-Deception and Self-Discovery in Field Work," 209.

18. Jean Duncombe and Julie Jessop, "'Doing Rapport' and the Ethics of 'Faking Friendship,'" in *Ethics in Qualitative Research*, ed. Melanie Mauthner, Maxine Birch, Julie Jessop, and Tina Miller, 107–22 (London: Sage, 2002); see pp. 118–19.

19. Jane Ribbens, "Interviewing: An 'Unnatural Situation'?" *Women's Studies International Forum* 12, no. 6 (1989): 579–92; see p. 587.

20. Ribbens, "Interviewing: An 'Unnatural Situation'?" 589.

21. Pamela Cotteril, "Interviewing Women: Issues of Friendship, Vulnerability, and Power," *Women's Studies International Forum* 15, nos. 5–6 (1992): 593–606; see p. 599.

22. Wendy Rickard, "Oral History—'More Dangerous Than Therapy'?" 43.

23. Thomas J. Cottle, "The Life Study: On Mutual Recognition and the Subjective Inquiry," *Urban Life and Culture* 2 (1973): 344–60; see p. 351.

24. Daniels, "Self-Deception and Self-Discovery," 204.

25. Sherry Thomas, "Digging beneath the Surface," *Frontiers* 7, no. 1 (1983): 54.

26. Daniels, "Self-Deception and Self-Discovery," 206.

27. Blanca Erazo, "The Stories Our Mothers Tell: Projections of Self in the Stories of Puerto Rican Garment Workers," *Oral History Review* 16, no. 2 (Fall 1988): 23–28; see pp. 26, 28.

28. Daniels, "Self-Deception and Self-Discovery," 202–3.

29. Ann Phoenix, "Practising Feminist Research: The Intersection of Gender and 'Race' in the Research Process," in *Researching Women's Lives from a Feminist Perspective*, ed. Mary Maynard and June Purvis, 49–71 (London: Taylor and Francis, 1994); see p. 57.

30. Phoenix, "Practising Feminist Research," 57.

31. Mary Stuart, "'And How Was It for You, Mary?'" 82.

32. Micaela di Leonardo, *Varieties of Ethnic Experience: Kinship, Class and Gender among California Italian-Americans* (Ithaca, NY: Cornell University Press, 1984), 37.

33. Michael Roper, "Analysing the Analysed: Transference and Countertransference in the Oral History Encounter," *Oral History* 31, no. 2 (Autumn 2003): 20–31; see p. 21.

34. Roper, "Analysing the Analysed," 24.

35. Ronald Grele, "History and the Languages of History in the Oral History Interview: Who Answers Whose Questions and Why?" in *Interactive Oral History Inter-*

viewing, ed. Eva M. McMahan and Kim Lacy Rogers, 1–18 (Hillsdale, NJ: Lawrence Erlbaum, 1994); see p. 14.

36. Valerie Yow, "'Do I Like Them Too Much?' Effects of the Oral History Interview on the Interviewer and Vice-Versa," *Oral History Review* 24, no. 1 (Summer 1997): 55–79; see p. 79.

37. Paul Buhle, letter to author, November 14, 1992.

38. John Blassingame, "Using the Testimony of Ex-Slaves: Approaches and Problems," *Journal of Southern History* 41, no. 4 (November 1975): 487.

39. Blassingame, "Using the Testimony of Ex-Slaves," 489.

40. Phoenix, "Practising Feminist Research," 55.

41. Phoenix, "Practising Feminist Research," 64.

42. For popular presentation of research findings, see Deborah Tannen, *You Just Don't Understand: Women and Men in Conversation* (New York: William Morrow, 1990); Barbara Bate, *Communication and the Sexes* (New York: Harper & Row, 1988); Barbara Westbrook Eakins and R. Gene Eakins, *Sex Differences in Human Communication* (Boston: Houghton Mifflin, 1978). Robin Lakoff argues that men and women come from different cultures in *Language and Woman's Place* (New York: Harper & Row, 1975). See also Daniel N. Maltz and Ruth A. Borker, "A Cultural Approach to Male-Female Miscommunication," in *Language and Social Identity*, ed. John J. Gumperz, 196–216 (Cambridge: Cambridge University Press, 1982); see p. 196.

43. Don H. Zimmerman and Candace West, "Sex Roles, Interruptions and Silences in Conversation," in *Language and Sex: Difference and Dominance*, ed. Barrie Thorne and Nancy Henley, 105–29 (Rowley, MA: Newbury House, 1975); see pp. 116 and 123.

44. Zimmerman and West, "Sex Roles, Interruptions and Silences in Conversation," 117–18, 123.

45. Pamela Fishman, "Interaction: The Work Women Do," in *Language, Gender, and Society*, ed. Barrie Thorne, Cheris Kramarae, and Nancy Henley, 89–101 (Rowley, MA: Newbury House, 1983); Lynette Hirschman, "Male-Female Differences in Conversational Interaction" (paper presented at the annual meeting of the Linguistic Society of America, San Diego, CA, 1973); both as cited in Maltz and Borker, "Cultural Approach to Male-Female Miscommunication," which summarizes research findings on women asking questions; see p. 197.

46. H. M. Leet-Pellegrini, "Conversational Dominance as a Function of Gender and Expertise," in *Language: Social Psychological Perspectives*, ed. Howard Giles, W. Peter Robinson, and Philip M. Smith, 97–104 (Oxford: Pergamon, 1980); see p. 98.

47. Zimmerman and West, "Sex Roles, Interruptions and Silences in Conversation," 125; Leet-Pellegrini, "Conversational Dominance as a Function of Gender and Expertise," 102.

48. Sally Hughes, letter to author, October 19, 1992. See also a discussion by Alex Pang on interviewing scientific elites, "Oral History and the History of Science: A

Review Essay with Speculations," *International Journal of Oral History* 10 (November 1989): 270–85.

49. Leet-Pellegrini, "Conversational Dominance as a Function of Gender and Expertise," 97.

50. Hughes, letter to author, October 19, 1992.

51. Hughes, letter to author, October 19, 1992.

52. See Maltz and Borker, "Cultural Approach to Male-Female Miscommunication," 198, for a summary of the research on men's communication style in cross-sex casual conversation.

53. Maltz and Borker, "Cultural Approach to Male-Female Miscommunication," 202.

54. Research findings summarized by Maltz and Borker, "Cultural Approach to Male-Female Miscommunication," 198.

55. Judith A. Hall, "Gender Differences in Decoding Nonverbal Cues in Conversation," *Psychological Bulletin* 85 (July 1978): 845–57.

56. Maltz and Borker, "Cultural Approach to Male-Female Miscommunication," 198.

57. Leet-Pellegrini, "Conversational Dominance as a Function of Gender and Expertise," 98.

58. Jack W. Sattel, "Men, Inexpressiveness, and Power," in Thorne, Kramarae, and Henley, *Language, Gender, and Society*, 119.

59. Sattel, "Men, Inexpressiveness, and Power," 120.

60. Maltz and Borker, "Cultural Approach to Male-Female Miscommunication," 209–10.

61. For a general discussion of this, see Tannen, *You Just Don't Understand*, 276. For comment on the research, see Sattel, "Men, Inexpressiveness, and Power," 122.

62. Fran Markowitz and Michael Ashkenazi, "Sexuality and Prevarication in the Praxis of Anthropology," in *Sex, Sexuality, and the Anthropologist*, ed. Fran Markowitz and Michael Ashkenazi, 1–21 (Urbana: University of Illinois Press, 1999); see p. 1.

63. Rosemary O. Joyce, *A Woman's Place: The Life History of a Rural Ohio Grandmother* (Columbus: Ohio State University Press, 1983), 27.

64. Deborah Tannen, "Ethnic Style in Male-Female Conversation," in *Language and Social Identity*, ed. John J. Gumperz, 217–31 (Cambridge: Cambridge University Press, 1982); see p. 217.

65. Deborah Schiffrin, "Jewish Argument as Sociability," *Language in Society* 13, no. 3 (1984): 311–25; see p. 317.

66. Mark Hansell and Cherryl Seabrook Ajirotutu, "Negotiating Interpretations in Interethnic Settings," in Gumperz, *Language and Social Identity*, 85–94; see pp. 93–94.

67. Arthur A. Hansen, "A Riot of Voices: Racial and Ethnic Variables in Interactive Oral History Interviewing," in *Interactive Oral History Interviewing*, ed. Eva M. McMahan and Kim Lacy Rogers, 107–39 (Hillsdale, NJ: Lawrence Erlbaum, 1994).

68. Rosengarten, "Stepping over Cockleburs," 115.

69. Rosengarten, "Stepping over Cockleburs," 127.

70. Rosengarten, "Stepping over Cockleburs," 128.

71. Ronald Grele, Studs Terkel, Jan Vansina, Alice Kessler Harris, Dennis Ted-lock, and Saul Benison, "It's Not the Song, It's the Singing," in *Envelopes of Sound: The Art of Oral History*, 2nd rev. ed., ed. Ronald Grele (Chicago: Precedent Publishers, 1985).

CHAPTER SEVEN

Varieties of Oral History Projects: Community Studies

You may choose to interview with the objective of writing an individual's bi-ography or the history of a small group like a family, or you may choose to in-terview with the desired outcome a study of an entire community. Although interviewing techniques will be the same, the overall design of the research will be different for each kind of project. The special problems that biogra-phies and family studies present are discussed in the next two chapters. In this chapter, you will find discussion on studies of communities—a large group of people who share an interest, or participate in the same movement, or town, or particular kind of work, company, or institution, or live in the same place. There is also a concept developed lately, the "community of memory": people who might not have been in the same place or shared the same experience but bond because they are committed to recovering memories of the same historic experience—"memory workers" of the Holocaust, for example.[1]

When this kind of writing is historical in nature and its targeted audience is the community itself, it is referred to as *public history*. Definitions of public history vary. Jill Liddington, writing for the British journal *Oral History*, in-formally surveyed practitioners of public history to find current thinking about it. She found that there is no one answer to the question, What is pub-lic history?[2] Linda Shopes, a historian at the Pennsylvania Historical and Museum Commission, points out that public history can be undertaken ei-ther by scholars/researchers or by local citizens documenting their own his-tory, although often in consultation with scholars.[3] In other words, public history is defined by its audience—the public.

Public history is based on the same research methodology that is used in other research studies—there is no slackening because its aim is to inform the public rather than academicians. Liddington reminds us that public history does not mean "wider-audiences-at-any-cost, but rather an awareness of communicating appropriately to 'the public.'"[4] In the last half century, traditional histories and social studies have often been written for academicians or at least a highly educated lay public. And yet the lines are not so sharply drawn in reality as my statement suggests. The best academic histories have a wider audience than professors and students, and the best public histories have a wider audience, including academics, than the people written about.

Sociologists and political scientists have long had experience with commissioned research in special communities, and anthropologists and historians are becoming more and more involved in such commissioned projects. These commissioned projects may be researched and written under contract in which the commissioners' objectives are spelled out. This situation presents special problems for researchers and writers. Although ethical problems specific to commissioned studies were examined in the chapter on legalities and ethics, some different kinds of pressure are presented in this chapter.

Local history, once slightly denigrated by academicians, is now valued because it inevitably deals with transformation. Studies of communities, focused as they are on a particular group in a particular place, offer the great advantage of allowing us to see in detail how economic and social pressures common to a whole region affect people on a local level. We can understand the impact of nationwide and worldwide events on a community. We can glimpse a culture changing, detect the emergence of an identity shared by many in the community, and learn what meanings people have given places. Joseph Amato, in his book *Rethinking Home: A Case for Writing Local History*, stresses the power of community studies above all to help us understand what it is to be human:

People of every place and time deserve a history. Only local and regional history satisfies the need to remember the most intimate matters, the things of childhood. Local history carries with it the potential to reconstruct our ancestors' everyday lives: the goods, machines, and tools with which they worked, and the groups in which they were raised, in which they matured, celebrated, had ambitions, retired, and resigned themselves to their fates. It recaptures how they experienced the world through their senses: what they thought; how they felt; what they got angry, fought, and cursed about; what they prayed for; what drove them insane; and finally, how they died and were buried.[5]

Tensions in Community Studies

This is an important endeavor you are beginning. Let us say that you have chosen your community and your overarching question and you are ready to start the research process. Working in the traditional ways, scholars begin a project with a tentative list of topics they think are important and delve further into the subject by reading similar research. As scholars researching a community in which many members are living, we would miss an opportunity to learn if we began with a set list of topics. We would start off by telling them what was important in their history or present life instead of learning what they think is important.

The researcher is not just a passive recorder of information, however. He will pick up on topics informers mention that have relevance beyond the particular project. And he will also endeavor to get information on some topics narrators had not given much thought to before the interviewing process. Historian Kenneth Kann, while engaged in an oral history project on the history of the Jewish community in Petaluma, California, found that he and the narrators differed in what they thought was significant in the history:

> Some called attention to a great community political battle in the 1950s, when the right wing kicked the left wing out of the Jewish Community Center, which left the community split in two. But virtually no one called attention to the social consequences of the displacement of family chicken ranches by corporate poultry production in the 1950s. Everyone recalled the economic trauma of that period, but few had considered how the disintegration of their common economic base had greatly accelerated ongoing changes in family and community life. It required an outside perspective to see.[6]

Thus both researcher and community members brought different interests to the project. Kann recorded information about their interests as well as his own. So, the strategy for the oral history project is more of a shared experience than the traditional approach to historical research, where the source is primarily written documents. It can be different from early anthropological and sociological research in which the "subject" was fitted into a category. This is a recognition that in oral history research, members of the community, who are experts on their own experience, are natural resources for planning the topics to be covered. In the ideal collaborative process everybody contributes knowledge and everybody learns something.

Listening to members of the community that is under scrutiny and involving them in the beginning phase of the project is similar to sharing authority in the dialogic process within the interview itself. American historian Michael Frisch first used the term "shared authority" as the title for his collection of essays published in 1990 in which he was concerned specifically with a collaborative process in the interview.[7] I used the concept in the first edition of this book in 1994 to mean sharing the planning process with members of the community to be studied. Since then, the concept of collaboration in community research has been expanded in another direction to mean involving the community in sharing the process of analysis and public presentation. How much community members want to be involved in the ending stage of the project is a question that will be discussed later in this chapter. Especially at this most creative point in the research—the beginning—the input of community members is crucial for the researcher's learning new viewpoints to explore further.

However, as Kenneth Kann demonstrated, tension will probably arise between what researchers want to find and what people in the community want to emphasize. Barbara Franco, director of the Pennsylvania Historical and Museum Commission, describing efforts to bring scholarly research to public museums, says she found that scholars and citizens ask different questions about the past. (And, I think, about the present as well.) She concluded that the public searched for personal meanings, for evidence of values, incidents that would illustrate how ethical beliefs influence actions.[8]

Also, the public has too often been given a superficial account, and so this is what is expected. This so-called study delves into no problems and offends no one—a history where, to use David Henige's phrase, "seldom is heard a discouraging word."[9] But we, as researchers, want to tell the truth as we see it. However, if you are writing with the intention of publishing research on a company or institution for which you work or a town in which you live, you have to think about how much adverse reaction you can stand. Carol Kammen describes the questions she had as she began to write the history of her town:

> Was it a history I could tell? This question really is, do we tell the truth? Do we point to reverses in the past when we know that this is not the public's perception of what local history has been and should be? Do we examine unfavorable episodes along with more positive themes when a community generally expects that its local history will be promotional and make the community feel good about itself? Do we expose prejudice, stupidity, bad judgment, errors, or criminal behavior in the past? They are certainly topics dealt with in our newspapers today, yet I have rarely seen a local history that admits these things could have happened or were commonplace.[10]

It is important to explain your research project to groups in the community. There will be community members who object to including anything negative, as Kammen feared. These are the people who think the study should be "uplifting." Others may assume that the whole project is a waste of money—just some experts bent on confirming what they already know. This is the time for you to do some educating!

John Fox, a historian at Salem State College who was conducting interviews for a history of the Parker Brothers games, delivered talks to the "brown bag luncheons" company employees had. When I began the project on the history of the women's cooperative art gallery, I attended a meeting of the cooperative and explained what I was doing and how I would go about it. When I started working on the hospital history, the editor of the in-house publication wrote a little article about my project. Because I had this kind of advance publicity, people in this work community remembered something about the project and did not regard me as a complete stranger. I talked generally about my goals whenever I could. In the hospital halls, I wore a large button with the words "HISTORY: THE WORLD'S SECOND OLDEST PROFESSION." I explained to whoever would listen how a historian arrives at conclusions.

Tamara Hareven found when she was seeking narrators who had worked in the Amoskeag Mills in Manchester, New Hampshire, that people were puzzled and asked, "Why ask me? My story is not special." They consented to be interviewed because they wanted to help her. She and her coworkers organized a photographic exhibit of the mill buildings and workers. She comments on the difference this made:

> Attitudes changed drastically after the exhibit, "Amoskeag: A Sense of Place, A Way of Life," opened in Manchester. Although this exhibit was primarily architectural and was aimed at professionals and preservationists rather than at the larger public, it evoked an unexpected response from former and current textile workers in the community. It provided the setting for the former workers' public and collective identification with their old work place and it symbolized the historical significance of their work lives. . . . The sudden opportunity to view their own lives as part of a significant historical experience provided a setting for collective identification. Under these circumstances, interviewing ceased to be an isolated individual experience.[11]

The researchers found that the oral histories they recorded were of a different character than those recorded before the exhibit because the narrators were eager to talk to them. The narrators had assumed that everyone looked down on them because they were mill workers. Now they realized that others could be interested and see their work as part of the history of the nation. Hareven concludes, "The exhibit established our credibility as interviewers and laid the foundation for a continuing series of interviews with the same individuals."[12]

In practice, it is not always possible for historians to live in the community they are researching or even to stay long enough to do any preparatory work. Paul Buhle, a social and cultural historian, has interviewed radicals from a wide variety of movements, Yiddish cultural activists to labor-movement veterans to Hollywood screenwriters. His objective has been to record their personal histories for "An Oral History of the American Left," a national project centered at the archives of the Tamiment Library of New York University.

Buhle's narrators were members of a vibrant community or movement thirty to sixty years ago, but many individuals, now in old age, have moved to different parts of the country. Buhle cannot live in the community—often it has been dispersed. It has become a kind of "community of memory." His interviewing time in a specific place is very limited. He must therefore rely on local people the narrators know and trust to spread the word about his work and his purpose for the interviews. He finds a guide-adviser who will personally introduce him. Before the interview begins, he shows the narrator work that he has done, such as his *Encyclopedia of the American Left* and *Oral History of the American Left Guide*. He explains again the project at the Tamiment Library and his reasons for coming to record the life story.[13] Under these conditions, he has depended on others for advance educational work necessary for productive interviews and on the fact that local people have recommended him as a trustworthy person. His own reputation as a scholar of social and cultural history as well as labor history also comes into play here. His narrators know that he is serious and honest but also that they can trust him enough to disagree with his conclusions.

All of this illustrates that the ideal situation cannot always exist for the researcher, but it is still necessary within the real limitations to do some educating in the community at the beginning and all the way through. Knowing the significance of the project, narrators are more likely to take an interest. And once involved, they may want a truthful account to be the result of their work. Historians, ethnographers, sociologists, and anthropologists can stress that they want to help the community by providing information useful to its members.[14] We can create the expectation that this will not be a picture falsified to make it pretty but the closest we can get to the reality of the situation so that the information will be helpful. And then, of course, we must communicate to them our findings.

Informational Interviews

The best way to begin is to become informed as fast as possible by carrying out a literature review to find the relevant materials. One source to consult at the beginning is *Nearby History: Exploring the Past around You* by David E. Kyvig and Myron Marty, who discuss different kinds of sources, not only published materials such as books and newspapers but also unpublished documents such as census records and different kinds of federal records, and oral sources like folklore and oral history. They suggest questions about physical evidence like artifacts, landscapes, and buildings. You can find specific information on articles and books in a bibliographical essay on histories of cities and towns in their chapter titled "Linking the Particular and the Universal."[15] Here are the secondary sources that will alert you to possible topics to explore.

At the same time, conduct informational interviews (no recording, just taking notes) with individuals who have been directly involved in the community. Questions to ask during this first round of informational interviews include:

If you were writing this history, what events would you include?
If you were studying this particular industry here, what kinds of conditions would you describe? What events would you include?
What persons stand out in your mind?
What changes have you seen?
What would you like to learn from this study?
What do you hope such a history would do for you personally? What do you hope it would do for the community?

Return to the written sources (or your notes from the first perusal) and remind yourself of possible developments to explore. Scan your notes from the informational interviews to see what informants have left out. Returning to the informants, mention some of these topics to jog their memories, and see what significance these have for them. Other questions to ask in this second round of informational interviews are more specific and utilitarian:

Who knows a lot about this?
Who would you interview?
Who has kept a scrapbook or a file on this? Who might have kept photographs?
Where would I find the records you mentioned?

At the conclusion of these preliminary talks, compose a list of topics to be covered in the recording process. You have a list of possible narrators. Maybe, with luck, you also have a list of possibilities for locating written documents or published records or photographs not yet deposited in archives.

After this preliminary period in the research has been completed, write a letter to prospective narrators, stating the goals of the project—the community members' and yours. (Although this procedure was discussed in chapter 2, I will briefly review it here.) Explain who you are and give any endorsements from members of the community that you have permission to give. State clearly what will happen to the taped histories and your written research. Then request witnesses' help in the form of taped interviews. Explain why it is important to talk to people who lived through the experience. The letter should end with the notice that you will call.

The exception to this procedure is a situation in which the individuals have reason to distrust anything in print or to feel apprehension about such an invitation. Also, there are potential narrators who might not be able to read. Try to meet a friend of theirs to whom you can explain the project. Ask for help in making your purpose known and for an introduction so that you can explain the research in person.

Composing the Interview Guide

Let us say, then, that you are working on this introductory letter, getting to know people in the community, and preparing the advance educational events discussed above; meanwhile, you are searching the written sources and composing the interview guide. As you do this, ask yourself, "Who is being omitted? What is being neglected?"[16] What do I have uneasy feelings about?

If you are a historian, the questions in the interview guide will be inspired by the community members you have spoken to, your knowledge of similar historical events and of the historiography of the general topic, and your own interests. There will also be an awareness of the tension mentioned earlier about the kind of history you want to write and the kind of history other involved people want. If you are carrying out ethnographic research, the interview guide will reflect your own interests, the new insights gained from informational interviews and from living in the community, knowledge from your particular discipline, and your research purposes and the community's. One objective does not necessarily exclude the other, and you can structure the interview guide to reflect the different objectives. As the interviewing goes on, however, we learn more and evaluate and change the guide.

As you work on the interview guide, do not underestimate the value of informal conversation. True, you should not use specific information of a personal nature or information told to you for your ears only. And you have no release form—unless you send the informant a note and receive permission—but you can use general information and find lines of questioning to pursue. Later you can correct some assumptions you might have made on the basis of guarded recorded testimony. Keep a notebook in which you can, as soon as you get a chance, write down the comments you hear that you suspect will prove valuable and who said them in case you need to follow up later.

What you include in the guide at the beginning of this project is crucial. In his review essay on seven community histories published in the *Oral History Review* in 1989, Michael Gordon discusses the pitfalls of this kind of research. About one project, he writes that the researchers "dangle brief anecdotes before us and aspire to nothing more than regaling local audiences with stories of bygone days."[17] He explains that "public memories that serve individual, institutional, and community needs do not always contribute to historical understanding."[18] Jill Liddington is blunt: "There may be a point at which 'public' becomes 'popularization' becomes distortion."[19]

Make the guide broad enough to include the anecdotes that illustrate values the community wants spotlighted and recount individuals' deeds that set imaginations racing, but also include questions about historical developments that help us understand how past conditions evolved into the present situation. One way to evoke testimony about broad developments is suggested by Linda Shopes, in "Oral History and the Study of Communities: Problems, Paradoxes, and Possibilities": she says we might "conceptualize a community history project around a historical problem or issue rather than a series of life-history interviews." She explains: "A community is formed around the intersections of individual lives: What are the points of connection, tension, or alienation? What historical problem defines the community, and how can this problem be explored through questions to individual narrators?"[20] She poses the question crucial to community study: "How does one address an abstract concept or issue through the medium of lived experience?"[21] Consider, for example, the all-too-common phenomenon of the transformation of farmland into a suburb: What questions would you ask to get information about the impact of this on an individual's life? How would you connect your narrator's experience to the process of suburbanization going on all over the country?[22]

Look at this general question, for example: "How were gender roles changing?" In the guide, phrase the question specifically in terms of the narrator's experience—questions that request details. If you think about one aspect of change in gender roles, a shuffling of household responsibilities, you could ask questions like these: "Before you took a full-time job, what kinds of work did your husband do in the house?" And, "How were decisions about money made?" "After you began your full-time job, who picked the children up from the day-care center? Who cooked the evening meal? Who washed the dishes? Who bathed the children and prepared them for bed? Who washed the clothes and put them in the dryer? Who sorted clothes? Who cleaned the bathroom? How were decisions about money made then?" You might find that nothing changed, but in research a negative answer is significant, too.

Think of other specific ways changes in gender roles can be revealed. As the interviewing project goes on, you learn even more specific questions to ask. After the interviewing phase is completed, study all the interviews, looking for patterns in the answers to these questions. Read again other studies on change in gender roles and compare your findings to other research.

At the same time, we cannot overlook the importance of certain individuals who actively directed the community's course. On the occasion of the city's 350th anniversary celebration, Michael Frisch returned after years to Springfield, Massachusetts, where he had done his doctoral research, *Town into City: Springfield, Massachusetts, and the Meaning of Community, 1840–1880.* He knew that the "city's history requires remaining aware of what is happening outside the local context and understanding how that frame of reference becomes central to local self-definition." But Frisch's experience also led him to notice how certain individuals, occupying a position as leaders, defined for others what was happening, what ought to be done, and what was the "public good."[23]

In any community study, focus on the individual experience, but view your findings in a wider context. Investigate the economic and social changes that may have occurred, but also look for individuals or small groups who articulated what they thought were people's desires and then defined directions. Several general questions such as these can be a step to specific phrasing:

What are the connections between the community and the wider world?
How did this community share in experiences common to much of the nation?
How was this community unique?
Who were the individuals or groups that influenced the community's history?

In *Nearby History*, Kyvig and Marty's bibliographical essay in the chapter "Linking the Particular and the Universal" suggests the following general approaches:

How was modernization brought about?
To what extent was there economic and social mobility?
What were the patterns of migration into and out of the community?
How, and in what ways, was assimilation of immigrants brought about?[24]

Also consider such overarching questions as:

How was family structure changing?
What were the effects of changes in technology on working lives?

Choice of Narrators

The chapter on preparation for the interviewing project presents examples of how to select narrators for a community study. Historians will record the memories of the individuals who held positions of power in the community or company or movement, but they will also need to interview individuals at every level to get a complete view. In interviewing for a history of a college, I recorded the testimony of maintenance workers, retired and current college presidents, secretaries, librarians, professors, students, laboratory assistants, public relations people, members of the board of trustees, bookstore employees, the heads of student life, advisers, and so on. I tried to get information about college life from people with different vantage points, of different levels of power, and with different experiences. A variety of witnesses from different time periods indicated developments over time.

Prioritize when you draw up your final list of narrators. And alert yourself to people you are leaving out. Linda Shopes, in reflecting critically on her history of Baltimore neighborhoods after the passage of twenty years, realized that she and her coresearchers had not interviewed many people who had left the community. When they did interview the few who had left, they avoided questions about why they left and what they did not like about the neighborhood. They did not interview people who might have affected the community negatively—for example, developers and directors of lending institutions and businesses who had left the area. Their choice of narrators made a difference in their findings.[25]

Involving the Community

Shopes warns that unless your project is rooted in the community or linked to important centers of community life, your goals will have little meaning for others. The question is then: How can the researcher involve the community?

When Shopes and her coresearchers first began in 1977 to develop an oral history program at a senior citizens' center in a working-class Baltimore neighborhood, they hoped they could interest the senior citizens in learning oral history methods and becoming interviewers themselves. The researchers also hoped these citizens would help them locate written primary sources within the community. Although they made it clear that their goal was the publication of a popularly written local history, they found that at first people saw them as prying. Many did not share the researchers' enthusiasm for a community history and were not interested in being interviewed or learning to interview. History for them was what had happened to their own families and to the places and individuals significant to them in youth.[26]

Shopes and a graduate student started interviewing. After the interviewing period began, narrators, some of their friends, and a few younger people in the community became interested. Months passed, and Shopes began teaching a class to community residents in the skills of oral history interviewing. She found that they wanted to talk to each other—and especially to share reminiscences—as much as they wanted to talk about interviewing methods. Once they were in the field, although there was an interview guide, these community members as interviewers generally ignored the guide and let the narrators talk about what they wanted to. Not trained as historians, the interviewers lacked the background knowledge that would have enabled them to delve deeper into topics of a wider historical significance than the neighborhood. And neighborhood people interviewing their neighbors did not want to probe their narrators' worldviews; nor were they willing to question their narrators' interpretations of their collective experience.[27]

An important theme that emerged was personal survival; larger social themes were not as prominent. Narrators also wanted to talk about place (what was where and when) and tell stories of heroic efforts to sustain the family.[28] This emphasis on personal survival against odds is similar to the theme in Studs Terkel's collection of oral histories in Hard Times and may be a familiar experience to many oral historians. The researchers found, moreover, that their view of neighborhood was not in accordance with the narrators'. The narrators saw overlapping communities in their family, church, ethnic group, and work partners.[29]

The research team hired community oral historians, people who had grown up there and were still connected in some way and who had shown sensitivity to underlying meanings in testimony. They came to it with few prior assumptions and concentrated on gleaning whatever meanings were in the individual oral history. But the professional historians looked for specific information, quotations, or anecdotes to illustrate their own prior analysis.[30]

Shopes gives a realistic view of the difficulties likely to be encountered, but she does not mean that community history projects fully involving the residents at every stage are impossible. She urges that historians first become closely allied with neighborhood groups and in dialogue with them become sensitive to what interests people about their own history. These interests themselves suggest themes in social history. When the narrator strays from the interview guide and suggests her or his own topics, listen. Coordinate this testimony with the data gathered from traditional sources and compare and use this specific level of information to enhance understanding of the generalizations.

Special Research Situations

Studies of Ethnic Communities

If you are an outsider beginning to research the history of an ethnic community, first learn as much as you can about the culture. And even if you know the language and history, you may still have to build trust, as the following two examples illustrate. As mentioned earlier, Kenneth Kann studied an immigrant community in which three generations still lived in the same place. He comments:

> Nothing happens fast in oral history, especially when the oral historian is not a member of the community he is studying. Communities, and their members, have all kinds of experiences and views that are not for outside ears. The Petaluma Jewish community was particularly interesting to me because it was such an intensely lived collective experience, and because there was unusual continuity over generations, but that also made it less acceptable to me as an outsider. Oral history, if nothing else, requires truckloads of patience and perseverance.[31]

Antonio T. Diaz-Roys, in collecting ethnobiographies of Puerto Rican migrants to the United States, had to learn again the traditional ways of building trust in that community although he was an insider as far as that culture was concerned. He found that, at the beginning, his university affiliation made his respondents cautious lest they say something to devalue themselves in his eyes. He put away his tape recorder. He began to participate in a pattern of visiting: they came to see his family and he visited theirs. Gradually, a relationship of trust developed. He shared his own life story and they began to see why he had become interested in their lives. Only then did he reintroduce the recorder.[32]

And yet, even when all goes well, there is a tension within the interviewer: it is between analyzing, which causes distancing, and feeling guilt because she knows that this intellectual activity has not helped the community much, but at the same time, the project has benefited the researcher. Rina Benmayor, in her introduction to oral histories drawn from an interviewing project with Puerto Ricans in New York, says, "We have tried to be sensitive to the inherent contradictions of our positions as both university researchers and members of the very community we are studying."[33] I can see no way of reducing the tension except by finding a way to use the research to help the community.

In the above examples the interviewer came from the same culture but not the same community. Can the interviewer who is a complete outsider carry out productive interviews? In preparing for the "Oral History of the American Left" project, Paul Buhle learned Yiddish and read the newspapers that had been important to his narrators. He could talk about their past and even some current topics. His narrators recognized his deep interest in their lives, his sympathy for their idealism, and his scholarly expertise. The interviews were successful even though there were political and historical differences on specific issues.[34]

The outsider may also profit from reviewing the research on communication styles particular to a subgroup. Some subgroups have ways of communicating that the outsider may not be attuned to, such as the excessive politeness shown to strangers in a southern home. For example, "Y'all come to see us" should not be taken literally until you know the speaker well enough to judge whether she means it literally. Otherwise, you risk appearing at her front door and putting her in a state of shock. In some ethnic groups, an argumentative style is an indication that the narrator wants to establish a friendship on an equal basis with the newcomer. The outsider can be puzzled by behaviors characteristic of members of an ethnic group. For example, in a study of encounters between Americans and Japanese, hearing an American pay a personal compliment embarrassed the Japanese because they were used to keeping personal references out of a conversation. The Americans interpreted this reaction to the compliment as denial.[35]

The narrator will probably more readily trust the insider, but as Diaz-Roys learned, there is still work for the insider to do in explaining purpose and in becoming sensitive to nuances in personal relationships in the subculture he or she might have forgotten. The outsider can also carry out productive interviews if he or she is knowledgeable about the culture, is appreciative of it, and is able to communicate the purpose of the research (assuming that the purpose is agreeable to the community).

In the chapter on interpersonal relations, discussion showed how social class impinges on the interviewing situation. I remind you now that even if you are of the same ethnic group as the narrator, difference in social class will be felt and possibly expressed in some subtle way. Even if you feel you and the narrator are about on an equal level, keep in mind that we, as interviewers and interpreters of lives, assume a certain one-up position simply because we have intellectual power.

Work Communities

Consider also special problems involved in researching work communities. I base my definition of an occupational community, or work community, on the definitions of theorists such as historian Trevor Lummis and sociologists David Lockwood and Robert Blauner, as well as on my own experience in researching the history of a textile mill, a hospital, a college, and a women's cooperative art gallery. A work community is a group in which members have a strong identification with a specific kind of work, commitment to the same general goals, reliance on a code of behavior specific to the occupation, and a sense of belonging to a special group.[36]

Usually, the researcher steps into these "little worlds" without firsthand information on the occupation and without understanding what it means to the participants to be a part of this work community. As discussed above, the best way to proceed is by asking the group's long-term members what they thought was important in their history and what is important about the present. Often you will have to make a list of technical terms used in that occupation and learn them as quickly as you can.

Find out which individuals who are now active in the occupation as well as those who are retired are considered the most knowledgeable. Charles Morrissey argues that the researcher can best conceptualize a project by interviewing *former* members of the work community—for example, former members of Congress as distinct from current members.[37] They have acquired some perspective with the passage of time, and their jobs are not at stake. In any case, glean as much information about knowledgeable individuals as you can and keep a file folder with information on each. Also, for quick reference, maintain a card file on these potential narrators with addresses and telephone numbers.

Locate the places where people in the occupation go to talk—go there and listen. For the hospital history, I found it was the employee cafeteria. For the history of the women's cooperative art gallery, hanging around after gallery meetings and going to shows enabled me to learn a lot. For the college history, I discovered that the faculty dining hall was filled with stilted conversations of people who were wary of one another and that the "real talk" went on in small intimate groups meeting in private homes. Nevertheless, if I kept the conversation on the past—and far enough back in the past that a frank statement would not threaten their current situation—I could get general ideas about how people regarded a certain event or person. Wherever you go to listen, make sure people know you have an ulterior purpose: to record and write their stories. Let there be no misrepresentation of your role as researcher.

In recording the testimony of people presently employed in a work community, be cognizant of the fact that their jobs are at stake. In a small community, what someone says about someone else finds its way back to that person. Working relationships can be affected or company officials may judge a statement as proof of disloyalty and fire the speaker. As usual, tell the narrator where the tapes will go and who will have access to them. Be aware that when they talk about the near past and the present, they may have to be guarded. Historian Carl Ryant chose an industry in which the ownership was moving out of the community and workers felt a desire to tell their story.[38] This situation eliminated the problem of workers' vulnerability.

Other researchers have not been so unfettered. John Fox, historian at Salem State College, talking about his history of an insurance company, remarked, "I'm certain that in the minds of some employees, I am an agent of the employer."[39] I found in interviewing hospital staff members that they talked frankly and enthusiastically about their research projects or work on the wards but steered clear of comments about the administration. The guardedness of this testimony was revealed by the things they were willing to talk about off tape.

Indeed, most of us are interviewing in ongoing companies or institutions. Respect workers' needs to protect themselves: do not pressure them to reveal information that is potentially harmful to them. If they freely choose to reveal such information, knowing who will have access to the information, then record, of course. They want the information to be made known. In the case of a nursing home's abuse of patients, for example, employees knowingly risked their jobs to expose the violations. That was their choice. They interjected into the interviews their topic, and that was extremely valuable. If a topic is too dangerous for people currently employed to talk about, try to get usable on-tape information from people recently retired from the workplace. But even in this situation, people may be afraid that their frank discussions may put their pensions in jeopardy.[40] In the case of sensitive information, interviewers should offer narrators the option of closing the interview for a certain number of years. Or, at least, close certain parts. As interviewer, you can request permission to discuss the information from the closed paragraphs in a general way so that the identity of the informant cannot be known. (Give this section of your manuscript back to the narrator to see if what you have written is acceptable.)

Along the lines of interviewing workers currently employed, Robert Byington, who studies workers and organization of work, advises seeking endorsement from the union, not management.[41] Of course, this is not possible if you have been hired by management to write the history; but if you are a free agent, it is advisable to seek union approval, knowing that you still have to get permission from management to observe in the plant itself.

Commissioned Research

When you are commissioned to research and write a community study, those who pay the bill have ideas about what kind of history they want for their money. As a scholar, you know what you want, and that is based on your interests and your knowledge of the research literature on the topic. Ideally, the two approaches are similar; in reality, they may be antithetical. Sociologist Maurice Punch, who was commissioned to write the history of a school in Britain, found that even after several revisions of the narrative and analysis, he could not please the school's administrators. He cautions,

> Most sponsors, I would suggest, may find it painful to have their protective myths pierced. This should be borne in mind by inexperienced researchers who might learn the subtle art of not treading too irreverently, and too unnecessarily, on institutional corns. Furthermore, research students might learn that the research process from original aim to successful publication is not always a harmonious progression but can be beset with fieldwork difficulties and with struggles to have the findings accepted.[42]

When Carl Ryant, the late oral historian at the University of Louisville, was commissioned to write the history of the L&N Railroad, he was determined to record witnesses at every level in that work community. In an interview for Australian public radio, he explained,

We wanted to know how the change had taken place from passenger to freight, what had happened when steam engines disappeared and diesel engines came in their place, what it was like if you were a minority on a railroad (and in America most of the people who had what we would have called menial jobs, the porters, the workers in the dining cars, were Blacks). And we wanted to know what happened to women. . . . The railroad, I think, were a little suspicious of this. They never said no but they could not quite understand why we wanted to deal with such specific groups, whereas, they would have preferred us to talk only about nostalgic things, what the station was like.[43]

When Ryant asked for pictures, the railroad executives sent him pictures of past presidents. He replied, "This is very nice but I'd like pictures of Blacks and women working in the cars." They said, "We'll send them to you, but why do you want them?" He answered, "This illustrates a theme I want to deal with." He convinced them that that was part of the story too.[44]

In the preface to the history of a hospital community, I wrote that no effort had been made to gloss over mistakes, that it was by trying to succeed and failing that creative solutions were arrived at. One psychiatrist, important in the administration, owning veto power over the project, wrote in the margin of the manuscript that he rejected that approach as destructive. He had some objections on specific points also. I looked at those places in the manuscript and agreed with him that improvements in wording could be made. I made changes in the wording without altering the meaning. I did not delete accounts of troubles, however, and continued to argue the value of a credible history based on the testimony of people who had lived it. Actually another man, even higher in the institution's bureaucracy, prevented publication at that time, and it was only after he was fired several years later that the history was published.

Sometimes you fear that the book will never see daylight (as I did with the hospital history) if you are completely honest. You suspect that all your labor will be of no use to anyone. Still, even with these second thoughts, we face the fact that a less-than-honest account of the research findings profits no one. Often, however, it is possible to avoid trouble caused by the commissioners' desire to protect their image if you educate the commissioners about the difference between a public relations document and a serious research study. David Lewis and Wesley Newton, who wrote *Delta: The History of an Airline*, say that no company has gone through a long history without making mistakes. Not to confront and evaluate the effects of the mistakes is to produce a "puff job" that enlightens no one. They advise oral historians—at the very beginning—to make sure corporate executives understand this "risk of laying bare [the company's] past to objective scholarship."[45] Ryant's experience shows how once the commissioners understand that these goals will be helpful to them, they may see that obscuring the truth will defeat this purpose. I guess my experience shows that you stick to your guns and take the consequences—you survive.

Another way to get help educating the public about the purposes of the research and the nature of ethnographic research is to have an advisory committee or board. Ann Moyall, author of *Clear across Australia*, the history of Telecom Australia, the national telecommunications company, had a board set up. She insisted that the members include not only Telecom executives but also a professor of political theory who was an expert on communications and a historian respected for his work on technology. She also included an editor employed by an external organization. The board proved to be a great help. When one Telecom executive took chapters and rewrote them according to his view of history, the board was able to persuade Telecom that this would not produce the "scholarly and popular history" the company desired.[46]

An advisory committee as a group of people with different kinds of expertise can give various kinds of help. Jeremy Brecher says that his community and labor advisory panel during a research project on brass workers helped locate interviewees and find photographs and documents. They publicized the project and encouraged the research.[47]

Although board members can become valuable resources in educating the public, putting the researcher in contact with narrators, and consulting in the design of the research project, some caution is advised. In his *Oral History Program Manual*, William Moss suggests that the researcher must make it clear that the advisers' role should be to "advise and facilitate, not direct or obstruct."[48] The problem is that a much-involved board can take over the project.

Presentation of Findings

Ultimately, in researching and writing public history our purpose is to help people look at their past again and learn something valuable to them in the present. And for us, as researchers and human beings, we learn about our collective past and present. This chapter has dealt with the contributions of community members in the formulation of the project, the education of the community about the project so that differing goals are understood, and the narrators' interjection of topics during the interviewing process. Now we turn to the last stage: public presentation of information. Informing the public is of crucial importance—a community study is not complete without it. And public presentation may be your greatest challenge and a stimulus to your imagination and creativity. In this stage, the question arises: to what extent can the ideal of collaboration between researcher and community members be implemented? Two studies that focused on a collaborative process in interpretation and presentation are presented below.

Daniel Kerr founded a group to provide food for people living on the streets of Cleveland, Ohio, but he soon became interested in investigating the causes of such destitution. He wanted to take a different approach in his research than earlier studies of homelessness had taken, based as they were on observations by social service agency employees and academic researchers. He began the Cleveland Homeless Oral History Project with the aim of making the research a collaborative project with homeless people. He brought his mini-cassette tape recorder to the picnics his group sponsored for the homeless and began to focus on the life stories of four men. When he discovered that a public square had electrical outlets, he decided to bring a video camera and videotape the interviews there.

The next week, he showed the video on a television and VCR he brought to the square. The narrators wanted to have the interviews broadcast to other audiences of homeless people, and Kerr arranged to have one-hour interviews broadcast on the local college radio station each week. He then organized weekly workshops at a drop-in center to discuss this videotaped information. From these discussions a collective analysis emerged. He sums up the themes of these interviews as the narrators pinpointed them: "Every which way you look, people other than the homeless are profiting off of the institution of homelessness—be it the real estate developers, downtown leisure and retail business interests, the temp agencies, the prison industries, or the shelter providers."[49] Participants in these workshops went on to formulate ways to bring about change in the system.

In a project that resulted in a different kind of public performance, Alicia Rouverol interviewed prison inmates. One of her goals was to engage "our interviewees in the analysis of the interviews we generate and/or the creation of any products drawn from those interviews."[50] She uses the term "collaborative research" to describe her work, saying that it is close to "shared authority" but not the same process.[51] The prison where Rouverol's narrators lived is the Brown Creek Correctional Institution, an all-male, medium-security institution in Anson County, North Carolina. In 1996, while she was conducting an oral history workshop in the prison, the inmates expressed a desire to present the life histories to at-risk youth. They used the stories they recorded to create together a script for a play, "Leaves of Magnolia." She writes, "As we moved from interviewing to analysis of the transcripts and finally to the creation of the script, the inmates began increasingly to take ownership of the project, asserting their authority as experts of their own narratives."[52] They did indeed present their play to outside audiences.

However, convincing prison authorities at each step that the prisoners could undertake such a project was difficult, indeed, and sometimes controversy within the group of inmates was an obstacle. Rouverol describes how when disagreement arose, dialogue was essential if the project was to continue, and both interviewer and narrators learned from this dialogue. However, in giving such a brief synopsis of these projects, I have omitted the tremendous difficulties both researchers faced because of the research settings.

Rouverol acknowledges the responsibility she felt both toward fellow academics and toward the participants—each audience has its own expectations—and so the project had other forms of presentation, including her published academic article. Both of these creative, imaginative projects suggest that sharing decision-making authority in interpretation and public presentation can be appropriate, even under extremely difficult circumstances. But there are also projects in which such a high level of participation of all involved may not be possible or desirable on the part of the narrators or the interviewer. There may be times when the researcher cannot, in good conscience, present the narrators' viewpoints uncritically. Linda Shopes considers it impossible (or utter idiocy) to involve narrators in interpretation and presentation in such studies as Kathleen Blee's book based on interviews with Ku Klux Klan women.[53] Shopes concludes, "Collaboration is a responsible, challenging, and deeply humane ideal for some oral history work, but in certain kinds of projects, beyond a basic respect for the dignity of all persons, it seems not an appropriate goal."[54]

Looking Deeply and Critically at Your Collection of Oral Histories of a Community

Read your interviews over again and again, reaching for the sense of something important underlying the words of these oral histories. The rich meanings come to us only in this way. For example, Michael Frisch, in studying closely his interviews, noted the "emergence of the overarching, abstract notion of 'public interest' of Springfield, that is, a feeling shared by most citizens that there is a general good that takes precedence over private interests."[55] He tried to figure out what the community *imagined* as its limits, and then he could discern the effects of this imagining on its course.

I look for anecdotes, jokes, and repeated stories to see what meanings lie beneath the surface. In a city near mine, Durham, there is an often-told joke about a happy bachelor, heir to the Duke family's tobacco-processing fortune, who had shown no interest in marrying and producing a scion in the next generation but was much occupied with a woman of interesting reputation. The family was troubled. A family member told him, "Buck, she's slept with every man in town." Buck thought about this, worked his jaw to shift his cigar to the side of his mouth, and replied, "Hell, Durham is not such a big place." This is the self-deprecating, yet defiant, humor characteristic of the region—"Durham is *not* the Paris of the South," my Durham friends tell me, laughing. But also there is conveyed in this joke a sense of comfort in having one's being in a small town, even a sense of pride.

But I will not just dangle the anecdotes, as Michael Gordon warned. If I had undertaken a formal interviewing project in Durham, I would try to discern, reading carefully all the transcripts, a pattern in statements dealing with place. I would listen again to those statements in the tape for clues to feelings. I would ruminate over possible underlying meanings, especially suggestions of elements of shared identity and shared values and shared attitudes. And I would ponder what the jokes and anecdotes intimated, such as attitudes about the proper place in the community for woman's sexuality and yet fear of its wide possibilities that the joke here hints at.

Then I would try to figure out what this testimony omitted or glossed over. The historical accounts of Durham I have read often obscure the efforts of Durham industries, especially the textile mills and tobacco manufacturers, to defeat unionization. They do not mention the low wages paid to workers, or the long working hours, or the dust, heat, and humidity in the factories. They omit the effects of addiction to cigarette smoking—Liggett and Myers was a major industry there—and fail to mention details such as the fact that the cigarette companies gave a few free cigarettes each day to their hundreds of workers to "hook" them and thereby increase the local market. When I tried to help a friend who had bought a deceased cigarette worker's house (the worker had died of lung disease), we spent days washing the yellow stain off the ceilings and walls and then more time painting with a stain blocker. You can imagine the condition of the people's lungs who worked in the plant for thirty years and smoked. Instead of confronting this, local histories praise the cigarette barons for bringing prosperity to the city.

And I would ask, Whose point of view is represented here? Who has been left out? An oral history study by Dolores Janiewski on workers' lives in Durham, her 1979 dissertation at Duke University, "From Field to Factory: Race, Class, Sex, and the Woman Worker in Durham," does reveal working conditions, and so does an oral history project by students at North Carolina Central University, "Working in Tobacco: An Oral History of Durham's Tobacco Factory Workers."[56] Why are these histories different? The researchers tapped memories of people of a different social class in this city, working people who had not been asked before.

The Importance of Place

Like the research on Durham, community studies are often rooted in a geographic place. Interviewers find that narrators' memories are stimulated by mention of a place and that they anchor a memory to a place. Recent studies of place, its psychological significance especially, compel us to think differently about what a sense of place means in our lives. Kathleen Norris, in *Dakota: A Spiritual Geography*, writes of the North Dakota farm where she lives, "Where I am is a place where the human fabric is worn thin, farms and ranches and little towns scattered over miles of seemingly endless, empty grassland."[57] She searches to find the ways this place affects her thinking.

In *Rethinking Home: A Case for Writing Local History*, Joseph Amato reminds us, "Imprinted on a child's mind, home establishes vocabularies of senses, emotions, images, and metaphors that later express a lifetime's meaning."[58] He goes on to explain that home extends beyond the walls of a house to include the environment, historical era, and the material goods within it.

Dolores Hayden's *The Power of Place: Urban Landscapes as Public History* reveals the way that demolition or preservation of city buildings expresses a political statement: the neighborhoods demolished have been working-class and ethnic. Places preserved as historically significant rarely celebrate women's lives. Researchers of the Holocaust quickly become aware of the significance of absence of place—whole villages have been destroyed—in their narrators' psyches. The power of place, Hayden declares, remains untapped.[59]

Recommended Reading

General Discussion of Community Studies and Public History

Allen, Barbara, and Lynwood Montell. *From Memory to History: Using Oral Sources in Local Historical Research*. Nashville, TN: American Association of State and Local History, 1981. See especially the chapters on uses of oral history, ways to interpret conflicting accounts, and tests for validity in oral sources. The authors are folklorists, and the text is helpful in pointing to ways to handle legend and myth.

Blatti, Jo. "Public History and Oral History." *Journal of American History* 77, no. 2 (1990): 615–25. Author offers a model for public history productions based on oral history. Especially valuable are the criteria she provides for evaluating public presentations.

Baum, Willa. *Oral History for the Local Historical Society.* 3rd ed. Walnut Creek, CA: AltaMira, 1995. Straightforward, informative guide.

Diaz, Rose T., and Andrew B. Russell. "Oral Historians: Community Oral History and the Cooperative Ideal." In *Public History: Essays from the Field*, ed. James Gardner and Peter LaPaglia, 203–16. Among many informative articles in this collection, this is an especially insightful essay.

Frisch, Michael H. *A Shared Authority: Essays on the Craft and Meaning of Oral and Public History.* Albany: State University of New York Press, 1990. See especially "The Memory of History," pp. 15–27, a thoughtful essay on how public history can convey a sense of the past that does not obscure or romanticize but rather enables us to sort out the productive from the nonproductive so that we are able to create a different future than we might have had without this knowledge.

Gerber, David A. "Local and Community History: Some Cautionary Remarks on an Idea Whose Time Has Returned." *History Teacher* 13 (November 1979): 7–30. The author considers an element new in local history in the 1970s: the converging of academic and popular interests. He reviews the questions we ask about ethnicity and suggests goals such as researching local history to analyze "the interaction between various social processes, such as urbanization, industrialization, social mobility, or immigrant assimilation."

Gordon, Michael. "Seeing and Fleeing Ourselves: Local Oral Histories of Communities and Institutions." *Oral History Review* 17, no. 1 (Spring 1989): 117–28. Author provides an excellent review of work published in community history up to the end of the 1980s and suggests questions to ask about community studies.

Grele, Ronald. "Whose Public, Whose History?" *Public Historian* 3 (Winter 1981): 40–48. Grele considers questions raised about public history, "questions that go to the heart of the uses of history in the culture and processes by which historical consciousness is formed and expressed." He gives a brief history of the public history movement and discusses the role that public history may play.

Kammen, Carol, and Norma Prendergast, eds. *Encyclopedia of Local History.* Walnut Creek, CA: AltaMira, 2000. This volume, using the encyclopedia format, offers an excellent brief essay on public history (look under *p*) and other unusual discussions, for example, how local history is researched and regarded in different countries.

Karamanski, Theodore J. "Reflections on Ethics and the Historical Profession." *Public Historian* 21, no. 3 (Summer 1999): 127–34. Succinct, persuasive defense of public history: "All historians face the professional challenge of consciously serving Society" (p. 130).

Kelly, Robert. "Public History: Its Origins, Nature, and Prospects." In *Public History Readings*, ed. Phyllis K. Leffler and Joseph Brent, 111–20. Malabar, FL: Krieger

Publishing, 1992. This is a brief and useful history of the development of public history as a movement in this country.

Kyvig, David E., and Myron A. Marty, *Nearby History: Exploring the Past around You.* 2nd ed. Walnut Creek, CA: AltaMira, 2000. This is an excellent resource for locating written sources as well as suggestions for questions for oral history research. See especially the final chapter, "Linking the Particular and the Universal," which is a bibliographical essay, and look at the useful appendixes, which provide such aids as forms for requesting information from federal agencies and suggestions for using the World Wide Web.

Liddington, Jill. "What Is Public History? Publics and Their Pasts, Meanings and Practices." *Oral History* 30, no. 1 (Spring 2002): 83–93. This is a brilliant, easy-to-read brief tracing of the evolution of public history as a field in the United States, Britain, and Australia, and then a discussion of what "public" means and of the special problems and mission of public history.

Morrissey, Charles. "Public Historians and Oral History: Problems of Concept and Methods." *Public Historian* 2, no. 2 (Winter 1980): 22–29. Morrissey reminds readers that a "public historian is a professional historian, not a court historian" (p. 29).

Samuel, Raphael. "Local History and Oral History." *History Workshop* (Great Britain) 1 (1976): 191–208. This essay by the late outstanding historian Raphael Samuel on the uses of oral history in studying communities is a classic, still provocative and wise. Samuel asks questions about local history that point us in the direction of questioning our assumptions that have influenced what we see in the documents and assumptions based on what conforms to the expectations at the time the document was produced. He critiques different kinds of sources, for example, family papers, landscapes, demographic studies.

Shopes, Linda. "Oral History and the Study of Communities: Problems, Paradoxes, and Possibilities." *Journal of American History* 89, no. 2 (September 2002): 588–98. Author offers definition of community, describes problems of searching for extant collections of oral histories of communities, and offers solutions. She suggests questions to ask about extant collections and discusses the problems of organizing and conducting a community oral history project.

Trask, David, and Robert Pomeroy, eds. *The Craft of Public History.* Westport, CT: Greenwood, 1983. This reference work contains informative articles with excellent bibliographies.

Journals Devoted to Public History

Public Historian: A Journal of Public History. Sponsored by the National Council on Public History. Published by the University of California, Santa Barbara. Four issues per year.

Public History Review. Published annually in Sydney, Australia, by the Professional Historians Association, NSW, Inc. E-mail: cludlow@ozemail.com.au.

Oral History. See the section "Public History." University of Essex, Essex, UK. Published two times per year.

Radical History Review. Published by the Mid-Atlantic Radical Historians' Organization (MARHO) three times per year. Printed and distributed by Duke University Press, Durham, NC. See special section on public history.

Studies of Neighborhoods, Cultural Groups, and Towns, Based on Oral History

Boyer, Sarah. "Rock Hill, South Carolina; San Antonio in the 1920s and 1930s; Gadsen, Alabama." (Review essay.) *Oral History Review* 30, no. 2 (Summer–Fall 2003):143–44. Boyer, a member of the Cambridge Historical Commission, presents a brief critique of three community histories. Very useful for reminders of what *not* to do in this kind of research, especially omission of perspectives from diverse representatives of the community.

Broussard, Albert. "Oral Recollection and the Historical Reconstruction of Black San Francisco, 1915–1940." *Oral History Review* 12 (1984): 63–80. Broussard discusses the ways in which he used oral history to recover the history of a black community in San Francisco, especially to discover leaders and organizations that had been forgotten but were nevertheless pivotal in directing the community's course.

Buckendorf, Madeline, and Laurie Mercier. *Using Oral History in Community History Projects.* OHA Pamphlet Series 4. 1992. A brief guide, especially clearly written, that presents information on all aspects of a community history project. A good secondary source to start with. Send request for copy and information about the cost to Executive Secretary, Oral History Association, Dickinson College, Carlisle, PA.

Diaz-Roys, Antonio T. "Maneuvers and Transformations in Ethnobiographies of Puerto Rican Migrants." *International Journal of Oral History* 4, no. 1 (February 1983): 21–31. This article has excellent suggestions for learning about the targeted culture before undertaking interviews for a project.

Di Leonardo, Micaela. "Oral History as Ethnographic Encounter." *Oral History Review* 15 (Spring 1987): 1–20. This is an account of experiences interviewing in a California Italian American community. The resulting book is *The Varieties of Ethnic Experience: Kinship, Class and Gender among California Italian-Americans* (Ithaca, NY: Cornell University Press, 1984).

Hansen, Arthur. "Oral History, Japanese America, and the Voicing of a Multiplex Community of Memory." (Review essay.) *Oral History Review* 24, no. 1 (Summer 1997): 113–22. This is a review of four books that use oral history to document the history of Japanese American families and communities. Hansen points out the ways each study deals with transmission of community memories and values.

Kann, Kenneth. "Reconstructing the History of a Community." *International Journal of Oral History* 2 (February 1981): 4–12. Kann uses his experience in writing the history of an ethnic community—the Jewish community in Petaluma, California—to illustrate problems and solutions in community studies.

Kerr, Daniel. "'We Know What the Problem Is': Using Oral History to Develop a Collaborative Analysis of Homelessness from the Bottom Up." *Oral History Review*

30, no. 1 (Winter–Spring 2003): 27–45. This article occurs in an issue of the *Oral History Review* that focuses on the concept of shared authority—it is well worth reading the entire issue, articles and commentaries, because all deal with research in special communities.

Myerhoff, Barbara. "Telling One's Story." *Center Magazine* 13 (March 1980): 22–40. The author discusses her work among Jewish retirees in a community center. The book that is based on this research, *Number My Days* (New York: Dutton, 1978), is a gem.

Okihiro, Gary. "Oral History and the Writing of Ethnic History." *Oral History Review* 9 (1981): 27–46. Okihiro raises important questions about the use of oral history research in ethnic communities.

Rouverol, Alicia. "Collaborative Oral History in a Correctional Setting: Promise and Pitfalls." *Oral History Review* 30, no. 1 (Winter–Spring 2003): 61–85. An especially reflective article on handling disagreements and stalemates between interviewer and narrators and between interviewer and institutional authorities during the planning for public presentation of the research.

Serikaku, Laurie R. "Oral History in Ethnic Communities: Widening the Focus." *Oral History Review* 17, no. 1 (Spring 1989): 71–88. This is a very useful article on the ways oral history can inform a study of ethnic communities.

Shopes, Linda. "Oral History and Community Involvement: The Baltimore Neighborhood Heritage Project." In *Presenting the Past: Essays on History and the Public*, ed. Susan Porter Benson, Stephen Brier, and Roy Rosenzweig, 249–63. Philadelphia: Temple University Press, 1986. Shopes, in the context of her specific project, raises questions about researching community history in general, focusing especially on the involvement of the community itself.

Studies of Work Communities and Institutions

Aiken, Katharine. "Working and Living: Women and Mining Communities." (Review essay.) *Oral History Review* 26, no. 1 (Winter–Spring 1999): 119–25. In this review of six books on women in mining communities and on mining cultures, Aiken points out that these books reveal how men and women reinforced gender roles, how the dangerous nature of the work affected all family members, and why unionization was of crucial importance to the mining families.

Beik, Mildred. *The Miners of Windber: The Struggles of New Immigrants for Unionization, 1890–1930.* University Park: Pennsylvania State University Press, 1996. This study of a town dominated by the Berwind-White Coal Company, the site of poverty and desperate efforts to unionize, presents the insights of an excellent scholar and woman who grew up in the town. It is thoroughly documented, with oral history interviews an important part.

Bodnar, John. "Power and Memory in Oral History: Workers and Managers at Studebaker." *Journal of American History* 75 (March 1989): 1201–21. This article discusses the ways workers remembered important events in labor struggles.

Brecher, Jeremy. "A Report on Doing History from Below: The Brass Workers History Project." In Benson, Brier, and Rosenzweig, *Presenting the Past*, 267–77. Strategic plan for involving members of a work community in an oral history project, from introducing the project to presenting results of the research to the public.

Brecher, Jeremy, Jerry Lombardi, and Jan Stackhouse, eds. *Brass Valley: The Story of Working People's Lives and Struggles in an American Industrial Region*. Philadelphia: Temple University Press, 1982. This community study is based on an especially skillful interweaving of text and oral history.

Friedlander, Peter. *The Emergence of a UAW Local, 1936–1939: A Study in Class and Culture*. Pittsburgh: University of Pittsburgh Press, 1975. Friedlander discusses the value of repeated in-depth interviews with a principal narrator.

Gittens, Diana. *Madness in Its Place: Narratives of Severalls Hospital, 1913–1997*. London: Routledge, 1998. Gittens conducted sixty-five in-depth interviews with a wide range of people who worked, lived, or were confined in this mental hospital. She presents a fascinating study of this community and because of her reliance on oral history, offers some surprising observations.

Hareven, Tamara. "The Search for Generational Memory." In *Public History Readings*, ed. Phyllis Leffler and Joseph Brent, 270–83. Malabar, FL: Krieger Publishing, 1992. This is an account of an interesting research strategy in a project among former workers in the Amoskeag Mills in Manchester, New Hampshire.

Honey, Michael Keith. *Black Workers Remember: An Oral History of Segregation, Unionism and the Freedom Struggle*. Berkeley: University of California Press, 1999. This book is based on interviews with African American union members in Memphis, Tennessee, at the Firestone and International Harvester plants.

Kelen, Leslie G., and Eileen Hallet Stone. *Missing Stories: An Oral History of Ethnic and Minority Groups in Utah*. Salt Lake City: University of Utah Press, 1997. These ethnic groups are represented, although most narrators are American born: Ute people, African Americans, Jews, Chinese, Italians, Greeks, Mexicans. The cultural hegemony of the Mormon Church shows even in this history that is focused on working lives in ethnic communities.

Lummis, Trevor. "Occupational Community of East Anglian Fishermen." *British Journal of Sociology* 28, no. 1 (March 1977): 51–77. The author discusses the importance of a selection of narrators that includes a broad range of people who speak about the experience, including those who chose not to fish.

Riney, Scott. "Education by Hardship: Native American Boarding Schools in the United States and Canada." (Review essay.) *Oral History Review* 24, no. 2 (Winter 1997): 117–23. Riney reviews three books that use oral history to examine the historical situations of white-run boarding schools for Native Americans in the United States and Canada. Their purpose was to enforce conformity to the dominant culture. Oral histories from these enforced communities reveal strategies of resistance and accommodation.

Guides for Teaching Local History, Using Oral History Projects

Crothers, A. Glenn. "Bringing History to Life: Oral History, Community Research, and Multiple Levels of Learning." *Journal of American History* 88, no. 4 (2002):

1446–51. Crothers offers a way to organize a college survey course on American history by using oral history projects. Upperclassmen experienced in oral history interviewing act as mentors to the student researchers.

Lee, Charles R., and Kathryn L. Nasstrom, eds. "Practice and Pedagogy: Oral History in the Classroom." Special issue, *Oral History Review* 25, nos. 1–2 (Summer–Fall 1998). While not all the articles are focused on community history, general strategies for using oral history in classroom teaching are useful.

Metcalf, Fay D., and Matthew T. Downey. *Using Local History in the Classroom.* Nashville, TN: American Association for State and Local History, 1982. This work is brief on oral history, but the information on other primary sources is helpful.

Wood, Linda P. *Oral History Projects in Your Classroom.* Pamphlet in the series published by the Oral History Association, 1992. (To order, contact the Oral History Association, Dickinson College, P.O. Box 1773, Carlisle, PA 17013-2896, or e-mail: oha@dickinson.edu.) Useful suggestions for introducing and developing an oral history project in a secondary school classroom. Ideas for project topics, as well as useful forms, such as a project evaluation form, are offered.

Notes

1. Iwona Irwin-Zarecka, *Frames of Remembrance: The Dynamics of Collective Memory* (New Brunswick, NJ: Transaction Publishers, 1994), 56. Much of the book concerns a community of rememberers, the "memory workers" of the Holocaust.

2. Jill Liddington, "What Is Public History? Publics and Their Pasts, Meanings and Practices," *Oral History* 30, no. 1 (Spring 2002): 83–93; see p. 89.

3. Linda Shopes, "Oral History and the Study of Communities: Problems, Paradoxes, and Possibilities," *Journal of American History* 89, no. 2 (September 2002): 588–98; see p. 588.

4. Liddington, "What Is Public History?" 90.

5. Joseph A. Amato, *Rethinking Home: A Case for Writing Local History* (Berkeley: University of California Press, 2002), 3.

6. Kenneth Kann, "Reconstructing the History of a Community," *International Journal of Oral History* 2 (February 1981): 4–12; see p. 8.

7. Michael Frisch, *A Shared Authority: Essays on the Craft and Meaning of Oral and Public History* (Albany: State University of New York Press, 1990), xxii.

8. Barbara Franco, "Doing History in Public: Balancing Historical Fact with Public Meaning," *Perspectives*, May–June 1995, 5–8; see p. 6; Roy Rosenzweig and David Thelen, eds., *The Presence of the Past: Popular Uses of History in American Life* (New York: Columbia University Press, 1998) presents discussions on the general public's ideas about what history should be.

9. David Henige, "Where Seldom Is Heard a Discouraging Word: Method in Oral History," *Oral History Review* 14 (1986): 35–42.

10. Carol Kammen, *On Doing Local History: Reflections on What Local Historians Do, Why, and What It Means* (Walnut Creek, CA: AltaMira, 2000), 86.

11. Tamara Hareven, "The Search for Generational Memory," in *Public History Readings*, ed. Phyllis K. Leffler and Joseph Brent, 270–83 (Malabar, FL: Krieger Publishing, 1992); see pp. 277–78.

12. Hareven, "Search for Generational Memory," 277–78.

13. Paul Buhle, letter to author, November 14, 1992.

14. R. M. Keesing, "Anthropology in Melanesia: Retrospect and Prospect," in *The Politics of Anthropology: From Colonialism and Sexism toward a View from Below*, ed. G. Huizer and B. Mannheim, 276–77 (The Hague: Mouton, 1979), as quoted in R. F. Ellen, ed., *Ethnographic Research: A Guide to General Conduct* (London: Academic Press, 1984), 137.

15. David E. Kyvig and Myron A. Marty, *Nearby History: Exploring the Past around You*, 2nd ed. (Walnut Creek, CA: AltaMira, 2000).

16. Morrissey, manuscript notation, March 11, 1993.

17. Michael Gordon, "Seeing and Fleeing Ourselves: Local Oral Histories of Communities and Institutions," *Oral History Review* 17, no. 1 (Spring 1989): 117–28; see p. 118.

18. Gordon, "Seeing and Fleeing Ourselves," 119.

19. Liddington, "What Is Public History?" 90.

20. Shopes, "Oral History and the Study of Communities," 596.

21. Shopes, "Oral History and the Study of Communities," 596.

22. Shopes, "Oral History and the Study of Communities," 596.

23. Frisch, *Shared Authority*, 229.

24. Kyvig and Marty, *Nearby History*, 216–38.

25. Shopes, "Oral History and the Study of Communities," 590.

26. Linda Shopes, "Oral History and Community Involvement: The Baltimore Neighborhood Heritage Project," in *Presenting the Past: Essays on History and the Public*, ed. Susan Porter Benson, Stephen Brier, and Roy Rozenzweig, 249–63 (Philadelphia: Temple University Press, 1986); see p. 253.

27. Shopes, "Oral History and Community Involvement," 253–54.

28. Shopes, "Oral History and Community Involvement," 252.

29. Shopes, "Oral History and Community Involvement," 253 and 255.

30. Shopes, "Oral History and Community Involvement," 255–56.

31. Kann, "Reconstructing the History of a Community," 7.

32. Antonio T. Diaz-Roys, "Maneuvers and Transformations in Ethnobiographies of Puerto Rican Migrants," *International Journal of Oral History* 4, no. 1 (February 1983): 21–31; see pp. 21–23.

33. Rina Benmayor, "For Every Story There Is Another Story Which Stands before It," in *Stories to Live By: Continuity and Change in Three Generations of Puerto Rican Women*, 1–23 (New York: Hunter College of the City University of New York, Oral History Task Force, 1987).

34. Paul Buhle, letter to author, November 14, 1992.

35. D. Barnlund and S. Araki, "Intercultural Encounters: The Management of Compliments by Japanese and Americans," *Journal of Cross-Cultural Psychology* 16

(1985): 6–26. Quoted in Stephen P. Banks, Gao Ge, and Joyce Baker, "Intercultural Encounters and Miscommunication," in *"Miscommunication" and Problematic Talk*, ed. Nikolas Coupland, Howard Giles, and John M. Wiemann, 103–12 (Newbury Park, CA: Sage, 1991); see p. 111.

36. Robert Blauner, "Work Satisfaction and Industrial Trends in Modern Society," in *Labor and Trade Unionism*, ed. Walter Galenson and Seymour Martin Lipset (New York: John Wiley, 1960), 351; Trevor Lummis, "Occupational Community of East Anglian Fishermen," *British Journal of Sociology* 28, no. 1 (March 1977): 58–61; David Lockwood, "Sources of Variation," in *Working-Class Images of Society*, ed. M. Bulmer (Boston: Kegan Paul, 1975), 17.

37. Charles Morrissey, letter to author, March 11, 1993.

38. Carl Ryant, interview with Bill Bunbury for "Talking History," Australian Public Radio, Oral History Association Conference, October 10, 1991, Salt Lake City, Utah.

39. John Fox, paper delivered at the session "The Historian as Hired Gun," Oral History Association Conference, October 10, 1991, Salt Lake City, Utah.

40. Jeremy Brecher, Jerry Lombardi, and Jan Stackhouse, eds., *Brass Valley: The Story of Working People's Lives and Struggles in an American Industrial Region* (Philadelphia: Temple University Press, 1982), 277.

41. Robert H. Byington, "Strategies for Collecting Occupational Folklife in Contemporary Urban/Industrial Contexts," *Western Folklore* 3 (1978): 43–56.

42. Maurice Punch, *The Politics and Ethics of Field Work* (London: Sage, 1986), 75.

43. Ryant, interview with Bill Bunbury for "Talking History."

44. Ryant, interview with Bill Bunbury for "Talking History."

45. David Lewis and Wesley Newton, "The Writing of Corporate History," *Public Historian* 3, no. 3 (Summer 1981): 68.

46. Ann Moyall, interview with Bill Bunbury for "Talking History," Australian Public Radio, Oral History Association Conference, October 10, 1991, Salt Lake City, Utah.

47. Brecher, Lombardi, and Stackhouse, *Brass Valley*, 273.

48. William Moss, *Oral History Program Manual* (New York: Praeger, 1974), 20.

49. Daniel Kerr, "'We Know What the Problem Is': Using Oral History to Develop a Collaborative Analysis of Homelessness from the Bottom Up," *Oral History Review* 30, no. 1 (Spring 2003): 27–45; see p. 40.

50. Alicia J. Rouverol, "Collaborative Oral History in a Correctional Setting: Promise and Pitfalls," *Oral History Review* 30, no. 1 (Winter–Spring 2003): 61–85; see p. 74.

51. Alicia J. Rouverol, e-mail to author, July 23, 2004. Alicia read the paragraphs relative to her project and gave me invaluable help and suggestions.

52. Rouverol, "Collaborative Oral History in a Correctional Setting," 74.

53. Kathleen Blee, "Evidence, Empathy, and Ethics: Lessons from Oral Histories of the Klan," *Journal of American History* 80, no. 2 (September 1993): 596–606.

54. Linda Shopes, "Commentary: Sharing Authority," *Oral History Review*, 30, no. 1 (Winter–Spring, 2003): 103–10; see p. 109.

55. Michael Frisch, "Town into City: A Reconsideration on the Occasion of Springfield's 350th Anniversary, 1636–1986," in Frisch, *Shared Authority*, 191–201; see p. 198.

56. Dolores Janiewski, "From Field to Factory: Race, Class, Sex, and the Woman Worker in Durham" (Ph.D. dissertation, Duke University, Durham, NC, 1979). See her published book on this research, *Sisterhood Denied: Race, Gender, and Class in a New South Community* (Philadelphia: Temple University Press, 1985). See also Beverly Jones and Claudia Egelhoff, eds., "Working in Tobacco: An Oral History of Durham's Tobacco Factory Workers" (Durham, NC: History Department, North Carolina Central University, 1988.)

57. Kathleen Norris, *Dakota: A Spiritual Geography* (Boston: Houghton Mifflin, 2001), 7–9.

58. Amato, *Rethinking Home*, 17.

59. Dolores Hayden, *The Power of Place: Urban Landscapes as Public History* (Cambridge: MIT Press, 1995).

CHAPTER EIGHT

Varieties of Oral History Projects: Biography

"What a wee little part of a person's life are words and deeds, his real life is lived in his head"—so said Mark Twain.[1] The time is long past when the writer could just recount the deeds of the dead person, extolling his accomplishments in public life. Biographer Leon Edel remarks, "The public façade is the mask behind which a private mythology is hidden—the private self-concept that guides a given life, the private dreams of the self."[2] Now readers want to peep behind the mask, to understand the ways the individual sees himself or herself, the inner struggles and motivation, the way psychological makeup influenced the subject's interpersonal relationships, the interpretation the subject gave to life's events. Evidence for these concerns does not often appear in written documents unless the researcher has access to private correspondence and personal journals. And even when such written sources are available, they do not always contain passages in which the subject has set down such reflections. Oral history techniques of questioning about motivation, feelings, and meanings are an effective way to get this information, as well as the details of deeds and events. The in-depth interview is the research method that enables you, the researcher, to ask such questions of the subject.[3]

In this chapter, I discuss attitudes in academia about biographical research. I point out some techniques for using oral history to research biography. Agendas that both interviewer and narrator may have are discussed, as well as the effects of gender and culture on the narrator's and interviewer's agendas. Ways to relate to the subject's family members are gingerly offered.

Ethical questions inevitable in studying a life are explored. Finally, I draw on biographers' work for suggestions for topics in the interview guide and for some evocative questions.

Biography: Literature or History?

Biography is sometimes considered a literary genre; sometimes, history. Professor of English literature Paul Kendall, Richard III's biographer, declares, "Biography is a genuine province of literature."[4] Historian and biographer B. L. Reid defines biography as a branch of history because "its essence is fact and its shaper is time."[5] I argue that biography is an interdisciplinary endeavor: the biographer must use historical research methods and concepts but also employ psychological insights, sociological perspectives on the individual in the group, and anthropological ways of understanding the individual in his culture. To engage the reader in the narrative of the life under scrutiny, the biographer must attend to writing style and narrative techniques appropriate to literary work.

Biography is not fiction. Virginia Woolf reminds us that the fiction writer tells the reader, "Every character in this book is fictitious." No character in a biography is fictitious, and neither is any event. The biographer is an artist under oath—he cannot invent or lie about evidence. If anything is made up or anything significant about the life is omitted, the result is not a credible life history. There are truths to be learned in fiction, but in biography the truths must be evidence based. The art in biography is the creativity in the search for evidence, the arranging of evidence to present an engrossing narrative of this unique life, and the interpretation of it, but biography is also the presentation of an individual life in its relationship to a wider history.

A challenge to the veracity of biography comes from postmodernist theorists who argue that both narrator and biographer are products of their culture and therefore can work only within these limits and also that they *impose* a coherence on the wildly disparate events of a life. Furthermore, the biographer infuses the story with his or her own feelings, making every biography an autobiography. I grant that neither narrating subject nor biographer can reconstruct fully the life as it was lived, that we do operate within the boundaries of concepts drawn from our culture, and that we react emotionally to our subject. However, I do not think that relieves us of the responsibility to get as close to the lived experience as we can get by carrying out our research as fully and as conscientiously as we can and by scrutinizing our own attitudes about the subject and the research process.

Some postmodernists also contend that the narrator has no stable core, no consistent self.[6] But if we did not have some psychological stability, we could not function in daily life. Of course, the way we see ourselves is influenced by the culture—we judge ourselves by values learned in a culture, for example—and views of the self change in some aspects as we go through life stages. But at the foundation of our psychological makeup there is a consciousness of an irreducible, consistent self. I go back to 1981 to anthropologists L. L. Langness and Gelya Frank, who explain,

> But even though there are consequently many ways in which to see ourselves at any moment, undoubtedly there is a unity of some kind that binds together an individual's life. After all, we recognize other people not just because their name remains the same, or by their physical features, which also remain consistent to a degree, but also by their character. In time, as we get to know people, they become somewhat predictable and a pattern emerges. Similarly, we can recognize the pattern that makes us familiar to ourselves.[7]

Recently psychologist Jerome Bruner wrote about the way we see in ourselves an "irresistible sense of continuity over time and place." He also stresses that we pick up on expectations of others about us, and we are guided by cultural models of what selfhood should be. Bruner asserts that in some ways we may change our thinking about ourselves as the situation requires, but we nevertheless guard the basic feeling of coherence and continuity we have about ourselves.[8]

Why Research and Write Biography?

I confess that I followed my passion—biography—and only later asked the most basic question: Why do we, biographers and readers of biography, spend our lives studying someone else's? I realized I liked biography because the process of studying a life compelled me to establish a connection to another and to feel empathy with that person—an immensely enriching experience. As long as the effects of a historical event, say, a world war, a depression, or arrival in a strange country, were expressed in general terms, I found it hard to imagine the impact on individuals. Biographies enabled me to understand how these events were experienced by the people who lived through them.

In my own biographical research about two women writers, I tried to discern the way the individual writer's inner world that produced the literary works was influenced by gender, social class, historical moment, and culture and how, in turn, the writer influenced her culture. My first subject, Bernice Kelly Harris (1891–1973), was a conventional middle-class housewife and churchgoer in a small North Carolina town. She was an obedient wife and wrote only when her husband was not at home because her "scribbling" annoyed him—but she articulated in five of her seven novels for generations of women a central question: How much of myself must I give up in order to belong to you?[9] My other subject, Betty Smith (1896–1972), drew from her memories and psyche the account of growing up in a Brooklyn tenement that she wrote in her autobiographical novel, A Tree Grows in Brooklyn, and then influenced her culture as millions of readers began to think of their own experiences in its terms.[10]

For a time in the twentieth century, however, biography as a genre was not considered by academics as a research endeavor of much consequence, although the general public continued to read biographies. Many sociologists relied on survey research and statistical method and considered single case studies like biography misguided, but other sociologists in the United States, especially those connected with the University of Chicago early in the twentieth century, used interviews covering the subject's entire life as their data.

Now a new attitude about the worth of biography is emerging in academia. In the year 2000, a collection of essays by European sociologists, The Turn to Biographical Methods in Social Science, presented a fresh look: "Ethnography and biography explore process, rather than merely structure. It is because it is through single cases that self-reflection, decision and action in human lives can best be explored and represented that the case study is essential to human understanding."[11] Sociologist Brian Elliott argues, "Evidence from the official sources, the censuses and diverse enquiries of the state, evidence from the market research organizations, commercial pollsters, and others, evidence from sociological surveys and case studies can teach us much, but they do not take us close into the real, lived experience and uncover the intimate dynamics of the social world. But the biographical studies can do that."[12] Anthropologists seek studies of individual lives to understand how networks of relationships function and how seemingly shared assumptions and meanings actually vary with individuals.[13]

Analytical psychology has always built theory on the basis of individual case studies, but researchers were looking for pathology. Recently, across disciplines humanists have used the case study approach, and especially humanistic psychologists have used individual biography to look—not for pathology—but for normality, that is, to chart developments occurring normally at different life stages.[14]

Among historians, reluctance to value biographical study stemmed from emphasis on social movements or widespread conditions and on the use of statistical analysis.[15] But other points of view were expressed too. In 1968, David

Brion Davis, using Martin Luther as his example, argued that historians of culture should "examine in detail how the personality crises of a complex individual reflect tensions within the general culture and how the individual's resolutions of conflicts within himself lead ultimately to transformations within the culture."[16] Davis explains that biography can provide "a concreteness and sense of historical development that most studies of culture lack." Barbara Tuchman, speaking of the research for A Distant Mirror, her biography of the crusader Coucy, declares, "I knew that there in front of me was medieval society in microcosm and . . . the many-layered elements of Western man."[17] For her, biography "encompasses the universal in the particular."[18] Finally, many historians accept that individuals singly as well as collectively make decisions that change history. Biography lets us see why they made these decisions, how they made them, and how they got to that point.

Even scholars whose work is in the history of science now acknowledge the need for biographical research. Historian of science Thomas Hankins declares that biography can "tie together the parallel currents of history at the level where the events and ideas occur."[19] Thomas Soderqvist, biographer of the immunologist Niels K. Jerne, asserts that biographies of scientists can show us the way the scientist's mind works and the milieu in which she works. Especially a biography can reveal the necessity of independent thinking—the need to realize his unique talent and to make divergent judgments and unconventional choices.[20]

Biographers of writers have contended for decades with advocates of structuralism and poststructuralism. With an emphasis on the text itself and on the reader—which these two movements advocated—there was diminished interest in the writer. Interpreting the meanings of a literary work by pointing to the reasons an author came to write it seemed a futile exercise. Indeed, poststructuralists questioned whether there was any meaning in a life except what the biographer imposed on a chaos of bits of information.

Now with increasing discussion of the limitations of poststructuralism, there is a renewed appreciation of biography. Brian Roberts, in his book Biographical Research, attributes this change partly to postmodernism. Postmodernist theorists offer a "critique of grand narratives—dominant ideologies and social theories—and a stress on change, diversity, and uncertainty." Roberts argues that since we are living in a world where there is no shared reality, there is acceptance for exploring individual accounts of lives within their particular culture.[21] And so, despite their dismissal of the existence of a consistent self, postmodernists opened the way for us to take a closer look at society by focusing on the multiplicity of perceptions that biographical studies can offer.

Regardless of the ups and downs in the acceptance of the study of biography among academics, biographers and readers continue to pursue it. Perhaps most compelling is the hope that by studying other lives, we can better understand our own. Indeed, we seem to have a compulsion to tell the stories of our lives and to hear stories about other lives. Biographer Richard Ellman declares that to make sense of the seemingly haphazard events of a life, our own and others', is "an essential part of experience."[22]

Difference between Life History, Life Story, Autobiography, and Biography

The terms *life history* and *biography* are used to suggest two different things. A *life history* has been defined as the account by an individual of his or her life that is recorded in some way, by taping or writing, for another person who edits and presents the account.[23] Theodore Rosengarten taped Ned Cobb's life history and presented it in *All God's Dangers*. There is nothing new here except the technology: for centuries people have written their life histories at others' request. For example, British working women early in the twentieth century were encouraged by the Women's Cooperative Guild to write the stories of their lives. Margaret Llewelyn Davies edited and published these writings as *Life as We Have Known It*.[24] *Life story* may also refer to this kind of writing, and you may see it used interchangeably with the term *life history*.[25]

The biographer takes up the life history and autobiographical writings and personal documents, such as letters, and artifacts, such as a house, garden, furniture, and photographs, and fashions them into a narrative with a wider historical context than the individual life. Rosemary Joyce recorded the life history of an Ohio grandmother, Sarah Penfield, and then wrote a biography from it, presenting extended quotations from the oral history but also showing how Penfield was typical or not typical for her time and place.

Autobiography is an account told by the individual on her own initiative, not in response to someone else's questions. For the in-depth interviewer who intends to write a biography, autobiographical writings are a godsend. Critical writings on the craft of autobiography are presented in the collection of essays *The Culture of Autobiography: Constructions of Self-Representation*.[26] I have sought my subjects' autobiographical writings; I was aware, however, that although these were not done at someone's request, each writer had an audience in mind that shaped what she wrote—if the autobiography is not written for publication, the audience is oneself. In this chapter, I call your attention to publications on autobiography because the two processes, writing for oneself and taping a life history for someone else, are similar in that both involve the act of making meaning of life's events and describing a self in the process of thinking about and articulating experiences.

Why Tell This Life Story?

Your subject may ask you, "Why do you want to tell my life story?" Famous people expect that someone will want to write their biographies, but people not so famous may also be aware that their lives deserve to be known. Ned Cobb, a simple farmer without education, understood that his movement, the Sharecropper's Union of the 1930s, should have a place in history. When Theodore Rosengarten appeared in the Alabama countryside at the shed where Ned made baskets, Ned said, "I knew someday you'd come."[27] But Sarah Penfield, a farm woman who had known Rosemary Joyce for several years, was puzzled when she realized Joyce wanted her to be the subject of a book. Penfield thought of herself as just an ordinary grandmother.[28]

You may know with certainty that you are going to tape the life history of a famous person and write a biography on the basis of it. But with an unknown person in a routine interview for a research project, you may be surprised to find during the first hour that you have chanced upon a natural raconteur whose memory for details and vivid language make these interviews a rich source. When Rosengarten went to Alabama to research the history of the Sharecropper's Union, he had no idea he would publish a life history. Joyce knew Sarah Penfield for years before she decided that she would work on her biography. Sometimes it takes a while to realize that the temptation to work on the biography of an extraordinary narrator is too compelling to resist and that the life has something special to offer.

So, why tell this narrator's story? Barbara Tuchman justified her biographies on the grounds that the characters she chose were present at pivotal events in history and that the biography would help the reader understand the context for the important event. Rosengarten justified his book as the vehicle by which the deeds and life of a black sharecropper in the South could become known in history. Rosemary Joyce explained that in many ways Sarah Penfield's life showed the reader what it was like to be a farm woman in Ohio in the early part of the century. Sara Alpern began her study of *Nation* editor Freda Kirchwey because, she admits, "I wanted answers to all the questions I faced as a woman, historian, and mother."[29]

Sociologist Raymond Gorden suggests thinking about questions such as, Why have I chosen this life to study? What is the purpose of this research? Why have I selected these particular narrators?[30]

On the other hand, why would anyone agree to work with a researcher, revealing intimate details of a life? Psychologist Gordon Allport suggests the following reasons:

They sense an opportunity to provide justification for the way they have
  lived.
They desire to create order from disparate events.
They seek redemption and social reincorporation through confession.
They are pleased to be helpful in increasing knowledge of human lives.
They enjoy the aesthetic pleasure of expressing their thoughts in a unique
  way.
They like to give their own perspective on life.[31]

I add to this list that sometimes the narrator is pleased to have an account of his or her life to leave to grandchildren. Sometimes the narrator wants to set the historical record straight. But the reason may also be simply that we enjoy the opportunity to talk about experiences with an attentive listener. We want to make sense of our lives, and one way to do this is by explaining to others.

Setting Up Interviews, Involving the Narrator

Narrators, whether the subject herself or the people willing to talk about the subject, will want to know when you are going to appear on the doorstep. Researcher Ken Plummer advises the biographer/interviewer to decide with the narrator time and place of meetings, kinds of questions that will be asked, whether the person will receive a list of topics before the sessions begin, what leeway the narrator has to talk about what interests him or her, what the final product will be, and what control the person will have over the contents of the publication.[32] It is productive to tell the narrator the main topics you will bring up, as Plummer suggests. The narrator will start thinking about them and will add topics. But a list of specific questions should not be handed out if you want unrehearsed answers. I have found that the unrehearsed answers are the most revealing.

You may find yourself agreeing to work in some unorthodox ways as you negotiate an interviewing schedule and place. Rosengarten recorded Ned Cobb's testimony as Cobb made oak baskets in a shed. Joyce recorded Sarah Penfield's words as Penfield worked in her kitchen. One narrator I went back to many times preferred to talk when her housework was finished, and we could sit in the yard during summer in the late afternoons and drink iced tea and spend periods of time thinking silently. Another liked for me to sit at the huge round dining table in her apartment over her son's funeral parlor. Her dining room was a neighborhood meeting place, so there were interruptions. At first, my purist heart sank because I know that an interviewer needs a place to interview that is quiet and without interruption. But I learned to just turn off the recorder and be sociable when other people came in the room and then resume when the narrator and I were alone again. In all of these situations, the best interviews were obtained when the recording went on at a time and in a place most conducive to the narrator's relaxed mood and ability to concentrate.

As you have read several times in this book, during the interview, it is important that you as interviewer permit the narrator to interject topics other than those you have in the interview guide. Even the discussion of topics that seem far from your interests at first may offer clues to the personality of the speaker—and maybe evidence for a subject that will interest you as you reflect on all the information later.

Effect of the Narrator's Agendas and Psychology on the Interview

I have touched on initial reasons the narrator may have for beginning the project. Once the interviewing is under way, you may sense that there are motivations that are not so conscious. Both narrator and interviewer have biases, and an awareness of them will enable you to understand what is happening in the interpersonal relationship, to critique the oral document, and to look with a critical eye at your own interpretations. Biographer Andrew McFadzean reminds the oral historian, "The dynamics of an interview suggest that the outcome is often the result of a complex interplay between individual memories and personal agendas."[33]

In an oral history interview, what the interviewer is privileged to witness is a process by which the narrator reinforces, in some ways, an identity, or perhaps becomes aware of some aspect of identity only vaguely understood before. It is, of course, an endeavor in which we are all constantly engaged, but in the formal interview this is a focused action. The very act of reinforcing a sense of self results in a feeling of wholeness. From this wholeness of recounted experience, an identity—a feeling of "I am this kind of person"—is once again validated. Georges Gusdorf, who writes on the autobiographical form, insists that the process of composing a history of one's own life facilitates a discovery of the self: "My individual unity, the mysterious essence of my being—this is the task of gathering in and of understanding in all the acts that have been mine, all the faces and all the places where I have recognized signs and witness of my destiny. In other words, autobiography is a second reading of experience, and it is truer than the first because it adds to experience itself the consciousness of it."[34]

In oral history interviews for biography, the answers narrators give to your questions and the topics they choose to interject fit into the picture they have of their lives. The interviewer may also find that the narrator's choice of stories to tell may have something to do with personal myths. A personal myth is not a falsehood, psychologists say; rather it is a way by which human beings "organize their inner lives."[35] Psychologist Anthony Stevens in *Private Myths: Dreams and Dreaming* asserts that this is a good thing: "A good personal myth is an adaptive one: it affords an emotionally satisfying synthesis of one's personality structure with one's life circumstances, and promotes effective adjustment to reality."[36]

Agnes Hankiss, in her essay "Ontologies of the Self: On the Mythological Rearranging of One's Life History," shows how a narrator may create a view of the past that justifies a decision made then or even a present condition.[37] That is an ongoing process for each of us and is bound to affect oral history testimony. During one interview for the Smith biography, I soon realized that I would not be able to follow my interview guide at all—the narrator felt compelled to do something different than talk about Betty Smith. Sometimes an invitation to record a life history acts as a school reunion will, stimulating us to recall our own lives and compare. The narrator's agenda was to think through things that had happened to her some fifty years ago when she knew Betty Smith. Although our agendas were different, she did give me information that I used to establish a context for my subject's life.

Sometimes the narrator struggles to reconcile evidence from the past with present needs. Doris Kearns describes several versions Lyndon Johnson gave of his relationship with his mother. While Kearns was researching the Johnson biography, he would call her in the early morning hours when he could not sleep. He would re-create moments with his mother in the distant past, picturing her as "loving, sensitive, and spiritual." In the last year and a half of his life, he also gave Kearns images of a "demanding, ambitious, frustrated woman who had loved him when he succeeded for her and scorned him when he failed." But the next morning, in the clear light of day, he would call Kearns and declare that his mother was a wonderful woman who loved him unconditionally.[38] The contradictions in his testimony were revealing. His identity was that he had been a loved son and he needed to support that; on the other hand, he wrestled with painful memories that revealed the complexity of his relationship with his mother. For Kearns, learning this was more important than acquiring factual information about his mother.

Gusdorf advises, "One should not take the narrator's word for it, but should consider his version of the facts as one contribution to his own biography."[39] Johnson told Kearns that his great-great-grandfather died heroically at the Battle of San Jacinto in Texas. Later Kearns discovered that this ancestor had never even been at the battle and that he had died at home in his bed. Probably Johnson had not meant to lie, but he wanted a heroic ancestor and so, after telling the story many times, he himself came to believe it.[40] In these last years of his life, Kearns surmised, he may have needed a heroic family history to validate his own belief that he had been destined to be a leader.

Both friends and enemies have agendas that are not always transparent at the beginning of the interview—sometimes it is to pay back a debt. One man who had been a close friend of Joe Jones, Betty Smith's second husband, hated Betty Smith because, in his view, she treated this second husband badly. During the preliminary interview, he told me he remembered Joe's observations of her; but during the recording, he declined to reveal them. He began the interview by telling me he owed a lot to Joe Jones and then he created a saint. He chose not to reveal anything mean-spirited his friend might have said—even though he probably believed whatever his friend said was true—and he certainly did not want to tell me anything positive about Betty Smith that Joe might have said.

You may easily detect in an ongoing interview contradictions in the testimony. After the interview, when you have a chance to reflect on it, consider Ken Plummer's questions:

> Is unintended misinformation being given?
> Has there been any evasion?
> Does evidence suggest that the narrator is lying?
> Has a "front" been presented?
> How much has the narrator forgotten?
> How much of what is or is not revealed self-deceptive?
> Is the narrator trying to please you?[41]

Effect of the Interviewer's Agenda on the Interview

On the conscious, stated level, the biographer's agenda is to gather as much information about the subject as possible. But we can achieve a better understanding of our research process and of the resulting oral document and written biography if we can become aware of our other, perhaps not completely conscious, agendas. And there are plenty of chances for our agendas to influence the project: We decide what is important enough to ask about. We decide who will be interviewed. We select the information and interpret it.

For example, Alex Haley points out in his introduction to *The Autobiography of Malcolm X* how his questions affected the oral history. During the interviews, Malcolm X tried to project an image of himself as a critic of society, a thinker. Haley asked him questions about his childhood, his mother, his emotional life, so that Malcolm X comes across as a complex personality.[42]

A recent conceptual shift in academic disciplines that views subjectivity in research as a necessary component leads us to delve into the interviewer's effects on the research process.[43] For example, in the past no biographer admitted having a relationship of any kind to the subject unless it was a matter of a son writing about his father. A new intellectual climate emerged as many scholars became concerned with the biographer/interviewer's relationship to the subject. Thoreau's biographer, Richard Lebeaux, insists that a biographer seeks a subject in part on the basis of unconscious fulfillment of needs and then changes during the course of research as his or her own needs change. Lebeaux uses a striking metaphor to characterize the complexity and intimacy in the relationship of biographer to his subject: "Yes, biography for me has been a 'joining with reservations,' a 'marriage' of my life with Thoreau's; the relationship has lasted—not without some stormy arguments, separations, and passionate reconciliations."[44]

Affinity of biographer to subject can have its advantages. Historian Frank Vandiver speaks of "the biographer's spark of creation."[45] Without it, a biography is simply a factual account; with it, anthropologist Gelya Frank says, the biographer can achieve "a conceptual grasp of the subject."[46] Even with the most repellent individuals, the biographer must have some willingness to see the subject's world through his eyes. With this suspension of judgment during the interviewing, you will increase the likelihood of understanding the subject. During the interpretation and writing phase, you exercise your judgment.

Sometimes empathy arises without effort because the biographer shares some experience with the subject—perhaps both have been single parents or both have struggled with the same religious issues or both have done the same kind of work. There may be some shared philosophy of life or goal that attracts the biographer. Samuel Baron thought he chose to write a biography of the Russian intellectual and politician G. V. Plekhanov because he just needed a suitable subject for a doctoral thesis. Whenever he was asked, "Do you like Plekhanov?" he bristled. Only years later did he realize, "I knew relatively little about Plekhanov when I made my choice, but I was certainly aware that he devoted his life to study, writing, and politics, with Marxism as his lodestar, in an effort to change his world for the better. It would seem that I chose Plekhanov because I sensed a resonance between his life history and my life plan."[47]

In *The Challenge of Feminist Biography*, Lois Rudnick writes that it was during a dinner conversation with a friend one evening about her research for a biography of Mabel Dodge Luhan that she gained a sudden insight: "I realized that Luhan appealed to the side of my imagination that likes to fantasize about being the queen of my own universe, with the money, creative power, and imperious will to do good and interesting things, to know adventurous people, to influence my times, and to live on the edge—psychologically and politically." During the course of the research, she came to understand that "one of its most paradoxical delights was entering worlds that helped to explain my own but that were at the same time the antithesis of my own."[48]

How does affinity to the subject affect the interview? During the research for the biography of Bernice Kelly Harris, I realized that I had begun to like her very much and became afraid that my liking her would make me reluctant to hear negative things about her. I started asking my narrators to tell me something she had said or done that was unkind or false. But in fact she was an ethical and compassionate person; and even if she did not like someone, she had such self-control no one would have known. My narrators struggled to think of something. No matter how hard I pressed, I could not elicit negative information. Of course, people don't like to speak ill of the dead, but examples of her kindness cropped up so consistently in the oral testimony, regardless of my questions, that I took them seriously. I sought corroboration for the narrators' views of her in the written records—especially letters to her and the letters she wrote.

For the biography of Betty Smith, I felt like debating the narrators who disparaged her as a hack who would write stories for romance magazines. I wanted to say, "You don't know what it's like to raise two children alone. If you were in the same situation, you, too, would have sold stories where you could." But I clamped my lips shut as I became aware of my need to defend her and realized that I should not let my empathy for her affect the interview. (But I wonder if my body stiffened when I heard criticisms like this of her.)

In researching textile workers in the mill village, I sought to understand my own roots. And in choosing to interview the women only, I gave as a conscious motivation the fact that women talk more readily to another woman about some issues than they do to men. That was true, but, unconsciously at the time, I created an opportunity to experience the pleasure of entering the world of women, of re-creating the warmth and sense of "we are women to-gether" I had known as a child in my mother's kitchen. As the project went on, I sought reassurance in the way each woman saw her life as a whole, integrating the crises, putting them into perspective, at a time when I was confronting crises in my own life. But possibly my unconscious agenda biased my questioning—leading me to avoid asking questions that embarrassed them, for example—and the resulting written account may have been skewed in the direction of presenting too positive a picture. This was something I was not aware of at the time.

During the research process, maintain an ongoing dialogue with yourself. Write it out in your journal and then let the writing "cool" before you return to it. Consider Ken Plummer's advice in *Documents of Life* and ask yourself:

> How have my own attitudes impinged on the interview? My religious values, political views, general assumptions, theories and expectancies? [I also ask here, how has the interview been affected by my conscious and barely conscious reasons for choosing the subject in the first place?]
> How has the interview been shaped by my personality—for example, need for approval, hostility, or anxiety to get the interview finished?
> How has it been shaped by my appearance and body language?
> How has the interview been shaped by my age, gender, class, race?
> That a certain kind of nonverbal communication was going on?
> That we knew each other before the interviewing began?
> That the interview was held in a certain place?[49]

Emotional investment is a good thing, but become aware of what is happening. Changes in your body alert you to your own heightened emotion during an interview. You look down and see your hand clutching the arm of the chair. Or, you feel your face flushing or your heart beating a little faster. Or, your foot is swinging. (Observe the same nonverbal signs in the narrator.) You can ask yourself, What was I feeling so intensely about during that discussion? The answer may point you to your own agenda.

The Effect of Gender on Questions and Interpretations

Since images of women and men are socially constructed, the interviewer has to keep in mind cultural influences. In the introduction to *The Challenge of Feminist Biography*, the editors insist, "Because society tends to value male models of achievement and behavior more than it values female models, a woman's gender may exercise greater constraints on the way her life evolves.

Failing to consider this difference distorts, if not falsifies, any account of a woman's life."[50]

In earlier centuries, biographies were written by men about famous men. Writers and readers expected a biography to be about a statesman, a general, an explorer, a scientist, an artist or writer, a business tycoon. Since these occupations were usually closed to women, they could not fit into categories meriting biographies. Now writers and readers are more open to looking at the lives of ordinary men and even ordinary women who respond in extraordinary ways to life's challenges. Oral history is an especially effective way of revealing these lives because ordinary men and women rarely write their autobiographies. Recently collections of brief biographies of ordinary women (who turned out to be extraordinary) based on oral history have appeared, such as *Walking on Fire: Haitian Women's Stories of Survival and Resistance*, which informs us of women's strategies for resisting a brutal political regime.[51]

Furthermore, biographies used to be focused on external events deemed appropriate to the subject's gender. Even in the rare biographies of women who were notable in government service or in a profession, the biographer seemed to have a hard time choosing appropriate themes. Linda Wagner-Martin says that when she compared biographies of Franklin and Eleanor Roosevelt, she noted that Franklin's biographers treated such topics as his political decisions, associations with other political leaders, outcomes of his governing abilities. Eleanor's biographers treated family relationships, domesticity, and social events. Readers could conclude that Franklin did not concern himself with his small children, or feel emotional loneliness, or glimpse his inadequacies, or indulge in extramarital affairs. What was usually downplayed or omitted altogether from biographical studies of Eleanor were her creative ideas, influence on political decisions, leadership on a world level, and inspiration for social change.[52]

Now readers of biography recognize the indissoluble link between the private and the public worlds and expect the biographer to discuss these. Because of women biographers' work, such topics as details of daily living, feelings about private and public events, and relationships are no longer ignored, even in biographies of men.

Special conditions of women's lives, previously omitted, are being treated in biography, especially the importance of friendships for women. Research suggests that men form close friendships that are different from the friendships women have. Men's friendships are based on sharing activities;[53] women's friendships are based on talk, confidences, and sharing of feelings. And men's friendships may not play as important a role in their lives as friendships do in women's lives. Men in crisis may respond in a "fight-or-flight" mode; women in crisis turn to other women in a "tend-and-befriend" mode.[54]

It is obvious that women have been shunted away from work defined as appropriate for men, and even within the workplaces open to them, they have been paid less than men and denied equal access to promotion. But there are other less obvious influences that the biographer should consider. For example, Carolyn Heilbrun warns against accepting the "marriage plot" as the foremost component for a happy life for a woman. When we do so, we put accomplishments in second place.[55]

I thought about the "marriage plot" in the biographical research I did. Betty Smith could have stayed married to her first husband or married a new man who would provide security; instead, she was determined to make a living as a writer—the "marriage plot" was not her first priority. Some observers might conclude that she paid a price for her independence, and I could have taken the easy way out and attributed her unhappiness to the failure to sustain a marriage. Asking narrators and reading her letters and autobiographical writings, I found she expressed no complaint about her decision to maintain her independent lifestyle. (She married a third time and supported him.) She was not a happy person, but this was caused by the existential anxiety within her. Other biographers have had to confront society's assumption that a woman has to be in a relationship with a man to be a complete person,[56] and sometimes the subject does feel that, sometimes not. Something can be learned from exploring the influence of this assumption in your interviewing.

Another related assumption that Heilbrun questions is that once a woman has finished raising children and has entered middle age, her usefulness declines and her life winds down. Now women's biographers note that great bursts of creativity may occur late in women's lives. Both of my subjects were in their late forties when they wrote their first novels, and in their fifties and sixties they were active, creative, productive women. Joyce Antler's biography of Lucy Mitchell shows that Mitchell's seventies and eighties were the most productive years of her life.[57]

Lyndall Gordon, biographer of Virginia Woolf and Charlotte Brontë, presents examples of the set stories of traditional biographies of women that continue to influence our thinking: "the romantic doomed-genius story (for the Brontës); the quaint-spinster-story (for Emily Dickinson); the child-abuse/frigidity story (for Virginia Woolf)." But these set stories, she argues, do not reveal the "uncategorized ferment of hidden possibilities."[58] As interviewer, you can delve into the hidden, distinctive aspects of your subject's life. You can structure your interview guide so that it contains a range of questions about daily life and relationships—no matter how improper. And you can free yourself from society's assumptions about gender-appropriate work and behavior for both men and women. You can keep in mind instead that individuals have amazing ways of rounding the corners and negotiating the obstacles in their paths to satisfy their needs.

Interviewing Friends, Enemies, and Even the Onlookers

Interview all of them, but set priorities, of course. I have been assuming that your subject is alive and able and willing to talk. Alas, I have not been so lucky—both my subjects had been dead nearly thirty years when I began the study of their lives—and so the biographical research I have done has been dependent on oral history interviews with my subjects' friends, family members, associates, neighbors, observers, and enemies. But I would have sought these narrators even if my subjects had been living because a rich biography will offer multiple perspectives on the life.

Newspaper reporters know that they should seek out maids, servants, chauffeurs, and secretaries to the famous if they want information on what the person was like on a daily basis. Reporters find out how the individual handled crises from the people who served the subject, such as the subordinates in the organization. Beatrice Webb insists that the "mind of the subordinate in any organization will yield richer deposits of fact than the mind of the principal."[59] It is the subordinate, after all, who implements the subject's decisions and witnesses the consequences.

Take into account as you interview associates that impressions change over time. In comparing interviews with Lyndon Johnson's associates to those with John F. Kennedy's, Doris Kearns found that there was a marked difference: "The tendency of President Johnson's associates is to be critical, while the tendency of President Kennedy's associates is to be admiring." She surmised that this was not just a reflection of the different personalities of the two men. She writes, "The central figures in the Johnson circle seem to be trying to break free of the intimacy and the fusion they experienced with Johnson, trying to live a life of some detachment, proving that they deserve their liberty by criticizing their former master." On the other hand, Kennedy kept his political associates at some distance. Kearns suspected that his associates tried to insinuate bonds that were never there.[60] In any case, the association with "greatness" lends drama to one's own life, and that is an influence to watch out for in interviews.

There are people who knew your subject only briefly, but the glimpse they give you of the individual's actions at a certain time and place are revealing.

When historian Dee Garrison was researching her biographical study of Mary Heaton Vorse, a journalist and labor organizer, she went to Vorse's favorite home in Provincetown, Massachusetts. She interviewed many people—by design, both those who had liked and disliked Vorse. Garrison began to get a picture of her subject's effects on this little town. Vorse's former minister, recalling the opposition of townspeople when he marched in a local demonstration against the war in Vietnam, said, "The emotional support she offered me was very, very important to me at the time."[61]

Sometimes it is a remark during an interview with an onlooker that is the piece of the puzzle you were missing. Interviewing a townswoman during the research for Betty Smith's biography, I heard an observation of Betty Smith's appearing one spring morning at the Farmers' Market in an old black coat and carrying a large basket filled with vegetables. I realized at that moment that she was doing the food shopping and cooking for the five people living in her house then. I understood why she was having trouble finding time to work on her second novel. She was not just procrastinating.

Interview the enemies too. They will be biased, just as loyalists and defenders are, but underlying the account there may be deeds the subject's friends did not experience, and you will get a different perspective on your subject. In critiquing John Toland's biography of Hitler, David Mitchell noted that Toland had interviewed mostly Hitler's associates. Toland said that he interviewed Hitler's opponents, as well, but Mitchell argued that the emphasis was on the other side. He observes, "If he had interviewed primarily opponents and victims of the German tyrant, the emphasis of the biography would most certainly have been altered."[62]

Another reason to interview opponents is that you can better understand what your subject faced. You can place your subject's writings or political opinions, for example, in the context in which they were produced. You can know whose writing she or he was reading, whose arguments needed to be answered, or the kinds of personalities who had to be dealt with.

The Wider World in the Interview Guide for Biography

All of the people mentioned above will give the interviewer/biographer an understanding of the concerns of the time and place—the neighborhood, the town, local crises, and world developments. Although my interests were focused on the differences that social class, gender, and culture made in the lives of the two women I studied, I was reminded by such scholars as historian Marc Raeff to ask questions about the impact of world events on their lives.[63] I had to confront the question, How did living in this particular historical moment affect the subject's life? What difference did it make that she came to adult-hood during World War I, say, rather than 1968?

Bernice Kelly Harris did come of age during World War I. She grew up during the early years of the twentieth century and began teaching during World War I. She saw her students, nearly the same age as she was, go off to war and never come back. She reeled from the shock. She spent the years of World War II seemingly safe in Seaboard, North Carolina, near the coast. She learned to search for enemy airplanes, she rolled bandages, she cut and sewed clothes for the women of besieged Leningrad, and daily she sat at a table helping people with ration books. She wept over every death overseas of Seaboard men, saying that each death "destroyed a world."[64] I don't think it is by chance that her worst depression descended on her in 1943.

In the interview guide, include the questions that will give you informa-tion on the ways that historical events impinged on this person's life. Not to place the individual in a historical context is to wrench the life from its meaningful place, to isolate the person in a strange way.

Placing the Subject in the Context of Gender, Race, Class, and Culture

Ask yourself, How is this individual typical for his or her gender, race, social class, cultural group? Other questions to be concerned with are, How is this in-dividual different from what would be expected in her age group? Or, in what ways does the person share psychological needs with other people of the same gender and life stage? In what ways is the person unique? Indeed, an important fact impinging on the in-depth study of a life is the phenomenon of develop-mental stages, that is, the different stages at which human beings have specific emotional needs and life tasks to complete. On this topic, two excellent stud-ies to consult are Daniel Levinson's *Seasons of a Man's Life* and George Vail-lant's *Adaptation to Life*.[65] Levinson published the counterpart to his book on men in *Seasons of a Woman's Life*, but the study goes up only to age forty-nine.[66] Erik Erikson's work on stages was the pioneering study and continues to be en-lightening, while Gail Sheehy's *Passages: Predictable Crises of Adult Life* is a pop-ular, very readable version of the research data.[67] Knowing the literature on human development will enable the researcher or writer to place the subject in the context of emotional needs of others in the same age group. For the ways that people in specific cultures and at specific times experience stages, look at Glenn Elder and Janet Giele's work on life course research.[68]

Carol Gilligan at the Harvard Graduate School of Education studied eleven-year-old girls at a private school, showing how the influence of our culture constricts their choice of future work and how it affects their sense of worth.[69] Her study of moral development in women, *In a Different Voice: Psychological Theory and Women's Development*, is an exposition of the particular ways women in our society react to important ethical dilemmas.[70] *Meeting at the Crossroads: Women's Psychology and Girls' Development*, by Gilligan and Lyn Mikel Brown, explores the psychological crisis girls go through as they move from childhood to womanhood. Gilligan and Brown point out how important relationships are at this stage and, by implication, at every stage: "Girls watch the human world like people watch the weather. Listening in to the sounds of daily living, they pick up its psychological rhythms, its patterns."[71] Other studies of women's lives, although not longitudinal, may prove useful to you, such as *Women's Ways of Knowing* and *Educated American Women: Self-Portraits*.[72]

All of these studies stress the reality of change over the life course. The oral history interview, by requiring the narrator to discuss developments over time, opens up the possibility of a dynamic interpretation of a life.

Possible Ethical Implications in Biographical Research

Although you may not know what the final product will be, you should discuss possibilities with the narrator. I give the main narrators the opportunity to review the parts of the manuscript in which they are quoted before I send it off for anyone else to see. Narrators can advise me of errors. And I want to know how their interpretations differ from mine and thereby get the chance to think mine over again. Even more important, I want to give them an opportunity to see personal information I have used before it becomes public. I do not, however, give anyone the right of veto over the entire manuscript.

If someone wishes to protect himself, that is certainly understandable. Researcher Dan Bar-On reminds us, "In such a delicate kind of research, we hold the meaning of people's lives in our hands."[73] What private details of a person's life are necessary to the biography will be for you to judge. Thomas Cottle sums up this uneasy situation: "The dilemma of preserving privacy while publicly recording the way lives are led is unresolved and will remain unresolved."[74]

Especially in biographical research, there is the matter of invasion of privacy. If your subject means to tell you, that is one thing. If someone else tells you details about your subject, that is something else. Search for other evidence: if true, consider whether these details are necessary to convey the personality of the individual or provide the context in which he or she acted.

Consider the costs to living persons. And think about the possibilities of a libel suit.

Historian Sara Alpern revealed the fact that her subject, Freda Kirchwey, an editor of the *Nation*, and her husband, Evans Clark, had open extramarital relationships. But Alpern also made the decision not to disclose the names of the persons involved. However, she agonized over including—in a discussion of the effects of the death of a young son on Kirchwey—the subject's statement that this son was her favorite. Alpern did not want to hurt the feelings of the surviving son. When this son read the manuscript, he asked Alpern to put the quotation back in, saying that she owed the reader that information.[75]

Sometimes the biographer has to ask herself what is important for the reader to know. When Victoria Glendenning was doing the research for a biography of poet Elizabeth Bowen, she visited a woman whose deceased husband had had a love affair with Bowen. The widow had invited Glendenning, saying she had Bowen's love letters to him. She gave Glendenning a choice: the writer could quote from the letters and not name him, or she could say Bowen had the affair with the named man and not quote from the letters. Glendenning chose to quote from the letters and not name him. The choice of words, the writing style, the details revealed an important aspect of Bowen's life at the time and her state of mind then. The name of the man was not necessary to the understanding of Bowen.[76]

Anthropologist James Clifford considered the matter of an illegitimate son of a biographical subject who was not aware of his paternity. Clifford suggests that perhaps in cases like this the biographer should consider preserving the evidence in archives, and not publishing it while the individual affected by it is still living. He urges biographers to consider the subject's own reasons for secrecy.[77]

While I am determined to include all evidence necessary to an understanding of my subject, I, too, have omitted specific information tangential to my subject's life that would harm a living person. In the Betty Smith biography, I discussed her distress when she found out that her daughter, then nearly nine months' pregnant, had received a warning from her physician that the pregnancy was so problematic that the baby might have to be extracted in pieces. When I sent the manuscript to the now grown-up granddaughter, she asked that I omit that line. I did omit it, saying simply that Betty Smith was distressed about a possibly dangerous development in her daughter's pregnancy. But in another case, I refused to delete discussion of an event because it was squarely about Betty Smith and I judged it of great importance in her life.

Legal Issues Specific to Biography

There are legal issues in biographical research to be concerned about too. When I began the biography of Bernice Kelly Harris, there were no restrictions on her letters, which were in the University of North Carolina's Wilson Library in the Manuscript Department. Her heirs could have prevented me from quoting extensively from the novels and plays, however, because they held copyright. They generously gave permission, but if they had not, I could have whittled down the quotations from the novels and plays, or paraphrased, and still had a viable biography. I had a rich collection of oral histories with release forms.

When I started work on the biography of Betty Smith, I saw the notice at the front of her collection of documents in the Manuscripts Department at the University of North Carolina that all letters and all writings, published and nonpublished, were under copyright owned by her heirs. Since I had had such a good relationship with Harris's heirs, I brushed this notice aside. I obtained release forms for the oral histories I recorded with members of the family and all narrators. However, I eventually realized that heirs who have copyright to every word in the subject's documents, published and unpublished, have leverage to control the content of the biography.

Read the fine print before you begin a biography. Make sure you have not only release forms for the recorded oral interviews but also permissions for the written documents you will use in the biography.

Effect of the Research on Relationships within the Subject's Family

Often the inclusion of details about private experience gets the biographer into trouble with the subject or the subject's family. One consideration is based on how well known the subject was. Ulick O'Connor states the problem clearly:

> A question however which must always concern the biographer is to what extent does he have to take into account the matter of living relatives and their susceptibilities. It seems fair to say that this decision can have something to do with the sort of person who is the subject of the biography. The great statesman, writer or artist has after all placed himself in the public domain to an extent that in order fully to comprehend his position in relation to the circumstances and age that bred and shaped him, it can be necessary to deal with material that many relatives and friends would prefer to see left alone.[78]

As an example, O'Connor says he had discussed in a page and a half in his biographical study of Brendan Behan the attraction Behan felt toward both sexes. O'Connor believed that it was necessary to discuss Behan's unusually active sex drive because that was part of his ferocious appetite for pleasurable experiences in life. And Behan himself talked about this openly. After publication of the biography, some family members were angry, but Behan's mother's comment was, "Aren't we all human?"[79]

Consider also that biographical research, like family history research, is an extremely complex matter because each of your subject's family members has a unique relationship to her. At the same time each is also influenced by societal expectations. The editors of *The Challenge of Feminist Biography*, in discussing in their introduction the problems women's biographers face, write, "Some children, we found, blanked out everything negative about their mothers, others everything favorable. Because society still expects mothers to be more responsible for domestic life than fathers, might children judge mothers more harshly than fathers?"[80] And every family has its own secrets and myths, and members may feel the need to be protective of these.

And now to the important question: how does a biographer maintain good ongoing relationships with the biographical subject's family? For the biography of Bernice Kelly Harris, I had begun the documents search—a real pleasure because I was reading her interviews for the Federal Writers Project—before I spoke to members of her family. The archivist gave me the names of her family members living then, and I wrote letters introducing myself and explaining my reasons for wanting to write the biography. I made a courtesy call to the closest relatives and requested permission to interview them at a later date. A couple of times I sent notes informing them of the progress of the research and writing. At the conclusion of the work, I returned to each one the portions of the manuscript in which he or she had been quoted and the entire manuscript to the principal narrators in her family. They were very helpful in correcting errors. I also advised and helped the executor of the estate to obtain copyright for an unpublished novel of Bernice's. After the manuscript biography was finished, a few relatives voiced some specific objections—they did not want me to mention that Bernice Kelly Harris drank alcohol or that she suffered from depression, and they wanted more discussion on her role as a leader in the Baptist Church. However, they made no attempt to prevent publication. I was pleased when her much loved niece and nephew came to a symposium to honor Harris and presented me with her silver letter opener as a gesture of appreciation for my work.

Relationships with Betty Smith's family did not go as smoothly. I conclude that my correct, friendly, but not too close relationships with Harris's family members were a preferable way to proceed. Consider also that a too close personal relationship with one family member makes the others identify you with that person. And too close a personal relationship leads that person to think that you will write the biography she wants—after all, you are a friend, aren't you?

It is inevitable that the biographer will have a different interpretation of the life than individuals in the subject's family. Family members may take offense because you have a different view, and they may not be as tolerant as Behan's mother.

But you cannot escape a close personal relationship with the living biographical subject. The person may want to control access to information and to make final decisions about what to include. An authorized biography is suspect in the eyes of readers because they expect that anything unpleasant or less than respectable has been toned down or omitted. Make it clear to the subject that you will be responsible in this research, that your biography will be based on all available evidence, that you will not exaggerate intentionally, that you are not seeking to sensationalize, and that your goal is not a television miniseries with all its possibilities for inventing so the drama can attract an audience. Educate family members about what a scholarly biography looks like. Give the person some samples of your writing you have already published. If he or she declines to be a narrator or to help with this project, you may have to turn to others who know the subject to obtain oral history interviews and use these along with the written documents (read the fine print about rights to these, of course.)

Topics and Questions to Be Included in an Interview Guide

Every biographical subject is unique, and your choice of topics will be based on the unique experiences of this life. But for general questions to ask yourself, you could look for suggestions in Catherine Parke's *Biography:Writing Lives*:

> How did the person's private and public lives relate to and influence one
> another?
> How did childhood affect the adult life?
> To what degree is the subject conscious of shaping forces in the life?
> How did cultural and historical events and context affect the life?[81]

You will be wondering what was happening in your subject's inner life. Look at Robert Atkinson's questions in *The Life Story Interview*. These are the questions he used in his interviews for life histories of elders at the Center for the Study of Lives at the University of Maine. Under the heading "Inner Life and Spiritual Awareness," he suggests such questions as, "Have you ever felt the presence of a spiritual guide within you?" And, "What is your view on why there is suffering in the world?"

Under general topic headings, such as "Birth and Family of Origin," "Cultural Setting and Traditions," "Social Factors," "Education," "Love and Work," he offers some questions appropriate for a sociological interview with an educated narrator, such as, "What cultural influences are still important to you today?" Although these questions are class bound, others are not and can evoke rich answers in in-depth interviews with different kinds of narrators, such as, "What was it about her or him that made you fall in love?" And, "What is important to you in your work?" "Why do you do this work?" On "Major Life Themes," consider his thoughtful questions, such as, "What was the most important thing you have had to learn by yourself?"[82]

Paul Thompson, in *The Voice of the Past*, offers questions used in his study of life stories, with a focus on work, "A Life Story Interview Guide." Especially useful is his conceptual framework for topics, such as "Long-Distance Migration," "Grandparents' Generation," "Siblings/Cousins/Uncles, Aunts," "Daily Life in Childhood," and "Community and Class."[83]

All of these are topics and questions I return to again and again. In spite of the difficulties of researching and writing biography, I pursue biographical research—and oral history as a main component of it—because the process is a compelling adventure and what I learn always turns out to be beyond my expectations, often beyond my imagination. I agree with David Bakan, who writes, "The most significant truths about human beings inhere in the stories of their lives."[84]

Recommended Reading

Alpern, Sara, Joyce Antler, Elisabeth Israels Perry, and Ingrid Winther Scobie. *The Challenge of Feminist Biography: Writing the Lives of Modern American Women*. Urbana: University of Illinois Press, 1992. This collection of ten essays by feminist biographers presents a discussion of how their research and writing evolved; it argues that private and public life are inextricably intertwined and that the biographer cannot ignore the pervasive influence of gender in both men's and women's lives.

Atkinson, Robert. *The Life Story Interview*. Thousand Oaks, CA: Sage, 1998. Useful questions to ask; a sample analysis of a life history is offered.

Bar-On, Dan. "Ethical Issues in Biographical Interviews and Analysis." In *Ethics and Process in the Narrative Study of Lives*, ed. Ruthellen Josselson, 9–21. Thousand

Oaks, CA: Sage, 1996. Thoughtful, perceptive discussion of ethical issues in biographical work.

Bruner, Jerome. "The Autobiographical Process." In *The Culture of Autobiography: Constructions of Self-Representation*, ed. Robert Folkenflik, 38–56 (Stanford: Stanford University Press, 1993). Instructive essay by a psychiatrist who is also a humanist and scholar.

Chamberlayne, Prue, Joanna Bornat, and Tom Wengraf, eds. *The Turn to Biographical Methods in Social Science*. London: Routledge, 2000. A collection of essays that are essential reading for anyone in the social sciences who is considering writing a biography.

Clifford, James L. *From Puzzles to Portraits: Problems of a Literary Biographer*. Chapel Hill: University of North Carolina Press, 1970. This offers an account of how the author tracked down leads and followed hunches; it is both fun to read and informative.

Cohler, Bertram. "Personal Narrative and Life Course." In *Life-Span Development and Behavior*, vol. 4, ed. P. Baltes and O. Brim, 205–41. New York: Academic Press, 1982. This essay uses psychoanalytic theory to explain how transitions are accommodated in the telling of one's life.

Cottle, Thomas J. *Private Lives and Public Accounts*. Amherst: University of Massachusetts Press, 1977. See especially the first chapter, pp. 3–26, for a thoughtful introduction to research for a biography.

Crapanzano, Vincent. "Life Histories." *American Anthropologist* 86, no. 4 (1984): 953–60. This essay stresses that when we analyze a life history, we are analyzing a text, not a social reality, and this text is itself the product of a complex collaboration.

Erikson, Erik. *Childhood and Society*. New York: Norton, 1963. See chapter 7, "Eight Stages of Man," pp. 219–34, for a brief explanation of each of Erikson's stages.

Feinstein, David, Stanley Krippner, and Dennis Granger. "Mythmaking and Human Development." *Journal of Humanistic Psychology* 28, no. 3 (Summer 1988): 23–50. Authors trace the history of the concept, define and discuss three basic premises about personal myths, and offer a case study to illustrate how the concept of personal myth can be used in therapy.

Geiger, Susan N. "Women's Life Histories: Method and Content." *Signs: A Journal of Women in Culture and Society* 2 (Winter 1986): 334–51. This review article offers instructive commentary on life histories.

Glendenning, Victoria. "Lies and Silences." In *The Troubled Face of Biography*, ed. Eric Homberger and John Charmley. London: Macmillan, 1988. This essay deals with such gritty issues as what the biographer leaves out.

Gordon, Lyndall. "Women's Lives: The Unmapped Country." In *The Art of Literary Biography*, ed. John Batchelor, 87–98. Oxford: Clarendon Press, 1995. An account that sensitizes us to the effects of gender in the study of biography.

Gusdorf, Georges. "Conditions and Limits of Autobiography." In *Autobiography: Essays Theoretical and Critical*, ed. James Olney. Princeton, NJ: Princeton University Press, 1980. This is a brilliant discussion of the relationship of past events to the present in the narrator's mind.

Hankins, Thomas. "In Defence of Biography: The Use of Biography in the History of Science." *History of Science* 17 (1979): 1–16. A gem of an essay—describes the developments in attitudes about biography of scientists.

Hankiss, Agnes. "Ontologies of the Self: On the Mythological Rearranging of One's Life History." In *Biography and Society*, ed. Daniel Bertaux. Beverly Hills, CA: Sage, 1981. This essay shows how a narrator may create a myth system about the past that enables him or her to justify a present condition.

Hunt, David. *Parents and Children in History: The Psychology of Family Life in Early Modern France.* New York: Basic Books, 1970. For an overview of Erik Erikson's theory of human development, see chapter 1, "The Psychological Background: Erik Erikson's Theory of Psycho-Social Development," pp. 11–17.

Kaufman, Sharon. *The Ageless Self: Sources of Meaning in Late Life.* Madison: University of Wisconsin Press, 1986. The author shows in detail the process by which individuals integrate and accept the diverse experiences of a lifetime, so that they achieve the final stage of development outlined by Erikson.

Langer, Elinor. "Coming to Terms." *Pequod: A Journal of Contemporary Literature*, nos. 223–24 (1987): 209–40. The author discusses omissions in her subject's memoir as well as her relationship to her dead subject. She confronts the question, Do you keep the secret your subject kept?

Langness, L. L., and Gelya Frank. *Lives: An Anthropological Approach to Biography.* Novato, CA: Chandler & Sharp, 1981. See especially the section "Biography and the Structure of Lives" for a discussion of the way individuals have a unity within that helps them select and make sense of memories.

Lebeaux, Richard. "Thoreau's Lives, Lebeaux's Lives." In *Introspection in Biography: The Biographer's Quest for Self-Awareness*, ed. Samuel Baron and Carl Pletsch, 225–48. Hillsdale, NJ: Lawrence Erlbaum, 1985. An account of how a biographer seeks a subject to fill his own needs and then changes the interpretation as his own life changes.

Lepore, Jill. "Historians Who Love Too Much: Reflections on Microhistory and Biography." *Journal of American History* 88, no. 1 (June 2001): 129–44. Witty, incisive essay on the way a biographer unconsciously allies with the subject or someone in the subject's life.

Mitchell, David. "Living Documents: Oral History and Biography." *Biography* 3 (April 1980): 283–96. This article discusses the uses of oral history in writing biography and presents outstanding biographies based on oral history.

O'Connor, Ulick. *Biographers and the Art of Biography.* Dublin: Wolfhound Press, 1991. This has several interesting chapters, but see especially the discussion on dealing with untrue accounts written by the subject (pp. 90–98).

"Oral History and Biography." (Book review symposium.) *Oral History Review* 18, no. 1 (Spring 1990): 93–109. This symposium contains an introduction to biography by Linda Shopes and reviews of six recent biographies. It is informative for the connections between biography and oral history and for characteristics of effective biographical writing.

Pachter, Marc. "The Biographer Himself: An Introduction." In *Telling Lives*, ed. Marc Pachter, 2–15. Washington, DC: New Republic Books, 1979. This is an incisive essay on the effects of the writing of biography on the biographer.

Plummer, Ken. "Doing Life Histories." In *Documents of Life*, Contemporary Social Research Series, ed. M. Bulmer, 7 (London: Allen and Unwin, 1983). A sensitive and sensitizing essay on biographical research and analysis of life histories.

Quilligan, Maureen. "Rewriting History." *Yale Review*, Winter 1988, 259–86. This is a review of five biographies of women and a discussion of the way prominent women have a double burden: not only to be unique but also to be representative.

Roberts, Brian. *Biographical Research*. Buckingham: Open University Press, 2002. A comprehensive textbook on biographical research, written with clarity and style.

Schwarz, Ted. *The Complete Guide to Writing Biographies*. Cincinnati, OH: Writer's Digest Books, 1990. The chapter on ethics, "How Can You Say That about Them?" offers specific examples.

Shore, Miles. "Biography in the 1980's." *Journal of Interdisciplinary History* 12, no. 1 (Spring 1981): 89–113. The author presents a brief history of approaches in biographies and sets forth criteria for judging the use of concepts from clinical psychology to analyze life history data.

Sitzia, Lorraine. "A Shared Authority: An Impossible Goal?" *Oral History Review* 30, no. 1 (Winter–Spring 2003): 87–101. A reflective account of the interviewer's relationship with a narrator in a biographical study that took six years and resulted in a book and other forms of public presentation. The forces that affected Sitzia's relationship with her narrator, as well as the ways they shared direction of the project, are candidly discussed.

Smith, M. Brewster. "Selfhood at Risk: Postmodern Perils and the Perils of Postmodernism." *American Psychologist* 49, no. 5 (May 1994): 405–11. Brewster discusses debates among psychologists about postmodernist views of the self. While he is not concerned about stability of the self, he does stress that ideas about the self are culture bound. He deplores the hopelessness engendered by some postmodernist writers.

Soderqvist, Thomas. "Existential Projects and Existential Choice in Science: Science Biography as an Edifying Genre." In *Telling Lives in Science: Essays on Scientific Biography*, ed. Michael Shortland and Richard Yeo, 45–84 (Cambridge: Cambridge University Press, 1996). An essay, indeed a volume, of crucial importance to anyone interested in biographies of people in science.

Thompson, Paul. "Life Histories and the Analysis of Social Change." In *Biography and Society*, ed. Daniel Bertaux, 289–306. Beverly Hills, CA: Sage, 1981. This article offers an account of the ways individual biographies can be used for a study of social change.

Wagner-Martin, Linda. *Telling Women's Lives: The New Biography*. New Brunswick, NJ: Rutgers University Press, 1994. Perceptive discussion of the changes in writing biography where gender is concerned.

Watson, Lawrence C. "Understanding a Life History as a Subjective Document: Hermeneutical and Phenomenological Perspectives." *Ethos* 4, no. 1 (Spring 1976): 95–131. Discussion on the ways in which the biographer brings his or her own background, intellectual interests, commitments, sensitivity to dialogue, and ability to re-create insights to the interpretation of the subject's life.

Weidman, Bette S. "Oral History in Biography: A Shaping Source." *International Journal of Oral History* 8 (February 1987): 41–55. This article discusses the ways oral history influences the presentation of the life in a biography.

Notes

1. Mark Twain, quoted in J. R. R. Christie and Fred Orton, "Writing on a Text of the Life," *Art History* 11, no. 4 (December 1988): 545–62; see p. 559.

2. Leon Edel, *Literary Biography* (London: R. Hart Davis, 1957), 33.

3. Bette S. Weidman, "Oral History in Biography: A Shaping Source," *International Journal of Oral History* 8 (February 1987): 41–55; see p. 50.

4. Paul Murray Kendall, "Walking the Boundaries," in *Biography as High Adventure: Life-Writers Speak on Their Art*, ed. Stephen B. Oates, 32–49 (Amherst: University of Massachusetts Press, 1986), 33.

5. B. L. Reid, *Necessary Lives: Biographical Reflections* (Columbia: University of Missouri Press, 1990), 4.

6. For a discussion of this view and rejoinder, see M. Brewster Smith, "Postmodern Perils and the Perils of Postmodernism," *American Psychologist* 49, no. 5 (May 1994): 405–11.

7. L. L. Langness and Gelya Frank, *Lives: An Anthropological Approach to Biography* (Novato, CA: Chandler & Sharp, 1981), 108.

8. Jerome Bruner, "Self-Making Narratives," in *Autobiographical Memory and the Construction of a Narrative Self: Developmental and Cultural Perspectives*, ed. Robyn Fivush and Catherine A. Haden, 209–25 (Mahwah, NJ: Lawrence Erlbaum, 2003); see pp. 210–11.

9. Valerie Yow, *Bernice Kelly Harris: A Good Life Was Writing* (Baton Rouge: Louisiana State University Press, 1999).

10. Valerie Yow, *Betty Smith and "A Tree Grows in Brooklyn"* (submitted for publication).

11. Michael Rustin in Prue Chamberlayne, Joanna Bornat, and Tom Wengraf, eds., *The Turn to Biographical Methods in Social Science* (London: Routledge, 2000), 49.

12. Brian Elliott, "Biography, Family History and the Analysis of Social Change," in *Time, Family and Community: Perspectives on Family and Community History*, ed. Michael Drake, 44–63 (Oxford: Blackwell for the Open University, 1994); see p. 47.

13. Chamberlayne, Bornat, and Wengraf, *Turn to Biographical Methods in Social Science*, 8.

14. George E. Vaillant, *Adaptation to Life* (Boston: Little, Brown, 1977).

15. See, for example, Pierre-Philippe Bugnard, "Les retrouvailles de la biographie et de la nouvelle histoire," *Schweizerische Zeitschrift fur Geschichte, Revue suisse d'Histoire* 45, no. 2 (1995): 236–54. And Guillaume Piketty, "La Biographie comme genre historique," *Vingtieme Siecle* 63 (1999): 119–26.

16. David Brion Davis, "Recent Directions in American Cultural History," *American Historical Review* 73, no. 3 (February 1968): 696–707; see pp. 704–5.

17. Barbara Tuchman, "Biography as a Prism of History," in *Telling Lives: The Biographer's Art,* ed. Marc Pachter, 132–47 (Washington, DC: New Republic Books, 1979), 136.

18. Tuchman, "Biography as a Prism of History," 136.

19. Thomas Hankins, "In Defence of Biography: The Use of Biography in the History of Science," *History of Science* 17 (1979): 1–16.

20. Thomas Soderqvist, "Existential Projects and Existential Choice in Science: Science Biography as an Edifying Genre," in *Telling Lives in Science: Essays on Scientific Biography,* ed. Michael Shortland and Richard Yeo, 45–84 (Cambridge: Cambridge University Press, 1996), 75–77.

21. Brian Roberts, *Biographical Research* (Buckingham, PA: Open University Press, 2002), 5.

22. Richard Ellman, *Literary Biography* (Oxford: Clarendon Press, 1971), 19.

23. Roland Barthes, "Death of the Author," in *Image, Music, Text,* ed. and trans. Stephen Heath, 142–48 (New York: Hill and Wang, 1977); see p. 148.

24. Margaret Llewelyn Davies, *Life as We Have Known It* (London: Hogarth Press, 1931; New York: W. W. Norton, 1975).

25. Robert Atkinson, *The Life Story Interview* (Thousand Oaks, CA: Sage, 1998), 7.

26. Robert Folkenflik, ed., *The Culture of Autobiography: Constructions of Self-Representation* (Stanford: Stanford University Press, 1993).

27. Theodore Rosengarten, lecture, University of Rhode Island, Fall 1978.

28. Rosemary O. Joyce, *A Woman's Place: The Life History of a Rural Ohio Grandmother* (Columbus: Ohio State University Press, 1983), 48.

29. Sara Alpern, Joyce Antler, Elisabeth Israels Perry, and Ingrid Winther Scobie, *The Challenge of Feminist Biography* (Chicago: University of Illinois Press, 1992), 162.

30. Raymond L. Gorden, *Interviewing: Strategy, Techniques and Tactics,* 4th ed. (Chicago: Dorsey Press, 1987), 165–73.

31. Gordon Allport, *The Use of Personal Documents in Psychological Science* (New York: Social Science Research Council, 1942), 69–74.

32. Ken Plummer, "Doing of Life Histories," in *Documents of Life,* Contemporary Social Research Series, ed. M. Bulmer, 7 (London: Allen and Unwin, 1983), 93.

33. Andrew McFadzean, "Interviews with Robert Bowie: The Use of Oral Testimony," *Oral History Review* 26, no. 2 (Summer–Fall 2001): 29–46.

34. Georges Gusdorf, "Conditions and Limits of Autobiography," in *Autobiography: Essays Theoretical and Critical,* ed. James Olney (Princeton, NJ: Princeton University Press, 1980), 38.

35. David Feinstein, Stanley Krippner, and Dennis Granger, "Mythmaking and Human Development," *Journal of Humanistic Psychology* 28, no. 3 (Summer 1988): 23–50; see p. 27.

36. Anthony Stevens, *Private Myths: Dreams and Dreaming* (Cambridge, MA: Harvard University Press, 1995), 202.

37. Agnes Hankiss, "Ontologies of the Self: On the Mythological Rearranging of One's Own Life History," in *Biology and Society*, ed. Daniel Bertaux, 203–9 (Beverly Hills, CA: Sage, 1981), 203.

38. Doris Kearns, "Angles of Vision," in Pachter, *Telling Lives*, 90–103; see p. 101.

39. Gusdorf, "Conditions and Limits of Autobiography," 36.

40. Kearns, "Angles of Vision," 98.

41. Plummer, "Doing of Life Histories."

42. Alex Haley, introduction to *The Autobiography of Malcom X* (New York: Ballantine, 1964), 390.

43. Valerie Yow, "Do I Like Them Too Much?" *Oral History Review* 24, no. 1 (Summer 1997): 55–79.

44. Richard Lebeaux, "Thoreau's Lives, Lebeaux's Lives," in *Introspection in Biography: The Biographer's Quest For Self-Awareness*, ed. Samuel Baron and Carl Pletsch, 225–48 (Hillsdale, NJ: Lawrence Erlbaum, 1985).

45. Frank Vandiver, "Biography as an Agent of Humanism," in Oates, *Biography as High Adventure*, 50–64; see p. 50.

46. Gelya Frank, "'Becoming the Other': Empathy and Biographical Interpretation," *Biography* 8, no. 3 (1985): 189–210; see p. 197.

47. Samuel Baron, "My Life with Plekhanov," in Baron and Pletsch, *Introspection in Biography*.

48. Lois Rudnick, "The Male-Identified Woman and Other Anxieties: The Life of Mabel Dodge Luhan," in Alpern et al., *Challenge of Feminist Biography*, 116–38; see p. 131.

49. Plummer, "Doing Life Histories," 180.

50. Alpern et al., *Challenge of Feminist Biography*, 7.

51. Beverly Bell, *Walking on Fire: Haitian Women's Stories of Survival and Resistance* (Ithaca, NY: Cornell University Press, 2001).

52. Linda Wagner-Martin, *Telling Women's Lives: The New Biography* (New Brunswick, NJ: Rutgers University Press, 1994), 6.

53. Robert A. Lewis, "Emotional Intimacy among Men," *Journal of Social Issues* 34, no. 1 (1978): 108–21.

54. Shelley E. Taylor, Laura Cousino Klein, Brian P. Lewis, Tara L. Gruenewalk, Regan A. R. Gurung, and John A. Updegraff, "Biobehavioral Responses to Stress in Females: Tend-and-Befriend, Not Fight-or-Flight," *Psychological Review* 107, no. 3 (2000): 411–29.

55. Carolyn Heilbrun, *Writing a Woman's Life* (New York: Ballantine, 1989).

56. Rudnick, "Male-Identified Woman and Other Anxieties," 122, 125–26.

57. Joyce Antler, "Having It All Almost: Confronting the Legacy of Lucy Sprague Mitchell," in Alpern et al., *Challenge of Feminist Biography*, 97–115.

58. Lyndall Gordon, "Women's Lives: The Unmapped Country," in *The Art of Literary Biography*, ed. John Batchelor, 87–98 (Oxford: Clarendon Press, 1995).

59. Bearice Webb, *My Apprenticeship* (London: Longman, Green, 1926), 409.

60. Kearns, "Angles of Vision," 98.

61. Dee Garrison, "Two Roads Taken: Writing the Biography of Mary Heaton Vorse," in Alpern et al., *Challenge of Feminist Biography*, 5–78; see p. 73.

62. David Mitchell, "Living Documents: Oral History and Biography," *Biography* 3 (April 1980): 283–96; see p. 291.

63. Marc Raeff, "Autocracy Tempered by Reform or by Regicide," *American Historical Review* 98, no. 4 (1993): 1143–55.

64. Quoted in Valerie Raleigh Yow, *Bernice Kelly Harris: A Good Life Was Writing* (Baton Rouge: Louisiana State University Press, 1999), 141.

65. Daniel J. Levinson with Charlotte Darrow, Edward B. Klein, Maria Levinson, and Braxton McKee, *The Seasons of a Man's Life* (New York: A. A. Knopf, 1978); George Vaillant, *Adaptation to Life* (Boston: Little, Brown, 1977).

66. Daniel J. Levinson, *Seasons of a Woman's Life* (New York: A. A. Knopf, 1996).

67. Erik Erikson, *Childhood and Society* (New York: W. W. Norton, 1963); see chapter 7, "Eight Stages of Man." See also Gail Sheehy, *Passages: Predictable Crises of Adult Life* (New York: E. P. Dutton, 1976).

68. Glenn Elder and Janet Z. Giele, *Methods of Life Course Research: Qualitative and Quantitative Approaches* (Thousand Oaks, CA: Sage, 1998).

69. Carol Gilligan, *Making Connections: The Relational Worlds of Adolescent Girls at the Emma Willard School* (Cambridge, MA: Harvard University Press, 1990).

70. Carol Gilligan, *In a Different Voice: Psychological Theory and Women's Development* (Cambridge, MA: Harvard University Press, 1990).

71. Lyn Mikel Brown and Carol Gilligan, *Meeting at the Crossroads: Women's Psychology and Girls' Development* (Cambridge, MA: Harvard University Press, 1992).

72. Mary Field Belenky et al., *Women's Ways of Knowing: The Development of Self, Voice, and Mind* (New York: Basic Books, 1986); Eli Ginsberg, *Educated American Women: Self-Portraits* (New York: Columbia University Press, 1966). See also Nadya Aisenberg and Mona Harrington, *Women of Academe: Outsiders in the Sacred Grove* (Boston: University of Massachusetts Press, 1988); although not a developmental study, the oral history testimony does point to connections between life stages and an academic woman's thinking about career.

73. Dan Bar-On, "Ethical Issues in Biographical Interviews and Analysis," in *Ethics and Process in the Narrative Study of Lives*, ed. Ruthellen Josselson, 9–21 (Thousand Oaks, CA: Sage, 1996), 20.

74. Thomas Cottle, *Private Lives and Public Accounts* (Amherst: University of Massachusetts Press, 1977), 11.

75. Sara Alpern, "In Search of Freda Kirchwey: From Identification to Separation," in Alpern et al., *Challenge of Feminist Biography*, 159–76; see p. 173.

76. Victoria Glendenning, "Lies and Silences," in *Troubled Face of Biography*, ed. Eric Homberger and John Charmley, 49–62 (London: Macmillan, 1988); see p. 51.

77. James Clifford, *From Puzzles to Portraits: Problems of a Literary Biographer* (Chapel Hill: University of North Carolina Press, 1970), 124.

78. Ulick O'Connor, *Biographers and the Art of Biography* (Dublin: Wolfhound Press, 1991), 76.

79. O'Connor, *Biographers and the Art of Biography*, 77–78.

80. Alpern et al., *Challenge of Feminist Biography*.

81. Catherine Parke, *Biography: Writing Lives* (New York: Twayne, 1996), xiv.

82. Robert Atkinson, *The Life Story Interview* (Thousand Oaks, CA: Sage, 1998), 43–53.

83. Paul Thompson, *The Voice of the Past: Oral History*, 3rd ed. (Oxford: Oxford University Press, 2000), 309–23.

84. David Bakan, "Some Reflections about Narrative Research and Hurt and Harm," in Josselson, *Ethics and Process in the Narrative Study of Lives*, 5.

CHAPTER NINE

Varieties of Oral History Projects: Family Research

Oral history can be like the light that shines on a family in a seventeenth-century Dutch painting as family members go about their daily tasks. Indeed, it is the daily life of the family—experiences that no one thought important enough to write down—that can be illuminated in the oral history interview.

Relationships among family members, motivations, fears, strong feelings, the vivid memories about an individual's words or actions at some important moment can be sought in oral history questioning, as well. Scholars who study the family emphasize the importance of family stories that contribute to the shaping of individuals' lives. Usually, these are not written down but simply told by one generation to the next. Oral history facilitates the taping and preservation of stories unique to a family.

Family history, when you research your own family, can be richly rewarding. A student in my class, a woman of Italian American heritage, decided to write a three-generational history of herself, her mother, and her maternal grandmother. The grandmother, whom she at first saw as an old woman whose values differed in important ways from her own, became to her through the interviewing process a young woman—in photographs looking much like her granddaughter—with many of the same hopes and fears. The student drew closer to her grandmother in a way she had not thought possible.

This is one reason, creating a bridge across generations, that teachers assign oral history projects on family history to students. Another reason is to give students the opportunity to increase appreciation of their own cultural heritage. Another is to offer a project that makes students aware that history is something that happens to them, that it is not just something written in a textbook. Still another reason is to give students in social science an opportunity to observe and analyze interaction in this small unit of society that influences social interaction on other levels, as well. It is an effective way for students to learn the methodology of historical research or to gain experience in ethnographic research.

Many of us, no longer students, undertake family history projects involving extensive interviewing in a research population ostensibly because we know that an understanding of a culture depends on understanding its most basic unit. On another level, we seek answers to questions about our own families that we were vaguely aware of as children but which pique our interest or trouble us in adulthood. Often, in these wider research projects with many families, we ask the questions that give us insight into our own.

Individual family history has been looked at sometimes with disdain by professional historians. There are good reasons for this: too often in the past such publications have been mere laudatory accounts, skimming the surface of serious issues, masking the unpleasant events, whitewashing the less-than-respectable deeds. And the scope has been narrow because there was little concern with how the individual family was affected by and participated in the history of the wider world. But family history, thoroughly researched, that confronts and deals with serious concerns, presents an honest account, and places the individual family in a wider historical context can be enlightening. Because there are recently published family histories that do just that, critics in the historical profession have become interested in individual family histories. Beyond this consideration, however, there is something compelling about studying families. Historian Michael Kammen says about John Demos's *The Unredeemed Captive: A Family Story from Early America* that this study is "a great drama with a human face, one that touches us because it is personalized and particularized."[1]

Psychologists, sociologists, folklorists, and anthropologists have also begun to take an interest in individual family history. More than half a century ago, in a public lecture in 1949, Oscar Lewis talked about the need for sociologists and anthropologists to study individual families. He had been thinking about the best way to "study the individual and understand his relationship to the culture." He argued that a study of the family could help "bridge the gap between the conceptual extremes of the culture at one pole and the individual at the other." The researcher could see in this social unit how individuals work together or refuse to do so; defy, carry out, or change wider societal norms; and create behavioral expectations characteristic of that unit. Lewis concluded, "It is in the context of the family that the interrelationships between cultural and individual factors in the formation of personality can best be seen."[2]

In Lewis's approach to the study of the family, a dynamic model is required that involves delving into a history of the family. Anthropologist Christie Kiefer, in researching and writing an ethnographic study of three generations in Japanese American families, aimed at "viewing personality as a lifelong process that dynamically interacts with cultural and historical change."[3] Using the in-depth interview with individuals in families and also observing community life, she investigated her "respondents' perceptions of their own past" to find out how "these perceptions affect relations between the generations."[4] She describes her general approach: "I show how intellectual habits related to age, sex, culture, and social class affect the way people see their history and how they act toward each other."[5]

Family history has been referred to as a "high-risk endeavor."[6] To get the honest, well-researched account that will make the effort worthwhile requires understanding and sensitivity. In writing this chapter, I have been conscious of the fact that the readership may vary from the historian reconstructing a social history of the family, to the sociologist or anthropologist using a limited number of families as case studies, to the family member seeking to understand his or her own personal history. Whatever the purpose, each of us must be aware of what our intervention into this small group can do. On a more specific level, differing purposes at times require different considerations, and I try to address these. However, each of us has had meaningful contact with a family, and I make the assumption that information about researching one's own family will be of some interest to every reader. On the other hand, those of us researching our own families can learn from social scientists studying families from a different vantage point.

Finding Families for Social Science Research

For your own family history, you will probably interview all interested relatives, but social scientists do not have such an easily defined and accessible research population. Some researchers have contacted heads of agencies in a targeted community and asked these individuals to introduce them to families they think might be interested.[7] Others have asked clergy or physicians to recommend them to families, but according to the nature of the project, this may put the minister or doctor in an awkward position because of the relationship of trust and confidentiality he or she often has with families.[8] Often family members are reluctant to commit themselves to such a project, believing that they must have some special problem that has caused them to be singled out or fearing that they will have to reveal intimate details of their lives. Researcher Reuben Hill persuaded the director of the Minnesota Family Study Center at the University of Minnesota to write a letter telling families who had had contact with the center how important Hill's research was to an understanding of families. The director stressed that this was a study of three generations in the same family, that it was difficult to find three generations in one geographical area, and that the help of these families would be greatly appreciated.[9] Interviewers found that this letter from a respected organization resulted in goodwill toward the research project and a willingness to participate.

British sociologists J. M. Pahl and R. E. Pahl, studying the impact of a man's managerial career on the family, contacted the men during the time they were in a program at Cambridge and later when they had been active in their careers several years.[10] By sending questionnaires to both husbands and wives early on (before they even planned to conduct in-depth interviews), the Pahls aroused interest in the project. I suspect that the purpose of the research—which did not imply that the families were chosen because they were in trouble—made this less threatening. And because the researchers invited everyone who had been in the course to participate in the research, the narrators could assume that they were like everybody else—a comfortable feeling when family matters are going to be discussed.

Introduction of the Project to the Family

The consideration of utmost importance for the social scientist is trust. This will require an explanation of the ways that anonymity and confidentiality will be maintained. Also, the social scientist usually does not involve subjects in the editing of research studies, but with this kind of research, in which you use extremely personal information from in-depth interviews, such involvement of narrators may be warranted. Although you disguise the individuals' names, those talked about may recognize themselves. If at all possible, let them see the part of the manuscript relevant to them before publication. Give them the reassurance at the beginning that you will do this.

Although I have been referring to "the family" as if it were a monolithic entity, nothing could be farther from the truth. If you are interviewing in your own family, you know that each family member is an individual with his or her own thoughts about a family history. At the very beginning of a family interviewing project, it is advisable to take into account the feelings of differing personalities. Folklorist and family historian Margaret Yocum thinks that introducing the project to one's own family is "the biggest emotional hurdle for a field-worker." She advises the researcher to consider three issues: (1) What do you already know about different family members' reactions to recording and writing a history? (2) How do members react when you talk about your desire to write such a history? (3) Is it better to propose the project to the whole family at a gathering or to small groups of individuals?[11]

I would discuss the project with small groups of family members. At these informal meetings, ask what questions the family members have about the family's history. Discuss your purpose and your research strategy fully with family members. Undoubtedly, you will be asked to clarify. Tell them (1) what your purpose is, what you want to learn; (2) how each member can help you in the interviewing, research, and editing; (3) whom you will record; (4) how you will deal with sensitive family issues; and (5) what you will do with the material.[12] Listen to the topics they offer; tell them the topics you are interested in and explain why. Consider their suggestions about topics and which members to record.

You have been reading secondary sources on family studies and family histories. (You will find specific books in the list of recommended reading at the end of the chapter.) Start your records search: birth certificates, baptismal records, marriage certificates, death certificates, wills, land deeds, census data, immigration records. These are the steel girders to support the framework you build. David Kyvig and Myron Marty in *Nearby History: Exploring the Past around You* provide forms for requesting federal census records and such documents as ship passenger arrival records.[13] States have records such as birth and death; counties will likely have marriage records—the relevant departments are usually referred to as vital records. With this factual information secured, you can construct a chart showing family members' relations to each other, with important dates noted with each name. Once you have made decisions about the general topics you will pursue, think about specific questions that will help you get information. (Questions are suggested at the end of the chapter.) You are ready to compose the interview guide.

Inspiring Narrators' Interest in Participating in the Research

If you are researching a history of your own family, in explaining your project, you may want to do as Yocum suggests and compare the family history to a genealogy, simply because genealogy is something most people are familiar with.[14] You can point out that a family history will give a more detailed picture than a genealogy. Explain, for example, that genealogy gives important information, such as birth dates, marriage partners and dates, births of children, deaths—but not how anybody felt about those events. You might also show members other family histories or studies of families to give them specific examples of what you want to do.

Understanding may not be achieved easily, however. Micaela di Leonardo, not intending to write her own family's history, but to do some practice interviews with the aim of saving the tapes for the family, approached her uncle Tony. He consented to be interviewed but never understood her purpose. She describes the encounter: "Tony, an interviewer's nightmare, began as soon as I turned on the tape recorder—'All right, I'm just gonna give you one chapter and you better get it down'—and proceeded to discourse as he pleased, about what he pleased, for hours, refusing to answer my questions. He then called all my aunts and told them I was going to make thousands of dollars from his interview and that he wanted his share."[15]

Di Leonardo's experience is a reminder that even when you think an individual in the family understands what you are doing, that might not be so. You have to explain once again. Yocum advises the family researcher to ask to see the family Bible; poems and stories members wrote or loved; crafts such as carvings, quilts, and gardens; and possessions such as scrapbooks, photograph albums, and personal collections.[16] Ask the person to talk about these artifacts and take notes. More problematic are legal papers: most people will show a birth certificate but might be reluctant to bring out a divorce decree. Do not insist: get the record from the appropriate county government office. If you take a photograph to study, get it copied immediately and return the original.

The research activity discussed above has a double purpose: the family members' interest in their own history is awakened, and the researcher learns a lot through artifacts and discussion about them. Researchers must not take without giving something back, however. If you are writing a history of your own family, Yocum suggests making holiday greeting cards with quotations from the members or making for each a photograph album of family history. You might write a paper on the family's folklore and give each member a copy.[17] Another gift is a booklet of family recipes with anecdotes about them. By doing this, you show that you value the preservation of family traditions.[18]

If you are a social science researcher, you will need to interest family members so that they will want to devote time and effort to the interviews. Celia Deschin found that family members in her study of a suburban community became intensely involved "only when questions in the interview touched upon aspects of the individuals' lives about which they felt concern, conflict, or other emotional involvement."[19] In explaining the research questions that you have, you could show how the information gained will be useful to the families interviewed as well as to the wider community.

As in researching one's own family, it helps rapport to make a gesture of respect. If you are able to make photographs—for example, of the original family home—make a copy for each family member. As the research progresses, send the narrators in the families you are researching a letter telling them how the research is coming along and what conclusions seem to be emerging.

Research Strategies with Husband and Wife

You have introduced the project on your own family history at informal meetings of several family members and listened to them reminisce and spark one another's memories while you recorded or took notes. You have composed the interview guide and are ready to begin interviewing. Now is the time to record with one member only. The in-depth interview is different from the focused interview in a small-group setting: the intensely personal, reflective nature of the in-depth interview requires one-on-one interaction.

I argue against interviewing husband and wife together because the responses of one spouse are influenced by the presence of the other. More important, conjoint interviews are at the top of the scale for high-risk endeavors, because some things may be articulated by one spouse that hurt the other's feelings. Sociologist Richard Gelles found that conjoint interviews in his study of domestic violence exacerbated the enmity between two marriage partners.[20] Only if the research purposes require observation of family interaction would such a research design be warranted.[21]

Sociologist Theodore Greenstein, in *Methods of Family Research*, urges researchers to be aware that responses may depend on the role an individual plays at the time of the interview: "Interviewing adults in the presence of their children, for example, might produce very different results from those we might obtain by interviewing the same adults in the presence of their own parents." He also suggests that some topics, such as child abuse and domestic violence, may not come to the fore—he calls these "backstage behaviors."[22]

Sensitivity to Members' Feelings versus Need to Present Evidence

Inevitably, as you listen and ask questions in these interviews, you will brush against the skeleton in the family closet. Kristie Miller, in researching the biography of her maternal grandmother, Ruth Hanna McCormick, found that her mother's father had committed suicide. The physician had been induced to list cardiac infarction on the death certificate, and the family had kept its secret for forty years. By the time Miller began to do the research, family members had accepted the fact of the suicide and the harmlessness of telling the truth about it.[23] Miller was saved by the passage of forty years.

Indeed, passage of time is an important consideration: you may feel freer to bring the skeleton out if the members of that generation are deceased. When your family history deals with recent events, you have some alternatives. The preferred one is to discuss the skeleton with family members, deciding on wording that is acceptable. Another is to promise to withhold public distribution for a stated length of time. But obscuring the truth is not an alternative if your goal is a credible history. If, as a social scientist, you are presenting a limited number of case studies, you should discuss with family members ways to convey the troublesome information in a general way while maintaining confidentiality in specific matters.

Another problem is antagonism between two members. Kristie Miller was bent on interviewing her mother's sister even though her mother had not spoken to this sister for years. She found that reestablishing contact with the aunt and interviewing her at length brought back to her a valuable personal relationship she might never have reclaimed otherwise.[24] Presumably, her valid excuse—the writing of the grandmother's story—made this acceptable to her mother. You have to trust and hope that your impartial interviewing of all family members of a certain generation will show that you are just interested in recording each person's story—rather than wanting to record evidence to support one side. However, you may have to make that explicit.

Often family members have different memories of the same event, and almost always they have different interpretations. The challenge is to present these different views in such a way that no one feels slighted. When you write the study, use the oral history testimony in a way that demonstrates that each narrator's individuality is appreciated. Show that diversity in interpretation is expected and enriching. Consider the situation and point of view of each one. Although the following example is simple, it shows an approach that can be used: John accompanied his father to the office each day and observed him interacting with businesspeople and associates. His judgment was that he was a hard man to deal with. Ellen, then ten years old, ran to meet her father when he came home in the evenings. To her, he was affectionate and teasing.

Also, the passage of time and subsequent life experiences influence testimony. When Joyce Antler was researching the life of Lucy Sprague Mitchell, a leader in early childhood education, she was surprised to hear

Mitchell's adult children disparage her parenting. One son, then sixty-five, admitted that it was in his adulthood, when he was disappointed in the way his career had gone, that he became resentful of his mother.[25] In researching a biography of Jessie Daniel Ames, a leader in interracial reform organizations in the South in the 1920s and 1930s, Jacquelyn Hall found written evidence of the love Jessie Daniel Ames felt for her sister in their youth. This was corroborated by family members' testimony. But Ames's writings in middle age emphasized resentment against her sister. Part of this stemmed from Ames's memory that her sister had been their father's favored child, and part came from her adult rejection of a model of femininity she identified with her sister.[26]

This kind of highly problematic situation has to be dealt with gingerly if one or both parties are living: one possible way is to indicate that you understand that lives and relationships changed over time, that some family members drifted apart as they encountered their own separate challenges, that because of different experiences over time they cannot now see things in the same way.

Interviewing Techniques with Family Members

Interviewing in one's own family is different in an important way from other kinds of oral history interviewing. The interviewer has a lifelong relationship with the narrator and a mutual identification with the same family. The good or bad reputation of one family member affects the other family members. The emotional hurt that one member sustains has consequences of some sort for others. You, as interviewer, must be especially sensitive to the ramifications of your close identification with your narrators and of the narrator's close identification with you.

Often, there is already a level of trust, but you can give further assurance of your determination to maintain confidentiality. In his book *Recording Your Family History*, William Fletcher advises giving the narrator in a family history the original tape to keep. This is not the usual practice, but in this situation it may be advisable, as he explains: "It helps build trust and emphasizes by direct action the confidentiality that exists between the two of you. You want to stress that the tapes are for your narrator first, and that you want him or her to feel completely sure that feelings of privacy come first."[27]

The narrator may want you to delete a part. You could offer the alternative of deleting the designated part in a copy that others may see, but not in the original that the narrator keeps. However, if he or she insists on deletion, you must delete, but indicate on tape that there is a deletion at that particular point. You could hope that several weeks later, the narrator may be feeling differently about telling you the same story and say it on tape again and not request deletion. Often, repeating a story in your mind makes it less shocking. In any case, when the interviews with this individual are completed, make duplicate copies of the tapes even though there are deletions and return the originals to the narrator. Whatever the situation, do not discuss the content of the tape with anyone until the family member has signed a release.

I am not advising letting a narrator keep the tape if you are a social scientist researching others' families: in this situation, stress your professional role and define the tape as necessary to your research. After the research has been completed, you may wish to offer a copy of the tape to the narrator as a gift, but that is a matter different from the situation above. As researcher you need to keep the original as long as your research is in progress and then to deposit it in archives.

If this is your family, it is a good idea to interview your favorite relative first, because you will be more relaxed as you become familiar with your interview guide.[28] If this is a social science research project, choose someone who seems most amenable to the project. In either case, you need a goodwill ambassador vis-à-vis the other members of the family.

Begin the interview with nonthreatening questions, such as date and place of birth, people significant in childhood, favorite games. Wait until the individual reveals confidence in his or her ability to respond and to trust you before you attempt the hard questions. Even then, you may not be inclined to ask a hard question, and the narrator may not feel like answering it. Tell the narrator how you feel about introducing this troubling topic and give him or her a chance to describe to you feelings about discussing the matter. Explain the significance of the topic in the overall study. The family member may need time to think this one over.

Also, there will be times when the narrator is reluctant to go into detail. A gentle phrasing of a "why" or "how" question is appropriate. I have said, "Help me to understand this." You can try a gentle probe: probing will not necessarily wreck the relationship if this is done sensitively and in the spirit of collaboration in an important endeavor. Anthropologist Karen Fields's experience in recording and publishing a life history of her grandmother, Mamie Garvin Fields, *Lemon Swamp and Other Places: A Carolina Memoir*, is a good example of this process. The memoir begins with childhood in a black community in Charleston, South Carolina, in the 1890s and ends with Mamie Fields's retirement from teaching in 1943. There were several subjects on which Karen Fields and her grandmother did not see eye to eye:

As we drew chapters from transcripts, we discussed some matters vigorously. Upon rereading certain passages, Grandmother Fields would say, "We must add to this"—if, for example, we had neglected the accomplishment of some respected local person. Or she would write, "Let's leave this out"—if, on mature reflection, a comment seemed too strong, or if an observation threatened to resurrect some long-dead sentiment that she deemed well dead. "Why?" I would demand. Discussing the reasons why showed me aspects of belonging to a Southern community that would not have occurred to me to ask about, while showing us both differences between our standpoints. These discussions deepened our understanding of the human context in which we were working and of each other. Needless to say the arrival of deepened but unsought understanding caused us to dismay at times, for it meant rewrapping packages we had thought already tidy.[29]

At the beginning of each session, ask if there are things about the last interview the family member would like to add. The questions you asked in the previous session stimulate memory as the narrator reflects on them later. At the end of each session, suggest topics you will discuss in the next session: "Next time, let's talk about the first years in Brooklyn, what your aunts and uncles were doing then and what family get-togethers were like." Encourage the narrator to add the topics she would like to discuss. These general hints will get the narrator to start thinking and remembering, looking for photographs and letters.

Ask also for the names of people in the community who knew family members well—the customers who regularly came into the family shop over the years, teachers who taught individuals in the family, and so on. By talking to them, you can get not only information but also a sense of how people outside the family thought of various family members. A clearer picture of relationships between family and community members emerges.

Whether you are interviewing in your own family or you are a social scientist interviewing in many families, keep a personal journal in which you express your feelings day by day during the project. Much of this information from the interviews is confidential, so you cannot talk about it with others: you will have to "talk" to yourself via your journal. Feelings from childhood long forgotten suddenly pop up—testimony on family matters awakens them. You may remember from the chapter on memory that recall of an incident that was accompanied by strong emotion can make you feel as if it were happening in the present. Let a little time elapse after you write a description of what you are feeling and the testimony that caused this; then read and ponder what you have written. This process may alert you to an important question to ask in interpretation, and it definitely will help you understand why you are relating to the family member in the way that you are.

Use of Artifacts and Photographs in Interviewing

In interviewing family members, observe rituals, listen to stories, and search for artifacts—these can be powerful stimuli to questions and revealing answers. This became clear to me when my brother, Robert Yow, a genealogist, and I went to visit a distant relative, then in her nineties. She mentioned that she still had her great-grandfather's New Testament, the one he had carried in his hip pocket when he was fighting in the Civil War. We were curious because most of the family were Quakers and pacifists. How did this man feel about going against family values? She brought out his New Testament for us to hold. My brother asked if the ancestor had ever talked about his feelings about fighting. She replied that seeing the book reminded her, "Yes, he always said that was wrong and he wished he hadn't done that." She then remembered that as an old man, he refused a pension because he said it was wrong to take arms against a brother. This artifact might have led us to another source, but we were too moved and thinking too hard about what she had just said to ask to see his correspondence with the government. We missed an important document.

An example of how potent use of artifacts can be in interviewing is presented by Ruth Polk Patterson, in her family history, *The Seed of Sally Good'n: A Black Family of Arkansas, 1833–1953*. Patterson relied on oral history interviews in which family stories of her ancestors were told to her, and she sought to corroborate this information with other sources, such as interviews with neighbors, letters, official records, artifacts, excavation of the family home (with the resulting drawings of the layout), and remains such as pieces of china cups. All of these became clues in the detective work of finding the evidence for the family history.[30]

Photographs are the kinds of records that most people keep, and you will find that they do indeed stimulate the narrator to remember. You can ask specific questions, such as, "Why was the photograph taken at this time? Why does the big sister hold the little sister—were they very close when they were children? After they grew up? Why does this son stand beside his mother while this son stands beside his father? Were these their best clothes? What were their everyday clothes like? The house looks different in this picture from the way it looked in the earlier one: how did the house change over the years?"

To reach for meanings underlying the testimony, I strongly recommend that you read Marianne Hirsch's book *Family Frames: Photographs, Narrative and Postmemory*, especially her beginning chapter on Roland Barthes's *Camera Lucida*.[31] She discusses Barthes's view that a photograph is a "physical, material emanation of a past reality . . . it authenticates the reality of the past and provides a material connection to it." Hirsch asserts that a photograph of a family both reveals family cohesiveness and further enhances a sense of togetherness; it both chronicles family rituals and becomes a part of the rituals.[32] Although in Hirsch's book you will not find specific questions to ask, you will be alerted to depths of meaning that will inspire interpretations of the photograph and of the narrator's thoughts about the photograph.

The late British historian Raphael Samuel, in his brilliant *Theatres of Memory*, remarks of family photographs, "They are posing not for the viewer but for themselves, projecting an image, however idealized, or fantasized, of what they believed themselves to be."[33] You might wonder, What is the image this family wanted to project? How is this family photograph similar to other family photographs of that period? How is it different?

In *Family Secrets: Acts of Memory and Imagination*, Annette Kuhn uses her own family's photographs to discuss the layers of meaning inherent in the images: "Bringing the secrets and the shadows into the open, allows the deeper meanings of the family drama's mythic aspects to be reflected upon, confronted, understood."[34] Kuhn contends that we must understand the context, must ask such questions as, Who took this picture? Who was not in the picture? What does this photograph not show? And to you, the reader, she poses this question: "What happens, then, if we take absences, silences, as evidence?"[35] And on another level, she advises considering the question, What were the particular society's expectations of such a picture? What are the connections between the personal image and the wider world? As an example, she connects the photograph of herself in the dress she wore when she was eight to the photograph of Queen Elizabeth, taken on the same day, the coronation.[36]

Although Bibles and photographs are kept and people define them as important, be alert to other possibilities—such things as a scrap of paper with a grocery list found at the bottom of a trunk or a faded paisley shawl or a broken toy or a tattered account book or a diagram of a garden. Artifacts can lead you to ask questions you had not thought of. Ask about a grocery list: "Are these the only things people usually bought at a store? What did they raise themselves or make at home?" About a wooden toy: "Who made this? Who was it made for? Was this a special relationship in the family? Why do you think this was kept in the family when other toys were not?" About a diagram of a garden: "Whose garden was this? I see only flowers here—does this mean that the woman had a vegetable garden somewhere else or that she did not have to worry about raising her own vegetables? Where did she get her seeds? How did she learn to garden? Who worked with her?"

Also important is the way that family members helped one another. When you see the cash register receipt stuck in the back of a cookbook, you may remember to ask how the family survived when there was no cash, what limits were set on spending and who set them, how goods were shared, how services were offered or asked for, how payment was made—for example, in delayed payments of cash, services, or goods?

Those slides and home movies you slept through as a child—look at them again with family members who were participants. Ask them to explain why they took the shots that particular day. Find out if there were family members who refused to be filmed and why. Ask what they are feeling as they look at themselves at that period of their lives. This window on their life can inspire you to ask new questions and them to talk.

Family Folklore

Smithsonian colleagues Steven Zeitlin, Amy Kotkin, and Holly Cutting Baker collected family folklore and presented types in A Celebration of American Family Folklore. They were particularly interested in family sayings, which they describe as "the poetry of everyday life."[37] These convey family values and indications of feelings about individuals. One family recalled the origins of a saying: The family drove down to a river where the boys were getting ready to begin a boat trip. Just as they were leaving, one son kissed his sister on the cheek and said, "Goodbye, Sis. Tell Ma the boat floats." From then on whenever a family member called home to assure others that things were all right, he said, "Tell Ma the boat floats."[38] The saying expresses the confidence that individuals in the family care and will want to know what is happening to a family member. This is an example of an important family value carried on from one generation to the next.

Storytelling is another indication of family values or ways of interacting. In A Celebration of American Family Folklore, the authors remind readers that often people remark after a harrowing experience, "At least it will make a good story." They analyze this process: "Our family stories make it possible to laugh over incidents that were anything but funny at the time, and the laughter signals that the trauma has been incorporated into the daily round of family life."[39] The story will have a meaning in the context of the particular family. Ask each narrator after he or she tells the story, "What do you think is the meaning of this story?"

Often a story will characterize an individual in one broad stroke. For example, family members tell the upcoming generation a story about the grandmother who realized that the granddaughter had not done that day's chore of collecting eggs from the henhouse. The grandmother swore at her, "May ye never have a hen!" That granddaughter left the farm and lived in cities all her life. Was the interaction between grandmother and granddaughter a liberation from the hard work of a farm? Perhaps, but in that family, it was an indication of the personalities of the two individuals.[40] Zeitlin, Kotkin, and Baker comment, "[The family stories] enable us to simplify the complexities of a family member's personality into an easily remembered, easily communicated narrative."[41] The pitfall is that these brief glances simplify too much. The complexity of a character is not revealed. It will be up to you, the interviewer, to get the details that present more complete evidence about an individual.

Along with stories, family myths serve a purpose, such as to reinforce a distinguishing characteristic of the family, to teach a family value, or to save a reputation. "We were rich then." Or, "Your grandfather was known as the smartest man in town—why, he invented the washing machine." Or, "We were always known for our hospitality." Or, the one in my family, "Your grandmother never let a person leave her house hungry." I've spent a lot of time cooking, believing on the basis of this myth that I, as a woman in this family, am expected to do this.

You may unconsciously accept the myths in your own family, as I did, because they are a part of your way of thinking about the world or because they stimulate family pride that you also feel. Or you may be a social scientist studying a particular family from a greater emotional distance. In any case, check these myths out. They may contain a kernel of truth that you can corroborate with other kinds of evidence. On the other hand, they may present an account that is demonstrably false yet revealing of a family need and therefore true in an important way.

Also consider family rituals such as the gatherings at weddings, funerals, reunions, and special holidays as evidence of certain kinds of interaction among members. In A Celebration of American Family Folklore, religious and secular rituals are described as ways that "real emotional business is transacted." The authors explain, "Stories are told, nicknames bantered, photos taken and perused. For some families these may be their only way of expressing kinship."[42] Go and be both participant and observer. Take field notes on questions you want to ask your narrators about these rituals. Look for all of the ways that kinship is expressed. Ask the participants when you get to the interview what the rituals mean to them.

Thus, the family historian and any ethnographic researcher would do well to consider all kinds of folklore as evidence. Distinguish this from factual information about an actual event, however. Here the emphasis will be on meanings. To be meaningful, a story does not necessarily have to be verifiable. For factual information about events, look for corroborating evidence in written records; compare the oral accounts with other kinds of evidence, such as letters, photographs, official documents, and newspaper accounts. Check dates for accuracy.

Confronting Differences in Interpretation with the Narrator

Differences about interpretations arise as soon as family members read what you have written. When you as interviewer-writer accurately record and present an event in the manuscript but the narrator strongly opposes your interpretation, you can engage in a dialogue with the hope of coming to an understanding of each other's position, not necessarily an agreement. Folklorist Katharine Borland recorded the life history of her grandmother, Beatrice. Beatrice described an event that took place in the grandstand at a horse race in Maine. The young Beatrice, attired in frilly dress, gloves, hat, and carrying a purse, bet on a horse against her father's advice. Her horse won and won again in the second heat while the men around her grew more and more dismayed. When her horse won for the third time, she threw hat, gloves, and purse to the wind.[43]

Her feminist granddaughter interpreted the situation as one in which women were granted only "partial participant status." Beatrice had defied this and bet—"the narrated event takes on the dimension of a female struggle for autonomy within a hostile environment." Beatrice's throwing away gloves, hat, purse—the trappings of femininity—symbolically acted out her rejection of encumbrances placed on women's behavior.[44] When the grandmother read this, she was shocked by this interpretation and accused her granddaughter of interjecting into the story her own values.[45]

Borland says that in retrospect she wished she had played that segment of the tape for her grandmother and asked her what meaning she gave it. She also suspected that in part her grandmother's strong feeling about the interpretation came from "loss of authorial control." Borland regretted that she had "assumed a likeness of mind when there was in fact a difference."[46] Later, grandmother and granddaughter went over the manuscript again; and the grandmother admitted that although she had not thought about the events in her life in that way, some of what Borland had said was "very true."[47]

This experience points to the danger of the researcher's presenting an interpretation of an event in a family history as the only one and of reading into a situation in the past a present view. This does not mean the researcher should keep silent about her or his own interpretation, but Borland rightly advises checking with the narrator about meaning and distinguishing the narrator's from the interviewer-writer's interpretations.

Social scientists studying many families can also check interpretations. Chaya Piotrkowski, in preparing the manuscript for *Work and the Family System: A Naturalistic Study of Working-Class and Lower-Middle-Class Families*, discussed a draft with most of the research families. He explains his reasons for doing so: "Although it was costly, the benefits of such a collaboration for the research investigation cannot be overestimated. Sociocultural bias in interpretation becomes much less problematic, as does the danger of misunderstanding. Such a process also helps guide the course of research, and there is less chance of emerging with a description that is not grounded in the experience of those it purports to represent."[48]

Suggested Questions to Ask in Family History Research

Ruth Patterson's family history is an informative one for the public because the individuals, although caught up in family aspirations and their own desires, are always seen against the background of national events and local customs. You will need to consider broad themes like this as you plan the interview guide. William Fletcher in *Recording Your Family History* suggests organizing questions about family history into three broad categories: (1) typical life cycle and "life crisis" events—courtship and marriage, births of children, work and career experiences, decisions in middle age, retirement; (2) historical events and your narrator's experience of them—for example, the two world wars, the Depression, war in Korea and Vietnam, rapid change in technology; (3) personal values, experiences, and life philosophy—for example, religious experiences, affiliations, community, life experience lessons, generational differences.[49]

Linda Shopes suggests a slightly different organization that emphasizes social relationships and community: (1) the impact of major historical events and trends; (2) relationship of various aspects of social life, such as work, religion, community life, or class status and mobility, to individuals within the family; (3) structure and dynamics of family life; and (4) folklore by which a family preserves and uses its experiences.[50]

Often a roughly chronological approach is the most useful way to organize an interview. When the narrator is remembering a certain era in her life, living in a certain place during that time, living with certain people, then the researcher can ask the appropriate questions within the selected broad themes. If the narrator has her or his own organization, however, you, as researcher, can fit your questions into it. Because recollections often spring from the way people associate one thing with another in their minds, narrators often abandon chronological sequences in choosing what to remember. A woman may want to concentrate on the life stages of each child rather than on her own, and she may see herself in the context of interaction with the child. A man may want to discuss first the highlights of his career and return to discuss childhood second because he sees childhood as secondary in importance to the career.

If you are researching your own family, specific questions such as the following probably have come to mind: "Why did my great-grandparents come here? How did they survive those first years? What did they want for themselves and for their children? What were their decisions and their values that went into the process of making my parents the people they were? How was a family culture built up? Where did it come from? In what ways did family members communicate with one another? What behaviors were expected of a man and of a woman? How have such influences affected my life?"

William Fletcher's *Recording Your Family History* and Jim Watts and Allen F. Davis's *Generations: Your Family in American History* both offer suggestions such as these: In talking about people and events in any life situation, ask, "What was a typical workday like?" Or, "What was a typical Sunday like?" Probe with specific questions: "When did you get up? What did you do? Who prepared the food? Was this the big meal of the day? What did you eat? Who was there?"[51] Such specific questions as, "How were people seated at the table?" can be very useful. Seating arrangement is an indication of status within the family: sometimes women did not sit at all. And headship indicates level of power or, at least, the person to which the group makes a show of respect.

Discover the roles each family member would be expected to take. In discussing the adolescent years, ask such questions as, "What were your chores around the house as a girl? What were your brothers' chores? What were you allowed to do for fun? What were your brothers allowed to do? Did your mother and your father indicate to you what they expected you to do in your adult work? Did you think about what you wanted to be? What did you see as the possibilities? Were there other family members who talked to you about what you might do in adulthood?"

The influence of outside institutions can be explored. In our secular times, we may discount religious experience, for example, but this was a part of the lives of older generations. I asked my narrators who had been children in a North Carolina mill village before World War I what they had gotten out of church attendance. One woman remarked of her minister, "He made me feel important." This was no small feat in a mill village population where the saying in the nearby town about mill workers was, "Don't get close—you'll get lint on you."[52]

Questions about games and stories are productive of many kinds of revelations. In the same project discussed above, I was struck by the narrators' ingenuity and originality in childhood. They made their own games from natural materials—there was no money to buy toys. They covered rocks with moss and made "stuffed sofas" for doll furniture. They made their dolls from corn cobs. They then invented life dramas that these dolls played out. They had marriages and funerals for the corncob families in which they practiced the behavior that would be expected of them as adults—for example, someone would deliver an eloquent sermon, someone would cry.[53] I learned much about the norms of this group from asking questions about children's play. And questions about childhood play revealed things about family relationships and the personalities of individuals, such as which aunt let children play in her house and dress up in adult clothes and shoes, which one let the children jump up and down on the beds, which one insisted on silence and obedience.

When the discussion focuses on childhood and adolescence, you have an opportunity to discover family expectations about acceptable behavior and appropriate gender roles. Ask questions such as, "What would have been your mother's attitude toward premarital sex or teenage sex? How did she let you know?"[54] Watts and Davis suggest asking, "How important was it in your generation to become a father? A mother?" And inspired by Piri Thomas's account of growing up in *Down These Mean Streets*, they offer this question: "What does 'becoming a man' mean to you?"[55]

Information about family survival is important to all family members. Ask who took care of sick family members, how the family got along during periods of unemployment, what effects there were when a wage earner left the family. In this context, ask how the family survived the Depression. Did the family lose a home? A farm? How did this affect the women? The men? Find out how the two world wars (and others) affected the family.

So many families in the United States, Canada, Australia, Britain, and western European nations have experienced immigration that you are likely to deal with this in studying any family. For immigrant groups, get as much background information on the particular group as you can. Studies such as these will give you clues about specific questions to ask. In your questioning, search for motivation. Find out how the immigration was accomplished and what family members' expectations were, as well as the details of the encounter with the new culture. Watts and Davis suggest asking, "For your grandparents, what did 'making it' in American society mean? What did it mean to your parents? What does it mean to you?"[56] Migration within a country also characterizes our era. For a history of black families in the United States, for example, find out how the individual family members accomplished the move from South to North, who helped them in this transition, what kinds of experiences were different in the new setting, what their hopes were, how they survived.

And ask the hard questions about social injustice, such as, "Was your family ever under attack by another group—for example, the Ku Klux Klan?"[57] And even harder, "Do you know if your grandfather ever joined the Klan?" Or, "Were you denied that job because you were not a man (or the right color or did not attend the right church or have the right kinship ties or speak the right kind of English)?"

The questions suggested here do not even begin to cover all the possibilities. In your background reading about the particular culture the family comes from and in your reading of other family histories, biographies, and manuals on family history mentioned here, you will find questions applicable to your own study. Search and be open to all kinds of areas to explore; then write out an interview guide with the broad themes significant to you and, within them, the specific questions you need answered. Decide how you will vary the guide to make it appropriate for each family member you interview.

Evaluation of Family Members' Oral Histories

As you ask these questions during an interview, there will be times when something does not ring true or contradicts another narrator's testimony. You may also find contradictions in the narrator's statements on the same subject. In writing your own family's history, even though you love these narrators— each of them significant in some way in your life—you must carefully evaluate the oral history. It is a document, a primary source to be approached critically. Of course, you compare one narrator's testimony to others', and you search for other kinds of evidence to dispute or corroborate statements that you suspect may not be factually true. Akemi Kikumura, from her experience in writing a biography of her mother, advises using direct observation and comparing what you observe with what is being told to you. She also suggests repeatedly asking the same question of a narrator over a long period of time.[58] The narrator may think things through or check on him- or herself and arrive at a more accurate answer. Or something may happen that will make the narrator decide to answer your question more candidly.

There is the phenomenon that Mario Puzo calls "retrospective falsification."[59] Social scientists sometimes use the term *biography reconstruction* or *retrospective interpretation*. The motivation for this reconstruction of experience to suit the narrator stems from the desire of family members to paint a picture of family life that teaches what they want the next generation to learn. This way of presenting the past in such a way that it satisfies current need is not a characteristic unique to family history, of course. But if it is essentially a picture that other evidence does not support, then you must beware of perpetuating it. Sometimes you, as a member of the family, share its values and want to believe the "retrospective falsification." Be conscious of this possibility as you evaluate the oral history testimony. What the narrator says is true for him or her at that moment or is what he or she wishes were true. You must find out if the evidence bears it out before you present it as an evidence-based picture for everyone in the family, generations to come.

Advantages of Studying Family History

I have pointed out potential problems as roads to avoid or choose with caution, but the journey is worth taking. Consider the advantages in researching your own family: family members will tell you things they would never tell an outsider. Kikumura, an American-born woman from a Japanese family, describes her mother as "a woman of Meiji Japan, born in an era when Confucian ethics tenaciously gripped the moral fabric of that country."[60] She found that both generational and cultural differences separated her from her mother, and she felt that she was both "outsider" and "insider." Still, her mother's biography could not have been written by anyone else: "Given the purpose of my research and the kinds of data I wanted to collect, I firmly believe that my study could not have been completed by anyone other than a member of my immediate family. When I asked my mother if she would have revealed her life experiences to anyone other than a close family member, she replied, 'No! You don't disclose your soul to a tanin (a nonrelative).'"[61]

Certainly the rewards for this research are rich. This is a journey into your family's past, but it is also an exploration of yourself—of the stories, rituals, relationships, and values that influence your own way of looking at the world. And the process itself of going over a life together is a means of coming to understand family members and drawing closer to them. Kikumura comments on the effects of this process for her: "The Life History turned out to be a very transformative experience for me, for in the process, I was able to reshape many of the negative images that society had ascribed to people of color and I was drawn closer to my mother, my family, and my community."[62]

Collecting the tapes that compose an oral history of the family or writing a history is a gift to the generations that come after us. It is a personal, intimate gift. And in this sense, the advantage of doing this kind of historical research is unique.

For the social scientist who has studied by means of in-depth interviews a limited number of families, the work is also rewarding. As Oscar Lewis pointed out, "In the description of the various family members we see real individuals as they live and work together in their family group rather than as averages or stereotypes out of context."[63]

Summary

Family relationships are forever (just a reminder). Therefore, the family researcher must be highly sensitive to each member's feelings and motivations in this kind of project. It is crucial that introduction of the project is done so that cooperation or at least acceptance is achieved, but you cannot sacrifice honesty about your purpose in order to get cooperation. Education of family members about the uses of the family history and research methods is necessary whether you are researching your own family history or carrying out a research project involving many families. And your own self-reflection as the project goes on will teach you much. The best family histories will reveal the ways the general culture interacts with the unique family culture and how both impinge on the psychological makeup of each family member.

Recommended Reading

Overviews of Family History

Bate, Kerry William. "Family History: Some Answers, Many Questions." *Oral History Review* 16, no. 1 (Spring 1988): 127–30. In this brief review essay, Bate raises questions about two recently published family histories—one, *The Seed of Sally Good'n: A Black Family of Arkansas, 1833–1953*, is mentioned in this chapter—and thereby suggests questions we can ask about other family histories.

Drake, Michael. *Time, Family and Community: Perspectives on Family and Community History.* Oxford: Blackwell for the Open University, 1994. An excellent collection of articles by scholars in a range of disciplines.

Gordon, Michael, ed. *The American Family in Social-Historical Perspective.* 2nd ed. New York: St. Martin's, 1978. Rich collection of articles on the history of the American family as historians have viewed it. A useful introduction to this special field of social history that spans from Philip Greven's article on family structure in seventeenth-century Andover, Massachusetts, to "A Mother's Wages: Income Earning among Married Italian and Black Women, 1896–1911," by Elizabeth Peck.

Greenstein, Theodore N. *Methods of Family Research*. Thousand Oaks, CA: Sage, 2001. Author's intended audience is undergraduate and graduate students in sociology: he discusses ways to go about research and to understand research results. See especially the discussion on qualitative research methods, chapter 7 (pp. 97–107) and chapter 4, "Using the Internet to Study Families" (pp. 49–58).

Hareven, Tamara K. "Recent Research on the History of the Family." In Drake, *Time, Family and Community*, 13–43. Hareven surveys long-held ideas about the history of the family and shows how new research modifies them. She suggests questions that arise from current research that point to future research. (Her longer version of this article is "The History of the Family and the Complexity of Social Change," in *American Historical Review* 96, no. 1 [1991]: 95–124.)

———. "The Search for Generational Memory." In *Public History Readings*, ed. Phyllis K. Leffler and Joseph Brent, 270–83. Malabar, FL: Krieger Publishing Company, 1992. This is an excellent essay on the need individuals have for "vicarious linkage with the historical group experience"; it presents an analysis of the appeal of such autobiographical histories as *The Autobiography of Malcolm X* and *Roots*.

Thompson, Paul, and Daniel Bertaux, eds. *Between Generations: Family Models, Myths and Memories*, vol. 2 of *International Yearbook of Oral History and Life Stories*. Oxford: Oxford University Press, 1993. Very useful articles concerning families' experience in different nations but reveals overall the power of the family to transmit values and expectations from generation to generation. See especially Anne Muxel, "Family Memory: A Review of French Works on the Subject," pp. 191–97, for a brief, general account of questions French historians of the family are asking. Paul Thompson in "Family Myths, Models, and Denial in the Shaping of Individual Life Paths," pp. 11–38, discusses using life histories to discover "the process and scope of intergenerational transmissions."

Vinovskis, Maris A. "American Families in the Past." In *Ordinary People and Everyday Life: Perspectives on the New Social History*, ed. James B. Gardner and George Rollie Adams, 115–37. Nashville, TN: American Association for State and Local History, 1983. This article is an overview of scholarly works on the family, with a bibliography pointing to specific studies.

Using Oral History in the Classroom to Research Family History

Cuthbert, David. "Undergraduates as Historians: Family History Projects Add Meaning to an Introductory Survey." *History Teacher* 7 (1973): 7–17. In this specific and helpful article, Cuthbert includes the handout he gives to his classes, the release form he uses, and questions his students ask.

Elliott, Brian. "Biography, Family History and the Analysis of Social Change." In *Time, Family and Community: Perspectives on Family and Community History*, ed Michael Drake. Oxford: Blackwell for the Open University, 1994. In this excellent, brief article, Elliott surveys present trends in family history research, argues for the relevance of family and biographical studies, and presents his own strategies in teaching students how to research their family history and connect this to worldwide events.

Jeffrey, Kirk. "Write a History of Your Own Family: Further Observations and Suggestions for Instructors." *History Teacher* 7 (1974): 365–73. Jeffrey points out in brief essay form the difficulties of assigning a family history in a one-semester course but includes reasons for having students write a family history nevertheless.

Metcalf, Fay D., and Matthew T. Downey. "Teaching about Families with Local History Sources." In *Using Local History in the Classroom*, 129–49. Nashville, TN: American Association for State and Local History, 1982. This could be termed "using the history of a family to teach local history." The chapter includes some specific information on using such sources as federal census data.

Zemelman, Steven, Patricia Bearden, Yolanda Simmons, and Pete Leki. *History Comes Home: Family Stories across the Curriculum*. York, ME: Stenhouse Publishers, 2000. Although this volume, designed for middle school students, scarcely pays attention to oral history, it does offer practical advice on other aspects of researching family history appropriate to this age group.

Suggestions for Family History Projects

Finnegan, Ruth, and Michael Drake. *From Family Tree to Family History*. Cambridge: Cambridge University Press in association with the Open University, 1994. Excellent guide to family research and although centered on British families, has applications for families in other places as well. Look especially at chapter 1, "Starting from Where You Are," and chapter 2, "Going Further: Tactics and Strategies."

Fletcher, William. *Recording Your Family History*. New York: Dodd, Mead, 1986. Fletcher suggests several hundred questions. My qualm is that some of these as phrased are "leading questions," but the ideas behind them are still useful.

Kikumura, Akemi. "Family Life Histories: A Collaborative Venture." *Oral History Review* 14 (1986): 1–7. This article deals mainly with the interpersonal relationships of interviewer and family members but also contains some suggestions on interviewing strategies.

Oblinger, Carl. *Interviewing the People of Pennsylvania: A Conceptual Guide to Oral History*. Harrisburg: Pennsylvania Historical and Museum Commission, 1978. In this helpful guide, refer especially to appendix C, "Family and Work Interview," pp. 70–80.

Martin, Peter, Gunshid G. Hagestad, and Patricia Diedrick. "Family Stories: Events (Temporarily) Remembered." *Journal of Marriage and Family* 50 (May 1988): 533–41. The authors' research indicated that family stories are mainly about personal events rather than historical events of a broader nature; 75 percent of stories their subjects told were about grandparents, only 20 percent about great-grandparents, and farther back, only about 4 percent.

Miller, Robert L. *Researching Life Stories and Family Histories*. Thousand Oaks, CA: Sage, 2000. Miller presents a history of the life study approach in the discipline of sociology. Chapters 3 and 4 offer information on the collection of family histories and life histories, and chapter 5 presents an analysis of a life history.

Shopes, Linda. "Using Oral History for a Family History Project." In *Oral History: An Interdisciplinary Anthology*, 2nd ed., eds. David K. Dunaway and Willa Baum, 231–40. Walnut Creek, CA: AltaMira, 1996. Shopes provides a brief, but helpful, introduction to the use of oral history in researching family history. She offers a sample form for each family member's information to help with the researcher's record keeping.

Watts, Jim, and Allen Davis. *Generations: Your Family in Modern American History*. 3rd ed. New York: Knopf, 1983. The authors present selections from family histories—both scholarly histories and autobiographical writings—with introductions and suggested questions based on the selection.

Yocum, Margaret R. "Family Folklore and Oral History Interviews: Strategies for Introducing a Project to One's Own Relatives." *Western Folklore* 41 (October 1982): 251–74. The article contains specific information on this important step.

Use of Artifacts in Studying Family History

Hirsch, Marianne. *Family Frames: Photographs, Narrative, and Postmemory*. London: Routledge, 1997. Hirsch's comments on the photographs will take your breath away. Once recovered, you will find your mind racing with the questions this book suggests you ask of photographs. Her words can indeed "empower us to imagine what's behind the surface of the image" (p. 2). You will be inspired not only to ask your family members certain questions about the photographs but also to look at their replies in new ways.

Kuhn, Annette. *Family Secrets: Acts of Memory and Imagination*. London: Verso, 1995. A strikingly original and insightful approach to analyzing photographs is presented here. Using principally photographs of herself taken by her father, she interprets the images in terms of the psychological struggles of mother, father, child, thereby delving into the feelings these images evoke. Kuhn does an excellent job of showing the reader the importance of the societal context for a photograph.

Kyvig, David E., and Myron A. Marty. *Nearby History: Exploring the Past around You*. 2nd. ed. Walnut Creek, CA: AltaMira, 2000. You will find in this volume useful questions for interviewing family members and for placing families in a background of local history. The authors provide caveats for determining authenticity and potential usefulness of various kinds of artifacts.

Lesy, Michael. *Time Frames: The Meaning of Family Photographs*. New York: Pantheon Press, 1980. Interesting and unusual interpretations of family photographs are presented.

Samuel, Raphael. *Theatres of Memory* (London: Verso, 1994), 366. See especially "In the Eye of History," pp. 315–36, and "Scopophilia," pp. 364–77. These chapters are about analyzing historic photographs but will give you insights into contemporary photographs—ever afterward, we cannot "take photographs on trust or treat them as transparent reflections of fact" (p. 329).

Taft, Robert. *Photography and the American Scene.* New York: Dover, 1964. First published 1938. This is a history of photography that gives the characteristics of photographs at different times in history. If you are trying to date a family photograph, this may help.

Outstanding Family Histories Based on Oral History

Broussard, Albert. *African-American Odyssey: The Stewarts, 1853–1963.* Lawrence: University Press of Kansas, 1998. This carefully researched history of three generations in an elite African American family reveals the intersection of culture, time, and unique personality. While experiences of the older generation could not be documented by oral history, the second and third generations' experiences are. This family history reveals how hard work and education do not necessarily produce success when race prejudice is involved.

Garceau, Dee. *The Important Things of Life: Women, Work, and Family in Sweetwater County, Wyoming, 1880–1929.* Lincoln: University of Nebraska Press, 1997. Using oral histories as well as records, such as the local newspapers and county manuscript census, Garceau discusses women's efforts to maintain family and community. She shows how kin networks provided for families suffering from loss of jobs or injuries or death and how women bowed to family pressures in choice of mate and in applying for land grants so that they could eventually extend their parents' or brother's or husband's land.

Kessler, Lauren. *Stubborn Twig: Three Generations in the Life of a Japanese Family.* New York: Random House, 1993. Kessler does use oral history research in this study of her own family. She reveals how families deny or downplay tragic events—in this case, Japanese Americans' internment during World War II—in an effort to weave them into a larger pattern of meanings that allows them to continue their lives. (See review by Arthur Hansen in the *Oral History Review* 24, no. 1 [Summer 1997]: 113–22.)

McLellan, Marjorie L. *Six Generations Here: A Farm Family Remembers.* Madison: State Historical Society of Wisconsin, 1997. Author uses family photographs, archival records, artifacts, and interviews to show how a particular family, the Kruegers, originally from Germany (Pomerania), living on a Wisconsin farm, "constructed and used their past in order to articulate a shared identity" (p. 3). This is beautifully illustrated by extensive use of family photographs, and the text presents family history in its complexity.

Porter, Marilyn. "Mothers and Daughters: Linking Women's Life Histories in Grand Bank, Newfoundland, Canada." *Women's Studies International Forum* 11, no. 6 (1988): 545–58. Porter conducted in-depth interviews with several generations of women in the same family to find out how women's work had changed and how the women experienced these changes. She explores the nature of the relationship between mothers and daughters and calls attention to the use of oral history as a method for discovering relationships within families.

Notes

1. Michael Kammen, comments on the dust jacket of John Demos's *The Unredeemed Captive: A Family Story from Early America* (New York: Alfred A. Knopf, 1995).

2. Oscar Lewis, "An Anthropological Approach to Family Studies," in *The Psychosocial Interior of the Family*, 3rd ed., ed. Gerald Handel, 119–28 (New York: Aldine, 1985); see pp. 120–23.

3. Christie W. Kiefer, *Changing Cultures, Changing Lives: An Ethnographic Study of Three Generations of Japanese Americans* (San Francisco: Jossey-Bass, 1974), ix.

4. Kiefer, *Changing Cultures*, xx.

5. Kiefer, *Changing Cultures*, xx.

6. Judith Worth, "The Use of the Family in History," *New England Social Studies Bulletin* 34 (1976–1977): 19–22.

7. Elizabeth Bott, *Family and Social Network: Roles, Norms, and External Relationships in Ordinary Urban Families* (London: Tavistock, 1957), 16.

8. Bott, *Family and Social Network*, 13–14.

9. Reuben Hill, *Family Development in Three Generations: A Longitudinal Study of Changing Family Patterns of Planning and Achievement* (Cambridge, MA: Schenkman, 1970), 122.

10. J. M. Pahl and R. E. Pahl, *Managers and Their Wives: A Study of Career and Family Relationships in the Middle Class* (London: Penguin, 1971), 6–7.

11. Margaret R. Yocum, "Family Folklore and Oral History Interviews: Strategies for Introducing a Project to One's Own Relatives," *Western Folklore* 41 (October 1982): 251–74; see p. 255.

12. Yocum, "Family Folklore and Oral History Interviews," 255.

13. David E. Kyvig and Myron A. Marty, *Nearby History: Exploring the Past around You*, 2nd ed. (Walnut Creek, CA: AltaMira, 2000).

14. Yocum, "Family Folklore and Oral History Interviews," 260.

15. Micaela di Leonardo, "Oral History as Ethnographic Encounter," *Oral History Review* 15 (Spring 1987): 1–20; see p. 10.

16. Yocum, "Family Folklore and Oral History Interviews," 260.

17. Yocum, "Family Folklore and Oral History Interviews," 262.

18. Yocum, "Family Folklore and Oral History Interviews," 265.

19. Celia S. Deschin, "Some Further Applications and Suggested Principles," *Social Work* 8 (April 1963): 14–18; see p. 17.

20. Richard Gelles, *The Violent Home* (Newbury Park, CA: Sage, 1987), 37–38.

21. Linda A. Bennett and Katharine McAvity, "Family Research: A Case for Interviewing Couples," in Handel, *Psychosocial Interior of the Family*, 75–94; see pp. 82–87. See also J. Collins and B. Nelson, "Interviewing the Married Couple: Some Research Aspects and Therapeutic Implications," *British Journal of Psychiatric Social Work* 8, no. 3 (1966): 46–51; Graham Allen, "A Note on Interviewing Spouses Together," *Journal of Marriage and Family* 42 (February 1980): 205–10.

22. Theodore N. Greenstein, *Methods of Family Research* (Thousand Oaks, CA: Sage, 2001), 10.

23. Kristie Miller, "Ruth Hanna McCormick: A Life in Politics" (paper presented at annual meeting of the Oral History Association, October 17, 1992, Cleveland, Ohio). See Kristie Miller, *Ruth Hanna McCormick: A Life in Politics* (Albuquerque: University of New Mexico Press, 1992).

24. Kristie Miller, discussion during the session on biography, annual meeting of the Oral History Association, October 17, 1992, Cleveland, Ohio.

25. Joyce Antler, "Having It All, Almost: Confronting the Legacy of Lucy Sprague Mitchell," in *The Challenge of Feminist Biography*, ed. Sara Alpern, Joyce Antler, Elisabeth Israels Perry, and Ingrid Winther Scobie (Urbana: University of Illinois Press, 1992), 106.

26. Jacquelyn Dowd Hall, "Lives through Time: Second Thoughts on Jessie Daniel Ames," in Alpern et al., *Challenge of Feminist Biography*, 139–58; see pp. 150–51.

27. William Fletcher, *Recording Your Family History* (New York: Dodd, Mead, 1986), 11.

28. Alan J. Lichtman, *Your Family History* (New York: Vintage, 1978), 49.

29. Mamie Garvin Fields with Karen Fields, *Lemon Swamp and Other Places: A Carolina Memoir* (New York: Free Press, 1983), xii.

30. Ruth Polk Patterson, *The Seed of Sally Good'n: A Black Family of Arkansas, 1833–1953* (Lexington: University Press of Kentucky, 1985).

31. Marianne Hirsch, *Family Frames: Photographs, Narrative and Postmemory* (London: Routledge, 1997).

32. Hirsch, *Family Frames*, 6–7.

33. Raphael Samuel, *Theatres of Memory* (London: Verso, 1994), 366. See especially "In the Eye of History," pp. 315–36, and "Scopophilia," pp. 364–77. These chapters are about analyzing historic photographs but will give you insights into contemporary photographs, as well.

34. Annette Kuhn, *Family Secrets: Acts of Memory and Imagination* (London: Verso, 1995), 6.

35. Kuhn, *Family Secrets*, 13.

36. Kuhn, *Family Secrets*, chapter 5, "A Meeting of Two Queens," 59–83.

37. Steven Zeitlin, Amy Kotkin, and Holly Cutting Baker, *A Celebration of American Family Folklore* (New York: Pantheon, 1982), 150.

38. Zeitlin, Kotkin, and Baker, *Celebration of American Family Folklore*, 150

39. Zeitlin, Kotkin, and Baker, *Celebration of American Family Folklore*, 19.

40. Zeitlin, Kotkin, and Baker, *Celebration of American Family Folklore*, 16.

41. Zeitlin, Kotkin, and Baker, *Celebration of American Family Folklore*, 14.

42. Zeitlin, Kotkin, and Baker, *Celebration of American Family Folklore*, 164.

43. Katharine Borland, "'That's Not What I Said': Interpretive Conflict in Oral Narrative Research," in *Women's Words: The Feminist Practice of Oral History*, 63–75 (London: Routledge, 1991); see pp. 65–67.

44. Borland, "'That's Not What I Said,'" 67.

45. Borland, "'That's Not What I Said,'" 67–69.

46. Borland, "'That's Not What I Said,'" 69–72.

47. Borland, "'That's Not What I Said,'" 73–74.

48. Chaya S. Piotrkowski, *Work and the Family System: A Naturalistic Study of Working-Class and Lower-Middle-Class Families* (New York: Collier, 1978), 26.

49. Fletcher, *Recording Your Family History*, 2.

50. Linda Shopes, "Using Oral History for a Family History Project," in *Oral History: An Interdisciplinary Anthology*, eds. David K. Dunaway and Willa Baum, 238–47 (Nashville, TN: American Association for State and Local History, 1996); see pp. 240–41.

51. Jim Watts and Allen F. Davis, *Generations: Your Family in American History* (New York: Alfred A. Knopf, 1978); Fletcher, *Recording Your Family History*, 48.

52. Valerie Yow (listed as Valerie Quinney), "Childhood in a Southern Mill Village," *International Journal of Oral History* 3, no. 3 (November 1982): 167–92; see p. 186.

53. Yow, "Childhood in a Southern Mill Village," 168.

54. Fletcher, *Recording Your Family History*, 26.

55. Watts and Davis, *Generations*, 27.

56. Watts and Davis, *Generations*. See section 3, "The American Dream," pp. 34–68.

57. Watts and Davis, *Generations*, 51.

58. Akemi Kikumura, "Family Life Histories: A Collaborative Venture," *Oral History Review* 14 (1986): 1–7; see pp. 5–6. The biography of her mother is published as Akemi Kikumura, *Through Harsh Winters: The Life of a Japanese Immigrant Woman* (Novato, CA: Chandler & Sharp, 1981).

59. Quoted in Watts and Davis, *Generations*, 48–49.

60. Kikumura, "Family Life Histories," 4.

61. Kikumura, "Family Life Histories," 3.

62. Kikumura, "Family Life Histories," 7.

63. Lewis, "An Anthropological Approach to Family Studies," 123.

CHAPTER TEN

Analysis and Interpretation

As you are evaluating the oral history document, studying the text closely, and indexing the tape, you begin to be aware of how the narrator is recounting experiences—how he or she is selecting details and organizing them, where there is a pause and then a change of topic, what expressions are repeated. Because this is a guide for collecting information and we have the space of one chapter only for analyzing the oral history document, I do not treat analysis in depth. However, as you begin to discern patterns, this is a good time to consider analytical approaches across disciplines. This is a most creative period for the researcher-writer. John and Lynn Lofland use the terms "surrender" and "discipline" to describe the process of analyzing: "The surrender entails opening yourself up to your personal sensibilities, insights, and proclivities, as these interact with the data. The discipline entails channeling and evolving these personal interactions with the data in terms of relevant units of analysis, appropriate questions, and the constraints of what is interesting."[1]

Analytical Approaches across Disciplines

Often scholars using the in-depth interview as a research method look for recurring themes, symbols, imagery, myths, and rhetorical devices. An example of the use of symbols in individual testimony can be found in folklorist Patrick Mullen's book *Listening to Old Voices: Folklore, Life Stories, and the Elderly.* Mullen shows how a narrator talked about the event that began his career as an auctioneer at age eleven. In that year of his life he also witnessed an exhumation of a grave and looked down into the face of a man dead ten years—an unforgettable confrontation with death. In the closing years of his own life, the narrator chose these two incidents to recount, symbols of his beginning his adult life and of his awareness of its end.[2] Raphael Samuel and Paul Thompson, in *Myths We Live By*,[3] present discussions on analyzing symbols and myths in a life review.

One way to analyze a life history is to discern the roles the individual played. L. L. Langness and Gelya Frank present a discussion about this in a review of anthropologists' analyses of life histories in *Lives: An Anthropological Approach to Biography*.[4] David Mandelbaum, drawing from his study of the life of Gandhi, suggests considering the parameters of a person's life, the principal turnings, and the person's characteristic means of adaptation. He cautions that these should be seen in the context of the sociological and cultural structures within which the life unfolded.[5]

In *The Research Act: A Theoretical Introduction to Sociological Methods*, Norman Denzin uses the work of sociologist Kimball Young and L. L. Langness to describe another approach to analyzing life histories: Young examined the life histories in terms of the individuals' developmental history, that is, life stages and life experiences, but he looked also at the inner life, for example, self-concept and values. He viewed each life history as a complete world, but there is much working back and forth between life histories in the collection, comparing the case specific and the general. Denzin's approach is closely related. In his 1984 book *Interpretive Biography*, Denzin discusses the ways individuals identify turning points in their lives, "epiphanies": (1) the moment that changes your life; (2) the moment that has been building when you know change is irrevocable; (3) the "minor epiphany," a symbol that brings insight to understanding an event or a person; and (4) those episodes that compel you to relive an event and give it meaning.[6]

In an article in the *Journal of Interdisciplinary History*, Miles Shore suggests a psychoanalytic approach but defines the conditions that should be present before attempting this kind of analysis of a life history. Shore cautions that psychological interpretation can be considered when (1) otherwise inexplicable events can be explained by psychological factors, (2) enough information is given in the document to warrant this kind of interpretation, (3) the researcher has a degree of mastery of psychological matters, and (4) a psychoanalytic concept can be applied to the specific life history so that the concept enhances understanding. He suggests considering such occurrences as developmental crises, loss, disappointment, life change precipitating emotional distress, and manifestations of physical and psychological illness. Especially he calls attention to the personal myth, explaining this as the set of less-than-conscious motivations that influence attitudes and behavior that form a pattern as the individual goes through life stages.[7]

If you are working with oral histories from many individuals, looking for patterns and hoping to develop a theory from your data, consider still other models. Sociologists Leonard Schatzman and Anselm Strauss suggest taking notes during the process of data collection on possible ways to analyze—rather than waiting until the end and then looking over all the data. They see this as leading to a process whereby data are placed in classes: "Probably the most fundamental operation in the analysis of qualitative data is that of discovering significant *classes* of things, persons and events and the properties which characterize them."[8] (I interpret their use of the word "class" to be similar in meaning to the term currently in use, *categories*.) The researcher then finds the links between categories and begins to form organizing schemes.

The example Schatzman and Strauss give is drawn from research on a hospital. The researchers started with a category, "Scheduled Encounters among Hospital Staff"; but they found that most encounters occurred incidentally and around the time of the occurrence of a new or problematic event. They then set up a new category termed "Incidental Encounters."[9] For Strauss, collecting data and forming ideas about what it means go on at the same time.

Still another model to consider is the historian's. If the researcher is using a collection of life histories, usually gathered around a general topic such as an occupation or movement or historical event, it is the common meanings of the shared experience that are sought—and also the meanings unique to the individual. Alessandro Portelli states this succinctly: "The fact that a culture is made up of individuals different from one another is one of the important things that social sciences sometimes forget, and of which oral history reminds us."[10]

Virginia Yans-McLaughlin, with the late labor historian Herbert Gutman, directed an in-depth interviewing project with three hundred immigrants and migrants to New York City and their children—African Americans, Jews, Italians, Irish, Germans, and Puerto Ricans. In analyzing about one hundred Italian and Jewish oral histories from this project, she was interested in finding out "the social processes and contexts from which these accounts of the self emerged." She suggests that a fruitful analytical approach is to look for "(1) the way in which the speaker organizes the past, present, and future time during an interview; (2) the way in which the speaker describes himself or herself in relation to the past; (3) the way in which the speaker describes, or fails to describe, interaction with objects and persons of the past; and (4) the interaction of the two sets of scripts, the historian's and the speaker's."[11] Of course, we must figure out not only what the narrator's cultural scripts are but also what our own are. Considerable self-reflection is required always.

In similar research, Ronald Grele, in "Listen to Their Voices: Two Case Studies in the Interpretation of Oral History Interviews," compared two oral histories of Jewish garment workers, drawn from a project on the history of labor union activity in New York City.[12] One narrator, Mel Dubin, told the story of his involvement in the garment industry and in the International Ladies Garment Workers Union, in the context of the history of New York. Grele found that although Dubin lived into the 1970s, he ignored strikes after the 1910 strike—the one particularly significant to him. Dubin's narrative has a theme: Jews and Italians learned to sew in Europe in a mythic past and brought with them their skills and fighting spirit. Now that they are dying out, the backbone of the garment industry—the union—and the city are weakening. Grele notes that actually New York never depended on one industry, and garment manufacture itself was well established before the great immigration period of Jews and Italians. Historically inaccurate, Dubin's narrative nevertheless suggests the central myth with which he makes sense of his working life.

For comparison Grele presents another life story interview from this collection of oral histories of New York working-class people that describes some of the same historical events. This narrator, Bella Pincus, does not locate meaning in a mythic past but points to a specific historical past in czarist Russia. While Dubin stresses electoral and union politics as a means by which the working class can assert power, Pincus points to militancy as the only way a working person can gain political power. Grele observes, "To Bella power originates in people opening their world for themselves, not in elections and the good graces of officials." There is no inevitable decline in this view: the world continues to be an "arena of dramatic conflict."[13]

The interpretations of their similar historical experiences differed for these narrators, but they were both involved in a process—the construction of a past usable for them personally. Grele points to the way analysis revealed that shared historical memories overlie a deeper level, the particular vision of the experience—the "complex structures of historical memory."[14] Grele was concerned about the process whereby myth becomes history and this becomes ideology. His question is useful to us as oral historians: how does the narrator recount a shared historical experience yet wrest from this a unique meaning consonant with his or her personal vision?

Alessandro Portelli has shown how individuals used symbols held collectively to convey the meaning of their struggles together.[15] In his article on the testimony of a working man in Italy, "The Best Garbage Man in Town: Life and Times of Valtero Peppoloni, Worker," Portelli offers the reader extended excerpts from a single oral history and presents his interpretation. His purpose is to show "how a single life story relates to broader and shared patterns of culture, and how the common, shared elements relate to what makes this story both representative and unique."[16]

Portelli's narrator, Valtero Peppoloni, begins his life story with an account of his father's arrest for political reasons in the 1920s and his father's subsequent loss of his job. The whole family had to move to Terni, where it was still possible to get factory jobs, but his father died shortly after the move. As a child, Peppoloni stole apricots from the landlady's tree to right the injustice in the way his mother and her family were treated as sharecroppers and servants. Peppoloni went to work as a teenager, and his story is focused on work and wresting justice from an unjust society. Portelli looks closely at the structure of Peppoloni's narration and finds that it proceeds in a linear way, but also, within this broad outline, there is a circular recurrence of theme, and the stages of development of the narrative build on each other. For Peppoloni, the main theme that underlies the account of events is this: "Let's do our work first, our duty . . . then we'll claim our rights and struggle for them."[17] Portelli finds that "the deeper level of the narrative, therefore, is one of consistency and continuity."[18]

Portelli views Peppoloni's account as falling into "shared narrative patterns, structures, and motifs."[19] He can see it as a story representative of the workers' lives at that time and in that place, but he also realizes that it is personal and unique: "What makes this story intensely personal is, in the end, the fullness, depth, and intensity of its personal use of shared cultural traits."[20] Portelli's implied question to ask of any oral history is indeed useful: how does this oral document use shared narrative patterns and themes from a specific culture and at the same time describe fully and vividly a unique experience?

A Close Look at an Individual Oral History

My work has been both with content analysis of a collection of interviews and also with a close look at the individual oral history, and I combine approaches of a couple of disciplines. I offer here as an example an oral history project on the history of a women's cooperative art gallery I carried out in the late 1980s when the cooperative was fifteen years old. The gallery was the seventh in the nation in the early 1970s to be founded by women, for women artists. Up to that point, women had a hard time getting their work shown in museums, and often they could not sell their work because gallery owners would not even look at it. Usually the gallery owner said something like, "We already have a woman's work here. We can't use any more." At the annual exhibition of contemporary art at the Whitney Museum in 1970, only 5 percent of the artists represented were women, and this was typical of major exhibitions. Women started showing their work at street fairs and hanging paintings in small public spaces or college libraries. In 1972, women artists in New York set up a cooperative art gallery, Artists in Residence (AIR), and their gallery became a model for other women throughout the nation.

The gallery I studied, the Hera Gallery, was begun by ten women in Wakefield, Rhode Island, a small town far from New York, the center for art in the United States. These ten artists were housewives or part-time instructors or graduate students with little money, but they pledged what they could and converted an old laundry into a gallery. Nobody expected it to last, but it is ongoing today. I was hired to write a straight narrative history of the founding of the gallery as part of the celebration of their fifteenth anniversary. But personally, I was interested in finding out how these artists came to believe in their work to the point of making the sacrifices necessary to start a gallery and to sustain it year after year. And I wanted to know how belonging to and working for a woman's cooperative gallery changed their personal lives and their work. I was also intrigued by their commitment to egalitarian structure and wanted to know how that worked in practice.

I carried out in-depth interviews with the ten founding members and with ten additional members, as well as six more interviews with the artists' husbands and community people. With these oral histories and many informal conversations, I entwined other documents, such as gallery logs, minutes of meetings, correspondence, and photographs. I also used participant-observation data because I attended gallery meetings and show openings.

Not having a computer at the time and being a hands-on, literal-minded person, I cut up by hand a copy of each transcript and placed the segments in loose categories according to the interview guide's topic headings. I found out that I needed to add new topic headings, as well. As I read through all the segments again under each topic heading, I further discriminated according to the thought of the segment and formed many smaller headings. I could then examine all the answers that dealt with the particular topic—I just picked up that pile. When the categories did not shed light on the information, I changed categories and headings and shuffled all the piles. You can carry out the same process using a computer's copy and paste function.

For many topics, the answers were the same for all or a huge majority of narrators, and so it was easy to arrive at generalizations. For example, all of the narrators voiced the conviction that the women's cooperative art gallery was justified because of the difficulty women had in getting gallery owners or museum curators to look at their work. All talked about the effects of sustaining the gallery on their personal life: They felt guilty about taking money from the family budget to pay monthly dues. They also felt guilty about taking time from the family so they could work on art or go to the gallery. On the other hand, they said they felt freer in their artistic expression—they were not trying to impress the New York art establishment and they felt supported by fellow gallery members in taking risks.[21]

If I had wanted to delve into a deeper level to understand the psychological reasons why these women artists made the first sacrifices to set up the gallery and continued to make sacrifices to sustain it, I would have looked more closely at each oral history. Sociologist Daniel Bertaux and historian Isabelle Bertaux-Wiame, who studied bakers in France, were interested in the careers of the general group "bakers," and not interested in details of individual cases. They were not seeking explanation at a psychological level, as Bertaux states: "We always tried to have bakers and bakers' wives focus upon what they had *done* in life (practices) rather than what they thought about it."[22] But examination of motivation in the study of women artists is appropriate and enlightening because this movement started with the *decision* of women to take action. The consequence was important: the decisions of individuals in the Hera group and others in this nationwide movement changed the way people regarded women artists' work. The movement inspired art historians to ask different questions than they had asked before, which meant that it not only forced people to look critically at the power structure in the contemporary art world but also prompted new research on the history of artistic production.

Look closely now at one of these life stories: here is a brief narrative about the interviewing situation and then extended excerpts from one transcript. First I used a pseudonym, but when I sent the draft of this chapter to the artist, she told me to use her real name. Most of my questions were prompted by a need for information to write the commissioned history of the gallery. Indeed, the frame for this oral history is the interviewing project for a history of the women's art gallery, and the stated audience is not only the researcher but the members of the gallery itself and also the general public.

Perhaps we can, metaphorically speaking, put our heads together to analyze this document: we can ferret out categories and themes in the testimony. We can arrive at an interpretation. Space is limited, so this transcript has had to be edited to the extent that parts not relevant to the central concerns of the project are omitted: these omissions are indicated on the transcript. However, the progression of the dialogue was as it is presented here; nothing has been rearranged. Both narrator and interviewer are comfortable expounding and so articulate that there are not many "uh's" or false starts on the tape, but the clearly audible ones have been noted on the transcript, and long pauses have been noted. Brief pauses and scarcely audible "uh's" have not been noted. I have used standard English spelling most of the time because that is the way both spoke.

At the time of the interview, Marlene Malik was a faculty member in the art department of a private New England university and had attained national recognition as an artist. The interview took place in her home. She had met me at the gallery and had supported the interviewing project's aim. In those brief prior meetings, I had developed a liking for this narrator because of her sense of humor and her candor. I did not know anything about Marlene's personal life, however, and so this interview was a surprise (to put it mildly). Marlene's children, now grown, were in the house at the time, and her husband arrived home near the end of the interview. Before and after the interview, I had some interaction with family members and was struck by the relaxed feeling among them and by Marlene's very obvious affection for, and pride in, each one.

YOW: Usually we begin by asking the narrator some questions about childhood and growing up because fifty years from now when people listen to the tape, they'll want to know who you are. So. Where you're coming from, to use the current phrase. Where were you born?

MALIK: Chicago, Illinois. April Fool's Day, 1940. I assume you want me to go on. (laughs)

YOW: (interviewer chuckles) Did you grow up in Chicago?

MALIK: Yeah, I grew up in Chicago. I'll have to . . . (pause)

YOW: Tell me about your growing up. Where did your father work? (interruption by daughter)

MALIK: I was born in a bathtub to a schizophrenic mother and a gambler father who had TB, apparently. I grew up in foster homes in Chicago, and I grew up—no, at first, I was in an orphanage for the first four years of my life. And then I grew up in foster homes. So I never knew my parents. I had no memory of them. The only way I found out about them was when I was eighteen, a sister of mine—my only sibling—uh, wrote a letter to the agency that was my guardian and said, "I'm looking for my long lost sister." That's how, you know, I got to know the family history a bit. I lived in a lot of foster homes. In fact, I tried to remember how many and I can't remember. I suppose I should really try and remember.

YOW: These were usually working-class families?

MALIK: Middle-class and then, of course, as you can certainly predict, I was a very difficult youngster and became very rebellious during my teen years and I was a runaway. So, you know, every time I would run away, that was another foster home. It was difficult, but anyway I ended up when I was about fifteen in what they call a unit, which is a modified orphanage. (brief interruption by her other daughter) Where was I? Anyway, the last three years, from the time I was fifteen to eighteen, I stayed with a very, very wonderful couple. I feel like they sort of saved my life. And it was in fact then that I began to get into art. And one of the things all during the time I was growing up was—the arts were magical. I could have no feeling for religion. As far as I was concerned, God had died years ago. So, religion didn't mean a thing to me and I feel real hostile about organized religion in general and am an avowed atheist. But art and the arts, they were magical. That was where truth lay.

YOW: How did you come in contact with the arts?

MALIK: Well, it's funny because that's the weird part. Because these were not very, you know, classy folks. But I suppose if you're an orphan and a foster kid, they sort of do things more for you, in a way. I mean, it's a weird kind of dichotomy.

YOW: Like, these families would buy you some crayons and paper?

MALIK: Yes, but it wasn't the crayons and paper, I don't ever remember that being significant. I remember going to the ballet! Or, to an art museum. Maybe even these were school trips. (telephone rings, brief interruption) Uh, but those were like magic moments, and they meant a lot to me. So, there were two things that were very interesting to me: one, the arts, and I felt that truth really lay there. And the other thing is I really wanted to be a doctor. In fact, I was thinking about this recently. (laughs) But it seemed like I could never do that. And I couldn't, you know, there was no way. I would go from high school to high school so my educational background was a mess. But I knew I was bright enough. So, uh, it was a difficult thing. But anyway, the arts became finally what I felt most comfortable with and seemed a possibility for me because you didn't have to do anything to be an artist. You could just *be* an artist.

YOW: At the time you were staying with the lovely family, from age fifteen to eighteen, did you take art lessons at all?

MALIK: No, huh-uh.

YOW: Did you go to the Art Institute on your own?

MALIK: Yes, yes! All the time. It was like a temple for me. It was a place of peace and quiet and contemplation. And I honestly felt that that is where the truth was. I would look at those El Greco paintings of

Toledo which Chicago had—you're from Chicago? (interviewer shakes her head no) You know the area? (interviewer nods yes) Ahhh! Great! I mean, that museum is heaven! It is heaven! I mean, some of the best stuff is there. You know what else is important? I saw the movie *Lust for Life*. I mean, I know it affected a lot of people. I know it did. That movie was so incredible. And that was another thing I realized, that art could affect people, that film can affect people. Art can affect people. You can make a real difference. You can say something through art that you can say through nothing else. Except maybe music. But it's really special and it really has an effect. So, I mean, I'm still romantic about art. I think it's just the greatest thing.

YOW: Uh, I'm wondering how you got into this. I mean, did you go to college and . . .

MALIK: OK. Yeah, educational background. I started taking night classes at the Art Institute.

YOW: How old were you?

MALIK: Eighteen.

YOW: You'd graduated from high school?

MALIK: I'd graduated from high school. And I, you know, nothing big in art in school. Nothing. No, no one ever thought I had talent. Nobody ever paid attention to me in that way.

YOW: How were you supporting yourself?

MALIK: I had a job.

YOW: Doing what?

MALIK: Strangely enough, I was working for an art studio. Commercial art studio. They were doing wood engravings. In fact, that's a funny story, how I got that job. It was a small, little studio. And they were looking for a girl Friday who could do everything, answer phones, do bookkeeping. I knew nothing, knew squat about bookkeeping. But I knew I could answer a phone. OK, so I get in there for the interview and it was run by two brothers and one of those brothers wanted desperately to be an artist himself and was a painter. And so he showed me a painting and he said, "What do you think of this work. I mean, who do you think influenced it?" And I said, "Well, I think. . . . " You know, I gave him a crit! This little eighteen-year-old who knew nothing! NOTHING! He was so impressed he hired me on the spot. Anyway, they were very good to me. Really nice. Incredible. And when I wanted to take courses, they would give me time off. And I just learned bookkeeping—that was no big deal.

[Summary of the narration that follows:

Of the two brothers who hired her, one was married with four children. She saw his struggle to make a living, paint, and take care of his family, but she also understood that he loved his family *and* his art. He later became a college dean and achieved recognition as an artist, as well.

She took painting courses at the Art Institute; she thought they were deadly. She started taking courses at Roosevelt University and excelled in her sociology course but decided art was more about sociology than sociology was about sociology. When she began to work for a psychology professor at the University of Chicago, the institution allowed her to take courses free.

While she was working and taking courses, she met her future husband, a graduate student doing his research at the Fermi Laboratory. They married in 1963. They thought she would stay home and take care of children and the house. They did indeed have children—three—but she kept painting at home. Finally she decided to go back to school. Although this was not their original plan, her husband was supportive. He finished his doctorate and obtained a faculty position at a New England university. They moved to Rhode Island, where she finished her college degree.]

MALIK: I didn't get into sculpture until I was in graduate school. What happened was, at the university here there was—I had been taking painting and there were a couple of older women. Two of them, Bernadette and Connie—the three of us became very good friends. And I think we were very, very supportive of one another. We were all in painting. Connie was the star. Not me, I was never a star. Connie was the star. When you see her paintings, you will faint. They were so beautiful. And it comes very easy for her. Art for me has always been a struggle. It's never come easy for me. I never thought that I had talent. I still don't. Although now people think I do, just goes to show. (smiles) (interviewer chuckles) Such bullshit.

[Digression: Marlene talks about her friends' art.]

MALIK: Towards the end of my career at the university, I took a sculpture course with a guy named Richard Calabro. That may ring a bell for you. (interviewer nods) He was great because he had a sense of adventure. He was a great art teacher. And anything you wanted to play around with was OK with him. In fact, he was enthusiastic.

YOW: He was supportive with you?

MALIK: Incredibly supportive with me!

YOW: With all his students or with you particularly?

MALIK: I don't know if he was supportive with—it's hard for me to tell. Somehow *I* felt his support. I think he was interested in what I had to say. I had never felt that from anybody else. In fact, there's another guy there named [in consultation with narrator, name is deleted] who, uh, I had shown some early stuff to and he said, "Uh-huh," and walked away. So, I never asked him again for any kind of criticism. You learn quickly who you can talk to and who you can't.

Whereas, Calabro, it was like, "Go for it!" "God! That sounds interesting. Do it!" You know, "Try it out." And in many ways I think I've modeled myself on his attitude as a teacher. Because I thought he was so good. NOTHING was impossible. NOTHING! And, you know, a sense of humor went along with it, too. "Hey, that sounds good!" Also, I had come to call it a day with my painting. I had gotten very hard edged. I was no longer using oils. I was using high-gloss enamel and primary colors and using very geometric shapes. Anyway, it seemed like a dead end. It seemed like—I mean, the imagery was bulldozers. There was an important reason for those bulldozers. I thought they—it was about power and the power of those machines which was so incredible. But . . . (stops)

YOW: What year did you graduate from . . .

MALIK: Nineteen—you know, you're real bad with dates. I can't even remember my kids' ages. Seventy, uh, wait a minute, I graduated from RISD [Rhode Island School of Design] in '79. '76! And then [after graduation from college], I spent a year, no, six months, at home. No, I applied for a grant at the Rhode Island State Council on the Arts. Just out of a whim, when I graduated. And I got it!

YOW: Grant to individual artists?

MALIK: Yeah, and I was so shocked by it—that I got it.

YOW: What did it pay for?

MALIK: Materials. You know, it's not a huge amount. It's just an incredible honor.

YOW: Did it pay for child care?

MALIK: No! Are you kidding? (laughs) We're talking art grants. They still don't. I think at that time it was $2,500. It's only $3,000 now. It's totally ridiculous. But anyway, I think that was a great boost. I applied to graduate school—and didn't get in the sculpture department! Didn't get in! Uh, I can't remember who said to me, "Don't accept 'no' as an answer," but somebody—I should remember that because it's important. Because they said, "Don't ever accept 'no' as an answer. If you can't get into the front door, go through the back door." So, I, uh, I applied to another program, got in, spent a year in that program, reapplied, and got into the sculpture program.

YOW: Where was that?

MALIK: RISD. It was just a different program. It was like the education program. And then at that time a change happened. A woman came into the sculpture department . . .

[Brief digression, instigated by interviewer, on head of the college, who, although a woman, did not help women students.]

MALIK: Part of my program was in the sculpture department although I wasn't working for an MFA, I was working for an MA. And I told her [new sculpture department head who was a woman] what happened. She said, "That's ridiculous. You get into the MFA program." So, I ended up with an MFA in sculpture.

[Narrative continues with description of her women's consciousness-raising group, which had, at the time of the interview, been going on for twenty years. It is still going on.]

MALIK: One of the problems I had about going to graduate school was that I had three young children at home. I had a lot of guilt. I had a lot of difficulty justifying that kind of thing even though my husband was supportive. I thought that I was a lousy mother and they [her consciousness-raising group] were the ones that did say, "Don't even think about it, don't even hesitate. Go." It helps. Also, they would listen to my fears, you know. I think it's been invaluable to all of us and moving in our lives. Sometimes you need somebody to just say, "Go!"

[Digression on the parents' cooperative school.]

YOW: Did you experience any discrimination in graduate school because you are a woman?

MALIK: Oh, absolutely, I think in the process of the selection, the fact that I couldn't get into the sculpture department until a woman was a chair. I mean, there's no question about it in my mind that they were not going to take—in fact, my work was slightly feminist at that time.

YOW: What do you mean?

MALIK: Well, it was dealing with, uh—well, that really is disgusting. It wasn't the big macho steel stuff, welded steel that was so acceptable during those years.

YOW: How would you describe your work then?

MALIK: It was a very mixed medium. I was using salt and glass and wires and threads. Threads—I mean that gets close to real questionable sculpture materials and, uh, doing smaller pieces. Size is a big thing, too. So those macho guys from the foundry were not going to take a woman who was doing this kind of work into the school.

YOW: What do you think male artists valued in sculpture?

MALIK: I think during those years they valued big, brawny—uh, macho—hard stuff to make. HEAVY! Heavy was important. (laughs)

YOW: That you had to weld?

MALIK: That you had to weld and be into casting, bronze casting, or you weren't really a sculptor. Fortunately there were some men who were breaking those stereotypes at that time. And I have to give credit to them because it was happening. Uh. And they were being more acceptable. I mean in a way they did pave the way for a lot of us. We didn't do it in a vacuum although we'd like to think we did. Yeah.

Analysis and Interpretation ᔒ 295

YOW: You were among the founding members, were you not?

MALIK: Yes!

YOW: When do you first remember hearing talk about the possibility of, um, founding a woman's art gallery?

MALIK: It was in that consciousness-raising group. There were several things going on. One of the members—Bernice, in fact, that you'll talk to— she had been going on and on about opening a restaurant. She still goes on and on about opening a restaurant. (laughs) She's a psychologist. It was a fantasy of hers and I think she was always toying with that idea. At the same time, we women artists were toying with the idea of communicating more, getting together more, doing something together. And, you know, again we didn't think this up in a vacuum. It was already in the air. There were women co-op galleries: AIR, I think, was the first we heard of and it was a very exciting kind of phenomenon. Uh, so at some point somebody said, "Well, why the hell don't you do it?" You know, just do it. Again, it's that kind of an attitude: nothing's impossible. Just go and do it. Which I wish I would remember more often actually. (laughs) Uh . . .

YOW: You don't remember whose idea it was?

MALIK: I hate to tell you this, and I'm really embarrassed to say that.

YOW: Are you the one who said, "Let's . . . ?"

MALIK: I think I'm the one that finally said, "OK, enough talking. Let's go for it." But, you know, I think other people remember it differently. I guess at that point I made the commitment in my head so I felt like I did it. I don't know. But it was right after that. That was at Mary Jane's house.

YOW: And this was your, your women's consciousness-raising group?

MALIK: Yes.

YOW: What do you think might have been your next step in this process?

MALIK: My next step?

YOW: The group's.

MALIK: To find a place.

YOW: You all decided that night, at Mary Jane's house, to look for a place?

MALIK: Yes, yes. Roberta was going to do it. And Merle.

YOW: Do you remember, uh, why anyone thought a gallery could succeed in a little rural county?

MALIK: I think everybody thought it was a ridiculous idea. I think that we were sort of goaded into it.

YOW: Goaded? What do you mean?

MALIK: Yeah, by other women who said, "What's the matter with you? Talk is cheap. Put up or shut up." I think everybody thought it was a totally ridiculous idea and I think we thought we were doing it for ourselves and not for the community.

YOW: Why? Why would it be good for yourself—to take on a responsibility like that?

MALIK: I think all of us had problems, uh, in exhibiting. In fact, we were ready to make a step in terms of professionalism. This seemed like an easy entrée. Easy. (laughs) A plausible entrée, a possible entrée. It was ridiculously difficult. (laughs) But you know naïveté is sometimes . . . (long pause)

[Digression on experience of exhibiting that her friends had encountered. Discussion of problems of converting the Laundromat into a gallery, especially of how desperate they were for money.]

YOW: I wanted to ask you how decisions were made in the group. There were ten of you in the group.

MALIK: Yeah, yeah.

YOW: How you all made decisions.

MALIK: I think we sort of bumbled through it. One of the things that, uh, we didn't want from the very beginning was a leader. That was clear. No one person should be president. It had to be a co-op. But very quickly it became clear that some people would do more work and some people would take more responsibility. And hopefully the responsibility would sort of be what people were good at. So, (pause) I don't know, it didn't always work out that way. And I think what happened was, because Roberta was willing, a lot of it was dumped on her. She was so good at it. And responsible and willing and able. (laughs)

[Digression: discussion on meeting schedules and on contemporary artists and definitions of a feminist artist. Description of her duties at the gallery—hanging shows, gallery sitting, getting out mailings, etc.]

YOW: Who took care of the children while you were doing that?

MALIK: Good question. (laughs) I think a lot of it was done while they were in school, and in between my classes, or my husband. He watched them. I would say, "Saturday, I've got to go to the gallery. You have to take care of the kids." But unfortunately the poor guy was already used to that because I was already a student. I think those years were very hard, and I think he put up with a lot of shit. (laughs)

[Discussion about the name of the gallery. Arguments in the gallery about definition of art versus craft. Desperate problem of money to sustain the gallery. Problems of selling art. More discussion on what is feminist art.]

YOW: Other issues—did you debate at all the admission of men to leadership [in the gallery]?

MALIK: Yes, yes. I love a debate! I love a good argument so I probably was in on all of them. (laughs) And I always had an opinion about something. Ah, yeah, I think those issues were very important. I still think about them. And I did agree that there was a kind of discrimination and when I heard people talk about backlash, you know, with the blacks, I felt sympathetic to that. I think there is a problem with that. I also agree with affirmative action, though— you know that you have to give those who have been downtrodden a break. Which is a justification for the feminist, for the women's gallery, and for the de facto discrimination [at Hera]. On the other hand, it bothers me a great deal—I mean, I've heard men artists in the neighborhood talk about how they are shut out and don't even want to go into Hera. I feel sympathetic to that. So—(pause).

YOW: And yet, there have been male artists exhibiting at Hera.

MALIK: Oh, yeah, originally I think the thinking was, "Well, if they are not in the power structure, then it's OK." Somehow I felt that was OK. They didn't have—they couldn't be in the power structure. But they shouldn't be directly discriminated against, except, you know—you and I know—that that's bullshit, too. Keeping them out of the power structure is simply what men have done with women so I mean there are these disgusting arguments and you go back and forth and back and forth. You want to do what's right, but what's right isn't always (pause) right. From one point of view, it's right; from another point of view, it's not right.

[Discussion on other things that were debated. From gallery members, she received support and useful critiques of her work. She learned a lot—for example, she became more accepting and respectful of others' ideas. Pressure of having an exhibition date imposed self-discipline.]

YOW: Did you ever feel like during this time that you started exhibiting and started teaching, and so forth, that it was difficult to be a married woman and an artist?

MALIK: Hahhh! I still think it's difficult. I think that every artist needs a good wife. And I would love to have a good wife. And I'm incredibly jealous of men who have good wives that are supportive and do the shit work. You know, that every artist needs to do. I think it's impossible. I mean, as supportive as my husband is, there are times when he drags his feet about going to an exhibition and rightfully so. I mean, I dragged him to many, many things and there were times when I did not want to go to his things. So, I mean, I think he is very supportive and yet he's still not a good wife. You know what I mean? I mean a *good* wife. (laughs)

YOW: What would a good wife do?

MALIK: Well, you know what I mean. I'm being facetious. And in fact I'm being very nasty about the whole thing. The point is that what you see with male artists is that their wives are out there hustling for them and doing the paperwork and filing the slides and writing the letters and entertaining the dealers and encouraging and taking care of the kids. And pretending like he's a big deal. That kind of thing. (laughs)

YOW: Did you ever feel like Hera should shake the community up?

MALIK: Yes.

YOW: How did you want them to shake it?

MALIK: I wanted this to be a little pearl in amongst the rhinestones, I guess. I think—maybe I was more radical then and have quieted down over the years. But I think I also wanted to shake them up as to what women can do. I mean, that we could get that together. Even as it was happening, I thought it was a miracle and I still do, given the problems.

[Conversation about sense of community within the gallery. Exchange of shows with other cooperative galleries. Reviews in arts magazines. Discussion about Marlene's students, in general.]

YOW: What do you see as the New York influence, even in so remote a place as this little town?

MALIK: Well, I guess I go along with the idea that for a period of time—not so much now but then—that New York was the Mecca of the art world. So, all of us were influenced. I mean, the whole country was influenced by New York art. And being in the Northeast, you can't ignore it. You have to go. It's a powerful, powerful draw.

YOW: Does the New York scene, particularly, let's say, the three or four galleries who sell, do they set the standards for what is art?

MALIK: Sure, sure.

YOW: For what is acceptable in sculpture?

MALIK: Absolutely. Oh, absolutely. There's no question about it. Now things have changed a little and I think during the seventies something very exciting happened. Artists were avoiding the gallery system and the museum system and were doing sited works. S-I-T-E-D.

YOW: What does that mean?

MALIK: Out in the hinterlands. Out in the desert. Out in the woods. Out in, you know, just (pause) essentially avoiding the whole art market. This to me was the most exciting thing that I had ever, ever heard of in my life. If you could avoid, bypass those New York bastards, or those gallery bastards, who, to me, ah—I don't know, they're like car salesmen. (laughs) As I say, I'm shy, I don't go and push myself. So, I didn't know how to deal with this whole thing. So, sited sculpture seemed to me like the most wonderful "out" where I could do my work and avoid all that other crap so I immediately went into that. That's what I do.

YOW: OK, tell me about it. Describe to me what you do.

MALIK: Well. (long pause) It's—I will work—the world is my exhibition space, in other words. The woods are my exhibition space. The street is my exhibition space. Well, I see you glancing over here. (interviewer is looking at a photograph) That was a piece that was done right here on the road where one early Sunday morning I got out there and laid these glass blocks down on the road, photographed it, and then blocked off the road, put a sign, photographed it, moved the bricks, and put them somewhere else, blocked off the road, photographed it. It was—the piece is difficult to describe because it only exists in slide form. It's a very old piece. And I mean you couldn't exhibit it in a gallery if you wanted to. It doesn't exist as a piece. And to me that was exciting to avoid that kind of system. Then, uh . . . (long pause)

YOW: Now, the piece that I'm seeing displayed in your living room looks to me like a photograph of . . .

MALIK: Yeah, it's a color Xerox actually.

YOW: Color Xerox. But it's placed under milky glass so you have the feeling—of (pause) being wet. Feeling like you're immersed in water and you're seeing the scene through water.

MALIK: Yeah, yeah. Actually it's an interesting piece. It was called, uh . . . (pause)

YOW: Like twelve [feet] by twelve. No, more like twelve by eighteen.

MALIK: Oh, now I remember the piece. It was called My Life as a Divided Highway. It was a very autobiographical piece. In fact, those glass blocks at some point go over my three kids. They loved to participate. At least they did at that time. I had them lying down on the road and the glass blocks went right over them. What you're looking at is just a fragment of the piece. Sort of a memory. The piece really doesn't exist anymore.

YOW: I see what you mean about going out in the woods and the road and making art. And, uh, whoever comes by sees it and it's therefore exhibited.

MALIK: Right. It's for the people. Not for the goddamned art market. No one can buy it. No one can own it. And I love that idea. I love that idea! And now my work is supported mostly through grants. And teaching.

[Discussion on granting agencies. Description of a sculpture she made for a festival in Atlanta that will be destroyed at the end of the festival. Discussion on the gallery's history after its founding. Ends with interviewer thanking narrator.]

Reflections on This Interview

Now I will take a step away from the interview and regard the transcript as dispassionately as I can. I will refer to myself as "the interviewer," hoping that this distance obtained by using the third person designation will help me to be a little objective, at least. But in my present role as analyzer, I will stay with the "I." In other words, in this analysis, I am two people: the one looked at critically and the one who is doing the looking.

Literature professor Marie-Francoise Chanfrault-Duchet says that a narrative is difficult to accomplish in an oral history interview because in a "real narrative" the narrator organizes the memory to give it "coherence and significance."[23] I argue just the opposite: in an oral history interview, narrators answer by telling stories, although sometimes these are little stories within the larger frame of an interview, the encompassing story. In the interview with Marlene, the interviewer does ask questions based on an interview guide, but the narrator answers and then elaborates, introduces a new subject, and delivers a commentary on the new subject. The interviewer follows her lead and asks questions about the new subject. At one point, the interviewer questions Marlene about a date because she is trying to remember what style of painting was dominant in those years so that she can see Marlene's painting in a context. Marlene says, "You know, you're real bad with dates." (A fair statement.) She proceeds to talk about what she wants to talk about. This narrator dominates the interview with ease and does indeed give her story coherence and significance.

First, look at the plot of this life story: the beginning, middle, and end. The interviewer has indicated a chronological structure for the interview by going to the beginning of life by asking first where the narrator was born. Marlene picks up on this chronological treatment of the life and proceeds to discuss growing up, marriage, education, founding of the gallery, and finally coming into her own as an artist. The narrative ends with her declaration that she loves the fact that she can defy the art establishment. It's a progression from helplessness as an orphaned infant to strength and defiance as a mature woman.

The interviewer could have begun the interview by asking about the founding of the gallery, but I do not think that would have elicited the background information desired. Marlene might have chosen not to continue the narration in a chronological order, however, but this seemed to be her inclination. She seemed to be thinking in terms of "what was I doing then?" or "what came next?"

Chanfrault-Duchet suggests searching for key phrases, that is, the "formal markers that accent the narrative."[24] In two narratives by working-class women, Marie and Germaine, who lived in the same French town during World War II, Chanfrault-Duchet showed how they repeated such key phrases as "one was obliged to" (Marie) or "I did not want to . . . but what could I do?" (Germaine).[25] These women did not see themselves as actors. One of Marlene's repeated phrases is "I mean." She does indeed see herself as an actor in the drama of her life and she insists on her interpretations. Her expressions of "I mean" emphasize what she is saying. She also repeats "you know." Sociologist Marjorie DeVault interprets "you know" as a request for understanding.[26] Looking over the transcript, it seems to me that Marlene repeats this phrase when she seeks understanding and affirmation.

It is interesting that at the beginning of her marriage, her expectation was that she would not have a career. She simply accepted the cultural script that women will not be significant contributors to art. And yet, she was self-aware enough to know that she needed to paint and finally defiant enough of societal expectations to seek education in art. This was not a step taken by many other women of her generation who had talent. Sociologist Marianne Paget interviewed both men and women artists and found that women doubted their right to be artists, thought such high ambition was wrong, and did not expect that they could make great paintings. Women expended much energy in just trying to live with such doubts. Men, on the other hand, felt no agony over aiming high and had no doubt about their right to be artists. They expected to make great paintings. Paget believes that men's anguish comes late in life when they realize they have failed to be the great artists they expected to be; but women's anguish comes at the beginning and all the way through a life.[27] During the interview, the interviewer should have explored in greater depth the process whereby Marlene arrived at the determination to make art her career.

Self-concept is an important reason, I think, why Marlene was able to live with doubts about expressing herself in art. In the transcript I searched for descriptions of self-concept because I wanted to know what kind of person puts so much time and effort into a common endeavor such as a women's cooperative gallery and takes such risks. Using an overall category, Self-Concept, I studied the testimony and detected the appropriate subcategories and placed in each the relevant self-statements:

I Am Unconventional.
Birth on April Fool's Day (not just April 1).
"I was born in a bathtub to a schizophrenic mother and a gambler father."
"I was a very difficult youngster and became very rebellious during my teen years and I was a runaway."
"I am an avowed atheist."
She chooses to bypass the usual route toward exhibiting work, "those New York bastards, or those gallery bastards."

I Am Defiant.
Challenge to interviewer at the beginning, after she says she was born on April Fool's Day: "You still want me to go on?" (She scoffs at the interviewer and also at whatever other listeners the interviewer has just alluded to.)
Choice of materials to work with that are different from the expected: when others were making sculptures of welded metal, "I was using salt and glass and wires and threads."
Choice of sited work, as opposed to work made to please a gallery owner: "The world is my exhibition space."
"I also wanted to shake them [the community around Hera] as to what women can do."

I Am a Risk Taker.
She cites with approval the art professor who said, "Try it out."
She declares several times, "Nothing is impossible."
She thinks it is important that someone said, "Don't ever accept 'no' as an answer."
She admits that she was the one who said, during the discussion about founding a woman's cooperative art gallery, "Let's go for it."

I Have a Sensitivity to the Beautiful.
"Art and the arts, they were magical. That was where truth lay."
"I realized that art could affect people, that film can affect people."
"You can say something through art that you can say through nothing else."
"I'm still romantic about art; I think it's just the greatest thing."
"When you see her paintings, you will faint. They were so beautiful."

I Have a Sense of Justice.
"Fortunately there were some men who were breaking those stereotypes at that time. And I have to give credit to them."
About her husband taking a lot of responsibility for home and children, "I think he put up with a lot of shit."
About denying men power in Hera, "I also agree with affirmative action, though—you know that you have to give those who have been downtrodden a break. Which is a justification for the feminist, for the women's gallery, and for the de facto discrimination."

Brian Roberts, in *Biographical Research*, advises interpreters of the oral history document to look for the contradictions. The narrator is very much disturbed at this point: if she is to think of herself as fair and just, how can she practice the very discrimination she has hated? She makes the statement, "Keeping them [men] out of the power structure is simply what men have done with women so I mean there are these disgusting arguments and you go back and forth." A sharp difference occurs in her narrative, which up to now has been confident and straightforward: "You want to do what's right, but what's right isn't always right. From one point of view, it's right. From another point of view, it's not right." Clearly, she feels extreme ambivalence on this point.

She admits that she does not feel good about saying male artists have the advantage because each has a good wife: "I'm being very nasty about the whole thing." Her sense of justice pulls her back from consciously dealing in stereotypes, but still she is organizing her thoughts along these lines, describing what she sees as behavior acceptable in this subculture.

Marlene Malik has felt the blows of discrimination in the art world because she is a woman, but she does not want to focus on this. She alludes to being out of vogue as far as sculpture was concerned because male artists who made heavy, massive objects dominated the field. Consequently she was denied access to the sculpture department at her graduate school. She had not yet started to exhibit at the time of the gallery's founding, but she was very much aware of the difficulty her fellow women artists were experiencing in persuading anyone to even look at their work. Still, she conscientiously gives credit to the men who helped her in her art career.

She is fiercely egalitarian but has to admit that the work in the gallery is not being shared equally. She remarks, "And I think what happened was, because Roberta was willing, a lot of it was dumped on her." Shortly after that, she laughs. The interviewer interpreted that as a nervous laugh.

The interviewer presses Marlene about the effects of her commitment to art on her family life and about her need for help from her husband. At first, Marlene makes a joke about needing a good wife, indicating that she realizes she has needed her husband to be something he cannot be. Then she thinks of an example, but it is a very nice example: he "drags his feet about going to an exhibition." I wonder what is not being said—and also why I, as interviewer, did not pursue this line of questioning. Possibly the good feeling I had about Marlene prevented me from following up on this subject because I sensed that my narrator did not want to discuss the matter in detail. I suspected that the narrator's reluctance might have been caused by an expectation of dredging up some painful feelings. Reflecting on my own way of relating to others, which carries over to the interview, I see how my reluctance to cause someone pain impinged here.

Now, looking at this transcript after the passage of nearly fifteen years, I regret that I did not ask the narrator to meet me at a place other than her home for a second interview. Away from children and family, Marlene might have talked more candidly about the frustration of bearing the primary responsibility of children and house and at the same time pursuing art. When we talked after this chapter in manuscript was sent to Marlene, she remarked, "I let him off easy, didn't I?" There is a social transformation of the family going on then and now—and one specific aspect is organization of work—that I should have documented in detail in each of these individual oral histories.

Marlene was caught in a dilemma: does a woman choose self-expression or nurturing?[28] Society defines woman's work as nurturing. A woman may try to do both, but inevitably self-expression most often takes a secondary place in her life. Paget, describing her research with artists, concludes, "If women choose a small art and a woman's place, they see their art as small, always their compromise. Yet if they choose a high art, they choose against a life world."[29]

I expected a liberal use of spoken metaphors because I had seen Marlene's witty comments in the gallery log, such as from the day Marlene was gallery sitting when her own show was up and she wrote, "Looking around the room [at her own pieces], it's like sitting with my selves."[30] She had said she wanted the women's gallery to be a "pearl in amongst the rhinestones." The gallery owners were like "car salesmen"—for them, art is only a commodity; profit is their concern.

But Marlene expressed in art, not words, the anguish she felt about leaving her family to make art and leaving artistic work to devote her energies to the family. Her most trenchant metaphor was expressed in the medium most meaningful to her. Suddenly in the interview, when Marlene observed the interviewer staring at a photograph, she felt she had to explain what this photograph of a particular sculpture was all about. Its title, *My Life as a Divided Highway*, came as an afterthought as she described the sculpture. The full meaning of her earlier statement about feeling guilty about leaving her children to devote her time to art is expressed in the act of placing glass blocks over her children as they lie on the road. This highway is divided so that it runs in two directions: she must decide which way she should be going. And what happens to a highway? You run over it. The children lying there, only palely visible under the glass, are in danger of being run over.

Even the photograph of this sculpture is overlaid with a milky glass so that the viewer gets the feeling of being immersed—if the feeling had been expressed in words, it would be, "I'm in water over my head."

Marlene thus shows us in sculpture the depths of emotional pain she felt in trying to be an excellent mother to small children and excellent wife to a much-loved husband and at the same time a dedicated artist. Her sculpture conveys these feelings much better than my glib phrases about the guilt women artists felt. Oral history has a way of hurling us beyond the safe wall of our general statements.

Many of her sculptures, like My Life as a Divided Highway, were built for the site and with the purpose of being dismantled at a designated time. She thus expresses in disposable materials the concept that nothing lasts. I can only speculate about this conviction's relation to the temporariness of her early life when she was moved from foster home to foster home. Also it may be an expression of her wish to prevent her sculptures ("my selves") from being owned or controlled by anyone. This situation in adulthood is an antidote metaphorically to her childhood, when some state-appointed authority "owned" her, but now she owns herself and her work. As an undergraduate, she ceased painting because her paintings were about images of power. She was so repelled by the thought that she stopped talking about this in the interview.

More information on the conditions of the foster homes and institutions she lived in and about Marlene Malik's feelings then and now about these places could have been pursued, but not necessarily with good result. Marlene told the interviewer that she would try to remember, but the interviewer had the feeling that she would do this in her own time. The interviewer acted like a social scientist and asked her a question about social class, but this exchange required a feeling response on the part of the interviewer. (For this, I should lose my license to practice oral history—if I had one.) Still, the interviewer sensed that the narrator was not going to talk about the worst aspects of being in foster homes. Only when the foster parents were loving was Marlene ready to talk about the situation.

In the same way, Marlene avoids dwelling on discrimination in the art world. She has gone through her life refusing to emphasize the worst aspects of what is done to her—it's a survival skill. She simply refuses to play the role of victim, either as an inmate in a foster home or as a woman in the art world. She does not deny acts of denigration against her, but she refuses to think of herself, or let us think of her, as a victim.

Marlene's marginal status vis-à-vis the art establishment because of her gender is like her lifelong condition of being on the fringes of society. As an orphan, she has been on the margin of this society from the beginning. She does not hesitate to call someone a "bastard" or say "hell" or "bullshit"—she wants to show she does not have to conform to the norms of "niceness" in our society. She does identify with other women artists at Hera and sees the group as "us" against "them" (New York gallery owners and museum curators). She consciously defies these arbiters of taste in art by deliberately choosing sited work: "The woods are my exhibition space. The street is my exhibition space." This defiance of the art establishment she finds "exciting."

I have examined the testimony that indicates self-concept—as well as the words that suggest uneasiness around certain topics. Main points of the self-concept—a risk taker, a defiant person, a person with a sense of justice—are consonant with her expressed motivation in starting the women's cooperative art gallery: her commitment to art, her expressed need for a supportive community of women artists, for an active role in reversing the injustice against women artists, and for a place to show her own work.

One theme of Marlene Malik's life story I see from scrutinizing the categories is this: art is essential in my life. There is another, equally dominant theme: I can judge and defy any authority I do not respect. Given these themes in her life story, I understand why this narrator put her most scarce resources—money, time, and energy—into a gallery that would challenge the art establishment.

But running deep under these stated themes is a dark current, alluded to in words, expressed in art: I chose to be a dedicated artist in defiance of society and paid a price. My construction of categories helped me to understand on one level, but they could have masked the underlying meaning of this life story. In this case, I was hit on the head with this underlying theme when I chanced to see the photograph of the highway sculpture. I am reminded of how important it is to relate the personal testimony to the life context it is drawn from. The experience with this narrative teaches me to keep reading and reflecting on the narrative to discover meanings deeper than the surface ones.

I intended to end this discussion with Marlene's reflections—I wanted her to have the last word about the analysis and interpretation. When Marlene read the chapter, she was pleased and said, chuckling, "I learned some things about myself." I asked if these were good or bad. She replied, "Interesting—I hadn't thought of these before." I wanted to ask, "what things?" but Marlene hurried on. Sometimes researchers find that they and the narrators tend toward a consensus rather than conflicting interpretations. In this case, though, Marlene was too candid throughout for me to believe that she was trying to "be nice"—niceness is not her style. She enjoys a debate too much to pass up a chance to engage if she believes that is warranted.

She wanted to tell me what was happening in her life now, and I wanted to know, and so the conversation took a new turn. I assume that as an artist, she does not consider words her métier, although she expresses herself very well indeed, and she would rather leave the responsibility for the words with me and go on to talk about a more exciting endeavor—art.[31] In this case, sharing interpretation was just not what she was interested in doing.

In the analysis, I have looked at plot, key phrases, structure of the narrative, context of the life, self-concept, contradictions, omissions, choices, desires, metaphors, symbols, and the influence of the individual's work. This process of analyzing as I have described it does not negate other themes that you may detect if you construct different categories to arrive at an analysis or if you look for different occurrences in the narrative—such as turning points. In any investigation of another's life, ways to analyze are a choice of the interpreter, and the resulting interpretations are never definitive.[32]

Recommended Reading

Atkinson, Robert. *The Life Story Interview*. Thousand Oaks, CA: Sage, 1998. Look especially at pages 57–74 in the chapter "Interpreting the Interview," where the author reminds us that the old standbys of quantitative research may not be appropriate for judging the life story interview, suggests other ways to judge, and briefly surveys a number of theoretical approaches to analyzing and interpreting the life story.

Bruss, Elizabeth. *Autobiographical Acts: The Changing Situation of a Literary Genre*. Baltimore, MD: Johns Hopkins Press, 1976. Although autobiography and oral history testimony are not the same, you will find the author's "Tool Kit" for analyzing self-statements interesting and helpful.

Chanfrault-Duchet, Marie-Francoise. "Narrative Structures, Social Models, and Symbolic Representation in the Life Story." In *Women's Words: The Feminist Practice of Oral History*, ed. Sherna Berger Gluck and Daphne Patai, 77–92. New York and London: Routledge, 1991. Author suggests that in analyzing a life story, we must look at key phrases and patterns, the kind of narrative model that is used, and myths. She then presents a condensed version of two different life stories and offers an analysis.

James, Daniel. *Doña María's Story: Life History, Memory, and Political Identity*. Durham, NC: Duke University Press, 2000. James presents a highly edited transcript of the life story of a woman who worked in the meatpacking plants in Brazil (beginning in 1944), raised her children, and took part in political action as well as worship in her church. In the second part of the book, he offers interpretive essays.

Lieblich, Amia, Rivka Tuval-Mashiach, and Tamar Zilber. *Narrative Research: Reading, Analysis, and Interpretation*. Thousand Oaks, CA: Sage, 1998. The authors' conviction is that narrative research differs from positivistic research in that no single, absolute truth is possible when human experience is studied.

Plummer, Ken. *Documents of Life 2: An Invitation to a Critical Humanism.* Thousand Oaks, CA: Sage, 2001. In analyzing life stories, Plummer discusses characters, themes, plots, genres, and the storyteller's point of view.

Portelli, Alessandro. *The Death of Luigi Trastulli and Other Stories: Form and Meaning in Oral History.* Albany: State University of New York Press, 1991. See especially the chapter "The Best Garbage Man in Town," where the author demonstrates one way to interpret a single life story in relation to the individual's specific group and culture.

Mishler, Elliot G. "The Analysis of Interview-Narratives." In *Narrative Psychology: The Storied Nature of Human Conduct,* ed. Theodore R. Sarbin, 233–55. New York: Praeger, 1986. Mishler offers an interview he had carried out, analyzing it in terms of language and context, especially the interpersonal relationship. Most interesting is the comparison he makes between this man's interview and the interview Anita Mishler recorded with the man's wife.

Roberts, Brian. *Biographical Research.* Buckingham, UK: Open University Press, 2002. See especially the chapter "The Narrative Analysis of Lives." This chapter provides definitions of narrative analysis, discusses time and myth in life stories, and presents briefly different models for interpreting the life story.

Rogers, Kim Lacy. "Critical Choices in Interviews." *Oral History Review* 15, no. 2 (Fall 1987): 165–84. Insightful discussion on interpretive conflict, effects on narrators when they hear or read interviewers' interpretation of their lives, reasons why interviewers should respect their own interpretations even when these incur the narrators' displeasure.

Runyan, William McKinley. *Life Histories and Psychobiography: Explorations in Theory and Method.* New York: Oxford University Press, 1982. Author's aim is to "search for appropriately rigorous criteria and procedures for evaluating and improving our understanding of individual life histories" (p. 14). Very readable, well-reasoned text.

———. "Why Did Van Gogh Cut Off His Ear? The Problem of Alternative Explanations in Psychobiography." *Journal of Personality and Social Psychology* 40, no. 6 (1981): 1070–77. Runyan offers thirteen psychodynamic interpretations of the ear cutting and suggests ways to evaluate interpretations.

Smith, Sidonie, and Julia Watson. *Reading Autobiography: A Guide for Interpreting Life Narratives.* Minneapolis: University of Minnesota Press, 2001. Autobiography and oral history testimony are different if you look at formal definitions, but they are similar in that they require self-disclosure, so information about interpreting the oral history can be gleaned from this book. The authors state that life narrators perform several rhetorical acts: justifying their own views, defending their reputations, arguing against the accounts of others, settling old contentions, conveying information about themselves and their way of life.

Tagg, Stephen K. "Life Story Interviews and Their Interpretation." In *The Research Interview: Uses and Approaches,* ed. Michael Brenner, Jennifer Brown, and David Canter, 163–99. London: Academic Press, 1985. This article will be helpful mainly to sociologists. It surveys and explains approaches to interpretation of the life story interview—such ways as time sequence, script, parsing, coding, transition matrixes, thematic analysis, life story grids. If you are interested in using a computer to sort sentences into categories, look at pages 180–82.

Watson, Lawrence, and Maria-Barbara Watson-Franke. *Interpreting Life Histories: An Anthropological Inquiry*. New Brunswick, NJ: Rutgers University Press, 1985. Now a classic, deservedly so, this book presents among other aspects of interpretation of life histories a discussion on such matters as how the interpreter brings her or his own insights and experience to the interpretation of a life story.

Notes

1. John Lofland and Lynn H. Lofland, *Analyzing Social Settings: A Guide to Qualitative Observation and Analysis* (Belmont, CA: Wadsworth, 1984), 135.

2. Patrick B. Mullen, *Listening to Old Voices: Folklore, Life Stories, and the Elderly* (Urbana: University of Illinois Press, 1992), 238–40, 256–59.

3. Raphael Samuel and Paul Thompson, *Myths We Live By* (London: Routledge, 1990).

4. L. L. Langness and Gelya Frank, *Lives: An Anthropological Approach to Biography* (Novato, CA: Chandler & Sharp, 1981); see chapter 3, pp. 63–86.

5. David Mandelbaum, "The Study of Life History: Gandhi," *Current Anthropology* 14, no. 3 (1973): 177–206. Discussed in Langness and Frank, *Lives*, 71–72.

6. Norman Denzin, *Interpretive Biography* (Thousand Oaks, CA: Sage, 1989), 71. See also Denzin's *Interpretive Interactionism* (Thousand Oaks, CA: Sage, 2001), p. 145, for four types of turning points.

7. Miles F. Shore, "Biography in the 1980's," *Journal of Interdisciplinary History* 12, no. 1 (Spring 1981): 89–113; see pp. 96–103.

8. Leonard Schatzman and Anselm L. Strauss, *Field Research: Strategies for a Natural Sociology* (Englewood Cliffs, NJ: Prentice-Hall, 1973), 110.

9. Schatzman and Strauss, *Field Research*, 114.

10. Alessandro Portelli, "The Best Garbage Man in Town: Life and Times of Valtero Peppoloni, Worker," in *The Death of Luigi Trastulli and Other Stories*, 117–37 (Albany: State University of New York Press, 1991); see p. 130. First published in the *Oral History Review* 16, no. 1 (Spring 1988): 58–69.

11. Virginia Yans-McLaughlin, "Metaphors of Self in History: Subjectivity, Oral Narrative, and Immigration Studies," in *Immigration Reconsidered: History, Sociology, and Politics*, ed. Virginia Yans-McLaughlin, 254–90 (Oxford: Oxford University Press, 1990); see p. 274.

12. Ronald Grele, "Listen to Their Voices: Two Cases Studies in the Interpretation of Oral History Interviews," *Oral History* (Spring 1979): 33–42.

13. Grele, "Listen to Their Voices," 40.

14. Grele, "Listen to Their Voices," 39–40.

15. Alessandro Portelli, "Pecularities of Oral History," *History Workshop Journal* 12 (Autumn 1981): 96–107; see p. 100.

16. Portelli, "Best Garbage Man in Town," 117.

17. Portelli, "Best Garbage Man in Town," 128.

18. Portelli, "Best Garbage Man in Town," 127.

19. Portelli, "Best Garbage Man in Town," 137.

20. Portelli, "Best Garbage Man in Town," 137.

21. Valerie Raleigh Yow, *The History of Hera: A Women's Art Cooperative, 1974–1989* (Wakefield, RI: Hera Educational Foundation, 1989). The taped interview presented here is in the archives of the University of Rhode Island library.

22. Daniel Bertaux and Isabelle Bertaux-Wiame, "Life Stories in the Bakers' Trade," in *Biography and Society: The Life History Approach in the Social Sciences*, ed. Daniel Bertaux, 149–89 (Beverly Hills, CA: Sage, 1981).

23. Marie-Francoise Chanfrault-Duchet, "Narrative Structures, Social Models, and Symbolic Representation in the Life Story," in *Women's Words: The Feminist Practice of Oral History*, ed. Sherna Berger Gluck and Daphne Patai, 77–92 (London: Routledge, 1991).

24. Chanfrault-Duchet, "Narrative Structures," 79.

25. Chanfrault-Duchet, "Narrative Structures," 85.

26. Marjorie DeVault, "Talking and Listening from Women's Standpoint: Feminist Strategies for Interviewing and Analysis," *Social Problems* 37, no. 1 (February 1990): 96–116; see p. 103.

27. Marianne Paget, "The Ontological Anguish of Women Artists," *New England Sociologist* 3 (1981): 65–79; see pp. 68–69.

28. Paget, "Ontological Anguish of Women Artists," 68.

29. Paget, "Ontological Anguish of Women Artists," 68.

30. Yow, *History of Hera*, 9.

31. See Lynn Echevarria-Howe, "Reflections from the Participants: The Process and Product of Life History Work," *Oral History* 23, no. 2 (Autumn 1995); see p. 42.

32. For ways to evaluate a single oral history, see William McKinley Runyan, *Life Histories and Psychobiography: Explorations in Theory and Method* (New York: Oxford University Press, 1984), 152. For other ways to evaluate, see Amia Lieblich, Rivka Tuval-Mashiach, and Tamar Zilber, *Narrative Research: Reading, Analysis, and Interpretation* (Thousand Oaks, CA: Sage, 1998), 171–74.

CHAPTER ELEVEN

Conclusion of the Project

This last chapter presents discussion on evaluation of the interview, provisions for retrieval of information, and instructions for depositing tape and transcript in archives. I offer models for writing the face sheet and information sheet. I demonstrate one way to index a tape and also to compile a master index from the indexes in the total collection. I review techniques for transcribing and discuss transcribing problems. Finally, I advocate the necessity of making the tape and transcript available to other people and suggest criteria for choosing the place to deposit a collection of oral histories.

These are the finishing touches to the project: to leave these undone is like leaving the Mona Lisa without a head, not to mention a smile—just putting your brush down and wandering off, muttering, "Finished."

Evaluation of the Interview

This book has offered discussion on ways that interpersonal relationships, personal agendas, setting, memory, and interviewing techniques affect the quality of the interview. After the interview is completed, the interviewer needs to listen to the taped memoir objectively and evaluate it, asking questions about how the influences mentioned above have made a difference in the taped document.

Consider these approaches to evaluation: Try to corroborate the information on the tape with other documents, written and oral. Listen closely to the testimony to determine if there is consistency within the testimony. If there is a lack of consistency on some point, try to find the reason for this. Ask of the document, What has been omitted? Suppressed? Distorted? Consider also, in the light of what happened afterward, whether this testimony makes sense. Check on facts where you think memory may have been faulty.

Look at the narrator's credentials for the testimony on specific issues: Does he know what he is talking about? Is this firsthand information? How close was she to the events recounted? Think about the recorded testimony in the context of the life: How does the purpose of the narrator affect the testimony? How are reflections on the past influenced by the present situation? Are events or feelings remembered in such a way that they show the influence of present feelings—such as a feeling of abundance and well-being so that harder times in the past are minimized in the telling?

This kind of "filtering" occurred when my students and I were interviewing farm families. We heard much about loneliness and lack of social contacts from the older generations. We wanted to accept their conclusion that the present is a time of social isolation; however, in looking at the list of social activities in the community, we saw that there were plenty of chances for socializing. The older generation may not, in fact, have had as many organized groups in their young adulthood. Other reasons for their loneliness, which they did not emphasize, were that their children had grown up and many activities had involved the children, and their health and age did not permit them to stay up as late as many activities required. Therefore, we had to consider their current situation as they idealized the past in their lives when they went to Grange meetings, danced at the schoolhouse, and played cards with other couples late on Saturday nights.

Ask of the taped memoir how the relationship between interviewer and narrator affected the course of the conversation. Were they both aware of the historical significance of the document they were recording? Did social norms impinge on the interviewing situation and influence the testimony? (Taboos against discussing sexual experience with a stranger, for example, will certainly influence an answer.) Did interviewing conditions—the environment, others in the room, the narrator's health—affect the testimony? How did phrasing of the question influence the answer? How did the interviewer's skills—such as clarifying, following up on a topic, challenging—make a difference in the information offered? How did the interviewer's biases, expectations, and manner of relating to the narrator affect the interview? How did the same conditions on the part of the narrator affect the interview?

Looking at the in-depth interview objectively, evaluate its usefulness. Does this taped memoir offer a unique perspective? Does it contribute some insight or some richness of detail not found elsewhere? Is this the best means of acquiring this information? Finally, ask how the information in this interview might be of consequence and importance to people outside the project interested in the general research topic. (See the Oral History Association's "Oral History Evaluation Guidelines" in appendix B.)

This critique will be invaluable to you as you sift evidence for your own writing. The information will also be used to write interviewer's comments that accompany the tape when it is deposited, and it will be used as an introduction to the transcription. Whoever listens to the tape or reads the transcript will find your evaluation of it very helpful, indeed. (If you have promised confidentiality, of course, you must take care not to include information identifying an individual.)

Face Sheet and Information Sheet

The interviewer's comments and a brief biography of the narrator go on an information sheet that accompanies the tape. At the top is the information any listener will need to know: the title of the project, the general topic of the interview, the narrator's name (or pseudonym if required), birthplace, date of birth, occupation, and family members (if you are using the narrator's real name and can thus identify his family.) In addition, there is the interviewer's name, the date, and the place of the interview. Include a paragraph giving a brief biography of the narrator and then a paragraph in which you, as interviewer, provide information on the context for the interview. A face sheet is placed over this as a title page. All of this gives information necessary to orient the listener to the situation of the interview. (See appendix G.)

Index to Each Tape and Master Index

You need an index to the tape: without an index, any listener, yourself included, will have to guess where a certain conversation begins and then play with the fast-forward and reverse buttons on the machine until it can be located. With an index, you know that on side 1, around tape counter number 450, the narrator begins to discuss your topic of interest. (Tape counter numbers vary from recorder to recorder, so the number is approximate.) Any time that you spend indexing the tape will save you much more time as you begin to use the information.

Before you begin working with the tape—indexing or transcribing—make a copy and work from the copy; this way, if you ever erase something by mistake or the tape breaks, the original is always there intact. Indexing requires patient and careful listening. So much depends on sensitivity and judgment in gleaning what is important in indexing a tape that I urge you to compose this first index yourself. Make four headings: narrator's initials (or pseudonym), tape side number, tape counter number, and topics. Start your tape counter number exactly at zero as you start to play the tape. As the narrator begins to discuss a different topic or takes a different slant on the topic, type the tape side and counter number and the new topic heading. I like to write in some detail under the topic heading what the narrator discusses. In some cases, where I expect that I may quote the narrator directly, I transcribe the sentence. If you do not expect to transcribe the entire tape, then you can save time by transcribing now the sentences you expect to use later. (I have usually not had money for transcription later, but if you do, it is not necessary to transcribe anything at this stage. See appendix H for a sample tape index.)

There are computer programs for compiling a master index from the indexes to individual tapes in a project. But again, you have to arrive at a judgment about the words and phrases that are significant—a machine cannot do that for you. And a machine cannot discern ideas that are not expressed in the phrases or words for which you have commanded it to search. Compiling a master index of tapes on computer using the copy and paste function is not difficult. Now you will see the usefulness of having the narrator's initials beside the tape side and counter number on the individual tape index: as you copy and paste these horizontal slivers, each one describing a topic with side and number and narrator's initials, you lose no pertinent information. Paste the entry under the appropriate heading. (These headings are the topic titles that you had composed for the interview guide.) There will be topics that you did not anticipate, of course, and you make up the heading titles that fit the subjects the narrators discussed and paste them there.

You will end up with fifteen to twenty or more entries under each heading. Look more closely at the items within each heading. Decide which need to be divided along more specific lines than the general topic allowed. For example, I had a heading called "Opening of the Gallery" when I was working on the master index for the collection of tapes from the project on the women's cooperative art gallery. I was composing the master index manually, so under this heading, I had slips of paper from fifteen narrators who had described preparations for the opening. Under the same heading, I had another dozen slips from oral histories that gave accounts of the opening celebration itself. I realized that even though these were closely related, they were different subjects that required different headings. On the other hand, some conversations may appropriately go under two headings. Alphabetize the headings; under each heading will be all the accompanying entries. You have a master index to the tape collection. (A sample page of a master index is in appendix I.)

Later, as you use the information from the project and you want to know who said what on a topic, you have only to look at your master index to see under that heading the names of the narrators who talked about this, with the tape side and tape counter, and a brief description of what was said. Within a few seconds, you know which tapes and which segments to review. What a time saver! How clear patterns become!

Transcription

A transcription is the written form of a taped interview. There is much debate about whether a transcription is truly a primary source. Surely, the written version of a conversation is not the same as the spoken version. David Dunaway, in considering the relationship of transcription to tape, remarks, "The oral interview is a multilayered communicative event, which a transcript only palely reflects."[1] The transcription is thus at best a step removed from the original. An analogy I use is the difference between the original and a copy in someone's writing other than the author's of a twelfth-century document: for research purposes you use it, knowing some errors may have crept in, but if you ever get the chance to see the original, you study it and check the copy. For twentieth-century history, if it is possible to listen to the tape, that is preferable. And it is necessary in some projects: people studying oral language usage must hear the tape.

But often for research purposes, a scholar in history, education, anthropology, sociology, or education will find that a transcription suffices. Certainly I have been grateful to libraries that sent me photocopies of the transcriptions when I could neither travel miles to listen to the tapes nor afford the cost of having a tape collection duplicated for me. And for my purposes, the transcription was easier to handle because I did not have to put a tape on the machine to play back, hunt for the counter number, and transcribe. In archives, it is often easier to let the scholar read a transcript first so that the tapes are not put under stress from continuous rewinding, fast-forwarding, and so on. Once he or she identifies the crucial tapes, then these are made available. And in some cases, where the tapes are not stored properly, the sound fades and the transcript saves the document from being lost entirely.

Transcribing Techniques
The problem is that accurate transcription is painstaking and time consuming. It takes a high level of skill and good judgment to force an oral document

into a written form that has the degree of truthfulness necessary for research. However, good transcribing techniques, as well as good judgment, can be learned. There is a benefit when the interviewer is also the transcriber, because he or she is familiar with the narrator's speech and the interviewing situation. If you are the transcriber, but not the interviewer, then you will find it helpful to listen to the entire tape first to get a feeling for the speech patterns. Then listen ahead a bit so that you know what comes after the sentence you are working on: you get an idea of where it ends and where the meaning changes. Then rewind the tape to the beginning of the sentence, listening to the phrase, writing it down. When you have finished copying the sentence, listen again, making sure the word order is correct and that you have not left something out.

A transcribing machine is a godsend, of course. Earphones and a foot pedal make this a much easier process than struggling along, using your right hand to rewind and play while also writing or typing. A word processor contributes to the ease of making corrections as you listen, and you end up with a clean copy. If there are mistakes that an auditor or the narrator finds, these are easy to fix on computer. Also, if you can obtain a template for transcription, that helps. Rina Benmayor made a request to her university's technology support office for help in designing a template. The technician devised a template, using the "Style" function for Microsoft Word, which allowed the students to focus on transcribing what they heard rather than on getting the format correct. To switch from narrator to interviewer, they struck the Enter key and automatically started typing the new speaker's dialogue in the right place. In other words, they could transcribe tapes without stopping to format manually each time they switched speakers.[2]

Another possibility is to purchase software for transcribing. Because technology changes so fast that whatever I recommend will be obsolete within a year of the publication of this book, I hesitate to suggest anything. But there is, as of now, a program called Start-Stop (Start-Stop Universal Transcription Service) for less than two hundred dollars. You could search online at www.startstop.com or, if the address changes, on Google. There is also free transcription software called Express Scribe, available from NCH Swift Sound; this program reads directly from audio CDs. To find discussion on the latest technology, subscribe to the Oral History List Service (an online service of the Oral History Association at h-oralhist@h-net.msu.edu; it's free). But if you use this kind of technological help, you should go back over the transcript, listening to the tape. Machines do make mistakes because they are not discerning (see the fine points below), and they do not distinguish emotions of the speakers.

Reproducing Speech

The first version of a transcript should be verbatim. The goal is to reproduce as closely as possible the speech of the narrator. In doing this, one of the problems that arises is how to represent speech that is not standard English, the speech we are accustomed to reading. In *A Woman's Place*, Rosemary O. Joyce discusses tidying up a narrator's sentences: "Because faithful reproduction takes us one step closer to actual data, any deviation becomes an error." She adds, "It seemed to me a heightened form of snobbery not to use the vernacular, a subtle way of saying, 'Your speech is strange, and, rather than embarrass either of us, I shall make it proper—like mine.' Pure ethnocentrism! Better by far that we quote the bank president, and all of us, with accent intact."[3]

Stay as close as possible to the sound you actually hear. You may be writing down "goin'" and "havin'" many times, as well as "ain't" and bad grammar in such phrases as "spoke to him and I." If that was what was said, write it. And the narrator might have said, as Nate Shaw (Ned Cobb) did in *All God's Dangers*, that someone was a "low-down, half-assed scalawag."[4] Leave it in and spell it as closely to the way it sounded as you can.

In her article "Resisting the Editorial Ego" in the *Oral History Review*, Susan Allen expresses this adherence to the spoken version most forcefully:

> Oral history is what comes out of people's mouths, and it has to be captured accurately on paper; or else you violate the integrity of the interviewee, who has been kind enough to give you his or her time, and you violate the integrity of the medium. What is on the tape is what happened in the interview. What is on tape is what was actually said. It is history already written on the wind, and if you feel any responsibility to the truth, you must see that the original content gets onto the transcript.[5]

Special Problems in Transcribing

Do you include all the "uh-huh's" and "hmm's"? Yes, definitely, if the speaker was troubled, because these may indicate hesitation. If this is just his or her normal speech pattern, then leave enough in to show the pattern but not so many that the speaker's meaning is obscured.

There are "crutch" words and phrases that speakers use over and over again. Sometimes you can leave some of them out if you include enough to indicate the speech habit. "Well" is one; "you know" is another. Look at this example in which the transcriber has rightly left in every word:

QUESTION: Did you try to stop the argument?
ANSWER: Well, I couldn't do . . . Well, but it wasn't, don't you know, any of my business. No. I didn't try.[6]

Here the repetition of "well" is not just a speech pattern; the speaker is troubled about admitting something.

When I speak to my eighty-six-year-old uncle on the telephone, he continually says, "You follow me?" He just wants to make sure I understand what he is saying and, possibly, that I agree with him or at least find what he is saying reasonable. If I transcribed every one of these, the reader (not loving him as I do) would get annoyed, but I need to transcribe enough to show his habitual way of speaking. Allen rightly makes this distinction: If a stutter or a cough (and, I add, habitual repetition of a phrase) is not significant to meaning, it may be deleted.[7]

Still, be careful about habitual phrases. "You know" is a phrase often repeated in our conversations. I used to assume it meant nothing until I read the enlightening article by sociologist Marjorie Devault, "Talking and Listening from Women's Standpoint: Feminist Strategies for Interviewing and Analysis": "In many instances, 'you know' seems to mean something like, 'OK, this next bit is going to be a little tricky. I can't say it quite right, but help me out a little; meet me halfway and you'll understand what I mean.'" Devault concludes, "If this is so, it provides a new way to think about these data. 'You know' no longer seems like stumbling inarticulateness, but appears to signal a request for understanding."[8]

In the first, verbatim transcript, leave in the "you know's" and anything you think might have meaning. You will need it in your analysis. And even in a published transcript, leave in enough to show the narrator's way of expressing himself.

Sometimes the narrator will begin a sentence, stop, begin again. Do you leave in the false starts? Almost always that is appropriate. Sometimes the false starts indicate the way the narrator is thinking through the topic as he or she speaks. Look at this example: "I would say yes, we were all—I would have to say I think we were all in it together. It was a group cause."[9] The speaker hesitates, phrases the answer a little differently, and in fact qualifies the statement he originally intended. The first example given below may look like a meaningless false start, but when it is punctuated correctly in the second example, we see it is a meaningful beginning to a story.

1. Well, that goes back—my first bitter experience with John Lewis goes back to 1917.

2. Well, that goes back. My first bitter experience with John Lewis goes back to 1917.[10]

The second correctly conveys the narrator's meaning: "I will tell you a story from the past now."[11]

Advice in manuals has been to leave out a false start if it conveys nothing significant. Keeping to the goal of reproducing the actual speech as closely as possible on the verbatim transcript, I include the false starts almost always. An exception occurs when a narrator stutters or just has a habit of starting a sentence several times: leave in enough to indicate this speech pattern, but you may not have to leave in every false start if this makes the reading almost impossible.

Punctuation

Punctuating and creating sentences so that you do not misrepresent the meaning is another challenge. Joyce describes her method: she uses "nonstandard punctuation, with few commas, semicolons, and even periods, to convey the flavor of Sarah's expressivity—her rapid discourse and run-together phrases and sentences."[12] Short sentences, sentence fragments, and run-on sentences are the way human beings talk. Do not try to force them into standard written English.

Certain usages of punctuation marks are fairly standard in oral history. Use the three points of an ellipsis to show that the sentence remains unfinished. Look at this example:

SMITH: There's nothing more I can say, I mean . . .

If the narrator just trails off and does not complete the thought but begins a new sentence, use a period and then the three points of the ellipsis. With this period, you show the reader that the first thought is not part of the next sentence. If the incomplete sentence is a question or an exclamation, insert this punctuation mark and then the three ellipsis points.

SMITH: I don't think I want to say. . . . . I have already said more than I should.

SMITH: Anything more to? . . . I think I have already said more than I should.

Use a comma to show there was a brief pause, as in this example:

SMITH: In those days people didn't talk about such, didn't discuss, such things.[13]

Use a dash to indicate an interruption in thought:

> ROSS: As a child, I used to make hats out of oak leaves—those
> big old oaks had beautiful leaves—and fastened the daisies
> on the leaves with broom straws.[14]

A dash is often necessary to make the sentence understandable. In *Oral History: From Tape to Type*, Cullom Davis, Kathryn Back, and Kay MacLean give this example of the way using the dash instead of the comma can clarify meaning:

> I told Mr. Boardman, "You know, Mr. Smith, both of the two brothers and their father before them, had an undertaking shop right down on Fifth and Capitol."
> Or, I told Mr. Boardman, "You know, Mr. Smith—both of the two brothers and their father before them—had an undertaking shop right down on Fifth and Capitol."[15]

If there is a moment in the interview when the narrator has motioned you to turn the machine off, in parentheses write, "taping stopped at narrator's request." When there is an interruption, indicate that and the kind of interruption if it makes a difference. Here are two examples, one of which requires an explanation to the reader, who will want to know why there was a change in conversation: in the first one, the narrator lets the dog out; in the second, the man's wife enters the room.

> JONES: Did I tell you about the time I . . . (interruption). The time
> I was sent to the southern part of the peninsula?

> SMITH: Yes, I did go to Japan when I was on leave. I had a . . . (in-
> terruption when wife enters the room). What else did you
> want to know about combat duty?[16]

Underline words that the narrator has emphasized. When there are audible clues on the tape or you remember or have written down notes about the nonverbal gestures, write them in parentheses. For example, the sound of pounding can be heard on tape, and the interviewer has indicated that the narrator frowned at the same time:

> JONES: He was lying! (frowns and pounds the table)

Or, there is a distinct change in the voice:

BROWN: I loved him. (speaks softly)

Are brackets and parentheses interchangeable? No. In *Oral History: From Tape to Type*, there is an explanation for correct use of brackets and parentheses within the narrator's or interviewer's dialogue: Parentheses enclose descriptions of action or emotion that accompanied the interviewer's or narrator's words. Brackets are editorial comments needed for clarification.[17]

NARRATOR: I'll admit I was in trouble with the DMV [Department of Motor Vehicles] and I was worried.

Do not use punctuation and capitalization within brackets or parentheses when they occur within an oral history dialogue. Make these notations brief. In bracketed sentences outside the dialogue, use standard punctuation. (See oral history presented in chapter 10.)

NARRATOR: I'll admit I was in trouble with the DMV [Department of Motor Vehicles]. (shuffles his feet)

If the narrator consistently mispronounces a word, then spell it as it sounds and indicate in a footnote on the transcript what term is being referred to. For example, "The narrator here says 'sadistics,' which is a substitute for 'statistics.'" Last names needed to identify a person mentioned in the conversation are placed in brackets, as all clarifications are. Here is the way Davis, Back, and MacLean suggest doing this:

Original transcript:
We were on this strike fighting against an imposition that the coal company had imposed upon us where the loaders would add their loads 275 more pounds for the ton. . . .
Edited version:
We were on this strike fighting against an imposition that the coal company had imposed upon us where the loaders would [have to] add [to] their loads 275 more pounds for the ton. . . .[18]

As you transcribe, there will be times when, try as you might to understand, the words are just not audible. Leave a space on the transcript and pencil in "inaudible" within penciled parentheses. It may be that the narrator or someone else more familiar with the regional speech can help you out.

At the end of the transcribing process, listen to the tape once again as you read the transcription, word for word. Give close attention to word order.

This is the careful checking for accuracy that makes the transcription a worthwhile research tool.

Return of the Transcript to the Narrator

If you, as a historian, make a transcript, you should return it to the narrator for corrections. And ethnographers who plan to use direct quotations to illustrate points must be sure the phrasing is correctly transcribed. In any case, the researcher does not want to work with a faulty transcription. Inevitably you miss something, and this final check may save the narrator and yourself much trouble later. If you are a social science researcher whose project does not require deposit of the transcripts in archives, or if you are looking only for data to be coded and used in the aggregate, then you may not need to return the transcript. But you still need to be sure of the veracity of your data, so carefully check the transcription word for word as you listen to the tape.

Allen gives an example of a faulty transcription from a project when the narrator was talking about the first time that he met Chief Justice Fred M. Vinson: "My first meeting with Fred was at the Woodland Auditorium Convention [Lexington, Kentucky] and my first observation of him was when Ben Johnson and Billy Klair and some of the rest of them agreed to be for Happy [A. B. Chandler] for lieutenant governor when the fool was nominated, and I think he was nominated in 1931."[19]

The narrator was actually speaking of Ruby Laffoon. The narrator might have gone into print as having called Happy Chandler a fool if the transcription had not been checked. In this case, the interviewer and editor caught the error before the transcription went to the narrator, but it is just such a mistake that could cause everyone a lot of grief.[20]

Beyond that, there is an ethical issue here: when you commit something oral to print and deposit it in archives so that it becomes available to the public, the narrator has a right to see what has happened to her or his words. Everybody knows the taped version is an informal conversation: there is something about print that gives it a formality that taped sound does not have. Therefore, there has been a change and the narrator has a right to see what you have done.

When you send the tape and transcript to the narrator, present your expectation that the narrator will not delete material or change meaning. In this accompanying letter, say something like, "I want to be sure this is an accurate representation of your words. Please check to see whether I have misunderstood a word or have spelled a name or term incorrectly." Explain that this transcript should be as close to spoken words as you can make it. Remind the narrator that speech is different from written dialogue. You might even include a page from another transcript if you have the release form for it to show what a final transcript looks like.

Give the narrator a specified length of time to review the transcript—maybe one to three months, depending on circumstances. If there is no reply, advise him that the archivist wants to go ahead and bind the transcription and that you need to know his wishes immediately. Most of the time, a few minor corrections will be made and the document returned to you. Occasionally, however, there is trouble. In *Effective Interviewing*, E. Culpepper Clark warns interviewers not to be surprised if the reaction is negative. He presents an excerpt from a letter he received:

> You cannot imagine the state of shock I was in after first reading your transcription. Truly, I've never liked to hear myself on tape, but. . . . What I do mind is sounding like a bumbling, illiterate. . . . In other words what I'm trying to say is that I'm revolted to the point of nausea about the whole tape. . . . Please endeavor to realize that I am not trying to be unkind or that I am pompous about my intellectual opinions. I can only be myself—honest and plain—very plain spoken.[21]

After all the explanation you give, you will still encounter narrators like Clark's who will change the transcript until all the punch is gone out of it and it is simply a dull bit of prose, not even close to the actual taped dialogue. It is unethical for you to change the transcript back; but before you deposit it, place a note on the information sheet to warn readers that this is an edited document. Any words the narrator has inserted are placed in brackets; any deletions are indicated by placing a warning in brackets at the appropriate place in the manuscript. At times the narrator may want to add a great deal of material; place that extended material as an addendum to the transcript.

Sometimes you have a project in which the narrator cannot read the transcript for one reason or another. There may be a family member who can read it to him or her as the tape is played. Or you may go back and do that. If a family member or someone not connected with the project reads the transcript to the narrator, you will have to explain why a transcript is a rendition of spoken language, not intended to be in correct English or polished. Sometimes it is just not possible for the narrator to go over the transcript: as a last resort, try to get the narrator's permission for a knowledgeable person to listen to the tape and check the transcript.

Index the transcript using the copy and paste function on a computer, or if you happen to have Microsoft Word, follow the instructions for using the

"Mark Index Entry" and "Index and Tables." (See appendix J.) Compile a master index to the collection of transcripts in preparation for depositing the collection of tapes and their transcripts in the archives. You can use the same instructions given in appendix J to create a master index. A face sheet or title page, an information sheet (such as you prepared for the tape) that contains a brief biography of the narrator and interviewer's comments, and a table of contents should accompany the transcript as well. Readers even fifty years from now will want to thank you. Finally, be sure to send the narrator a copy of the final version.

By now you are probably shaking your head over the time spent on an oral history project. The usual time required for transcribing an hour-long tape is six to ten hours. Willa K. Baum, who directed the oral history office at the Bancroft Library, University of California at Berkeley, estimated that it takes a total of sixty-three hours to transcribe, audit, do final typing, proofread, visit and call the narrator (to get the corrected transcript back), write the letter of thanks, index the transcript, prepare the pages on the interview history (interviewer's comments), and gather all documents, such as the release form.[22] The cost of transcribing alone if you hire a transcriber will be about $25 per hour; for a sixty-minute tape, almost completely audible, requiring six hours' work, the bill will be $150. Transcription of a ninety-minute tape will be much more, certainly over $200.

Considering the expense of money and time, you probably will not transcribe all the tapes in your collection. Decide on priorities: the tape that has little of interest to the general public, contains long segments blitzed by electrical interference or annoying background noise, or is very general and not especially informative may not need to be transcribed. And you may not want to transcribe all of a tape: if there is a long section that is irrelevant, leave it out, but note that on the transcription in brackets, as in the following example.

[Portion not transcribed that consists of interruption caused by the passing of a heavy truck and ensuing conversation on noise level in neighborhood.]

It is also possible that certain segments are so intensely personal that the narrator does not want them transcribed or that you feel that, in so doing, you would cause the narrator harm—ask the narrator what she wants to do. If she wants to leave it out, indicate on the transcription the general topic not transcribed (just as you did on the tape):

[Here the narrator, Lizzie Borden, requests that the taped segment concerning incidents involving her parents be sealed.]

Publication of Oral Histories

I have stressed here the necessity of making the first transcript as close to a verbatim account as you can. For the publication of life stories, some editors/interviewers think it is acceptable to "clean up" the language. J. A. Progler, in his article for the *Oral History Review* on choices in editing, advises first typing an absolutely verbatim account and then deciding which "um's" to leave out. He shows how he types out the verbatim transcript and then its "next distillation." For publication he does still another distillation: here I present the verbatim transcription and the version for readers.

Verbatim Transcription

HILLER: Uh, well that was written in um, that was written in um, oh by the way, I should mention with the illiac, eh subsequent to the illiac suite we did some, we did some um, programming of um, of um, score composition, in other words how to lay out an actual score with musical notation and I went um, uh to a um, fellow in denver colorado his name was um, um, um, he was a composer, and he devised this thing. . . . [my ellipses][23]

(Progler has gone through a second distillation, which I do not show, in which he still leaves out capital letters at the beginning of the sentence and most punctuation.)

Distillation 3 for Publication

HILLER: Subsequent to the Iliac Suite we did some programming of score composition. In other words, how to lay out an actual score with musical notation, and I went to a fellow in Denver, Colorado, he was a composer and he devised this thing. . . . [my ellipses][24]

This narrator, Dr. Lejaren Hiller, is a composer and computer music specialist. The verbatim transcript with all of the "um's" does not correctly represent him; on the other hand, he had just suffered a serious illness that had made remembering difficult. Progler was right to delete some of the "um's" for purposes of offering the interview to the public, but it reads too smoothly to give the reader an indication of the difficulty Hiller was having. Progler might well have alerted the reader to the fact that this is a highly edited transcript and also given some information on the context, that is, Dr. Hiller's serious illness at the time of the interview.

For their book *Women of Crisis*, Robert and Jane Coles present their interviews with working-class women, using standard English. Oral historian Sherry Thomas describes her reaction to reading the book by admitting that she read thirty or forty pages before she realized the narrator was not a university-educated white woman but a black itinerant farm worker. She felt that the way the authors had transcribed the language "took away the reality of the woman's experience."[25]

Thomas insists that almost nobody carefully puts in all the g's at the end of a word. When you do that, and add prepositions to make the sentence read smoothly, you change the feeling of the personality of the speaker and obscure his or her reality.[26] Interviewer Marjorie Devault also charges, "Standard practice that smoothes out respondents' talk is one way that women's words are distorted; it is often a way of discounting and ignoring those parts of women's experience that are not easily expressed."[27] Would we believe Lu Ann Jones's narrators were ever real if she changed their words in *Mama Learned Us to Work?*[28] Would we glimpse what these farming women were up against in the troubled 1920s and 1930s South? Would we imagine their vulnerability in confronting their poverty and hardships if they spoke in perfect English?

After transcribing the words of black sharecropper Ned Cobb for the book *All God's Dangers: The Life of Nate Shaw*, Theodore Rosengarten said that he spelled the words the way they sounded to him. Certainly, he retained the rhythm of the sentences and the grammar that the narrator used. Listen to this example as you read out loud: "That teached me fair that a white man always wants a nigger in preference to a white man to work on his place. How come that? How come it for God's sake? He don't want no damn white man on his place. He gets a nigger, that's his glory. He can do that nigger just like he wants to and that nigger better not say nothin against his rulins."[29]

Some oral historians argue that you need only correctly convey the meaning, but what they publish after they have put the narrator's thoughts into their words is what *they* think was the meaning. Others argue that you have to put the prose in a form that the public can read easily. They prettify the text, correct the grammar, take out all false starts, rearrange to make the speech sound like a planned delivery. Readers will detect the falseness. The editor is implying, "Here are the words of this narrator." But they are not the narrator's words if the editor has changed them. And really this homogenizing takes the real feeling out of the narrator's words. It smacks of a power relationship whereby the one who controls access to publishing decides how the narrator should talk.

In the published version of an oral history transcript, when you are making decisions about what to present to the reader, stay as close to the narrator's words as you can while still having a readable text. The least possible tampering with the primary source—*according the most respect for the narrator's unique way of speaking*—is the best way.

Editors also rearrange the parts of the transcripts so that all of the discussion on one topic goes together and all of the discussion on another topic is placed together. The very questions asked, which would help the reader to approach the document critically, are omitted. Studs Terkel, the renowned journalist and author of many books based on oral histories, including the engrossing *Hard Times: An Oral History of the Great Depression*,[30] reacted to a question about his editing practices put to him by Ronald Grele, who headed Columbia University's oral history program:

> GRELE: [The narrators] respond to you—they respond to the questions you ask and by eliminating your questions, aren't you somehow obscuring the relationship that evolves there?
>
> TERKEL: No, because it isn't me. See, two things are involved: How do you get the truth about—again truth or fact—about the person. You've got to get it out. Sometimes my questions might intrude in print. I don't need it. Sometimes it's needed.[31]

In the preface to *All God's Dangers*, Theodore Rosengarten explains his method of selecting and rearranging passages and omitting his questions so that the narrative is presented unbroken:

> In editing the transcripts of our recordings I sometimes had to choose among multiple versions of the same story; other times, I combined parts of one version with another for the sake of clarity and completeness. Stories that seemed remote from Shaw's personal development I left out entirely. By giving precedence to stories with historical interest or literary merit I trust I haven't misrepresented him.
>
> Besides this hazardous selection process, my editing consisted of arranging Shaw's stories in a way that does justice both to their occurrence in time and his sequence of recollection. I tried, within the limits of a general chronology, to preserve the affinities between stories. For memory recalls kindred events and people and is not constrained by the calendar.[32]

Here two experts talk about leaving things out and rearranging: they are obviously troubled about this editorial process. Rosengarten is especially sensitive to the distortion that an editor can bring about by placing together stories for which the narrator had a different association in mind. These published versions of in-depth interviews can only be regarded as highly edited primary sources, as a second step removed from the taped interview, the original primary source (the verbatim transcript is the first step removed). Certainly both writers have made available to the public worlds of experience we might never have known but for their work. And they have presented others' words as a narrative so compelling that we are caught up in these worlds.

Did they not have to do what was necessary to accomplish this? Yes, but there are degrees of tampering with the order of development of thoughts. I acknowledge that in publication, the necessity of arranging segments of the taped memoir may sometimes occur because you want the narrative to progress along a straight line; a change in someone's actual wording is much less acceptable. At the least, in the preface to a book based on taped interviews, the author owes readers an explanation of the editing policy and information about location and accessibility of the original primary sources.

Citation of Oral History Interviews

As you write for publication, you will need to cite the oral history interviews. *The Chicago Manual of Style* advises including names of narrator and interviewer, date of the interview, and location of the tape or transcript.[33] We need to know the place where the interview occurred, and the *Chicago Manual* does suggest providing the place of the interview if it is known. However, there is no indication of tape side number and tape counter number.

> Amy Smith Hunt [pseud.], interview by John Jones, June 16, 1976, tape recording, Southern Oral History Collection, the University of North Carolina, Chapel Hill, North Carolina.

For the transcription, there is no transcript page number.

> Amy Smith Hunt [pseud.], transcription of interview by John Jones, June 16, 1976, Southern Oral History Collection, the University of North Carolina, Chapel Hill, North Carolina.

We use reference notes so the reader can check our evidence. If you want to listen to the segment of the tape that is quoted, you will have to listen to the whole interview because there is no tape side number and no tape counter number. Because the *Chicago Manual* does not require the place of the interview to be designated, there may be no indication of where the recording took place—was this a telephone interview with someone in one city talking to a respondent in a different city?

The *Oral History Review* and *Oral History* footnote differently from the *Chicago Manual* and from each other. Look at two footnotes in the same issue of the *Oral History Review* (Winter–Spring 2003):

Interview with RT (Los Angeles: Survivors of the Shoah Visual History Foundation, October 12, 1994).

Clarence Dailey interview, March 20, 2000.

Since the method of footnoting is not consistent from one authoritative source to another, I suggest you give the reader a complete citation that will help the person interested to locate not only the tape but also the quotation you have offered. The first number is the tape side number; the second, the tape counter number:

Elizabeth Bullock, oral history recorded by author, Seaboard, North Carolina, June 19, 1996, 1:065. Bernice Kelly Harris Papers, no. 3804, Manuscripts Department, Louis Round Wilson Library, University of North Carolina, Chapel Hill, NC.

The second time you footnote the oral history, shorten it:

Bullock, oral history, 2:040.

If you recorded with one narrator several times, include the date of the interview in the subsequent, shortened citations. Notice that I do not use just "interview" because this term can refer to an interview in which only notes are taken as well as to a taped interview. I have seen the terms "taped interview" and also "tape recording" used to clear up this confusion. Here is an example from the *Chicago Manual*:

Hunt, Horace [pseud.]. 1976. Interview by Ronald Schatz. Tape recording. May 16. Pennsylvania Historical and Museum Commission, Harrisburg.[34]

In most publications centered on oral history, the term "oral history" is used. Readers of such works know what the term means and so it seems to me a briefer, clearer representation of the document.

For an example of an even more inclusive citation, the format used by the University of California, Berkeley, to give full information about the main collection from which the individual interview is drawn, see appendix K.

Sharing Information

You have put much work into a project, having made sure that the project has a wider significance than just one person's or one local group's interests. By depositing the collection of tapes in a library or in archives, you can make sure your research continues to be useful even though your own work has come to an end. We are not isolated human beings: the endeavor we undertake to understand human experience is a common one. We need all the help we can get from others, and we give all the help we can. Sometimes the historian has been compared to the detective, which suggests an individual working alone. But the comparison obscures the "full spectrum of criminal investigation" that goes on; for a historical question, it is the work of many investigators over generations that builds the needed evidence.[35] It is worth your time to consult the American Historical Association's "Statement on Interviewing for Historical Documentation" (published on the Internet at www.historians.org/pubs/Free/ProfessionalStandards.htm#Statement%20on%20Interviewing).

Now researchers in other disciplines also recognize the importance of making their data available to others. Data from classic studies such as William Foote Whyte's *Street Corner Society* have been placed in archives and made accessible.[36] And granting agencies are beginning to require research data in social science projects to be deposited for other scholars' use.

In searching for a "home" for a collection, try to find out what kind of security system the archives have. Are tapes that are sealed in whole or in part, according to the narrator's wishes, likely to remain locked up? Are there adequate provisions for public access to the collection? For example, will these tapes appear in the library catalog? Are there machines in good enough condition for the public to play the tapes without breaking them? Will the institution make a copy available to the public, preserving the original? Does the curator understand the value of an oral history collection? Is the curator willing to bind the transcripts and to provide adequate means for preserving these documents?

An equally important question is this: is the curator willing to transfer analog audio tapes to digital files for preservation? Andy Kovolos, archivist at the Vermont Folklife Center, defines the "three golden rules" for preservation of sound recordings: (1) make a copy for preservation that is as close to the original sound as you can get it; (2) keep as much data about the original as possible; (3) save the file in a standard format and in an uncompressed form. He advises archivists to consult *The NINCH Guide to Good Practice in the Digital Representation and Management of Cultural Heritage Materials* (Humanities Advanced Technology and Information Institute, University of Glasgow, and the National Initiative for a Networked Cultural Heritage; available online at www.nyu.edu/its/humanities/ninchguide/).[37]

An important consideration in deciding where to deposit a collection of tapes is the kind of storage facility available for the tapes. Kevin Mulroy, at the Getty Center for the History of Art and the Humanities, advises that the climate in the storage room should remain at about 60°F, plus or minus five degrees, with a relative humidity of 40 percent, plus or minus 10 percent. If there are drastic changes in temperature or humidity, the tape may swell or shrink. This causes stress on the tape and affects the sound. Of course, tapes should not be placed next to heaters, but they also should not be left in direct sunlight or even artificial light lest there be enough heat to damage them. Tapes should not be stored close to conduits, electric motors, transformers, and other sources of magnetic energy. The storage and playback sites should be kept as dust free as possible, and no food particles or cigarette ash should be allowed to come in contact with the tapes.[38]

The plastic containers in which cassette tapes come offer protection. When they are placed in storage, avoid using metal shelving unless the metal has been grounded first. Wooden shelves are safer. With these recommendations in mind, you can talk over with the curator the environment in which the tapes will be maintained and judge whether this is a good place to put them.[39]

Discuss with the curator ways to publicize the collection's existence and availability. A library or archive that has funds to publish a guide to its oral history collections is providing a very useful bibliographic tool for the public. A copy of such a guide should be copyrighted and sent to the appropriate offices for inclusion in bibliographies of published collections. Unfortunately, the last edition of the *Oral History Index: An International Directory of Oral History Interviews* was published in 1990 by the Meckler Corporation (that publishing company has since been sold.)[40] Alas, even for work done before 1990, there are noticeable gaps. However, recently an oral history index by Alexander Street Press, *Oral History Online*, has been placed on the Internet, at www.alexanderstreet.com/products/orhi.htm. The aim of Alexander Street Press is to index all important oral history collections in English throughout the world. You can locate an oral history interview by interviewer's name and by narrator's name. The information is updated quarterly. An annual subscription fee is required to use this bibliography. However, Alexander Street Press also offers a free online resource, the *Oral History Directory*, at www.alexanderstreet2.com/oralhist/, which claims to give details of major oral history collections in English.

State and local historical associations should also receive notice of the collection, whether or not there is a publication. Finally, you may wish to speak at meetings of local and state historical associations and other professional meetings to let the public know what the project was about and what is contained in the collection.

Having made sure your work will continue to be helpful, like an artist, you can now put your brush down, step back and survey the picture, and truly say, "Finished."

Recommended Reading

Preparation of Tapes and Transcripts; Depositories

Allen, Susan Emily. "Resisting the Editorial Ego: Editing Oral History." *Oral History Review* 10 (1982): 33–45. This is the single most valuable article for information on problems in transcribing.

Baum, Willa K. *Transcribing and Editing Oral History.* Nashville, TN: American Association for State and Local History, 1991. This has long been a very informative book on transcribing and remains a useful book to consult.

Davis, Cullom, Kathryn Back, and Kay MacLean. *Oral History: From Tape to Type.* Chicago: American Library Association, 1977. Chapter 3, "Processing Oral History," has information on transcribing and auditing. The authors permit more editing than some current practitioners would sanction, but there is still much that is useful in this book, especially models for record keeping.

Dunaway, David King. "Transcription: Shadow or Reality." *Oral History Review* 12 (1984): 113–17. The author presents a thought-provoking discussion on the relationship of transcription to tape.

Kesner, Richard M. "Archives, Records, and Information Management." In *The Craft of Public History*, ed. David Trask and Robert Pomerory, 90–141. Westport, CT: Greenwood, 1983. Reference work with excellent bibliography.

Mulroy, Kevin. "Preserving Oral History Interviews on Tape: Curatorial Techniques and Management Procedures." *International Journal of Oral History* 7, no. 3 (November 1986): 189–97. This is an informative account of how to store and manage an oral history collection.

Smith, Allen, ed. *Directory of Oral History Collections.* Phoenix, AZ: Onyx Press, 1987. This is a very useful reference work: oral history collections are listed by state; there is an index to both subjects and narrators; authors give conditions of access, general holdings and specific "Notable Holdings," as well as contact information.

Stielow, Frederick J. *The Management of Oral History Sound Archives*. Westport, CT: Greenwood, 1986. Stielow traces the history of the preservation of sound archives (both interviews and performances), goes on to discuss the complexity of the problems, and suggests solutions. Useful, practical appendixes.

Public Presentation of Findings

Blatti, Jo. "Public History and Oral History." *Journal of American History* 77, no. 2 (1990): 615–25. Author presents a discussion of criteria for judging the presentation of findings that is practical and wise.

Franco, Barbara. "Doing History in Public: Balancing Historical Fact with Public Meaning." *Perspectives*, May–June 1995, 5–8. In this cogent essay, the author is concerned with the need to pursue rigorous scholarship in public places, such as museums, and at the same time engage the audience of nonhistorians.

Notes

1. David King Dunaway, "Transcription: Shadow or Reality," *Oral History Review* 12 (1984): 113–17; see p. 116.

2. Rina Benmayor, "Cyber-Teaching in the Oral History Classroom," *Oral History* 28, no. 1 (Spring 2000): 83–91; see p. 6.

3. Rosemary O. Joyce, *A Woman's Place: The Life History of a Rural Ohio Grandmother* (Columbus: Ohio State University Press, 1983), 10.

4. Theodore Rosengarten, *All God's Dangers: The Life of Nate Shaw* (New York: Avon, 1974).

5. Susan Emily Allen, "Resisting the Editorial Ego: Editing Oral History," *Oral History Review* 10 (1982): 33–45; see p. 35.

6. Davis, Back, and MacLean, *Oral History*, 53.

7. Allen, "Resisting the Editorial Ego," 35.

8. Marjorie L. Devault, "Talking and Listening from Women's Standpoint: Feminist Strategies for Interviewing and Analysis," *Social Problems* 37, no. 1 (February 1990): 96–116; see p. 103.

9. Davis, Back, and MacLean, *Oral History*, 51.

10. Davis, Back, and MacLean, *Oral History*, 51–52.

11. Davis, Back, and MacLean, *Oral History*, 52.

12. Joyce, *Woman's Place*, 20.

13. Valerie Yow (listed as Valerie Quinney) and Linda Wood, *How to Find Out by Asking: A Guide to Oral History in Rhode Island* (Providence, RI: State Board of Education, 1979), 28.

14. Yow and Wood, *How to Find Out by Asking*, 28.

15. Cullom Davis, Kathryn Back, and Kay MacLean, *Oral History: From Tape to Type* (Chicago: American Library Association, 1977), 53.

16. Yow and Wood, *How to Find Out by Asking*, 28.

17. Davis, Back, and MacLean, *Oral History*, 126.

18. Davis, Back, and MacLean, *Oral History*, 55.

19. Allen, "Resisting the Editorial Ego," 38–39.

20. Allen, "Resisting the Editorial Ego," 38–39.

21. E. Culpepper Clark, "The Oral History Interview," in *Effective Interviewing*, ed. Alexander Tolor (Springfield, IL: C. C. Thomas, 1985), 191.

22. Willa K. Baum, *Transcribing and Editing Oral History* (Nashville, TN: American Association for State and Local History, 1977), 18–19.

23. J. A. Progler, "Choices in Editing Oral History: The Distillation of Dr. Hiller," *Oral History Review* 19, nos. 1–2 (Spring–Fall 1991): 1–16; see p. 6.

24. Progler, "Choices in Editing Oral History," 8.

25. Sherry Thomas, "Digging beneath the Surface: Oral History Techniques," *Frontiers* 8, no. 1 (1983): 52.

26. Thomas, "Digging beneath the Surface," 52.

27. Devault, "Talking and Listening from Women's Standpoint," 107.

28. Lu Ann Jones, *Mama Learned Us to Work: Farm Women in the New South* (Chapel Hill: University of North Carolina Press, 2002).

29. Rosengarten, *All God's Dangers*, 511.

30. Studs Terkel, *Hard Times: An Oral History of the Great Depression* (New York: Avon, 1970).

31. Ronald Grele, ed., *Envelopes of Sound: The Art of Oral History* (Westport, CT: Greenwood, 1992), 36.

32. Rosengarten, *All God's Dangers*, xxiv.

33. *The Chicago Manual of Style*, 15th ed. (Chicago: University of Chicago Press, 2003), 705.

34. *Chicago Manual of Style*, 706.

35. G. S. Cause, "Collingwood's Detective Image of the Historian," in *Reassessing Collingwood*, ed. George H. Nadel, 57–77 (Middletown, CT: Wesleyan University Press, 1990); see p. 77.

36. William Foote Whyte, "In Defense of Street Corner Society," *Journal of Contemporary Ethnography* 21, no. 1 (April 1992): 52–68.

37. Kevin Mulroy, "Preserving Oral History Interviews on Tape: Curatorial Techniques and Management Procedures," *International Journal of Oral History* 7, no. 3 (November 1986): 189–97; see p. 192.

38. Mulroy, "Preserving Oral History Interviews on Tape," 190–93.

39. Mulroy, "Preserving Oral History Interviews on Tape," 193.

40. *Oral History Index: An International Directory of Oral History Interviews* (Westport, CT: Meckler Corporation, 1990).

APPENDIX A

Sample Interview Guide

Workers at Wurlitzter, World War II

I. Biographical Information

1. Birth, birthplace
2. Father's name; mother's maiden name; siblings
3. Birthplace: father, mother
4. Father's work; mother's work
5. Narrator's education
6. Family of origin: special remembrances such as a Christmas day, a family vacation, Sundays, birthdays
7. Family of origin: cultural life (favorite books, radio programs, church experience)
8. Chores as an adolescent, favorite social events as an adolescent
9. Marriage (date, spouse, where met)
10. Children (names, date of birth)
11. Work before the war

II. Work at Wurlitzer: Beginning Employment

1. Why did you go to work at Wurlitzer?
2. When did you begin work there?
3. In what department did you first work?
4. What shift did you work? How many hours? Overtime?
5. What did you do on your first job there?

6. Did you have prior training or special skills?
7. (If no) How did you train? How long did it take to learn your job? Who trained you?
8. Explain how you did your first job.
9. What did you like about it? Anything you worried about?

III. Production during the War

1. Would you explain what you did in your longest-held job in the plant during the war?
2. How did your work change in the conversion to war production from peacetime production?
3. How did you feel about this different way of working?
4. What was made in your department? In other sections on that floor? Do you know what was made on other floors?
5. Did employees usually know what was going on in other departments? How did they know?
6. What happened to the glider (or bat bomb, or glider wings, or army cots) after it was finished?
7. How was the finished glider transported?
8. Were the parts inspected? By whom? What happened to rejects? Were there repercussions for the workers?
9. Were there quotas? Were they met? What happened if the quota was not met?
10. Did there seem to be a shortage of workers? (If yes) How was this shortage dealt with?
11. How much time was allowed to do the job? Who set the time limits? How did workers handle this?
12. Were you ever aware of a shortage of materials?

IV. Organization of Work

1. Were any skills from prewar production useful in war production?
2. How were workers organized in the plant—did you have a foreman? What was his main job? Superintendent? How often did you see him in the plant? Director? Any contact with him?
3. How many workers were you working with?
4. Did you work with women?
5. What kinds of work did women do in the plant before the war?
6. What kinds of work did women do during the war?
7. Were women assigned to jobs that required long training?

8. Were women seen as bringing special skills to the job?
9. Were women clustered in certain areas of the plant?
10. Were men and women working together on tasks? Do you know of men who refused to work with women or minority groups?
11. Were there any women supervisors?
12. Were there things about the work situation that stand out in your mind that you would like to talk about?

V. Work Community

1. Did you have family members working in the plant? Did family members help each other get jobs?
2. Did you see your fellow workers outside of work?
3. What nationalities and minorities worked at the plant? Did they tend to work together? Socialize together?
4. What were the company-sponsored social activities?
5. Were you involved in company-sponsored activities? Separate activities for men and women?
6. How were new workers coming in treated? Were new male workers treated differently than new female workers?
7. Was there a special place where employees could take breaks and talk to each other? (If yes, were there separate places for foremen? For men and women?)
8. Did coworkers help each other out?
9. Did you make friends working in the plant? Would you tell me how this happened?
10. Did you ever observe incidents of unfairness? Did you ever observe incidents of real helpfulness and kindness?
11. Were there any celebrations at work for birthdays or anniversaries? What did foremen and supervisors think about this?
12. Did most workers attend the company-sponsored events for work awards or war victories?
13. How did people react to war news? Deaths from the war? How did management react? What effect did the good or bad news have on work morale?
14. Were there any social events or places in town that workers went to regularly?
15. Did you feel your income during the war was better than it had been during peacetime? (If so, any special things you did with extra money?)

16. How was your family life affected by the hours you put in at Wurlitzer?
17. Did your spouse also work? Where? Did this necessitate a new way of getting work done in the home?
18. How did you get to work?

VI. Motivation to Work at Wurlitzer during the War

1. Were you ever asked to do special things for the war effort at Wurlitzer?
2. Did management do anything to make people feel a part of the war effort?
3. Were you aware of absenteeism during the 1940s? (If no or yes) How do you account for that situation?
4. What, if anything, did management do to inspire workers to work harder?
5. Were you there in 1944 when the company received the Army/Navy E Award? What happened? How did you feel about the award? Do you recall things people said about it?
6. What were the things about defense work that impressed you? Anything that worried you?
7. At the time, were you thinking about safety on the job? Any company publicity about this? Did you consider possible health hazards in this kind of work? Any talk in the plant about this?

VII. Security

1. How would you describe security precautions in the plant before the war? After the conversion to war production?
2. How were you made aware of security?
3. Were you in a section that dealt with more sensitive production?
4. Were you aware of being closely watched? By whom, do you think? Were explanations given?
5. Were you given any information about cooperating in searches? Were you searched? How did you feel about that? Were searches a frequent occurrence?
6. Did security precautions differ according to what was made in the section?
7. Were you aware of any group that was watched more closely or excluded from sensitive projects?
8. Did you know of German Americans working in the plant? How were they treated?
9. Who were the guards? How were they chosen? How did you feel about these individuals?

VIII. Labor Relations

1. What would you say was the Wurlitzer Corporation management's attitude toward the workers?
2. How did you yourself get along with the managers and the superintendents, directors, chief engineers? (If narrator was promoted to this category later, ask how many contacts he or she might have continued with line workers and what kind.)
3. How often did workers get raises? What would a worker have to do to get a raise?
4. How was a personal disagreement between a boss and a worker dealt with?
5. What were the workers' complaints? How were they dealt with by management?
6. Were there things the management could have done for the workers? Anything you would have especially liked? Why?
7. Was there talk of starting a union? When? How did you hear?
8. What did you observe as workers' reactions to the possibility of forming a union? Management's reactions?
9. How was unionization portrayed by management? How about the newspapers?
10. What steps were taken to form a union?
11. Why do you think unionization did not take place?
12. Were workers' attitudes about working at Wurlitzer different during the war than they had been before?

IX. Wurlitzer after the War

1. When did you leave Wurlitzer? Why?
2. What changes in production that started during the war persisted in peacetime? How did those changes affect your job?
3. Did you know people who were laid off immediately after the war? Did they find other jobs? What happened to them?
4. What did you do during the time you were waiting to go back to work?
5. Did returning veterans get their jobs back?
6. Did many women remain in the workforce at Wurlitzer?
7. Did workers' attitudes change at Wurlitzer after the war?

X. Women-Only Questions

1. Were there any differences in working conditions for men and women?
2. At Wurlitzer, was there equal pay for equal work?
3. Did employment benefits for women differ from those offered to men?

4. Were there any incidences in which women were treated differently from their male coworkers by foremen?
5. What requirements were there concerning clothing to wear on the job? Did men also have special clothing requirements?
6. Did you feel that you had skills that came in handy when you were working in the plant?
7. Did a man train you for the job? What were men's attitudes about training a woman?
8. Did you ever hear male employees talking about having women in the plant? What kinds of things did they say?
9. How were you treated by male coworkers in the plant?
10. How did you feel about being able to do the work? Did you see changes in your attitude about the work as time went on? Did you start thinking about yourself in a different way? (Did this job make you want to work?)
11. What were the satisfying things about working at Wurlitzer? Hard things about the job?
12. Did you hope to continue working in this position after the war? Was it a job that would lead to the future?
13. What changes in your own life did the war bring for you?
14. Did women at Wurlitzer ever go places together after work? Visit on weekends? Celebrate birthdays?
15. Were most of your women coworkers from the same age group?
16. What shift did you prefer? Why?

I'd like to ask you now about ways you managed to work full-time and care for a family.

17. Were there any child-care services provided by the plant? Any social services? Nurse? Cot to lie down on?
18. Who took care of your children while you worked? How did you feel about being separated from them?
19. Were superintendents understanding about absences when a child or spouse or parent was sick? Do you remember any specific incidences?
20. Did you have help with cooking? Cleaning? Child care? Shopping?
21. Would you describe a typical workday during the war years?
22. Was your husband working in DeKalb? How did your husband feel about your working? How did your parents feel about your working? Your children?

23. Was the money you earned yours to do with as you liked? Did the money go into a general family fund? How were decisions made about spending money?
24. What kinds of things did you buy as a result of your having an income?
25. When the war was over, was there pressure for you to quit your job and return home?
26. How did your life change after the war was over?
27. If you could relive an experience at work during the war years, what would that be?
28. If you could relive an experience in the family during the war years, what would that be?

APPENDIX B

The Oral History Association's
Oral History Evaluation Guidelines

Program/Project Guidelines

Purposes and Objectives

a. Are the purposes clearly set forth? How realistic are they?

b. What factors demonstrate a significant need for the project?

c. What is the research design? How clear and realistic is it?

d. Are the terms, conditions, and objectives of funding clearly made known to judge the potential effect of such funding on the scholarly integrity of the project? Is the allocation of funds adequate to allow the project goals to be accomplished?

e. How do institutional relationships affect the purposes and objectives?

Selection of Recording Equipment

a. Should the interview be recorded on sound or visual recording equipment?

b. Are the best possible recording equipment and media available within one's budget being used?

c. Are interviews recorded on a medium that meets archival preservation standards?

d. How well has the interviewer mastered use of the equipment upon which the interview will be recorded?

Selection of Interviewers and Interviewees

a. In what ways are the interviewers and interviewees appropriate (or inappropriate) to the purposes and objectives?

b. What are the significant omissions and why were they omitted?

Records and Provenance

a. What are the policies and provisions for maintaining a record of the provenance of interviews? Are they adequate? What can be done to improve them?

b. How are records, policies, and procedures made known to interviewers, interviewees, staff, and users?

c. How does the system of records enhance the usefulness of the interviews and safeguard the rights of those involved?

Availability of Materials

a. How accurate and specific is the publicizing of the interviews?

b. How is information about interviews directed to likely users? Have new media and electronic methods of distribution been considered to publicize materials and make them available?

c. How have the interviews been used?

Finding Aids

a. What is the overall design for finding aids? Are the finding aids adequate and appropriate?

b. How available are the finding aids?

c. Have new technologies been used to develop the most effective finding aids?

Management, Qualifications, and Training

a. How effective is the management of the program/project?

b. What are the provisions for supervision and staff review?

c. What are the qualifications for staff positions?

d. What are the provisions for systematic and effective training?

e. What improvements could be made in the management of the program/project?

Ethical/Legal Guidelines

What procedures are followed to assure that interviewers/programs recognize and honor their responsibility to the interviewees? Specifically, what procedures are used to assure that:

a. The interviewees are made fully aware of the goals and objectives of the oral history program/project?

b. The interviewees are made fully aware of the various stages of the program/project and the nature of their participation at each stage?

c. The interviewees are given the opportunity to respond to questions as freely as possible and are not subjected to stereotyped assumptions based on race, ethnicity, gender, class, or any other social/cultural characteristic?

d. The interviewees understand their rights to refuse to discuss certain subjects, to seal portions of the interviews, or in extremely sensitive circumstances, even to remain anonymous?

e. The interviewees are fully informed about the potential uses of the material, including deposit of the interviews in a repository, publication in all forms of print or electronic media, including the Internet or other emerging technologies, and all forms of public programming?

f. The interviewees are provided a full and easily comprehensible explanation of their legal rights before being asked to sign a contract or deed of gift transferring rights, title, and interest in the tape(s) and transcript(s) to an administering authority or individual?

g. Care is taken so that the distribution and use of the material complies with the letter and spirit of the interviewees' agreements?

h. All prior agreements made with the interviewees are honored?

i. The interviewees are fully informed about the potential for and disposition of royalties that might accrue from the use of their interviews, including all forms of public programming?

j. The interviews and any other related materials will remain confidential until the interviewees have released their contents?

What procedures are followed to assure that the interviewers/programs recognize and honor their responsibilities to the profession? Specifically, what procedures assure that:

a. The interviewer has considered the potential for public programming and research use of the interviews and has endeavored to prevent any exploitation of or harm to interviewees?

b. The interviewer is well trained to conduct the interview in a professional manner, including the use of appropriate recording equipment and media?

c. The interviewer is well grounded in the background of the subject(s) to be discussed?

d. The interview will be conducted in a spirit of critical inquiry and that efforts will be made to provide as complete a historical record as possible?

e. The interviewees are selected based on the relevance of their experience to the subject at hand and that an appropriate cross-section of interviewees is selected for any particular project?

f. The interview materials, including recordings, transcripts, relevant photographic, moving image, and sound documents, as well as agreements and documentation of the interview process, will be placed in a repository after a reasonable period of time, subject to the agreements made with the interviewee and that the repository will administer their use in accordance with those agreements?

g. The methodologies of the program/project, as well as its goals and objectives, are available for the general public to evaluate?

h. The interview materials have been properly cataloged, including appropriate acknowledgment and credit to the interviewers, and that their availability for research use is made known?

What procedures are followed to assure that the interviewers and programs are aware of their mutual responsibilities and obligations? Specifically, what procedures are followed to assure that:

a. Interviewers are made aware of the program goals and are fully informed of ethical and legal considerations?

b. Interviewers are fully informed of all the tasks they are expected to complete in an oral history project?

c. Interviewers are made fully aware of their obligations to the oral history program/sponsoring institution, regardless of their own personal interest in a program/project?

d. Programs/sponsoring institutions treat their interviewers equitably by providing for appropriate compensation, acknowledging all products resulting from their work, and supporting fieldwork practices consistent with professional standards whenever there is a conflict between the parties to the interview?

e. Interviewers are fully informed of their legal rights and of their responsibilities to both the interviewee and to the sponsoring institution?

What procedures are followed to assure that interviewers and programs recognize and honor their responsibilities to the community/public? Specifically, what procedures assure that:

   a. The oral history materials and all works created from them will be available and accessible to the community that participated in the project?

   b. Sources of extramural funding and sponsorship are clearly noted for each interview of the project?

   c. The interviewers and project endeavor to not impose their own values on the community being studied?

   d. The tapes and transcripts will not be used unethically?

Recording Preservation Guidelines

Recognizing the significance of the recording for historical and cultural analysis and the potential uses of oral history interviews in nonprint media, what procedures are followed to assure that:

   a. Appropriate care and storage of the original recordings begins immediately after their creation?

   b. The original recordings are duplicated and stored according to accepted archival standards (i.e., stored in closed boxes in a cool, dry, dust-free environment)?

   c. Original recordings are reduplicated onto the best preservation media before significant deterioration occurs?

   d. Every effort is made in duplicating tapes to preserve a faithful facsimile of the interviewee's voice?

   e. All transcribing, auditing, and other uses are done from a duplicate, not the original recording?

Tape/Transcript Processing Guidelines

Information about the Participants

   a. Are the names of both interviewer and interviewee clearly indicated on the tape/abstract/transcript and in catalog materials?

   b. Is there adequate biographical information about both interviewer and interviewee? Where can it be found?

Interview Information

a. Are the tapes, transcripts, time indices, abstracts, and other materials presented for use identified as to the program/project of which they are a part?

b. Are the date and place of the interview indicated on the tape, transcript, time index, and abstract and in appropriate catalog material?

c. Are there interviewers' statements about the preparation for or circumstances of the interviews? Where? Are they generally available to researchers? How are the rights of the interviewees protected against improper use of such commentaries?

d. Are there records of contracts between the program and the interviewee? How detailed are they? Are they available to researchers? If so, with what safeguards for individual rights and privacy?

Interview Tape Information

a. Is the complete original tape preserved? Are there one or more duplicate copies?

b. If the original or any duplicate has been edited, rearranged, cut, or spliced in any way, is there a record of that action, including by whom, when, and for what purposes the action was taken?

c. Do the tape label and appropriate catalog materials show the recording speed, level, and length of the interview? If videotaped, do the tape label and appropriate catalog information show the format (e.g., U-matic, VHS, 8mm, etc.) and scanning system and clearly indicate the tracks on which the audio and time code have been recorded?

d. In the absence of transcripts, are there suitable finding aids to give users access to information on the tapes? What form do they take? Is there a record of who prepared these finding aids?

e. Are researchers permitted to listen to or view the tapes? Are there any restrictions on the use of the tapes?

Interview Transcript Information

a. Is the transcript an accurate record of the tape? Is a careful record kept of each step of processing the transcript, including who transcribed, audited, edited, retyped, and proofread the transcripts in final copy?

b. Are the nature and extent of changes in the transcript from the original tape made known to the user?

c. What finding aids have been prepared for the transcript? Are they suitable and adequate? How could they be improved?

d. Are there any restrictions on access to or use of the transcripts? Are they clearly noted?

e. Are there any photo materials or other supporting documents for the interview? Do they enhance and supplement the text?

f. If videotaped, does the transcript contain time references and annotation describing the complementary visuals on the videotape?

Interview Content Guidelines

Does the content of each interview and the cumulative content of the whole collection contribute to accomplishing the objectives of the program/project?

a. In what particulars does each interview or the whole collection succeed or fall short of the objectives of the project or program?

b. Do audio and visual tapes in the collection avoid redundancy and supplement one another in the interview content and focus?

In what ways does the program/project contribute to historical understanding?

a. In what particulars does each interview or the whole collection succeed or fall short in making such a contribution?

b. To what extent does the material add fresh information, fill gaps in the existing record, and/or provide fresh insights and perspectives?

c. To what extent is the information reliable and valid? Is it eyewitness or hearsay evidence? How well and in what manner does it meet internal and external tests of corroboration, consistency, and explication of contradictions?

d. What is the relationship of the interview information to existing documentation and historiography?

e. How does the texture of the interview impart detail, richness, and flavor to the historical record?

f. What is the nature of the information contributed? Is it facts, perceptions, interpretations, judgments, or attitudes, and how does each contribute to understanding?

g. Are the scope, volume, and representativeness of the population interviewed appropriate and sufficient to the purpose? Is there enough testimony to validate the evidence without passing the point of diminishing returns? How appropriate is the quantity to the purposes of the study?

g. How do the form and structure of the interviews contribute to making the content understandable?
i. To what extent does the audio and/or video recording capture unique sound and visual information?
j. Do the visual and other sound elements complement and/or supplement the verbal information? Has the interview captured processes, objects, or other individuals in the visual and sound environment?

Interview Conduct Guidelines

Use of Other Sources

a. Is the oral history technique the best way to acquire the information? If not, what other sources exist? Has the interviewer used them and sought to preserve them if necessary?
b. Has the interviewer made an effort to consult other relevant oral histories?
c. Is the interview technique a valuable way to supplement existing sources?
d. Do videotaped interviews complement, not duplicate, existing still or moving visual images?

Interviewer Preparation

a. Is the interviewer well informed about the subjects under discussion?
b. Are the primary and secondary sources used to prepare for the interview adequate?
c. Has the interviewer mastered the use of appropriate recording equipment and the field-recording techniques that insure a high-fidelity recording?

Interviewee Selection and Orientation

a. Does the interviewee seem appropriate to the subjects discussed?
b. Does the interviewee understand and respond to the interview purposes?
c. Has the interviewee prepared for the interview and assisted in the process?
d. If a group interview, have composition and group dynamics been considered in selecting participants?

Interviewer–Interviewee Relations

a. Do interviewer and interviewee collaborate with each other toward interview objectives?

b. Is there a balance between empathy and analytical judgment in the interview?

c. If videotaped, is the interviewer/interviewee relationship maintained despite the presence of a technical crew? Do the technical personnel understand how a videotaped oral history interview differs from a scripted production?

Technique and Adaptive Skills

a. In what ways does the interview show that the interviewer has used skills appropriate to: the interviewee's condition (health, memory, mental alertness, ability to communicate, time schedule, etc.) and the interview location and conditions (disruptions and interruptions, equipment problems, extraneous participants, background noises, etc.)?

b. What evidence is there that the interviewer has: thoroughly explored pertinent lines of thought? Followed up on significant clues? Made an effort to identify sources of information? Employed potential challenges when needed? Thoroughly explored the potential of the visual equipment, if videotaped?

c. Has the program/project used recording equipment and media that are appropriate for the purposes of the work and potential nonprint as well as print uses of the material? Are the recordings of the highest appropriate technical quality? How could they be improved?

d. If videotaped, are lighting, composition, camera work, and sound of the highest appropriate technical quality?

e. In the balance between content and technical quality, is the technical quality good without subordinating the interview process?

Perspective

a. Do the biases of the interviewer interfere with or influence the responses of the interviewee?

b. What information is available that may inform the users of any prior or separate relationship between the interviewer and interviewee?

Historical Contribution

a. Does the interviewer pursue the inquiry with historical integrity?

b. Do other purposes being served by the interview enrich or diminish quality?

c. What does the interview contribute to the larger context of historical knowledge and understanding?

Independent/Unaffiliated Researcher Guidelines

Creation and Use of Interviews

a. Has the independent/unaffiliated researcher followed the guidelines for obtaining interviews as suggested in the Program/Project Guidelines section?

b. Have proper citation and documentation been provided in works created (books, articles, audio-visual productions, or other public presentations) to inform users of the work about the interviews used and the permanent location of the interviews?

c. Do works created include an explanation of the interview project, including editorial procedures?

d. Has the independent/unaffiliated researcher arranged to deposit the works created in an appropriate repository?

Transfer of Interviews to Archival Repository

a. Has the independent/unaffiliated researcher properly obtained the agreement of the repository before making representations about the disposition of the interviews?

b. Is the transfer consistent with agreements or understandings with interviewees? Were legal documents obtained from interviewees?

c. Has the researcher provided the repository with adequate descriptions of the creation of the interviews and the project?

d. What is the technical quality of the recorded interviews? Are the interviews transcribed, abstracted, or indexed, and, if so, what is the quality?

Educator and Student Guidelines

Has the educator:

a. Become familiar with the "Oral History Evaluation Guidelines" and conveyed their substance to the student?

b. Ensured that each student is properly prepared before going into the community to conduct oral history interviews, including familiarization with the ethical issues surrounding oral history and the obligation to seek the informed consent of the interviewee?

c. Become familiar with the literature, recording equipment, techniques, and processes of oral history so that the best possible instruction can be presented to the student?

d. Worked with other professionals and organizations to provide the best oral history experience for the student?

e. Considered that the project may merit preservation, and worked with other professionals and repositories to preserve and disseminate those collected materials?

f. Shown willingness to share expertise with other educators, associations, and organizations?

Has the student:

a. Become thoroughly familiar with the equipment, techniques, and processes of oral history interviewing and the development of research using oral history interviews?

b. Explained to the interviewee the purpose of the interview and how it will be used, and obtained the interviewee's informed consent to participate?

c. Treated the interviewee with respect?

d. Signed a receipt for and returned any materials borrowed from the interviewee?

e. Obtained a signed legal release for the interview?

f. Kept her/his word about oral or written promises made to the interviewee?

g. Given proper credit (oral or written) when using oral testimony and used the material in context?

Source: Oral History Association, *Oral History Evaluation Guidelines,* pamphlet no. 3 (Carlisle, PA: Oral History Association, Dickinson College: adopted 1989, revised 2000), omega.dickinson.edu/organizations/oha/pub_eg .html#Oral%20History%20Evaluation%20Guidelines.

APPENDIX C

Principles and Standards of the Oral History Association

The Oral History Association promotes oral history as a method of gathering and preserving historical information through recorded interviews with participants in past events and ways of life. It encourages those who produce and use oral history to recognize certain principles, rights, technical standards, and obligations for the creation and preservation of source material that is authentic, useful, and reliable. These include obligations to the interviewee, to the profession, and to the public, as well as mutual obligations between sponsoring organizations and interviewers.

People with a range of affiliations and sponsors conduct oral history interviews for a variety of purposes: to create archival records, for individual research, for community and institutional projects, and for publications and media productions. While these principles and standards provide a general framework for guiding professional conduct, their application may vary according to the nature of specific oral history projects. Regardless of the purpose of the interviews, oral history should be conducted in the spirit of critical inquiry and social responsibility and with a recognition of the interactive and subjective nature of the enterprise.

Responsibility to Interviewees

1. Interviewees should be informed of the purposes and procedures of oral history in general and of the aims and anticipated uses of the particular projects to which they are making their contributions.

2. Interviewees should be informed of the mutual rights in the oral history process, such as editing, access restrictions, copyrights, prior use, royalties, and the expected disposition and dissemination of all forms of the record, including the potential for electronic distribution.

3. Interviewees should be informed that they will be asked to sign a legal release. Interviews should remain confidential until interviewees have given permission for their use.

4. Interviewers should guard against making promises to interviewees that the interviewers may not be able to fulfill, such as guarantees of publication and control over the use of interviews after they have been made public. In all future uses, however, good faith efforts should be made to honor the spirit of the interviewee's agreement.

5. Interviews should be conducted in accord with any prior agreements made with the interviewee, and such agreements should be documented for the record.

6. Interviewers should work to achieve a balance between the objectives of the project and the perspectives of the interviewees. They should be sensitive to the diversity of social and cultural experiences and to the implications of race, gender, class, ethnicity, age, religion, and sexual orientation. They should encourage interviewees to respond in their own style and language, and to address issues that reflect their concerns. Interviewers should fully explore all appropriate areas of inquiry with the interviewee and not be satisfied with superficial responses.

7. Interviewers should guard against possible exploitation of interviewees and be sensitive to the ways in which their interviews might be used. Interviewers must respect the rights of interviewees to refuse to discuss certain subjects, to restrict access to the interview, or, under extreme circumstances, even to choose anonymity. Interviewers should clearly explain these options to all interviewees.

8. Interviewers should use the best recording equipment within their means to accurately reproduce the interviewee's voice, and if appropriate, other sounds as well as visual images.

9. Given the rapid development of new technologies, interviewees should be informed of the wide range of potential uses of their interviews.

10. Good faith efforts should be made to ensure that the uses of recordings and transcripts comply with both the letter and spirit of the interviewee's agreement.

Responsibility to the Public and to the Profession

1. Oral historians have a responsibility to maintain the highest professional standards in the conduct of their work and to uphold the standards of the various disciplines and professions with which they are affiliated.

2. In recognition of the importance of oral history to an understanding of the past and of the cost and effort involved, interviewers and interviewees should mutually strive to record candid information of lasting value and to make that information accessible.

3. Interviewees should be selected based on the relevance of their experiences to the subject at hand.

4. Interviewers should possess interviewing skills as well as professional competence and knowledge of the subject at hand.

5. Regardless of the specific interests of the project, interviewers should attempt to extend the inquiry beyond the specific focus of the project to create as complete a record as possible for the benefit of others.

6. Interviewers should strive to prompt informative dialogue through challenging and perceptive inquiry. They should be grounded in the background of the persons being interviewed and, when possible, should carefully research appropriate documents and secondary sources related to subjects about which the interviewees can speak.

7. Interviewers should make every effort to record their interviews using the best recording equipment within their means to reproduce accurately the interviewee's voice and, if appropriate, image. They should also collect and record other historical documentation the interviewee may possess, including still photographs, print materials, and other sound and moving image recordings, if appropriate.

8. Interviewers should provide complete documentation of their preparation and methods, including the circumstances of the interviews.

9. Interviewers and, when possible, interviewees should review and evaluate their interviews, including any summaries or transcriptions made from them.

10. With the permission of the interviewees, interviewers should arrange to deposit their interviews in an archival repository that is capable of both preserving the interviews and eventually making them available for general use. Interviewers should provide basic information

about the interviews, including project goals, sponsorship, and funding. Preferably, interviewers should work with repositories before conducting the interviews to determine necessary legal arrangements. If interviewers arrange to retain first use of the interviews, it should be only for a reasonable time before public use.

11. Interviewers should be sensitive to the communities from which they have collected their oral histories, taking care not to reinforce thoughtless stereotypes nor bring undue notoriety to them. Interviewers should take every effort to make the interviews accessible to the communities.

12. Oral history interviews should be used and cited with the same care and standards applied to other historical sources. Users have a responsibility to retain the integrity of the interviewee's voice, neither misrepresenting the interviewee's words nor taking them out of context.

13. Sources of funding or sponsorship of oral history projects should be made public in all exhibits, media presentations, or publications that result from the projects.

14. Interviewers and oral history programs should conscientiously consider how they might share with interviewees and their communities the rewards and recognition that might result from their work.

Responsibility for Sponsoring and Archival Institutions

1. Institutions sponsoring and maintaining oral history archives have a responsibility to interviewees, interviewers, the profession, and the public to maintain the highest technical, professional, and ethical standards in the creation and archival preservation of oral history interviews and related materials.

2. Subject to conditions that interviewees set, sponsoring institutions (or individual collectors) have an obligation to: prepare and preserve easily usable records; keep abreast of rapidly developing technologies for preservation and dissemination; keep accurate records of the creation and processing of each interview; and identify, index, and catalog interviews.

3. Sponsoring institutions and archives should make known through a variety of means, including electronic modes of distribution, the existence of interviews open for research.

4. Within the parameters of their missions and resources, archival institutions should collect interviews generated by independent

researchers and assist interviewers with the necessary legal agreements.

5. Sponsoring institutions should train interviewers. Such training should: provide them basic instruction in how to record high fidelity interviews and, if appropriate, other sound and moving image recordings; explain the objectives of the program to them; inform them of all ethical and legal considerations governing an interview; and make clear to interviewers what their obligations are to the program and to the interviewees.

6. Interviewers and interviewees should receive appropriate acknowledgment for their work in all forms of citation or usage.

7. Archives should make good faith efforts to ensure that uses of recordings and transcripts, especially those that employ new technologies, comply with both the letter and the spirit of the interviewee's agreement.

Source: Oral History Association, Oral History Evaluation Guidelines, pamphlet no. 3 (Carlisle, PA: Oral History Association, Dickinson College: adopted 1989, revised 2000), omega.dickinson.edu/organizations/oha/pub_eg .html#Oral%20History%20Evaluation%20Guidelines.

Oral History Excluded from Institutional Review Board (IRB) Review

The U.S. Office for Human Research Protection (OHRP), part of the Department of Health and Human Services (HHS), working in conjunction with the American Historical Association and the Oral History Association, has determined that oral history interviewing projects in general do not involve the type of research defined by HHS regulations and are therefore excluded from Institutional Review Board oversight.

At the October 2003 Meeting on the Oral History Association in Bethesda, Maryland, George Pospisil of the OHRP's Division of Education and Development, explained the OHRP decision regarding the application of the "Common Rule" (45 CFR part 46), which sets regulations governing research involving human subjects. These federal regulations define research as "a systematic investigation, including research development, testing, and evaluation, designed to develop or contribute to generalizable knowledge." The type of research encompassed by the regulations involves standard questionnaires with a large sample of individuals who often remain anonymous, not the open-ended interviews with identifiable individuals who give their interviews with "informed consent" that characterizes oral history. Only those oral history projects that conform to the regulatory definition of research will now need to submit their research protocols for IRB review.

Following is the text of a policy statement that was developed by the Oral History Association and the American Historical Association in consultation with the OHRP. This policy applies to oral history that takes place within an institution that has filed a multiple project assurance with OHRP.

As one of the seventeen federal agencies that have signed on to the Common Rule, the Department of Health and Human Services deals most directly with the type of clinical research that the federal regulations were originally intended to cover, and its concurrence with the policy statement should set the way for a uniform interpretation by other federal agencies. Oral historians should make this statement available to department chairs, directors of graduate studies, deans, and other officers concerned with institutional compliance with federal regulations.

Donald A. Ritchie   Linda Shopes
Oral History Association   American Historical Association

Application of the Department of Health and Human Services Regulations for the Protection of Human Subjects at 45 CFR Part 46, Subpart A to Oral History Interviewing

Most oral history interviewing projects are not subject to the requirements of the Department of Health and Human Services (HHS) regulations for the protection of human subjects at 45 CFR part 46, subpart A, and can be excluded from institutional review board (IRB) oversight because they do not involve research as defined by the HHS regulations. HHS regulations at 45 CFR 46.102 (D) define research as "a systematic investigation, including research development, testing, and evaluation, designed to develop or contribute to generalizable knowledge." The Oral History Association defines oral history as "a method of gathering and preserving historical information through recorded interviews with participants in past events and ways of life."

It is primarily on the grounds that oral history interviews, in general, are not designed to contribute to "generalizable knowledge" that they are not subject to the requirements of the HHS regulations at 45 CFR part 46 and, therefore, can be excluded from IRB review. Although the HHS regulations do not define "generalizable knowledge," it is reasonable to assume that the term does not simply mean knowledge that lends itself to generalizations, which characterizes every form of scholarly inquiry and human communication. While historians reach for meaning that goes beyond the specific subject of their inquiry, unlike researchers in the biomedical and behavioral sciences they do not reach for generalizable principles of historical or social development, nor do they seek underlying principles or laws of nature that have predictive value and can be applied to other circumstances for the purpose of controlling outcomes. Historians explain a particular past; they do not create general explanations about all that has happened in the past, nor do they predict the future.

Moreover, oral history narrators are not anonymous individuals, selected as part of a random sample for the purposes of a survey. Nor are they asked to respond to a standard questionnaire administered to a broad swath of the population. Those interviewed are specific individuals selected because of their often unique relationship to the topic at hand. Open-ended questions are tailored to the experiences of the individual narrator. Although interviews are guided by professional protocols, the way any individual interview unfolds simply cannot be predicted. An interview gives a unique perspective on the topic at hand; a series of interviews offer up not similar "generalizable" information but a variety of particular perspectives on the topic.

For these reasons, then, oral history interviewing, in general, does not meet the regulatory definition of research as articulated in 45 CFR part 46. The Office for Human Research Protections concurs with this policy statement, and it is essential that such an interpretation be made available to the many IRB's grappling with issues of human subject research.

Source: Donald A. Ritchie and Linda Shopes, "Oral History Excluded from Institutional Review Board (IRB) Review" (The Oral History Association and the American Historical Association, 2004).

APPENDIX E

Model Record-Keeping Sheets

You will need a log for registering the tapes and a form for recording information in more detail about each narrator's interviews. Here are some ways of keeping records. Sample 1 is based on that shown in *Oral History: From Tape to Type*, by Cullom Davis, Kathryn Back, and Kay MacLean (Chicago: American Library Association, 1977), which I have modified.

Sample 1: Interview Data Sheet

Narrator: Address:
Telephone: Birthdate: Birthplace:
Interviewer: Place of Interview:

	Date	Total Time	Collateral Materials	Indexed
Introductory letter				
Telephone call				
Preliminary visit				
Interview 1				
Interview 2				
Interview 3				
Interview 4				
Release form returned				

Tapes received _____

Labeled _____

Collateral materials
   returned _____

Transcribing begun _____

Number of pages _____

Total time _____

Editing _____

Returned to narrator _____

Received from narrator _____

Reread by _____

Proofread _____

Corrected _____

Indexed _____

Table of contents _____

Transcription photocopied _____

Tape duplicated _____

Thank-you letter _____

Tape & transcript deposited _____

Duplicated tape & transcript sent to
   narrator _____

Final typing _____

Problems: _____

Special considerations: _____

Sample 2: Master Log for the Project

As you accumulate tapes, you need to know at a glance which ones have been processed, and what remains to be done for others.

MASTER LOG FOR PROJECT

Interviews	Date	Release form signed	Tape indexed	Copy of tape sent to narrator	Transcription begun	Transcription completed	Transcription sent to narrator	Transcription returned	Transcription corrected	Transcription retyped	Proofreading final	Table of contents	Transcription sent to narrator	Deposited in archives

Legal Release Forms

The following sample release forms illustrate the range of complexity in forms currently in use. The first is the form I have used as an independent scholar, working on my own and not on behalf of any institution or employer. Please notice that I must also use a deed of gift agreement for both narrator and interviewer to sign so that the taped collection can be deposited in the archives. The second form is a work made for hire agreement, drawn up by John Neuenschwander, for an interviewer interviewing on behalf of an employer.

I also include three forms that provide for release of the taped collection to archives. The first is a form from the Bancroft Library at the University of California, which the interviewer signs when the tapes are deposited. In the second, based on the interviewee permission form used at the University of Connecticut's Center for Oral History, the interviewee gives her or his tape to the archives. The third form presented here is used by the Baylor University Institute for Oral History to provide donation of the interview to the archives by both the interviewee and interviewer.

Release Form for Independent Scholarly Research

Release Form for Scholarly Research

In consideration of the work that Valerie Yow is doing to collect and preserve reminiscences of Betty Smith Finch, I give her permission to use the information from my taped recording in scholarly publications or presentations on the life of Betty Smith Finch.

I understand that my taped recording and any transcript made from it will be deposited in Betty Smith Finch's collection of letters and documents in the Manuscripts Division of the Louis Round Wilson Library of the University of North Carolina. I understand that the Manuscripts Division will allow qualified scholars to listen to my taped memories and read the transcript in connection with their research. I know that this may result in public presentations, including radio and television broadcasts and publication on websites.

Any listener or reader of the transcript of this recording should bear in mind that this is my spoken, not my written word. This agreement does not preclude any use that I may wish to make of the content or expressions contained in this recorded memoir.

_____   _____
Signature of Narrator and date   Signature of Interviewer and date

_____
_____
_____

Address of Narrator

Restrictions:_____
_____
_____
_____
_____
_____

Release Form for Interviewer Acting on Behalf of an Employer

Work Made for Hire Agreement

_____ (*name of archive, program or individual*) enters into the following agreement with _____ (*name of interviewer*) on _____, 2002.

The _____ (*name of archive, program or individual*) has conceived of an original work of authorship relating to the ongoing creation of oral histories. Therefore, _____ (*name of interviewer*) is specially ordered and commissioned to conduct oral history interviews, which are to be part of the _____ (*name of archive, program or individual*)'s collective and/or supplemental work or other category of work eligible to be treated as a work made for hire under the United States Copyright Act.

_____ (*name of archive, program or individual*) and the interviewer intend that the copyright in the work or works that the interviewer prepares is to be owned by the _____ (*name of archive, program or individual*), which is considered the author of such work or works as defined by 17 U.S.C. 201.

In consideration for the specially ordered and commissioned services to be performed by the interviewer, the _____ (*name of archive, program or individual*) agrees to compensate the interviewer as follows:

_____

_____

_____

By this written instrument the parties expressly agree that all interviews conducted by the interviewer pursuant to this agreement shall be considered a Work Made for Hire, as defined in 17 U.S.C. 101 (2).

IN WITNESS WHEREOF the parties have executed this agreement effective as of the date first written above.

Signature of Agent/Representative _____

Signature of Interviewer _____

Date _____

Source: John Neuenschwander, *Oral History and the Law* (Carlisle, PA: Oral History Association, 2002), 86–87.

Interviewer's Release of Documents to Archives

Donated Oral History Collection
The Bancroft Library
Regional Oral History Office
University of California
Berkeley, CA 94720

Interviewer's Gift to the Bancroft Library

I, _____ (Interviewer), do hereby give to the Regents
of the University of California for such scholarly and educational purposes as
the Director of The Bancroft Library may determine, copies of the tapes and
transcripts of the interviews listed on the attached Exhibit, including the
right to publish all or any portion of such material and to authorize others to
publish quotations.

This gift does not preclude any use which I or the narrator of each interview may want to make of the recordings of his or her interview(s).

Dated: _____

_____

Interviewer

_____
_____

Name & Address of Interviewer

Accepted for the Bancroft Library by:

_____

Division Head
Regional Oral History Office

_____

Dated

Subject of interview(s) _____

Interviewee's Release of Documents to Archives

Interviewee Permission Form

Center for Oral History
University of Connecticut
438 Whitney Avenue Extension
Storrs, CT 06269-1132

I do hereby give as an unrestricted gift to the University of Connecticut Center for Oral History for scholarly and educational uses the Director of the Center shall determine, including the use of the World Wide Web, the tape-recorded interviews and transcripts thereof recorded on _____. I also transfer to the Center and the University of Connecticut legal title and all literary rights including copyright. This gift does not preclude any use I may want to make of the information in the recordings and/or transcripts myself.

_____   _____
Signature of Interviewer and date   Signature of Interviewee and date

_____   _____
Name of Interviewer (please print)   Name of Interviewee (please print)

_____
Interviewee's address

_____
Interviewer's address

Restrictions:_____
_____
_____
_____
_____
_____
_____
_____
_____
_____

Release of Documents to Archives by
Both Interviewer and Interviewee

Deed of Gift Agreement

The purpose of the Baylor University Institute for Oral History is to gather and preserve historical documents by means of the tape-recorded interview. Tape recordings and transcripts resulting from such interviews, collectively entitled oral memoirs, become part of the archives of The Texas Collection of Baylor University. Oral memoirs will be made available for historical and other academic research and for public dissemination.

Participation in the Institute's projects is entirely voluntary and may be withdrawn at any time. If you have any questions regarding your rights as a participant, or have other questions regarding this research, please contact the Baylor University Committee for Protection of Human Subjects in Research, Dr. Lee Nordt, Chair, Baylor University, One Bear Place # 97344, Waco, TX 76798-7344. Dr. Nordt may also be reached at (254) 710-4288.

Either Part I or Part II of this document as agreed to by the interviewee will govern use of the materials generated from an oral interview.

Part I. Interviewee Deed of Gift—Unrestricted

I have read the above and understand that the tape recordings and transcripts resulting from this oral interview or oral interview series will become part of the oral history archives of The Texas Collection at Baylor University, where they will be made available for historical and other academic research and for public dissemination.

1. I hereby give, grant, convey, and consign this oral memoir to Baylor University as a donation for such historical and scholarly purposes as they see fit, including but not limited to, the exclusive rights of reproduction, distribution, preparation of derivative works, public performance, and display.
2. I hereby transfer to Baylor University legal title and all literary property rights to my oral memoirs including copyright.

I herein warrant that I have not assigned or in any manner encumbered or impaired any of the aforementioned rights in my oral memoir.

_____   _____
Interviewee (signature)   Date

_____
Name of Interviewee (typed or printed)

Part II. Interviewee Deed of Gift—With Restrictions

I have read the above and understand that the tape recordings and transcripts resulting from this oral interview or oral interview series will become part of the oral history archives of The Texas Collection at Baylor University, where they will be made available for historical and other academic research and for public dissemination.

I herein warrant that I have not assigned or in any manner encumbered or impaired any of the aforementioned rights in my oral memoir.

1. I hereby give, grant, convey, and consign this oral memoir to Baylor University as a donation for such historical and scholarly purposes as they see fit, with only the following restrictions:

Nature of restrictions on use of *transcripts* (attach additional sheet if necessary):

_____

_____

Nature of restrictions on use of *tape recordings* (attach additional sheet if necessary):

_____

_____

2. I hereby transfer to Baylor University legal title and all literary property rights to oral memoirs including copyright with only the following restrictions:

Nature of restrictions on use of *transcripts* (attach additional sheet if necessary):

_____

_____

Nature of restrictions on use of *tape recordings* (attach additional sheet if necessary):

_____

_____

_____   _____

Interviewee (signature)   Date

_____

Name of Interviewee (typed or printed)

Part III. Interviewer Deed of Gift

I will conduct the interview or series of interviews with _____ and have read the above. In view of the scholarly value of this research material, I voluntarily donate my portion of these oral memoirs to Baylor University and hereby transfer to Baylor University legal title and all literary property rights to the memoir including copyright.

_____   _____

Interviewee (signature)   Date

_____

Name of Interviewee (typed or printed)

APPENDIX G

Sample Face Sheet and Information Sheet

UNIVERSITY OF RHODE ISLAND

STATE ORAL HISTORY PROGRAM: HISTORY OF HERA

Oral History Interview

with

NATALIE KAMPEN

By Valerie Yow

The Hera Gallery, Wakefield, Rhode Island

July 18, 1988

Sample Information Sheet

UNIVERSITY OF RHODE ISLAND
STATE ORAL HISTORY PROJECT: HISTORY OF HERA GALLERY

General topic of interview: The making of an art historian. The intellectual ferment in South County in the early seventies. The place of Hera Gallery in the history of South County and in the lives of its founders.

NARRATOR: NATALIE KAMPEN   INTERVIEWER: VALERIE YOW

DATE: July 18, 1988   PLACE: Hera Gallery
                                               Wakefield, Rhode Island

PERSONAL DATA
Birthdate: 1944
Spouse: (divorced)
Occupation: college professor of art history

BIOGRAPHY

Natalie Kampen, at the time of this oral history recording, had just finished teaching at one university and was getting ready to take a new position as a director of Women's Studies at another. She had come to the community in 1969 with a master's degree in art history. During her years of teaching art history in the state, she had finished her Ph.D. in Art History and built a distinguished record of research and publication. Not a member of the Hera Gallery, she was, nevertheless, a consistent supporter and close friend to founding members. Her marriage had just ended at the time of this recording and the interview catches her on the point of a new career in administration and a new personal life.

INTERVIEWER'S COMMENTS

This recording by a very perceptive, articulate observer is invaluable for information on the intellectual ferment among women in South County during the seventies. While there is little specific information on the founding of Hera, the intellectual climate which made that possible is explained here. This testimony is straightforward; the point of view is that of a feminist art historian. Natalie Kampen's involvement continues to be that of a supporter and consultant to the gallery: and therefore she does not choose the role of noninvolved observer, but openly states her allegiance to the gallery and championship of women in the field of art. The candor of the interview may be in part a characteristic of the narrator's personality, in part a result of the preexisting friendship and trust between narrator and interviewer.

Note: Samples are used with permission from Alexandra Broches and Natalie Kampen.

Sample Tape Index

UNIVERSITY OF RHODE ISLAND
STATE ORAL HISTORICAL PROGRAM: HISTORY OF HERA

NARRATOR: NATALIE KAMPEN   INTERVIEWER: VALERIE YOW

Place: Hera Gallery   No. of tapes: 1
        Wakefield, Rhode Island   No. of sides: 2
                                         Length of tape: 60 minutes
Date: July 18, 1988

Initials	Side	Number Counter	Topic of Discussion
NK	1	002	Introduction
NK	1	008	Birthplace and birthdate Philadelphia, 1944
NK	1	010	Growing up place Philadelphia suburb
NK	1	012	Parents' work Father trained in ancient history, but worked as a certified accountant. Mother, an art and architectural historian.

NK	1	015	Siblings
			Sister, 3½ years younger. She is married and teaches neurophysiology at a medical school.
NK	1	020	Art education in childhood
			She was regarded as a promising child artist and was given art lessons. At fifteen or sixteen, she went to an art school in Philadelphia eight hours a day during one summer. She found out she did not want to do art as a full-time occupation.
NK	1	032	Ambition in childhood
			Her mother, a graduate student then in art history, took her to a lecture about art history. Natalie fell in love with art history. The lecture, given by Frederick Hart, was on paintings from the Italian Renaissance. The slides were so beautiful and the language was so vivid that she remembers the lecture almost word for word. She saw for the first time the "connection between the beautiful object and the beautiful question."

Note: Document reproduced with the permission of Natalie Kampen.

APPENDIX I

Sample First Page of a
Tape Collection's Master Index

Oral History of the Hera Gallery, Wakefield, Rhode Island

MASTER INDEX
Please note: the first number after the name of the oral history is the side
number; the second number refers to the tape counter number.

ADMINISTRATION AT HERA (*See also* Coordinator at Hera)
Broches 2:379. Gutchen 2:191. Richman 2:319; 3:060, 339.

ADMINISTRATIVE ASSISTANT AT HERA
Bodin 1:240. Chabot 1:288. Richman 3:060. Waterston 1:053; 2:266.

ADMISSIONS PROCESS AT HERA (*See also* Men and Hera, Admissions)
Barnett 2:280. Chabot 1:221; 2:035. Greene 1:311. Hackett 2:119. Jahn
2:138. Killilea 2:298. Malik 1:522. Powers 2:020, 034.

ART AND ART HISTORY WOMEN'S GROUP
Christofferson 1:225. Kampen 1:360. Killilea 2:025. Richman 2:241.

ART DEPARTMENT, UNIVERSITY OF RHODE ISLAND
Christofferson 1:075, 330. Cutting 1:075, 097, 109. Gelles 1:088. Greene
1:060, 075, 095, 108, 495. Gutchen 1:417. Hackett 1:148, 188, 295, 330;

2:285. Jahn 1:271, 305, 326. Kampen 1:532. Malik 1:177, 188. Pagh 2:042, 150. Powers 1:572. Richman 1:320. Rohm 1:340, 360, 405, 454, 609.

ART EDUCATION BEGINNING IN ADULTHOOD
Barnett 1:018. Gelles 1:099, 110, 163. Greene 1:060, 108, 124. Gutchen 1:409, 417. Hackett 1:092, 148, 188, 330. Killilea 1:158, 165, 181, 219. Malik 1:160. Pagh 1:112, 293. Richman 1:212.

ART EDUCATION IN CHILDHOOD
Bodin 1:062. Bornstein 1:202. Broches 1:064. Cutting 1:061. Gutchen 1:086, 115. Hackett 1:056. Jahn 1:064, 122. Kampen 1:020. Killilea 1:069. Richman 1:065. Rohm 1:021. Waterston 1:153.

Note: Used with permission from Alexandra Broches and Natalie Kampen.

APPENDIX J

Instructions for Indexing a Transcript Using a Computer

This is the indexing method taught to me by the Tape Transcription Center, 129 Tremont Street, Boston, Massachusetts. These instructions are applicable when you use a Microsoft Word program run on a PC.

1. After you have completed the last draft of the transcription, read it again, looking for particular words or phrases that indicate an important topic. Make a list.
2. Mark these words or phrases by highlighting them when each one appears first in the text. For example, in the transcript analyzed in the chapter on analysis and interpretation, I highlighted *art, artist, children, husband, gallery,* and so on, when each word first appeared as I read through the transcript.
3. Press the keys Alt, then Shift, then X. A box called *Mark Index Entries* appears. Look at the list of words you've jotted down. Type the first one in the subject box and any subentry you wish. Click *Mark All.* Close box.
4. Now your document will have weird little marks that look like a backward *P* all over it. On the task bar, click on the backward *P*. The weird little marks will disappear.
5. In order to finish creating the index, go to the end of the document. Press Control and Enter to obtain a hard page break. Type in "Index" at the top. Press Enter, Enter, Enter.
6. Click on the *Insert* menu, then *Reference,* then *Index and Tables.* Look on the right for *Columns.* Click on *1,* then *OK.* Word will collect the entries and sort them alphabetically.

Citing the Oral Histories

Below is the citation format used by the Regional Oral History Office at the University of California, Berkeley (Regional Oral History Office, 486 The Bancroft Library, University of California, Berkeley, Berkeley, CA 94720-6000).

Bibliographic citation for a single interview transcript:

Broussard, Allen E., *A California Supreme Court Justice Looks at Law and Society, 1964–1996*, typescript of an oral history conducted 1991–1996 by Gabrielle Morris, Regional Oral History Office, The Bancroft Library, University of California, Berkeley, 1997, 266 pp.

Footnote citation for a single interview transcript:

1. Allen E. Broussard, *A California Supreme Court Justice Looks at Law and Society, 1964-1996*, an oral history conducted 1991–1996, Regional Oral History Office, The Bancroft Library, University of California, Berkeley, 1997, pp. 134–136.

Bibliographic citation for one interview transcript in a multivolume oral history:

Silverman, Mervyn F., "Public Health Director, The Bathhouse Crisis: 1983–1984," typescript of an oral history conducted in 1993, in *The AIDS Epidemic in San Fran-*

cisco: The Medical Response, 1981–1984, Volume I, Regional Oral History Office, The Bancroft Library, University of California, Berkeley, 1995, 276 pp.

Footnote citation for one interview transcript in a multivolume oral history:

1. Mervyn F. Silverman, "Public Health Director, The Bathhouse Crisis: 1983–1984," an oral history conducted in 1993, in *The AIDS Epidemic in San Francisco: The Medical Response, 1981–1984, Volume I*, Regional Oral History Office, University of California, Berkeley, 1995, p. 117.

Author Index

Subject Index

About the Author

Valerie Raleigh Yow received her M.A. and Ph.D. in history from the University of Wisconsin. She trained in oral history methodology at the University of North Carolina's Southern Oral History Program. In addition, she studied adult development at the Harvard Graduate School of Education and psychology at Boston College.

With a sociologist, the late Hugh Brinton, and social historian Brent Glass, she carried out her first oral history project, "Families of Carrboro," in 1974–1975, concentrating on interviewing women mill workers. She trained interviewers and interviewed in the project on the history of women clerical workers in Rhode Island, sponsored by their national organization, 9to5. She has been associate director of the State Oral History Project in Rhode Island, as well as a faculty member at Brooklyn College, the University of Rhode Island, and Northern Illinois University.

Among her publications of research based on oral history are books for public history: *Patient Care: A History of Butler Hospital, 1957–1993* (1994); *Bryant College: The First 100 Years* (1993); *The History of Hera: A Women's Cooperative Art Gallery* (1990). Biographical studies include *Bernice Kelly Harris: A Good Life Was Writing* (1999) and *Betty Smith and "A Tree Grows in Brooklyn"* (submitted for publication).

Dr. Yow has served as consultant on numerous oral history projects and has delivered papers at annual conferences of the Oral History Association and the American Association for the History of Medicine. She is an independent scholar living in Chapel Hill, North Carolina, where she re-searches and writes histories and conducts a practice in psychotherapy. She works with local groups on issues pertaining to social justice, protec-tion of the natural environment, and education for peaceful solutions to international crises.